SUMMA PUBLICATIONS, INC.

Thomas M. Hines
Publisher

William C. Carter
Editor-in-chief

Editorial Board

Benjamin F. Bart
University of Pittsburgh

William Berg
University of Wisconsin

Germaine Brée
Wake Forest University

Michael Cartwright
McGill Universityd

Hugh M. Davidson
University of Virginia

Elyane Dezon-Jones
Washington University

John D. Erickson
Louisiana State University

Wallace Fowlie (emeritus)
Duke University

James Hamilton
University of Cincinnati

Freeman G. Henry
University of South Carolina

Norris J. Lacy
Washington University

Jerry C. Nash
University of New Orleans

Allan Pasco
University of Kansas

Albert Sonnenfeld
University of Southern California

Orders:
Box 20725
Birmingham, AL 35216

Editorial Address:
3601 Westbury Road
Birmingham, AL 35223

Homage to Paul Bénichou

Homage to Paul Bénichou

Edited by

Sylvie Romanowski and Monique Bilezikian

SUMMA PUBLICATIONS, INC.
Birmingham, Alabama
1994

Copyright 1994
Summa Publications, Inc.
ISBN 0-917786-98-X

Library of Congress Catalog Number 94-67074

Printed in the United States of America

Contents

I
Plays and Context

Contents (cont'd)

II
Values in Process

Acknowledgements

The Northwestern University Research Grants Committee has provided partial support for the publication of this book. We gratefully acknowledge this assistance.

—*S. R. and M. B.*

Tabula Gratulatoria

Homage to Paul Bénichou

ALBANESE, Ralph, Jr.
Allegheny College, Lawrence Lee
    Pelletier Library
ALLENTUCH, Harriet R.
ALVAREZ, Blanca Figueredo
AMBRIERE, Madeleine

BAKER, Susan Read
BEASLEY, Faith E.
BIRBERICK, Anne L.
BRODY, Jules

Collège de France, Paris
COLLINS-CLARK, Kathleen

DANIEL, George B., Jr.
DEFAUX, Gérard

GEMMATO, Geno R.
GETHNER, Perry J.
GUTWIRTH, Marcel
GOLDWYN, Henriette
GOODKIN, Richard E.
GOULET, Angela Stella-Marie
GOUVERNET, Gérard
GUERON, Jacqueline

HARTH, Erica
HARTLE, Robert W.
Heinrich Heine Universität, Düsseldorf
    Romanisches Seminär
HENEIN, Eglal

HOROWITZ, Louise K.
Harvard University, Department of
    Romance Languages
HUBERT, Judd D.

JACKSON, G. Donald
John Carroll University

KAHL, Mary C.
KOPPISCH, Michael

LALANDE, Roxanne
LEIBACHER, Lise H.
LEINER, Wolfgang
LETTS, Janet T.
LEVIN, Harry
LOCKWOOD, Richard
LYONS, John D.

MARGITIC, Milorad
Memphis State University Libraries
MESNARD, Jean
MUELLER, Marlies

NAVON-GORN, Rena
NORMAN, G. Buford

PATTY, James S.
PICHOIS, Claude
PROBES, Christine McCall

Tabula Gratulatoria (Cont'd)

Randolph Macon College, McGraw-
  Page Library (Ashland, Virginia)
REISS, Timothy J.
ROBBINS-HERRING, Kittye Delle
ROMERO, Laurence
ROOT, Tamara Goldstein
ROWAN, Mary M.

SANKOVITCH, Tilde
SULLIVAN, Martha H.
SWEETSER, Marie-Odile
SZOGYI, Alex

TOLTON, Cameron D. E.

VAN DELFT, Louis
VENESOEN, Constant

VERDIER, Gabrielle
VIALET, Michèle

Wallace Library, Wheaton College
  (Massachusetts)
WATANABE, Nancy Ann
WATERSON, Karolyn
WEAVER-LAPORTE, Ellen
WEED, Patricia
WILLIAMS, Charles G. S.
WOSHINSKY, Barbara
WYATT, Neal

ZARUCCHI, Jeanne Morgan
ZIMMERMAN, Eléonore

Introduction

Sylvie Romanowski and Monique Bilezikian

IL ÉTAIT UNE FOIS . . . once upon a time, there was a young lycée teacher in Oran whose task it was to teach French literature of the second part of the seventeenth century. His pupils had already read texts of the first half of the century, but not very well, according to their teacher, who found their understanding of Corneille to be superficial and false. So he decided to perform some remedial teaching and prepared some materials on Corneille, for he believed that the literature of the second part of the century could not be understood except with regards to the first. The later texts, he thought, aimed to destroy the heroic, glorious notions of the aristocratic self of Corneille; how they were in reality a *machine de guerre* against Corneille had to be properly understood if these later texts were to make sense. Thus our young teacher, Paul Bénichou, conceived of a textbook divided very classically into three parts: one on Corneille and his concept of the hero, a second part on the literature of the next generation as a demolition of the hero, and a third part on Molière, different from both in his understanding and valuing of human nature. And so it was that helping high school pupils understand Corneille as a context for later literature was the point of departure for the *Morales du grand siècle,* still a must-read for all scholars of French seventeenth-century literature.

It is nothing short of miraculous that a book of literary criticism published in 1948 and conceived about a decade earlier is still current and indispensable reading. What is this magic which makes the book unique and unduplicatable? If we knew the recipe for producing such a lasting critical work, we could make a small fortune selling the recipe to other scholars desiring such longevity for their own books. Having a great mind is a *sine qua non* prerequisite, of course. Being a lycée teacher is probably not. But in this case, even that turned out to be an advantage: not having to teach specialists, but younger minds made Paul Bénichou focus on what is important and fundamental, a return to basics. Being in Oran meant not having access to the most specialized libraries of the world, and hence relying more on one's own insights and analyses. Most decisively, according to Bénichou himself, was the fact that his book was meant for a nonprofessional audience of lycée pupils and teachers, and that any kind of critical or partisan philosophical jargon had to be strenuously avoided, as well as scholarly apparatus such as footnotes. Independence of spirit, reliance on one's own inner resources, and the pedagogical imperative were ingredients that contributed to the making of this unique book.

During the gathering storms of the 1930s, Paul Bénichou left for Argentina, where he continued to teach and to expand his manuscript. A first submission and rejection by Gallimard was followed by more reworking and a second submission. Persistence was rewarded as the book finally was published in 1948, a decade in the making. The rest, as they say, is history. While being also on the faculty of the Sorbonne, he accepted a half-time appointment at Harvard, which lasted form 1958 to 1978 and gave him an opportunity to influence a large number of students. With the present volume, these American students, friends, and colleagues are happy to return the favor, showing their deep gratitude, their debt, and their affection to Paul Bénichou.

The editors of this volume chose to impose minimal constraints on the authors, hence these essays represent a cross-section of the criticism of scholars of various ages who have been influenced in some measure by Bénichou's teaching and writing. As the essays themselves offer a variety of topics, there is no single common thread in all of them. Yet as a whole, the volume is not disparate, and it is not only because the essays all deal with seventeenth-century literature. It should be mentioned here that Bénichou had a second specialty in his teaching: nineteenth-century literature, especially romanticism, which cannot be reflected in the present volume. In a subtle, yet discernible way, the authors show, we think, two characteristics that might well reflect Bénichou's approach: first, an aversion to specialized jargon, and second, an attention to contexts, be they philosophical, moral, or intertextual.

These essays are grouped together in two sections. The essays in "Plays and Context" focus on theater in its interplay with seventeenth-century society and ideology, while those in "Values in Process" are concerned with changing literary and moral values within the seventeenth century and down to our own time. At the beginning, we have placed two essays that focus on the ideological context: Richard Goodkin takes up the always present and daunting question of comparison between Corneille and Racine, suggesting further development of Bénichou's analyses of heroism, and John Lyons examines the rules and *bienséances* concerning the representation of horror. The remainder of the essays variously treat questions of social codes, authority, and kingship. Harriet Allentuch explores manifestations of the sacredness of the monarch—the myths of sacred blood and the divinity of kings in Corneille's time. In his study of the *Querelle du Cid,* Milorad Margitić demonstrates the significance of the critics' social background and standing in relation to Corneille's. Read Baker weaves together themes of erotic, political, and rhetorical seduction in the context of the *code des généreux* in *Cinna.* Eléonore Zimmermann provides a reading of another ever-present but seldom examined question, the rivalry between Corneille and Racine over the topic of Bérénice. Timothy Reiss focuses on Racine's second play, *Alexandre le Grand,* and the problem of unlimited royal power, such as the young King Louis XIV seemed not yet to embody, but did in fact to a prescient young playwright. Sylvie Romanowski examines the links between sacrifice, royal power, knowledge, and modes of representation in *Iphigénie.* Barbara Woshinsky's essay continues the focus on the connections between royal power and sacred space in Racine's last play, *Esther.* The final essay of this section by Michael Koppisch examines the chaos produced in Molière's *Amphitryon* by desire, rivalry, and jealousy.

The second section, organized chronologically as well as thematically, comprises a variety of topics centered on questions of philosophical values undergoing change, either within the writer or from one period to the next. Gabrielle Verdier examines the transformations of esthetic values even within a relatively short time span, from the 1620s to the 1640s, as reflected in Sorel's own revisions of his stories. Liberty, that most fundamental value, is the concern of Marcel Gutwirth, who examines its various aspects in La Fontaine's fables. Two essays reflect on attitudes regarding war: Charles Williams recognizes Madame de Motteville's changing attitudes towards war during the troubled years 1643-48, while Marlies Mueller's essay surveys the fundamental change taking place at the end of the century from military heroic values based on warfare to a pacifism that takes us into Enlightenment critiques of war and violence. Two more essays take us into the eighteenth century. Judd Hubert describes the transformations of the folk tale into unbelievable tales of the marvelous that will find heirs in the eighteenth century's philosophical and parodic stories. Gérard Gouvernet demonstrates how Dufresny and Dancourt imitated Molière and at the same time avoided controversy. Moving into the nineteenth century, Ralph Albanese, Jr. shows how the republicans used Molière's theater for their education program. To conclude this volume with the modern period, Laurence Romero reminds us that classical plays are meant to be performed and that gifted directors can make these plays new and exciting to twentieth-century audiences.

In the *avant-propos* of his book *L'écrivain et ses travaux,* Paul Bénichou comments on the critic's interpretive function. To the literary critic who views literature as "un être multiple, qui nous enveloppe de toutes parts, que chacun doit aborder à sa façon et éclairer selon son pouvoir" (x), we dedicate this volume, which exemplifies our diversity of approaches and our dedication to the study of literature in its multiple aspects—social, historical, ideological, esthetic, and philosophical. As former students, as friends and colleagues in America, we express our debt and our gratitude to our *maître* whose study of seventeenth-century French literature provided an inexhaustible inspiration and a firm foundation to our writing, and whose warm and enthusiastic guidance over many years encouraged us to pursue our study of what will always be for us *le grand siècle.*

I

Plays and Context

1

My Brother, My Self: Heroic Ideology and Heroic Difference in Corneille and Racine

Richard E. Goodkin

I

IN SPITE OF THEIR FREQUENT PAIRING by literary historians and other students of literature, Corneille and Racine actually worked in quite different circumstances. Corneille's aesthetics were formed during the last decade of the reign of Louis XIII (who ruled from 1610 to 1643), a monarch frequently besieged in a time of political instability: "The three decades after 1620 were ones of almost permanent unrest involving every section of the population, . . . [which] all showed a willingness to resist royal pressure and intimidation with violence."[1] By contrast Racine came into his own a generation later, in the early 1660s, the first years of Louis XIV's independent rule (Mazarin died in 1661). This was a period of increasing centralization, stabilization, and consolidation of power in the person of the king.

If, as recent trends in literary criticism suggest, literature inevitably enters into a relation with the ideology of its time, how do these distinct conditions affect Corneille's and Racine's work as tragedians? Paul Bénichou, in his influential study, *Morales du grand siécle,* distinguishes between Corneille's hero, "that archetype of superhuman humanity which was the ideal model of the aristocracy so long as it remained faithful to its own tradition,"[2] and the subsequent "demolition of the hero"—mainly stemming from the pessimism of the Jansenists—"which consists of denying any heroic or divine prolongation of our nature" (*Morales,* 143). As Bénichou points out, the influence of Jansenism, which becomes particularly strong during the reign of Louis XIV, brings about "the

obsolescence of the old heroic ideal of the aristocracy" (155): "If a note of
pessimism dominates, this is because under the reign of Louis XIV, the
aristocratic superman was in bad shape" (156).

Bénichou thus answers the question of the difference in ideology
manifested by the two tragedians by making a contrast between the political
ideology implicit in Corneille's heroism and the lack of political ideology in
Racine:

> But, of course, at the time Racine was writing, the only kind of politics
> capable of sustaining a drama, the politics of *Cinna* or *Nicomède,* was
> dead. The time of aristocratic rebellion was past, and absolutism in its
> triumph has made the character of the heroic conspirator and the truisms
> of the politics of generosity obsolete. And that is why political drama
> has such a small role in Racine, in spite of Racine himself. (245)

Bénichou implies that Racine's tragedy bears no relation to a political ideology. But how might this view be modified and developed to accommodate
the recent work linking Racine to the constitution and execution of Louis
XIV's ideology of absolutism?[3]

I would like to address this question by way of the extremely useful
double definition of heroism given by Philippe Hamon in his work on literature and ideology:

> As we can see, the problem of the hero . . . has to do with both
> structural processes internal to the work (he is the character who is the
> most fully depicted, whose action is the most momentous, who appears
> the most frequently, etc.) and an effect of axiological reference to value
> systems (he is the character who the reader suspects assumes and
> incarnates the "positive" ideological values of a society—or of a narra-
> tor—at a given moment of the story). In the first case, the character-
> hero organizes the internal space of the work by establishing a hierarchy
> of its cast of characters (he is the "main" character in relation to minor
> characters); in the second case, the hero's antecedents are in the cultural
> space of the era, which he remains permanently "plugged into," and the
> hero serves as a point of reference for the reader, as an ideological
> "discriminator" (he is "positive" in relation to "negatives").[4]

According to Hamon, heroism can be based on a relation between the text
and its context—the hero may embody an ideology external to the work—or

on a system of differences within the text—the hero may be defined by differentiation from other characters in the work.

This seems to me to be a crucial distinction in terms of Cornelian and Racinian heroism. As Bénichou states, Corneille's heroes embody an ideal external to the plays themselves; but we might add that they are generally not strongly differentiated from other characters in the plays, many or most of whom seem also to embody—or at the very least to accept—a similar ideological frame of reference. By contrast Racine's heroes, while they might seem to be non-heroes in terms of political ideology, are strongly differentiated within their works: Andromaque, Britannicus, Iphigénie, and Phèdre (among others) are defined by a difference. What I hope to show in the present article is that this pure heroic difference of Racine's protagonists itself has a political content. Racine's heroic system is attached to a political ideology no less than Corneille's is, but that attachment is an attachment with a difference.

II

In an attempt to quantify the complex issue of ideological heroism and heroism through difference, I would like to focus on the problem of siblings in the tragedies of Corneille and Racine.[5] The sibling relation, an important organizing structure in the plays, throws into relief the relation between Corneille's and Racine's texts and their respective contexts, as well as the ramifications of that relation for the question of the two forms of heroism identified by Hamon. It also provides a microcosm of the larger question of the king's position during the reigns of Louis XIII and Louis XIV. Before turning to the strictly literary domain, let us situate the analyses of the plays in the context of the final years of the rule of Louis XIII and the early years of the reign of his elder son.

The reign of Louis XIII was plagued by the threat of revolt and overthrow from Louis's younger brother, Gaston d'Orléans, who, until the birth of the future Louis XIV in 1638, was in fact the heir to the throne. When Gaston came of age in 1626, he and his half-brothers were suspected of conspiring to assassinate Cardinal Richelieu, declare Louis's childless marriage to Anne of Austria invalid, and have Gaston marry the queen.[6] The exile in 1631 of Louis's and Gaston's mother, Marie de Médicis—herself a formidable opponent of Richelieu—only highlighted the conflict between the two brothers: "From 1631 on, once the old queen had removed herself from the political arena, Gaston would be a constant thorn in the king's side, an unremitting source of pain and torment."[7] Up until the death of Louis XIII in 1643, Gaston was perennially jockeying for an advantageous position against his brother, the king.

After the death of her husband, Anne of Austria, the mother of Louis XIV, did everything she could to ensure that her popular younger son, Philippe, would never challenge his older brother as her own brother-in-law had challenged his during the final two decades of Louis XIII's reign.[8] Philippe was essentially raised as a girl, often dressed in female clothing until well past adolescence,[9] and altogether reared "not to be the threat Gaston was to Louis XIII" (Moote, 283). Whereas Gaston and Anne were repeatedly suspected of planning to rid themselves of Louis XIII and to marry—when confronted by her husband about this, Anne is said to have responded wittily that she would have "gained too little from the exchange" (Moote, 193)—it is Louis XIV himself who is thought to have dallied with his brother's wife, Henrietta Stuart.

I have indulged in the narration of this miniature seventeenth-century soap opera partly to show how acutely sensitive the theater-going public must have been to the problem of sibling rivalry among the ruling classes, but my goal is not to make a direct link between the real-life conflict of Louis XIII and Gaston d'Orléans and the plays produced during this period, a connection that would run the risk of reducing them to *tragédies à clef*. In fact the relation between the plays and the dynastic conflicts of the court would seem to suggest an opposition, for the central conflicts of the plays are repeatedly resolved not by the victory of one sibling over another, but rather by the paternal figure of the monarch, a pattern which we see in all of the plays from the period 1637-43. Now it is certainly possible for literary texts to represent extraliterary phenomena by opposition: as Pierre Maranda has demonstrated, for example, the exploitation of younger siblings by older ones favored by the rights of primogeniture is reversed in folktales, which tend to portray younger siblings as victorious in some way.[10] But at any rate the dynastic issues of the period are too complex to reduce to a single criterion—one must not overlook the crisis of succession that nearly developed as a result of Louis's and Anne's two decades of infertility, headed off in the nick of time by the birth of two sons in the five years before Louis's death.

Rather than establishing a direct connection between the dynastic issues in the plays and those of the period, I would therefore like to use Hamon's model to suggest that the predominance of the figure of the paternalistic monarch in these plays is related to Corneille's ideological heroism—heroism by resemblance to an ethic which the viewer could place outside the text, that is, heroism composed of inherited norms. Racine's recurrent use of the motif of the enemy siblings, by contrast, has to do with his own form of heroism-through-difference, heroic identity in Racine coming purely from differentiating oneself within the framework of the play from one's siblings or sibling figures. Let us take a brief overview of some key tragedies of Corneille and Racine with particular attention to the sibling relation.

III

Corneille was an extremely prolific playwright whose theatrical production spanned a period of some forty-five years and was as varied in genre and quality as Racine's was uniform. Nonetheless, up to this very day, Corneille's reputation as a tragedian is based on a handful of plays all written during the final decade of Louis XIII's reign: *Le Cid, Horace, Cinna, Polyeucte,* and *La Mort de Pompée,* all produced in the period 1637-43. In one way or another, all of these plays rely heavily on the paternal figure of the king or ruler for their resolutions. In *Le Cid,* even though the fight between Don Diègue and Don Gomès has some features of a sibling rivalry—it is set off by the king's awarding of a position of honor to one man rather than the other and thus puts the two in the situation of competing for the king's recognition—Corneille goes out of his way to eschew what could resemble a fraternal confrontation by skewing the generations. Each man has a child of marriageable age—indeed, therein lies the play's conflict. But Corneille not only makes Don Diègue almost a generation older than his challenger—as the latter succinctly points out, "Si vous fûtes vaillant, je le suis aujourd'hui" (*Le Cid,* I, 3, 195[11])—but he also avoids letting the two fight it out directly: Don Diègue's son, Don Rodrigue, is put in as a proxy for his father, thus making the duelists even more uneven in age. And the conflict between the two feuding families is ultimately settled by the king as much as by Don Rodrigue's valiance; even in winning the duel Don Rodrigue could be said to do nothing more than confirm the king's correct judgment that his family is more worthy than that of Don Gomès.[12]

In all of the four plays that follow, *Horace, Cinna, Polyeucte,* and *La Mort de Pompée,* the *dénouement* depends ultimately upon the king or ruler. In *Horace,* the conflict is between siblings—Horace against his sister

Camille and his brother-in-law Curiace—but the power of siblings is ultimately subordinated to that of parents. Horace kills Curiace, and in a fit of
rage over her anti-Roman rantings he also kills his sister; but while this is
the dramatic climax of *Horace,* the *dénouement* of the play is determined by
two father-figures, Horace's father and the king of Rome, Tulle. Aside
from one lackluster speech in his own defense, Horace spends most of Act
V sulking silently onstage.

    Cinna is completely organized around the paternal relation, as the
revolt plotted by the title character is meant to avenge the father of his lover
Emilie, and the conflict is brought to an end when the paternalistic emperor
Auguste shows his *générosité* by forgiving those who have plotted a revolt
against him. Similarly, *Polyeucte* ends with the conversion of Félix, the
Roman governor of Armenia, and his daughter in response to the coura-
geous death of the Christian martyr Polyeucte, while *La Mort de Pompée*
concludes with César's purported closing of the unfortunate episode of
Pompey's death. In all five dramas, then, the tragic conflict is settled in a
way that is essentially paternalistic: the ruler establishes or reaffirms a hierarchy of priorities and values. The figure that Corneille repeatedly puts onstage at the height of his powers is the paternal figure of the monarch.

    Now if we recall Hamon's distinction between ideological heroism
and heroism through difference—all of Corneille's heroes from this period
falling into the first category—we can see the *dénouements* of these plays in
a new light. The basic reason the rulers are able to settle conflicts is not,
ironically, that they are strong figures of authority. It is rather that the plays
do not develop an extensive system of internal difference between the characters, that at some level all of them are in agreement, or at least can fairly
easily be brought into agreement. One reason Don Fernand, the Castilian
king, is able to foresee the reconciliation of Don Rodrigue and Chimène is
that the two lovers represent the same ideological position, as do, in fact,
the two combattants in the fatal duel, Don Rodrigue and Don Gomès. The
duel has a winner and a loser, but it is fought by two men with identical beliefs. Similarly, in *Cinna* and *Polyeucte,* although the conflicts themselves
might seem to be ideological ones, they are resolved by a harmonious realignment of perspectives rather than by a gesture of authority: Auguste's
générosité defuses Cinna's plan for revolt, and Félix's conversion to
Christianity is, precisely, a change of beliefs which erases the difference in
ideology fueling the tragedy's conflict.

    Horace, which features a violent struggle between a brother and a
sister, might seem to provide a counterexample to this pattern. But in fact

Horace's sister Camille, although she purportedly takes an anti-Roman position, fights her brother with such force, vehemence, and singleminded-
ness that the play seems to be going out of its way to tell us that the real
conflict in the drama is between two true Romans, Horace and Camille,
rather than between Horace and the Alban Curiace. Camille is inescapably
Roman even in her attack upon Rome: by successfully goading her brother
into killing her—his own sister—she erases the very distinction between
Roman and non-Roman which she was supposedly upholding, for she
forces her brother to kill her against his will—his later disclaimers notwithstanding—and so beats him at his own game. She disgraces him as a
Roman and thus dies a better Roman than he. The brother and sister cannot
be defined by a difference; they are essentially the same.

In *La Mort de Pompée,* too, we find a brother and a sister, Cléopatre
and Ptolomée, and while the Egyptian queen does take a position different
from her brother's in condemning his role in the assassination of Pompey,
she does her best to protect her brother from the consequences of his
actions. César's words of reproach to Ptolomée might be taken as emblematic of the sibling relation in much of Corneille's tragedy:

> . . . nos guerres civiles,
> Où l'honneur seul m'engage, et que pour terminer
> Je ne veux que celui de vaincre et pardonner,
> Où mes plus dangereux et plus grands adversaires,
> Sitôt qu'ils sont vaincus, ne sont plus que mes frères,
> Et mon ambition ne va qu'à les forcer,
> Ayant dompté leur haine, à vivre et m'embrasser.
> (*La Mort de Pompée,* III, 2, 914-20)

Siblings in Corneille are meant to be reconciled—to share or to come to
share the same system of beliefs—as much as they are potential adversaries.
The metaphor of the conquered becoming the emperor's brothers suggests
that one reason for Corneille's recurrent use of Roman history—and also,
by extension, for the generally harmonious relations between siblings—in
his tragedies might be the Roman policy of encouraging the vanquished to
become like their conquerors, to become Roman. Like the American melting
pot, this is a policy of assimilation to a shared ideology rather than a system
of identity through difference.

For Corneille, then, the sibling relation is a relation basically lacking
in dramatic charge; as Constant Venesoen puts it, "the myth of fraternal

hatred has no power over Corneille."[13] Before turning to Racine, let us look at a few illustrations of this hypothesis in Corneille's later tragedies.

In *Nicomède* (1651), the title character is at odds with his younger half-brother, Attale; the two brothers fight over the inheritance of power and over the love of Laodice, the queen of Armenia. But the fraternal rivalry, which, as it turns out, is basically powered by Attale's mother (*Nicomède,* IV, 2, 1180-83), is invented by Corneille in order to avoid incorporating a patricide into the play: Corneille's historical sources tell an Oedipal story in which Nicomède's father, Prusias, tries to have his son killed, and the son turns the tables and has his father put to death.[14] Now as early as *Médée* (1635), Corneille appears to have found patricide and infanticide extremely upsetting motifs,[15] perhaps in part because in tragedy they are frequently metaphors for a breakdown of inherited norms. In this light the fraternal rivalry in *Nicomède* becomes more or less a distraction from the more serious danger of intergenerational violence.

Indeed, in several cases fraternity becomes a kind of game for Corneille. In *Rodogune* (1644-45), the twin brothers Seleucus and Antiochus anxiously await their mother's disclosure of which brother is in fact the elder of the two. But her announcement that Antiochus is the elder is quickly followed by our discovery that she has simply named him the elder for her own purposes: "C'est lui que j'ai nommé l'aîné" (*Rodogune,* IV, 6, 1425). Even in a play apparently centered around the fraternal axis, it is the mother who is in control; it is she who has the power to determine the hierarchy of the two brothers.[16]

This destabilization of the sibling relation reaches its apogee in Corneille's version of the Oedipus story, *Œdipe* (1659). Even in this *Urgeschichte* of intergenerational violence, Corneille again appears to use the sibling relation as a diversionary tactic. Perhaps responding once again, as in *Nicomède,* to a need to draw attention away from the horror of patricide, Corneille gives Œdipe a sister named Dircé who wishes to marry Thésée and reclaim the Theban throne usurped by Œdipe, who she does not know is her brother. When an oracle is given stating that Laïus's blood must be shed to save the city, Thésée poses as Dircé's long-lost brother in order to prevent her from sacrificing herself. This leads to the almost comic situation in which Thésée quite openly vacillates between the role of brother and that of fiancé, and provides such immortal lines as Dircé's cry of despair: "Ah! Prince, s'il se peut, ne soyez point mon frère" (*Œdipe,* IV, 1, 1262); Thésée's remarkable response: "Sitôt que vous vivrez, je cesserai de

l'être" (IV, 1, 1266); and his unhelpful (if well-intentioned) statement to
Œdipe: "Seigneur, je suis le frère ou l'amant de Dircé" (IV, 4, 1487).

Racine picks up exactly where Corneille left off, for his very first
play, *Les Frères Ennemis,* also known as *La Thébaïde* (1664), takes up the
story of Oedipus as well, although, appropriately, some time later in the
myth. Just as Racine marks the start of a new generation of tragedy, he
starts off treating a recent theme of Corneille's but looks at the younger generation, the sons of Oedipus, focusing on a motif that will permeate and in-
form his entire theater: the enemy brothers.

The story of Polynice and Etéocle, Oedipus's feuding sons, raises
issues central to Racine's tragedy, in particular the issue of heroic identity-
through-difference. Where Sophocles and Euripides disagree about which
of the two sons is the elder,[17] Racine neatly makes them into twins; his play
is essentially about the brothers' insistence on differentiating themselves,
their refusal to be equal. By making the brothers into twins, Racine emphasizes their indistinguishability: what the play is about, then, is their need to
distinguish themselves in the face of their utter equality. *Les Frères Ennemis*
is a tragedy of pure, arbitrary difference, of difference in its most unmiti-
gated form.

What we are being told at the beginning of Racine's career is that the
tragic hero or heroine defines him- or herself with reference to an other who
he or she is not, an other who functions to create a difference even if no
fundamental difference exists. A brief overview of Racine's early theater
will show us to what extent the sibling relation—and, analogously, intra-
generational struggle as the locus of pure difference—is written into
Racine's tragedies.

Andromaque has no characters who are siblings, but one of the
ways Racine has revolutionized the play is to eliminate the very strong generational hierarchy which is found in one of his principal models, Euripides'
Andromache. In Euripides' play, the central conflict over the fate of
Andromache and her child is fought out repeatedly along the lines of a strict
generational progression: the young and fatuous Hermione argues with the
older Andromache, who then argues with Hermione's father Menelaos,
who then argues with Achilles' father, the ancient Peleus. The entire play
moves from young to old and is essentially intergenerational in structure.
Racine takes basically the same conflict and completely eliminates all generational difference: Andromaque, Pyrrhus, Hermione, and Oreste all appear to belong to the same generation, and while they are not siblings, they,

like the enemy brothers, are in some sense indistinguishable; Racine goes out of his way to underline the parallels in the situations of all four characters, each of whom is involved in a relation (or in some cases two relations) of unrequited love and each of whom spends much of the play hesitating over a course of action.

Andromaque's heroism is reminiscent of the enemy brothers in that her differentiation from the other characters is simultaneously decisive and arbitrary. As Racine's first version of the play demonstrates by having Andromaque confess her love for Pyrrhus in act V,[18] the Trojan queen is not immune to the disease of Racinian love: like all the others, she, too, wants what she cannot have (she admits her love only after Pyrrhus's death, of course). The revised version of the play, which has become standard, conserves Andromaque's silence on this point; the two versions taken together teach the same double lesson as *Les Frères Ennemis:* the arbitrariness of heroic difference—Andromaque is *not* fundamentally different from the others—and the absolute need for heroic difference.

Racine's next tragedy, *Britannicus,* marks an important evolution in the treatment of fraternity. In this play the evil Néron puts his virtuous stepbrother, Britannicus, to death. Néron and Britannicus are completely unrelated by blood, but Racine emphasizes their fraternity; the two men are called brothers no fewer than nine times in the play. As Jacques Scherer points out, "if [in *The Enemy Brothers]* the fraternal relation suggests murder, [in *Britannicus*] . . . the situation is reversed: a story of murder engenders in the poetic imagination something like a fraternal relation."[19]

In fact the fraternal relation in this play seems to be treated very differently from *The Enemy Brothers,* for in this play the two fraternal figures are presented as opposites: where Polynice and Etéocle are indistinguishable, Néron and Britannicus bear no physical or moral resemblance to each other. And yet certain elements in the play do suggest that Néron and Britannicus are secretly alike. It is clear that Néron's love for Junie, Britannicus's fiancée, is another example of the rule from *Andromaque* that one wants what is unavailable. What is less clear but no less true is the fact that Britannicus's and Junie's love is itself also based on that rule: Junie's wish to make Néron envious of the two lovers ("De faire à Néron même envier nos amours," *Britannicus,* II, 6, 718)[20] may seem like a case of simple hyperbole—our love will make even the man who has everything jealous—but it also suggests that the couple's reaction to being excluded from power is to create a reversed locus of value—Britannicus and Junie being the haves and Néron the have-not—in the realm of love.

Contrary to all appearances, what separates Britannicus and Néron, then, is not a fundamental difference in belief or ideology, but rather the positions of the two men relative to each other: Néron is politically "in" and sentimentally "out," Britannicus the reverse. And although the play presents Britannicus's innocence and idealism as a counterpoint to Néron's jaded, cynical perspective, the apparent difference becomes an arbitrary difference once we have understood that, to quote Roland Barthes, "There is much less a Neronian being than a Neronian situation."[21] It is being "in" or "out"—elements defining a system of differences rather than belonging to any ideological position—which in itself creates the difference between Britannicus and his "brother."

IV

The problem of siblings reaches its climax in the two plays written by Corneille and Racine on the same theme and at the same time: Corneille's *Tite et Bérénice* and Racine's *Bérénice* (both 1670). Legend has it that shortly before her death under mysterious circumstances, Henrietta Stuart, the wife of Louis XIV's brother Philippe, suggested to Corneille and Racine that they each write a play on the subject of Berenice, whose love for the Roman emperor Titus is reported by the ancient historians Suetonius and Cassius Dio. Whether or not this starting point for the two Berenice plays is apocryphal,[22] it is particularly appropriate that the king's sister-in-law be linked to this competition. For the resulting plays represent a sort of literary sibling rivalry between the two tragedians. Racine's *Bérénice* preceded Corneille's *Tite et Bérénice* by one week, and both playwrights knew of the existence of the other's project. These two plays, written simultaneously by two rival playwrights, provide what may be an unprecedented event in literary history, a kind of *folie à deux* disturbingly reminiscent of Polynice and Etéocle. For just as *Les Frères Ennemis* is a play about the impossibility (as well as the necessity) of heroic difference, Corneille's and Racine's sibling rivalry appears to result in a confusion of identities, a nondifferentiation: Corneille writes a play that is Racinian in structure, essentially a Racinian play, and Racine writes a play which in many ways is worthy of Corneille.

Corneille's play, first of all, is based on the theme of fraternal rivalry: he puts onstage Titus's brother, Domitian, who is his rival in love. Corneille's play is based on what we might call, inelegantly, a love parallelogram, a four-cornered figure in which two men and two women repeatedly change allegiances from a variety of motives; it is a figure eminently worthy of Racine, whose famous four-linked love chain in *Andromaque* (produced only three years before the two Berenice plays) is arguably what really brought him to prominence as a playwright. Corneille takes this love chain and fills in new names:

Andromaque: Oreste—Hermione—Pyrrhus—Andromaque
Tite et Bérénice: Domitian—Domitie—Tite—Bérénice

Conversely, Racine writes a play with characters as idealistic and noble as Corneille's usually are. Moreover he writes a play in which there are no siblings, a play based on the paternal relation rather than the fraternal or sororal one. In Racine's play, Titus's father has just died and Titus must decide whether he as emperor can allow himself to marry Bérénice in spite of Rome's law forbidding an emperor's marriage with a foreign queen. The position Titus comes to in the play is that of his late father. In a particularly Cornelian turn of events, he decides that the only way to be worthy of Bérénice is to give up his union with her; the play's conflict is resolved—to the extent that it is—largely by an ideological shift, Titus's and Bérénice's values brought into line with those of the deceased emperor.

Thus each of the enemy brothers writes a play which is in the image of his fraternal counterpart: Corneille writes a Racinian-style play about sibling rivalry and love triangles, and Racine writes one about the inheriting of paternal values. But Racine's play, while it has the appearance of a Cornelian drama of paternal authority, is the most Racinian of dramas, the play in which Racine truly comes into his own. Titus has no literal brother in Racine's play, but he does have a secret rival: Antiochus, another foreign prince who, like Titus, is in love with Bérénice. Now this secret rivalry, which is the closest Racine comes to Corneille's fraternal competition over Bérénice in his own play, is revealed to Titus only at the very end of the play, and only briefly: when Antiochus tells Titus that he, Titus's "faithful friend," is secretly his rival, Titus's only response—his final words onstage—is the exclamation "Mon rival!" (*Bérénice,* V, 7, 1443). And when Bérénice in this same final scene addresses the two men and reaffirms the need for all three lovers to separate, Titus says nothing, while Antiochus alone reacts, in the play's famous final word: "Hélas!" He alone is speaking for the two men.

In this sense *Bérénice,* a play devoid of biological or even adoptive brothers, more fundamentally explores the nature of fraternity in Racine than Corneille's drama, even though the latter is undoubtedly influenced by the squabbling siblings of Racine's early plays. Antiochus is Titus's secret brother: the two men, both in love with Bérénice, both condemned to lose her, are at some level no more distinguishable than Polynice and Etéocle, except that one allows himself to lament the loss of love to a political ideology ("Hélas!") while the other cannot and remains silent. Racine's *Bérénice* could be subtitled *The Secret Brothers.*

What is the relation of this covert return of the supposedly inoperative motif of sibling rivalry in *Bérénice* (a Freudian return of the repressed?) to the ideological shift, the inheritance of paternal norms, which ends the play?

What Racine's play is telling us is that ideology itself can be based on difference, a message that is particularly applicable to the court of Louis XIV, and specifically to the elaborate and seemingly gratuitous etiquette developed and exploited by the king in his consolidation of power. As Norbert Elias demonstrates in his masterful study of the French court under the *Ancien Régime,* the court of Louis XIV is an excellent example of the relativity of value:

> A study of court society reveals . . . that one's own value is a link in the chain of compulsions produced by the interdependence to which one is exposed. Philosophical and sociological theories often treat "values" as something inexplicable, something "ultimate" and "absolute." People, so it appears, decide in total freedom which values they will adopt. . . . What has been said here on court society can make it easier to understand the connections between power and social structures and values. . . . It is difficult to escape the compulsion to base one's personal goals on . . . social values and norms and to join in the competition for such opportunities.[23]

The underlying lesson of Racine's theater is that an ideological position, insofar as it is artificial, cannot be defined independently of a system of differences which—and it is here that belief systems which present themselves as absolute would undoubtedly protest—are in themselves arbitrary.

If *Bérénice* were truly to be a Cornelian play based on heroic ideology, the character of Antiochus would be unnecessary; from an ideological point of view the conflict is not one between Titus and Antiochus, but one between Titus and his father. And yet in Racine's hands the ideological shift, the inheritance of paternal norms, has an element of dissimulation, regret, and negation: Titus is *not* converted to his father's position (as Félix is converted to Christianity, thus restoring harmony between the generations), but rather forces himself (or perhaps is forced by Bérénice)[24] to assume it. When Antiochus comes to speak for Titus and to express Titus's regret, this single action sums up the two antithetical movements of the entire play, which starts with Antiochus telling Bérénice that he can no longer hold his love for her inside, that he must reveal it, and ends with Titus telling Bérénice that he can no longer reveal his love for her, that he must keep it hidden from now on because of his political position.

But the emotional impact of the play tells us that this opposition between Antiochus and Titus is artificial, for the play allows us to see inside Titus, to see what is happening behind his change in position. Titus is allowed to take a position, but we are allowed to see the artifice of that position, just as Titus is allowed to have—or perhaps cannot escape having—an alter ego that expresses that artifice. The play thus ends on a note of negation and loss,[25] feelings which might be thought of as foreign to an ideological position which, as Hamon points out, establishes a set of purely positive values. *Bérénice* makes us feel that ideology cannot abolish difference. It makes us aware of the fact that—*caveat rex*—ideology is not absolute, but rather relative.

V

What is the impact of this realization for the rest of Racine's theater? The motif of the secret siblings, forged by Racine's rivalry with Corneille in *Bérénice,* permeates the rest of his theater. It is in fact fathers and mothers who dominate in Racine's plays after *Bérénice*[26]—perhaps by highlighting the role of the father in that play, as opposed to Corneille's competing brothers, Racine himself comes to think of himself as a potential purveyor of parental authority.[27] But the sibling relation is driven into hiding rather than exorcised. In *Mithridate,* the rivalry of the brothers Xipharès and Pharnace, which early in the play (I, 3) very nearly reaches the fever pitch of the fatal confrontation of Etéocle and Polynice, is overshadowed but not resolved by the return of their father, Mithridate. *Iphigénie* ends with the revelation that Iphigénie's evil companion, Eriphile, is none other than her first cousin, a girl also named Iphigénie. Eriphile, I would like to suggest, represents Iphigénie's own feelings of inner rebellion, fury, and betrayal set off by her father's willingness to sacrifice her; the "other Iphigénie" embodies a resistance to the heroic ethic carrying the Achaians to Troy, a resistance no less important than the purported acceptance of that ethic by Agamemnon's daughter herself.[28] Even the conflict in *Phèdre* could be seen as stemming from the heroine's unsuccessful attempts to ensure that her story will not repeat the pattern of unhappy love which ruined the life of her sister, Ariane (*Phèdre*, I, 3, 253-54).

But the play which best sums up the difference between Cornelian siblings and Racinians siblings is *Athalie* (1691), Racine's final play and one of the last works to enter the canon of French neoclassical tragedy from the reigns of Louis XIII and Louis XIV. *Athalie* ends with the death of the blasphemous titular heroine and the accession of her virtuous grandson, Joas, to the throne. Joas is made to inherit the values of his adoptive parents, Joad and Josabet, rather than those of his murderous grandmother. Whereas Corneille's tragedies are about the meshing, or in some cases the realignment of ideology between the generations, Racine toward the end of his career emphasizes the need for adoption, a metaphor of the need for a break between the generations, the dangers involved in accepting inherited norms. The value of this metaphor is summed up by the final speech of *Athalie*, spoken by Joas's adopted father, Joad:

> Par cette fin terrible, et due à ses forfaits,
> Apprenez, roi des Juifs, et n'oubliez jamais
> Que les rois dans le ciel ont un juge sévère,
> L'innocence un vengeur, et l'orphelin un père.
>
> (*Athalie*, V, 8, 1813-16)

Once we have understood that Racinian tragedy is based on the need for difference, we may not be shocked by the following paradox: Racine's work taken as a whole suggests that the orphan has a father, but that the son or daughter has none, that the only form of acceptable paternity—itself a metaphor for the inheritance of norms—is adoptive paternity. Adoptive paternity is paternity with a difference; choosing the link between the generations means, precisely, having a choice, and choice is based on at least the possibility of difference.

It is not coincidental that this final speech links fathers and kings: seventeenth-century tragedy, with its usual sense of order, thus seems to return to one of its starting points, Corneille's early plays with their paternal monarchs. But here the king is not a father, but rather has a father, and a harsh one: if kings have a judge and orphans a father, the suggestion is that the judge of kings is in a paternal position, they in a filial one. Perhaps it is not surprising that Louis XIV did not like this play, that Racine's fall from favor—which some believe contributed to his death eight years later—may be traced to this moment. As we have seen, Louis XIV easily controlled his brother. He also controlled the aristocracy, and he did so largely by gathering them at Versailles and placing them in a dependent position similar to that of children fighting for attention from an all-powerful parent, himself.[29] What the king did to the courtisans was to make them into undifferentiated siblings; like Etéocle and Polynice, they were all the more insistant on their differences for being essentially the same, reduced to a position of subservience to the king. But by according favors the king was not actually recognizing differences but rather creating arbitrary differences in order to strengthen a hierarchy leading to a single value, himself.

What we see in the case of Louis XIV is the blurring of the distinction between ideological heroism and heroism through difference. Louis's ideology of power is based *not* on inherited norms, as his father's was, and as that of Corneille's heroes was. It is rather based on difference, on what we might call *absolute difference:* arbitrary, unfounded difference which draws attention to itself by its very unconnectedness to inherited norms, its need to create itself within its own generation, a very deep-seated constituent element of tragic heroism. Louis built his position through the establishment of an artificial value system based on difference, with himself as the positive value and the value of others consequently defined simply by proximity to the king-as-absolute-value.

We might call this evolution, reflected in the difference between Corneille's and Racine's theater, the *spatialization* of values at the expense of temporal (inherited) values that are breaking down. As Bénichou puts it:

> What the influence and the spirit of the court took away from tragic greatness because of the breakdown of heroism is partly compensated for by a new prestige—less high-minded, but poetically speaking perhaps even more powerful—which spread out [rayonnait] from the court itself, from the court of Versailles with its banquets and triumphs. Everything great resided in royalty, and people shared in it precisely because they were close to royalty. . . . The idea of heroic grandeur had given way in people's minds to the idea of *majesty.* Man touched the divine not so much through value as through power and happiness. This atmosphere made its way into Racine's work. (*Morales,* 248-49)

The only thing to be added to Bénichou's very accurate depiction of the difference between Louis XIV's court and his father's is, precisely, the recognition that this lack of innate or inherent value—concomitant with the establishment of value through proximity or difference—in itself has a relation to an ideology. It is perhaps one of Louis's greatest strokes of genius to base an absolutist system at least partially on an arbitrary establishment of value.

It is precisely this collapse of inherited norms that makes the king not into a father figure, but rather into a Racinian-style secret sibling, a sibling who establishes his priority without having any *essential* difference from his sisters and (br)others. Rather than placing value in the relation between the generations, Louis resorts to an atemporal system of value: descriptions of Louis's court with its glamour—what Bénichou calls its *rayonnement*—at times seem to look forward to the Hollywood star system, perhaps the most far-reaching example of the creation of a set of arbitrary heroic figures in world history. But once we have recognized the element of arbitrariness in Louis's establishment of himself as an ultimate value—or, more to the point, once the king's "siblings" have recognized it—the difference is not so much effaced as it becomes reversible. The parental relation is essentially irreversible and asymmetrical, the sibling relation mutual and reversible (ordering within the family notwithstanding). And when the reversibility of heroic difference does become recognized, the king (or, as in this case, his descendants) may be in for an unpleasant surprise.

To this extent perhaps the king's displeasure at Racine was a perceptive reading of *Athalie,* although the same reading might well have led to something more fruitful, a lesson about the perenniality of siblings (and of difference) and the basic unforeseeability of difference as a bipolar system. As Racine tells us in his preface to *Athalie,* thirty years after the action of the play, Joas will put to death Zacharie, his adoptive brother, an action covertly alluded to in the body of the play (*Athalie,* IV, 4, 1416). The orphan may have a father, as the last line of Racine's theater tells us, and may even find a certain freedom in not being limited to inherited norms. But there is an equally important lesson in the play's projection into the future—the future of the tragic ruler, Joas, and the future of the lineage of Louis XIV. Persisting in getting rid of one's siblings can become an irremediable act, for unlike a child or a parent one cannot oneself adopt a brother. And brotherhood itself, the locus of difference in Racine, can also form an ideology: *liberté, égalité, fraternité.*

NOTES

1 David Parker, *The Making of French Absolutism* (London: Edward Arnold, 1983), 95.

2 Paul Bénichou, *Morales du grand siècle* (Paris: Gallimard, 1948), 155. This and all translations from the French, unless otherwise noted, are my own.

3 See, for example, Louis Marin, *Le Récit est un piège* (Paris: Minuit, 1978) and *Le Portrait du roi* (Paris: Minuit, 1981).

4 Philippe Hamon, *Texte et idéologie: Valeurs, hiérarchies et évaluations dans l'œuvre littéraire* (Paris: Presses Universitaires de France, 1984), 47.

5 Space restrictions prevent me from discussing here Corneille's relation to his own brother, Thomas, a prominent playwright in his own right.

6 A. Lloyd Moote, *Louis XIII, the Just* (Berkeley and Los Angeles: University of California Press, 1989), 191.

7 Pierre Chevallier, *Louis XIII: Roi cornélien* (Paris: Fayard, 1979), 404.

8 Undoubtedly Anne's motives were partly (if not mainly) personal, as she herself hoped to keep a considerable degree of power even after her sons reached majority.

9 John B. Wolf, "The Formation of a King," in ed. John B. Wolf, *Louis XIV: A Profile* (New York: Hill and Wang, 1972), 3-4.

10 Pierre Maranda, *French Kinship: Structure and History* (The Hague: Mouton, 1974), 134.

11 This and all quotations of Corneille are taken from Pierre Corneille, *Œuvres complètes*, ed. André Stegmann (Paris: Seuil, 1963).

12 It has been suggested that *Le Cid,* which was heavily criticized by Richelieu's newly formed *Académie française,* may have drawn Richelieu's disfavor because of the drama's depiction of the aristocracy as acting fairly independently of the king. Nonetheless the play's resolution, with its dependence on the king, does set in motion the recurring pattern I am talking about.

13 Constant Venesoen, "Le Thème de la fraternité dans l'œuvre de Racine: un cas de dédoublement?" in ed. David Trott and Nicole Boursier, *L'Age du Théâtre en France* (Edmonton: Academic Printing and Publishing, 1988), 143, n. 15. What Venesoen fails to point out is that the sibling relation in Corneille is repeatedly subordinated to the parental relation, not simply to Corneille's habitual "civility."

14 See *Examen* of *Nicomède,* in Pierre Corneille, *Œuvres complètes,* 520.

15 Corneille reduces the scene of Medea's murder of her children to four lines, and his Jason, faced with the destruction of his posterity, commits suicide onstage. This despair at losing one's heirs may not be completely unrelated to events in the royal household: in 1635 Louis XIII and Anne of Austria had failed to produce a successor during some twenty years of marriage. It is also not inconceivable that the image of the mother as vengeful foreigner owes something to the disgraced and exiled Marie de Médicis.

16 It is difficult to resist pointing out—although this may well be coincidental—that *Rodogune* was produced during the early years of the regency of Anne of Austria who, as

we have seen, did in a sense determine (or at least strongly reinforce) the hierarchy of her two sons.

[17] Sophocles, *Oedipus at Colonus*, 374-76; Euripides, *Phoenissae*, 71.

[18] For this scene, which appears in the 1668 edition of the play, see Jean Racine, *Œuvres complètes*, ed. Raymond Picard, 2 vols. (Paris: Gallimard, Pléiade, 1950 and 1966), 1: 1088-89.

[19] Jacques Scherer, *Racine et/ou la cérémonie* (Paris: Presses Universitaires de France, 1982), 94.

[20] This and all quotations of Racine are taken from Jean Racine, *Théâtre complet*, ed. Jacques Morel and Alain Viala (Paris: Garnier Frères, 1980).

[21] Roland Barthes, *Sur Racine* (Paris: Seuil, 1963), 83. I am using this statement somewhat differently than Barthes does in his analysis of the play, but, I believe, in much the same spirit.

[22] Although in his biography of his father, Louis Racine does not name Henrietta, he says that "A princess, famous for her wit and her love of poetry, had enjoined the two rivals to treat this same subject" (Jean Racine, *Œuvres complètes*, 1:33). Even if the idea for the two plays is attributed to Henrietta spuriously, the fact that many of Corneille's and Racine's contemporaries believed her to be the source of inspiration is in itself significant.

[23] Norbert Elias, *The Court Society*, trans. Edmund Jephcott (Oxford: Basil Blackwell, 1983), 75.

[24] My analysis of *Bérénice* is artificially skewed toward the two male figures because of their sibling-like rivalry; Bérénice is actually far and away the single most important character in the play. See, for example, my "The Performed Letter, or, How Words Do Things in Racine," *Papers on French Seventeenth Century Literature*, 32 (1990), 89-93.

[25] Bénichou remarks on the feeling of loss or regret which one often finds at the end of Racine's plays (*Morales du grand siècle*, 249), but I would like to emphasize to what extent that feeling can be read as undermining an artificial position of heroic affirmation. Aside from *Bérénice* I would cite as other examples *Andromaque, Mithridate, Iphigénie, Phèdre*, and *Athalie*.

[26] For a recent study of the maternal relation in Racine's theater, see Constant Venesoen, *Le Complexe maternel dans le théâtre de Racine* (Paris: Lettres Modernes, 1987).

[27] The fact that Racine's play was a much greater success than Corneille's also might have something to do with this as well. Obviously my approach here is not a psychological one, but I am convinced that making his début as a tragedian as late as 1664, Racine at least initially thought of himself as a younger brother in relation to Corneille and other older tragedians. It is perhaps partly for this reason that Racine chooses Euripides as his aesthetic *alter ego* rather than Sophocles (his favorite playwright) or Aeschylus, since Euripides himself stood in a similar relation to the earlier generation of tragic poets in Athens. In Harold Bloom's terms, if Racine's early emphasis on siblings

reflects his own artistic anxiety with reference to the already-established tragedians of his generation, *Bérénice* and the subsequent emergence of parental figures marks Racine's "victory" over Corneille, who in *Tite et Bérénice* might be said to have "inherited" Racine's anxiety.

28 For a fuller development of this question, see my *The Tragic Middle: Racine, Aristotle, Euripides* (Madison: University of Wisconsin Press, 1991), 125-36.

29 See, for example, Jacques Levron, *La Vie quotidienne à la cour de Versailles aux XVIIe et XVIIIe siècles* (Paris: Hachette, 1965), 37-39.

2

The Decorum of Horror:
A Reading of La Mesnardière's *Poëtique*

John D. Lyons

IN REMINDING US OF THE "origines sanguinaires du monde féodal,"[1] Paul Bénichou pointed out the link between the ethos of a social order—the landed aristocracy—and the aesthetic foundations of the genre we call French classical tragedy. "L'horreur du spectacle se mêle d'admiration," writes Bénichou of Corneille's *Rodogune,* in emphasizing the need to understand the context and origin of conduct which seems morally repugnant and even revolting. Horror and bloodshed, however, are not concepts frequently associated with the dramatic values of seventeenth-century France. We have, in fact, not profited from Bénichou's pioneering remarks to investigate the conflict between an aristocratic morality based on violence and the constraints placed on the representation of that violence within an absolutist monarchical society. We know, of course, that the physical reenactment of violence and bloodshed on the seventeenth-century stage became infrequent, particularly after the criticism of *Le Cid.* We forget, however, the extent to which tragedy was inextricably linked to horror in the theory and practice of the French classical writers. As a result we stress such issues as the three unities, *bienséance* or decorum, and verisimilitude without considering them as a defensive apparatus designed to protect tragedy against its own origin in horror.

Horror has always been linked to the body. From the Latin *horrere,* "to bristle," to the definition of *horreur* in the *Robert,* "Impression causée par la vue ou la pensée d'une chose affreuse, et qui se traduit par un frémissement, un frisson, un mouvement de recul . . . ," horror designates the body's rather than the mind's reaction to some perception. The way horror is paired discursively in seventeenth-century writing leads quickly to the conclusion that particular kinds of visual stimulus lead to this physical reaction. Spectacle, as the domain of vision, has a privileged relationship to horror in the phrase *spectacles d' horreur* (the title of a popular collection of stories).[2] D'Aubignac censures "ces Spectacles pleins d'horreur"[3] and La Mesnardière writes of certain actions in tragedies as "Spectacles horribles . . . qui s'exposent à nos yeux des Actions detestables, qui nous font transsir d'horreur à l'aspect de leur cruauté."[4] The particular kind of sight that produces horror is clear from the expression that Voltaire denounced as a cliché, "le carnage et l'horreur."[5] Horror is associated with carnage, with the injury and dismemberment of bodies, and it seems almost as if the perceiver's reaction is a form of empathy, communication from body to body which bypasses the veneer of civility or the specific narrative motivation of the physical assault that is viewed to produce the physical symptoms of a personal involvement as participant in the event seen.

Plays of the early seventeenth century included copious incidents of staged violence, dismemberment, and cannibalism. "Le goût du sang et des cadavres" as Scherer calls it, not only dominates much of the reign of Louis XIII, but resisted early attempts to remove such sights from the stage about the time of *Le Cid*.[6] It is difficult for us to recall how widespread this practice was and therefore to account for the preoccupation—even the obsession—with carnage and horror in the theoretical writings of mid-century. Duels and combats are mild compared to the horrors catalogued by La Mesnardière, the theorist most absorbed by this issue: "les mouches s'attachent au corps . . . & sucent le sang de ses playes" (98), "les Gibets & les Roües . . . le spectacle des corps qui nagent dans leur propre sang . . . " (419), "Tantale y rostit ses enfant . . . " (222), etc.

One of the major problems of theorists trying to impose greater decorum on French tragedy was the origin of tragedy itself as historical legacy of a very different culture. Tragedy could not be rid of horror except to the extent that the physical enactment of certain crimes might be removed from the stage itself. In the plot and the words of the characters, horror remained as the basis of tragedy:

> Car il ne faut pas demander que les Personnes theatralles soient absolument vertueuses. La Scene reçoit les Tantales aussi bien que les Iasons, les Medées comme les Hecubes, les Phedres comme les Alcestes: Et puis qu'elle expose à toute heure de meschantes actions, & que les infidelitez, les incestes, les parricides & d'autres crimes de ce genre sont ses sujets ordinaires, il faut par necessité qu'elle admette des meschans,

& qu'ils y paroissent reuestus au moins de quelque partie de leurs
mauuaises habitudes.[7]

There is a double problem here, wound together in this list. On one hand
there is the relation between the tragic subject (or represented event) and its
historical or fabulous basis. On the other, there is the relationship between
the culture of seventeenth-century France and its bonds to the past, both
classical and post-classical.

The struggle for decorum is, in part, a battle of modernity against
the horror of antiquity.[8] D'Aubignac notes the role of ancient practice in
shaping what is meant by tragedy: "parce que les Tragédies ont eu souvent
des Catastrophes infortunées, ou par la rencontre des histoires, ou par la
complaisance des Poëtes envers les Atheniens, qui ne haïssoit pas ces objets
d'horreur sur leur Theatre . . . plusieurs se sont imaginés que le mot de
Tragique ne signifioit jamais qu'une avanture funeste et sanglante . . . "[9]
The project of seventeenth-century poetics was not to replicate but to correct
the tragedy of the ancients. As La Mesnardière proclaims boldly, "nous
n'avons pas entrepris de . . . montrer de quelle sorte ont écrit les vieux
Tragiques, mais de . . . faire comprendre comment ils ont deu écrire" (219).
The struggle against horror is an attack therefore on the history of tragedy,
on its theory and practice, but also on history itself in the political and even-
emential sense. Horror was contained in the "rencontre des histoires" as
well as in the taste of the Greek audience. The terrifying paradox, for the
modern—that is, seventeenth-century—mind facing the ancient requirements of tragedy is that the personae of tragedy had to be princes and kings
and yet the actions of tragedy had to be serious faults, mistakes, or crimes.
These elements seem incompatible, for whether the prince is mistaken or
criminal (and thus logically or justly punished) or whether the prince is the
victim of actions (and thus insufficiently strong or astute to avoid social disorder and harm), boundaries are crossed which, for the contemporaries of
Richelieu or Louis XIV, threaten the confidence in the structure of society
itself.

The "spectacles pleins d'horreur" which d'Aubignac describes as
impermissible for his contemporaries are very specifically violence done to
kings: "nous ne voulons point croire que les Roys puissent estre mechans,
ni souffrir que leurs Sujets, quoy qu'en apparence maltraittez, touchent
leurs Personnes sacrees, ny se rebellent contre leur Puissance, non pas
mesme en peinture; et je ne croy pas que l'on puisse faire assassiner un
Tyran sur nostre Theatre avec applaudissement, sans de tres-signalées

précautions . . . " (73). Horror therefore calls into question the very body of the king and traces the boundary where social disorder passes into physical disintegration. The other principal social structure which is affected by horror is the family, whose disaggregation is made manifest by the misuse, penetration, dismemberment, and incorporation of bodies—incest, parricide, cannibalism. These, the "sujets ordinaires" of Greek and Roman tragedy, must in some way be deflected, covered, repressed for the modern audience.

Yet even in the middle and late seventeenth century, horror and tragedy were frequently associated. A dictionary illustration of the figurative use of the word *tragédie* includes the revealing sentences "Il se joüe quelquefois d'horribles tragedies en ceste cour-là. Il s'y est joüé une sanglante tragedie."[10] Furetière illustrates the use of the word *horreur* with the sentence, "La Tragedie doit exciter de l'*horreur, ou de la pitié, selon Aristote.*"[11] This frank admission of tragedy's aim to excite horror encountered opposition in one of the major texts of dramatic theory in the seventeenth century, La Mesnardière's *Poëtique,* in which the author pronounces himself strongly against horror in tragedy, distinguishing horror from terror and pity, the desirable emotions. Engaging in a lengthy philological argument, La Mesnardière proclaims that Aristotle designated terror and compassion the emotions of a perfect tragedy, "sans jamais parler de l'horreur, ce sentiment odieux, & fort inutile au Theatre" (22).[12]

Because La Mesnardière gives more attention to horror than other major theorists of tragedy, it is worth considering at length the problems horror poses for his view of tragedy and the definitions and restrictions he sets forth. He follows Aristotle's lead in attempting to define tragedy largely on the basis of the emotions awakened in the spectator. Citing Aristotle's claim that tragedy should produce *Eleos* or *Phobos,* which he translates as *compassion* and *terreur,* La Mesnardière comments that terror is useful because it inspires repentance: "la juste Terreur excitée dans les esprits par les peines des criminels, produit un effet profitable, par le repentir qu'elle inspire aux vicieux" (22). This description of the useful emotion, *phobos,* distinguishes the effect produced in the mind from the presumably physical suffering inflicted on criminals. A series of relays is established between the physical and the mental or spiritual, and *phobos* is attached to this "higher" faculty. A second distinction made implicitly by La Mesnardière is that between the past and the future. In the case of criminals, both their misdeeds and their apprehension for those misdeeds are past, whereas the *vicieux* who watch or hear of the punishments have either not yet committed the crimes to which they are inclined or have not yet been caught. The fear awakened in them would be forward-looking and useful in preventing crime. These distinctions, though implicit in La Mesnardière's first approach to the problem, are important for the understanding of his complaints about the translation of *phobos* into *horror* by Aristotle's Latin interpreters. *Horror,* according to La Mesnardière, means "Crainte & Horreur," whereas Aristotle meant only to signify *crainte* (33). La Mesnardière thus pushes horror away, though without explicitly defining it, while he promotes fear as a useful spiritual and didactic concept: "la sagesse commence par la crainte du Seigneur." La Mesnardière's task of purifying *phobos*/fear of its associations with the repulsive, sensualistic, and physical horror is not an easy one. Over several pages he complicates his task by admitting that the Greek poets misuse their own language by confusing horror with a "follie semblable à l'Enthousiasme" (24). He admits further that Aristotle uses a verb "qui signifie *frissonner* . . . qui exprime le Frisson attaché à certaines fiévres, & d'où sans doute est venue le *Frigere* des Latins, qui a fait nostre mot François." *Phobos* makes us shiver, but is not the "sentiment meslé de dégoust, de mépris & d'aversion" designated by *Horror.*

In this tangle of distinctions, La Mesnardière resorts next to a moral criterion. Horror is provoked in the spectator by a scale of ethical values: "nous ressentons proprement ce que nous appellons Horreur, lors que nous voyons commettre une cruauté detestable, une infame trahison, ou quelque semblable bassesse, qui offense nôtre esprit sans épouvanter nôtre cœur" (25). Horror affects the mind or *esprit* of a spectator but does not produce fear. The type of affect induced by horror is somewhat unclear. Horrible spectacles offend the mind, whereas earlier they are said to provoke disgust, scorn, and aversion. It would be clear to La Mesnardière's readers that horror as moral offense and as disgust is based on the refinement of the viewer's sensibility and moral standards, since the opening comments of the *Poëtique* are explicit in stating that only those of elevated social station can appreciate tragedy, which the people will never understand (folios N-P). Utility and pleasure—*le profit et la volupté*—are one for the refined spectator. Horror is therefore both disagreeable to such a person and ethically offensive. Terror, on the other hand, is highly desirable. La Mesnardière counsels to

> bien émouvoir la Terreur; Et si la Fable qu'il expose, finit par la
> punition de la Personne detestable, il doit dépeindre en ses supplices de

si effroyables tourmens, & de si cuisans remors, qu'il n'y ait point de
Spectateur coupable du mesme crime, ou disposé à le commetre, qui ne
tremble de frayeur lors qu'il entendra les plaintes, les cris & les hurle-
mens qu'arrachent des maux si sensibles au criminel qui les endure. . . .
Pour représenter ces tourmens, qu'il s'imagine vivement les douleurs
d'un Ixion attaché sur une rouë, & celles d'un Promethée enchaisné sur
un rocher, où un Vautour affamé lui vient déchirer les entrailles . . .
(99-100)

The boundary—difficult as it is to recognize in the sensory manifestations—
between the horrible and the terrible is drawn with a view to the situation of
the aristocratic audience. Terror should induce repentance in the vicious, it
should "épouvanter notre cœur." The events represented in tragedy should
frighten princes: "Les Princes doivent seuls estre effrayez des disgraces
de leurs semblables, qui sont sévèrement punis pour leurs méchantes
actions . . . " (N). Horror is not fear, argues La Mesnardière, and therefore
will not alter the conduct of the prince. It does not hold forth an idea of what
is going to happen to them. Horror is, then, in a sense, provoked by events
without historical significance since horror does not awaken the comparative
and mimetic response through which princes learn to avoid falling into the
crimes of similar princes. This, rather, is the effect of tragic terror.

La Mesnardière's difficulties in defining and containing horror reveal, however, that this concept is indissolubly linked with spectacle.
Horror is provoked "lorsque nous *voyons* commettre une cruauté detestable
. . . " (25, emphasis added). Second, horror marks the boundary of some
form of tolerance, the point at which repulsion replaces desire or temptation.
Third, horror is not connected to the *interest* of the spectator in the sense
that he or she has something at stake. Terror or fear (*phobos*) proposes
some interchange between spectator and spectacle, offers, that is, some
chance that what is seen happening might happen in turn to the viewer. In
this respect we could read La Mesnardière's horror as offering an aesthetic
experience to the extent that the aesthetic, a category not invoked by thinkers
of La Mesnardière's time, offers a disinterested experience of perception.
Although La Mesnardière does not speak of the "aesthetic," he does situate
horror beyond both the pleasurable and the useful, thus conferring on it a
quality that resembles the "aesthetic distance" of later criticism. Indeed, La
Mesnardière's horror is akin to the sublime of the later seventeenth century.

Distancing horror and disconnecting it from the spectator's own fate
does not mean removing the physical destruction which may be associated

with horror. We should be careful not to confuse La Mesnardière's position with what we retrospectively define as the *bienséances* of French classical theatre. It would be easy to assume that La Mesnardière simply banished violence from the stage. Instead, La Mesnardière classifies deaths or "Spectacles funestes" into three types: generous, horrible, and hazardous spectacles. All these involve the staged representation of some potentially mortal action. La Mesnardière actually recommends that death be enacted on stage when it is *généreux*. For instance, he praises "la mort d'un jeune Prince, qui aprés mille regrets capables d'arracher des larmes des cœurs les plus insensibles, se tuë genereusement auprés du corps de sa Maitresse" (206), and it seems proper to him that in Seneca's *Phaedra* the queen dies on stage: "peut-on la voir mourir auprés du corps de ce Prince par un supplice volontaire, sans concevoir de la Terreur qui corrige puissamment les ames incestueuses de l'inclination qu'elles ont à ces detestables amours?" (207). La Mesnardière's impassioned defense of staged deaths leads him to praise enactments of suicides, death by lightning, ax-murder, and the crushing of children. Defending the ancients against Castelvetro, La Mesnardière writes: "nous lui découvrirons Que des dix Poëmes tragiques que les Latins nous ont laissez, il en détruit les six plus beaux, où la Scene est ensanglantée. Phedre s'y tuë dans l'*Hippolyte* en la presence de Thesée, & de tous ceux qui la contemplent. Megare & ses deux enfans sont écrasez aux yeux du Peuple dans l'*Hercule furieux*. Le desespoir d'Iocaste ensanglante le Theatre dans *la merveilleuse Edipe*. Hercule expire sur la Scene au sommet *du mont Œta*. Une Mere dénaturée massacre l'un de ses enfans à la veuë de tout le monde . . . " (208).

Such murders and suicides are supposed to be agreeable to the spectator for mimetic reasons; they provide examples for reenactment: "Il faut sans doute avoüer que les meurtres de cette espece n'ont rien qui ne soit agreable, ni mesme qui ne soit utile; & qu'ils ne mettent dans les ames que des exemples vertueux d'un repentir plein de justice, qui merite d'estre imité pour le moins dans les sentimens, puis qu'on n'en doit pas imiter les genereuses actions" (207).

La Mesnardière tempers his fervor for staged murders for practical and ethical reasons. The practical reasons to avoid murder on stage are that it is sometimes difficult and dangerous to carry them out. The hazardous spectacles are ones which risk the lives of the actors (202). A second practical reasons for not staging such scenes as the crushing of Megara and her children is that the machinery for death and torture may be more comical than tragic: "On ne met point au Theatre les espées, les gibets, les roües, le feu . . . il est tres-difficile d'imiter ces bourrelleries sans que la feinte en soit grossiere, & par consequent ridicule" (205).

The other grounds for banishing certain murders from the stage can be termed ethical and are joined to La Mesnardière's campaign against horror: "ne pouvant fournir que des exemples detestables de parricides & de meurtres accompagnez de cruauté, il n'excite dans les esprits qu'un transsissement odieux & une horreur desagreable, qui surmontent infiniment la Terreur & la Pitié qui doivent regner l'une ou l'autre . . . dans une parfaite Tragedie" (204). In contrast to the *généreux* spectacles of murder and suicide, which offer models of noble conduct, horror overwhelms the pity and terror which are based on what we would call identification. Horror paralyzes the beholders, makes them *transis*. It seems that horrible spectacles appeal solely to our sense of the present rather than permitting the mental imitation of beautiful murders by which we project them into our own first-person future. The playwright's challenge is not so much to eliminate horror totally from tragedy as to place it at an appropriate remove in order to temper horror's precedence over the other emotions.

La Mesnardière's preoccupation with horror seems to lead him into gratuitous multiplication of examples of the kind of act that is repulsive enough to provoke this emotion: "cette Mere qui trempa les mains dans le sang de ceux qu'elle avoit engendrez . . . égorger . . . la pitoyable Polyxene . . . " (204-05). Many of these examples concern visual representation as opposed to verbal representation of horrible acts in theatrical narrative. He blames Seneca for having placed Medea's infanticide on stage rather than offstage, yet La Mesnardière does not question the necessity for the acts themselves to be part of the tragic plot. He therefore reinforces the idea that horror is a fundamental component of ancient tragedy. Horror, it seems, cannot be eliminated, but by being placed out of sight it can be removed both from our presence and our present. The horrible deed which occurs offstage returns only in the past (and the past tense) through the relay of a character. The character is exposed to the horrible and may feel horror, but the spectator does not. This arrangement for relaying the information without provoking the revulsion of a horrible event conforms to what Spitzer called the "klassische Dämpfung."[13]

Yet, however much relegating horrible acts offstage may attenuate the paralyzing effect, tragedy cannot seem to be theorized without repeatedly encountering horror. La Mesnardière lists horror as one of several emotions that can be used in tragedy: "l'horreur, l'amour, la jalousie, l'ambition, l'envie & la haine, & d'autres pareils mouvements, peuvent encore estre

employés dans nostre Poëme tragique" (104). Towards the end of *La
Poëtique* La Mesnardière seems to be sufficiently troubled by his own recurrent appeal to horror to feel that he must redeem it somehow. It seems that
there are, after all, two kinds of horror, one good and one bad. Good horror confirms the spectator in his or her sense of superiority. This horror is
"une Passion qui nous fait abhorrer le vice par une haine constante, vertu-
euse, & qui nous plaist; à cause que nous sçavons bien que nous sommes
fort raisonnables dans un si juste sentiment" (324). The other horror is the
familiar paralysis which is, throughout, associated with disgust, "un
mouvement plein de dégoust & d'aversion, qui offense & blesse nôtre ame,
pour peu qu'elle soit généreuse; pour ce qu'elle ne peut souffrir ni l'excès
de la perfidie, ni celui de la cruauté qui causent ce transsissement" (324).
Not surprisingly, both forms of horror reveal the spectator's condition of
moral virtue and good taste. The distinction seems to be primarily a matter
of the spectator's pleasure at the revulsion he or she feels. We can even
suppose that the two kinds of horror are the same horror expressed in
different ways, since it is a pleasure to have sufficient *générosité* to be offended. The second horror is the price to pay as proof of one's taste. The
issue that remains open is the line between what is bearable, yet sufficiently
méchant to provoke the audience's abhorrence.

The line between the acceptable and the excessively horrible is even
harder to maintain when La Mesnardière describes as exemplary of good
tragedy a crime which has all the qualities elsewhere censured: atrocity,
blood, parricide, cruelty, and odiousness. Describing Euripides' *Electra,*
La Mesnardière praises the perpetrators' description of their atrocity in
killing their mother: "Après avoir répété comment la Reine leur Mere ouvrit
sa gorge devant eux pour émouvoir à pitié ceux qu'elle avoit mis au monde;
Après avoir répété les Raisons qu'elle avança pour condamner leur dessein,
les prieres qu'elle fist pour détourner leur cruauté, le pardon qu'elle de-
manda pour adoucir leur fureur: Bref aprés avoir retouché les pitoyables circonstances d'une action si barbare, ils éxagerent eux-mesmes l'atrocité de ce
forfait, pour se rendre plus odieux et moins dignes de compassion" (232).
The praise La Mesnardière heaps on this example is partly justified by the
conversion of horror into terror. If horror is the immediate revulsion felt by
the well-born for atrocities, then the repentance of Electra and Orestes
demonstrates the passage from an immediate, temporally present experience
to a past-and-future-oriented act of fear and shame. Looking now upon the
act they have committed, they fear the consequences of their act for the future. This temporalization can be seized in the terms of *honte* and *terreur,*

the sentiments that now dominate them. La Mesnardière accentuates the shift in time, the stark contrast between the son's and daughter's feeling before and after their deed: "Ils sont enfin si effrayez de leur sanglante execution, qu'ils ne peuvent supporter la seule veuë de ce corps qu'ils cherchaient avec tant d'ardeur avant que de l'avoir tué . . ." (232).

Horror, as disgust and aversion, appears as the reverse and complement of corporal desire. Horror is reverse eros. Like the erotic, the horrible is fixated on the body, and in tragedy both horror and eros are in some way placed outside the bounds of "normal" physical relations. In *Electra* Orestes and Electra ardently seek the body of their mother, which is partially undressed for them before they dismember it. After their mother's death they still relate to her physically in an abnormal way. Excessive interest in her body, which they will mutilate, gives way to excessive revulsion from that body. Like eros, horror concerns viewing bodies and the effect that view has on the physical sensations of the viewer. What makes Euripides' work acceptable to La Mesnardière is the movement beyond that fixation towards fear, *phobos*.

Orestes and Electra serve as mediators between horror and terror in two ways. First, they experience horror themselves at sights and acts which would provoke horror in any *généreux* spectator. By experiencing this sentiment themselves, within the world of the tragedy, they seem to discharge a function of disapproval which otherwise would have been passed on to the audience. Horror seems acceptable and even praiseworthy when it is *performed*. Therefore, within the tragic spectacle, it is rather the *horrible* than *horror* itself which should be banished or at least contained.

If we look at the example of horror with which we began in Bénichou's *Morales du grand siècle,* Corneille's *Rodogune* does fit La Mesnardière's description of horror in certain respects. As Bénichou observes, in the character of Cléopâtre, "c'est plutôt le mépris du bien et du mal qui est sublime" (40) rather than the queen's will itself. La Mesnardière never admits admiration for transcendence of the ethical, and, indeed, is heavily moralizing where Corneille insists on the pleasure of the audience and its admiration of spectacle. However, La Mesnardière certainly does see horror as resulting from radical departures from the ethical standard which reach the point of being useless or dangerous for the tragic audience. The horrible can only provide a pernicious example if it provides a model. In Bénichou's comment that Rodogune places herself beyond ethical standards, we find a recognition that the agents of the horrible are free from ethical concerns. Yet the well-born spectators of the horrible receive the impact of horror by viewing as through the window of their moral system, looking out at an alien species. This is one of the reasons La Mesnardière tries to screen horror by interposing the concept of terror, which grounds itself in the same kind of acts and scenes as horror but classifies them and enables the audience to relate to them according to their noble social standards. Cléopâtre does not attempt, nor does Corneille's play suggest, any overthrow of the institutions of justice or morality in general. Instead she acts alone and without regard for a future, general modification of social standards.

Cléopâtre's disdain for the future is conveyed clearly in her attempts to destroy her children. While she succeeds in killing only one, the project of eliminating the future and of bringing her dynasty to an end with herself could be seen as emblematic of horror as the force which reduces everything to the present, as the force which *freezes* in the *transsissement* to which La Mesnardière appeals repeatedly. Terror, as fear, in La Mesnardière's system appeals to the spectator's self-interest and sense of the replicable effects of actions. Cléopâtre's whole aim is to prevent replication, to deny the consequences of reproduction itself. At first glance, it may seem highly speculative to interpret Corneille's queen's parricide as an emblem or allegory of horror. Two reasons justify such a reading. First, throughout *Rodogune* there is the specter of horror. Corneille himself wrote in his *Examen* of the steps he took to eliminate or mitigate the incest in which the two male heroes seem to be involved.[14] Cléopâtre's act is indisputably horrible; Corneille refers to it more than once as "dénaturé"[15] The characters of the play describe what she does as belonging to the category of horror. Antiochus, speaking of his brother's death, calls it "l'horreur de cette mort" (v. 1798). Secondly, the paradigm of parricide is routinely associated with horror in La Mesnardière. We can therefore discern a nexus between the conceptual disjunction of horror from historical continuity and the horrifying disruption of genetic continuity which is expressed in the physical destruction of parents and children. This link is particularly strong when the parent destroys the child and therefore eliminates the future, which is the time in which the lessons of tragic action can be applied—the time of terror. Cléopâtre's act—that is, the two-phased act of killing her sons, after having assured the death of their father—is a horrible act because it reduces the world to the present of physical paralysis and disintegration.[16]

Perhaps the most striking demonstration of the implosion of history which occurs in horror—that is the freezing effect of the horrible act—is Cléopâtre's view of the future. We have seen that horror does not concern the future, and therefore it may seem contradictory to ascribe a view of the future to a dramatic figure chosen to emblematize horror. Some of Cléopâtre's last words reveal, however, that she wishes a future that is frozen into the horrific moment of her own death:

> Puisse le ciel tous deux vous prendre pour victimes,
> Et laisser choir sur vous les peines de mes crimes!
> Puissiez-vous ne trouver dedans votre union
> Qu'horreur, que jalousie, et que confusion!
> Et pour vous souhaiter tous les malheurs ensemble,
> Puisse naître de vous un fils qui me ressemble.   (V, 4, 1819-24)

Cléopâtre's most horrifying gesture is undoubtedly this refusal of reconciliation at the moment of her death, a mother's dying curse. She not only explicitly calls down upon her son *horreur,* but she takes the step of defining the ultimate horror: a child like herself! Unlike terror, which is the fear of an effect following from a specified cause, horror does not distinguish between cause and effect and therefore does not propose a means to avoid consequences. La Mesnardière carefully denies to horror the quality of fear while ascribing to horror revulsion, aversion, and disgust. Cléopâtre's dying words are an attempt to fix this moment of disgust forever so that—just as in nightmares in which enormous effort produces no movement—the future can only hold the *transsissement* of the moment of her dying.[17]

In centering a discussion of horror on La Mesnardière's *Poëtique* and then shifting to an example of horror in a Cornelian tragedy I cannot help feeling uneasy and unconvinced before La Mesnardière's utilitarian systematization of horror. This uneasiness is intensified by Corneille's apparent unapologetic delight in a play dominated by horror—he wrote that he preferred *Rodogune* to all his plays, "un effet de ces inclinations aveugles, qu'ont beaucoup de pères pour quelques-uns de leurs enfants" (200)—as contrasted with La Mesnardière's constant struggle to distinguish between scenes of horror and scenes of terror. In certain respects Corneille's Rodogune conforms to La Mesnardière's descriptions of horror, as we have seen, but a modern reader—as, perhaps, also a seventeenth-century reader—can surely be forgiven for not always being able to distinguish in the *Poëtique* between good terror and bad horror. There is a certain unpredictability to the classification. Although one can find consistency in the *a posteriori* arguments by which La Mesnardière justifies the category in which he places his examples, it seems unlikely that one could learn from the *Poëtique* to determine in advance how other examples would fit. La Mesnardière himself trips up occasionally, by ending descriptions of terror with a phrase like "mais sortons de ces horreurs."[18]

It does not seem farfetched to suppose that, despite La Mesnardière's repeated attempts to deny it, horror is the fundamental tragic sentiment. Indeed, precisely because it is fundamental, La Mesnardière tries to find ways to preserve horror within a didactic, Horatian view of tragedy. As a result, the erotic and horrific fixation on bodies, on their members and on blood, has got to be connected to the instructional purpose which recuperates these acts for historical knowledge. If La Mesnardière had been able to dispense altogether with horror he would not have had to devote so much of his text to terror nor would he have invented the categories of good horror and of the *spectacles généreux*. In order to enjoy the spectacles of carnage and of cruelty in tragedy, La Mesnardière creates his elaborate and confusing system of relays through which horror is converted to terror within tragedy rather than being passed directly to the audience. In this way an ethical framework is created to veil horror in a kind of translucence so that it can be enjoyed while releasing the audience from any responsibility for the acts committed before them.

Much of the difficulty of describing horror in a consistent manner comes from the *a priori* definition of the tragic audience as limited to princes. Because the spectator as well as the *personae* of tragedy are well-born and politically important and because the usefulness of tragedy consists of teaching applicable lessons to such an audience, an emotion which transcends class distinction is suspect from La Mesnardière's point of view. La Mesnardière never specifically denies that the common people may feel horror, but it is clear that they cannot feel tragic terror. Terror requires the spectator to identify sufficiently with the dramatic character to fear that the same fate awaits him or her. The common people therefore have nothing to fear from the fate of princes or princesses. Horror also, at times, seems to be related to class. The well-born are repelled by certain spectacles because of their highly refined sensibilities. Could horror be described as the noble recognition of a common humanity in which nobility yields to a class-free penchant for destruction? Or is it rather a recognition of the way the conduct of princes, with its privilege of violence subject only to the fragile regulation of self-control, must appear to the masses?

What distinguishes La Mesnardière's approach to the conservation of horror in an age of politeness is his willingness to represent spectacles of death and other physical degradation on stage. He does not adopt routinely the technique of visual concealment which characterizes most of Cornelian and Racinian theatre. La Mesnardière attempts instead to use nonvisual screening procedures to frame horror into an ethically acceptable form. In the process of doing this he emphasizes its importance for a seventeenth-century sensibility, and thus, I would argue, invites us to look again at the tragedy of the period. Tending to ignore the horrible, twentieth-century readers accentuate the relays or mediators which are carefully placed near the horrible, but not necessarily in such a way as to conceal it altogether. Whether it be the needle which Dorise thrusts into the eye of her assailant in *Clitandre,* the wound through which the valor of the deceased Don Gomès speaks to his daughter Chimène in *Le Cid,* or the bloody grass that testifies to the complete physical destruction of Hippolyte in *Phèdre,* acts or sights which can be expected to awaken disgust and aversion are common in seventeenth-century theatre. This horror is an aspect of classical drama that deserves more substantial recognition.

NOTES

1 Bénichou, Paul, *Morales du grand siècle* (Paris: NRF/Idées paperback, 1948), 40.

2 Jean Pierre Camus, *Les Spectacles d'horreur.* (Paris: A. Soubron, 1630. Reprinted by Slatkine Reprints, Geneva, 1973).

3 D'Aubignac, Abbé (François d'Hedelin), *La Pratique du Théâtre,* edited by Pierre Martino (Algiers: Jules Carbonel, 1927), 73.

4 La Mesnardière, H.-J. Pilet de, *La Poëtique* (Paris: Antoine de Sommaville, 1640; Reprinted: Geneva, Slatkine, 1972), 202.

5 Voltaire, *"Le carnage et l'horreur,* termes vagues et usées qu'il faut éviter. Aujourd'hui tous les mauvais versificateurs emploient le carnage et l'horreur à la fin d'un vers . . . " ("Remarque sur *Sertorius,"* in *Commentaires sur Corneille* [Paris: Firmin-Didot, n.d.], 489).

6 Scherer, Jacques, *La Dramaturgie classique en France* (Paris: Nizet, 1950; rpt. 1968), 415.

7 La Mesnardière, 222.

8 On the other hand, the horrible is clearly connected to the influence of Seneca on Renaissance tragedy. See Ronald Tobin, *Racine and Seneca* (Chapel Hill: North Carolina University Press, 1971). The important figure of Medea is conveyed to modern playwrights through Seneca, and Medea is crucial for the link of the "denatured" mother to horror. See Mitchell Greenberg, "Mythifying Matrix: Corneille's Médée" in *Corneille, Classicism & the Ruses of Symmetry* (Cambridge: Cambridge University Press, 1986), 16-36.

9 D'Aubignac, 143.

[10] Académie française, *Dictionnaire de l'Académie française* (Second edition. Paris, 1695; reprinted Geneva: Slatkine, 1968).

[11] Furetière, Antoine, *Essais d'un Dictionnaire universel* (Amsterdam, 1687; reprinted, Geneva: Slatkine, 1968).

[12] Gellrich, Michelle, *Tragedy and Theory. The Problem of Conflict Since Aristotle* (Princeton: Princeton University Press, 1988).

[13] "Racine's Classical *piano,*" in *Leo Spitzer: Essays on Seventeenth-Century French Literature,* translated by David Bellos (Cambridge: Cambridge University Press, 1983), 1-113.

[14] *Examen* in *Œuvres complètes,* ed. Georges Couton (Paris: Bibliothèque de la Pléiade, Gallimard, 3 vols, 1980-87), II, 202.

[15] *Examen* of *Rodogune* (199), where Corneille calls Cléopâtre herself "dénaturée," and the dedicatory letter where her act is called an "effet dénaturé" (196).

[16] Mitchell Greenberg appropriately refers to the "metaphysical quagmire" of late Cornelian tragedy in discussing the ending of *Rodogune,* 153.

[17] For a discussion of the horror created by the perspective of transgressing moral absolutes in *Rodogune,* see Pizzorusso, Arnaldo, "Rodogune: un teatro dell'orrore," *Prospettive seconde, studi francesi,* (Pisa: Pacini, 1977), 25-44. *Rodogune* can also be usefully discussed with reference to the emotion of fear, as in the master's thesis of Kendall B. Tarte, "The Articulation of Fear in Pierre Corneille's *Rodogune*" (University of Virginia, 1990).

[18] This is how he ends his discussion of the tourments which *should* be represented to "bien émouvoir la Terreur" (99) by imitating the punishments of Ixion and Prometheus. Yet is is not clear why or whether the punishment of Prometheus is itself good and deserved.

3

Sacred and Heroic Blood and the Religion of Monarchy on the Cornelian Stage

Harriet Ray Allentuch

> I kneele for help; O! lay that hand on me,
> Adored Caesar! and my Faith is such,
> I shall be heal'd, if that my KING but touch.
> The Evill is not Yours: my sorrow sings,
> Mine is the Evill, but the Cure, the KINGS.
> —Robert Herrick, *Hesperides* (1648)

EVEN THOUGH RATIONALISM IS a prominent intellectual trend in seventeenth-century Europe, magical and religious modes of thought survive tenaciously. In France this is apparent not only in the bizarre medical practices, witch trials, and black masses that coexist with the new physics, but in political thought where a cluster of myths surrounding kingship, a magico-theological inheritance from the middle ages, shows stubborn persistence.[1] According to this mystical constellation of beliefs, the king is God's lieutenant: he holds his position by heaven's decree and passes it on through the divinely ordained principle of primogeniture. It follows that he and his children are of a different nature from other mortals and, as vessels of sacred blood, merit veneration even when they abuse their powers. To question this mysterious transmission of sacred authority through the blood line is to oppose God's will and undermine the structure of His universe.

Of a piece with these beliefs is the conviction that monarchs display their sacred origin in their physical appearance and in the exercise of preternatural powers. Kingship is said to shine forth in their faces; royal legitimacy in their performance of miracles. The January 1, 1633, issue of *Le Mercure français* depicts Louis XIII in the midst of 300 sick people seeking his touch for its therapeutic effect.[2] The medieval assumption that contact with the king's hand cures scrofula, while fading in England, survives throughout the reign of the seventeenth-century French Bourbons and even beyond. Henry IV, Louis XIII, and Louis XIV touch thousands of Frenchmen.[3] God's will, it is believed, passes through their fingertips. By the same token, good kings are said to heal moral ills, inspire miraculous conversions, and bring peace to unquiet minds.

To what extent do the dramas of Pierre Corneille, coeval with the reigns of Louis XIII and XIV and the rise of the early modern state, reflect this medieval heritage of politico-religious fantasies, myths, and superstitions? There are no royal claps of thunder on the Cornelian stage. No Cornelian monarch makes the crops grow or the fishes multiply. But here and there, in plays adapted from ancient, medieval, and Renaissance sources and rethought to reflect seventeenth-century French attitudes, there are echoes, not only of the principles of absolutist monarchy, as rationalized in contemporary political writings, but of the tenets of monarchical religion whose claims have little to do with reason.

In some of Corneille's plays, for example, the blood of kings works magic. In *Œdipe,* the French playwrights's free adaptation of Sophocles' *Oedipus rex,* Corneille rewrites the Greek *dénouement* to create an Oedipus whose blood performs miracles. No sooner does the king strike out his eyes than the issuance of royal blood cures the Theban plague and three men are resurrected from the dead. Awe fills the characters on stage as they listen to this recital of miraculous healing:

> Là ses yeux arrachés par ses barbares mains
> Font distiller un sang qui rend l'âme aux Thébains.
> Ce sang si précieux touche à peine la terre,
> Que le courroux du Ciel ne leur fait plus la guerre,
> Et trois mourants, guéris au milieu du Palais,
> De sa part tout d'un coup nous annoncent la paix.
>   (V, 9, 1995-2000)[4]

Other Cornelian kings emanate an aura through their sacred character that moves the beholder and lingers in his consciousness. A virtuous usurper, Grimoald, rules in *Pertharite,* but he fails to obliterate the image of the king he has detroned. Pertharite has only to show his face to be revered; though he is a prisoner, his people cling to him. Grimoald, too, surrenders to the magic of the royal visage and feels the inner tremor a royal presence excites.

> Un Roi, quoique vaincu, garde son caractère,
> Aux fidèles Sujets sa vue est toujours chère;
> Au moment qu'il paraît, les plus grands Conquérants,
> Pour vertueux qu'ils soient ne sont que des Tyrans,
> Et dans le fond des cœurs sa présence fait naître
> Un mouvement secret qui les rend à leur maître.
>
> (V, 2, 1591-96)

According to Cléopâtre in *La Mort de Pompée,* the sacred blood works not only upon the beholder, but instinctively, upon the royal heart, infusing monarchs with courage and high principle: "Cette haute vertu, dont le Ciel et le sang/ Enflent toujours les cœurs de ceux de notre rang" (275-76).[5]   Nevertheless, some Cornelian kings betray their "natural instincts." Cléopâtre's brother, Ptolomée, for example, violates the law of sanctity when he orders Pompée's murder. This does not mean, says Cléopâtre, speaking for the religion of monarchy, that Ptolomée lacks divine inspiration, but that he has fallen under the influence of evil advisors who deafen the voice of the blood. By a magical transference of responsibility, the monarch's "nature" is never to blame. His blood is infallible, if it is heeded.

> Les Princes ont cela de leur haute naissance
> Leur âme dans leur sang prend des impressions
> Qui dessous leur vertu rangent leurs passions,
> Leur générosité soumet tout à leur gloire,
> Tout est illustre en eux quand ils daignent se croire,
> Et si le Peuple y voit quelques dérèglements,
> C'est quand l'avis d'autrui corrompt leurs sentiments.
>
> (II, 1, 370-76)

These expressions of monarchical religion—rulers born to perform miracles, infused with mana, endowed, if they listen to the promptings of their blood, with spiritual infallibility—conflict on the Cornelian stage with the representation of an aristocratic and stoic ethos according to which individuals prove their superiority in tests of physical or moral strength. Most of Corneille's enduring successes correspond to those plays in which his protagonists overcome exceptional adversity and make themselves larger than life. Moral dynamism, the impassioned exercise of the will, the resistance to oppression and the drive toward self-dominion have long been recognized as distinctively Cornelian. Heroic vision and heroic poetry unite in the pulsing alexandrines for which Corneille is famous. His most dramatically enthralling theater results from this union.

Of course Corneille's "self-made" heroes and heroines are themselves examples of a blood mystique. The term "généreux," so often applied to them, comes from the Latin *genus* and means, in its original sense, belonging to a stock or race. These figures are "bien nés," born with a predisposition for excellence. Their courage is stamped in their aristocratic blood. Rodrigue and Don Sanche, for example, are "formés d'un sang noble, vaillant, fidèle (*Le Cid,* I, 1, 12); their eyes glow with "l'éclatante vertu de leurs braves aïeux" (I, 1, 14). Cinna declares: "Je suis Romain, et du sang de Pompée" (*Cinna,* V,1, 1546). Emilie is ready to stand alone against Auguste and despite his favors, refuses to "sell her blood" (*Cinna,* I, 2, 84). Polyeucte's blood miraculously converts unbelievers.

Still, there is an important distinction to be made between Corneille's aristocratic protagonists and many of his monarchs. The hero or heroine's triumphs may be anticipated, but they are never ready-made. Heroic "mana" flows not solely from "nature" but from painful choices and extraordinary exploits; these are expected to end only with death. Those monarchs who heed their blood have only to show themselves to accomplish miracles; the heroic aristocrat, like the aged Roman general Sertorius, goes on struggling, overcoming obstacles, transcending wayward passions. In the famous lines where Rodrigue identifies his father's blood with his own, there is no passive acceptance of his destiny. Rodrigue is spurring himself to show his superiority in action.

> Cette ardeur que dans les yeux je porte,
> Sais-tu que c'est son sang? le sais-tu?
> . . . .
> A quatre pas d'ici je te le fais savoir.
> *Le Cid,* (II, 2, 403-05)

Rodrigue stands here at the opening moment of a career of restless self-enlargement. Many of Corneille's kings, defined by sacred blood and semi-divinity, have only to be themselves to achieve enlargement.

Thus we can discern two conflicting ontologies at work in Corneille's theater—one religious, attached to hereditary monarchs and representing a descent of being from above; another, no less "racist" in its expression, but heroic, representing an unending struggle to create oneself.[6] The contradiction runs throughout Corneille's serious theater and is a persistent feature of his dramaturgy. At the same time a diachronic reading reveals patterns in the rise and fall, conflict and combination of these ontologies. The emphasis falls now one way, now the other at different moments in the playwright's long career. At times the heroic ethos predominates, overshadowing the worship of kings; elsewhere monarchical religion comes to the fore; on occasion the two are fused. Where magic and religion dominate and there is no trial by fire, the playwright's creative imagination rarely soars. Where his principals strive to achieve an identity of their own making, the magic of drama often prevails.

During the first and most successful phase of Corneille's dramatic career (1629-42), the theme of heroic self-fashioning clearly dominates. Here Corneille seldom dwells upon the divine nature of kings. *Cinna* is the only play of the period in which a sovereign is ardently celebrated in religious language. For the most part, in Corneille's early tragedies, aristocratic heroes are sundered by conflicts they struggle with in resonant poetry. Kings prove crucial to the action in *Le Cid* and *Horace:* they reintegrate the hero into the community, pardon his transgressions and enlist him in the service of the state. But they are respected rather than held in awe and their role is primarily utilitarian. They dispense justice and quiet the passions; the aristocratic hero commands the spotlight.[7]

In *Cinna,* however, Corneille works an important change, fusing hero and monarch. Auguste, an aristocrat who has battled his way to the throne, becomes a sacred emperor. To plot his hero's transformation in dramatically exciting and convincing terms, Corneille gradually directs attention away from the group of young aristocratic conspirators, whose plot against the emperor initially engages the audience's sympathies, and toward the ruler himself, who is locked in a moral crisis. This crisis emerges first against the background of the consultation scene, where the emperor confesses his uneasiness with a power seized in combat and held by force. Later, after the revelation that those he has loved best conspire against him, he again examines his life in a soliloquy that pits his younger self, the usurper Octave, still addicted to violence and demanding revenge, against Auguste, the emperor, responsible for public order. Peace comes to the state and legitimacy to the monarch as the result of an act of self-dominion.

Auguste separates himself entirely from Octave when he refuses to renew the cycle of violence. Moreover, by pardoning those who betray him, he sacrifices the passions glimpsed in earlier scenes—wounded feelings, humiliation, rage—and establishes a new model of moral courage. Corneille represents Auguste's change in the language of battle; it is a "victory," but the enemy Auguste conquers is himself. The emperor memorializes his triumph in Corneille's most famous ontological proclamation:

> Je suis maître de moi comme de l'univers.
> Je le suis, je veux l'être. O Siècles, ô Mémoire,
> Conservez à jamais ma dernière victoire.
> (V, 3, 1696-98)

Auguste is the only monarch on the Cornelian stage who, lacking the sacred blood, makes himself sacred by heroic means. Immediately following his willed "rebirth," religious notes resound; he works miracles upon the conspirators. Emilie extolls his healing powers, evidenced in her own sudden moral change, her "repentance" and "recovery of sight." Her long-held hatred dissipates as she embraces a new conception of the state and Auguste's sovereignty finds validation in the magic he works upon her.

> Et je me rends, Seigneur, à ces hautes bontés,
> Je recouvre la vue auprès de leurs clartés,
> Je connais mon forfait qui me semblait justice,
> Et ce que n'avait pu la terreur du supplice,
> Je sens naître en mon âme un repentir puissant
> Et mon cœur en secret me dit qu'il y consent.
> (V, 3, 1715-1720)

Before the curtain falls, prophecies are heard on stage. The power of divination descends upon Livie who speaks for the gods: Rome "n'a plus de vœux que pour la Monarchie" (1770). As Auguste changes, so too does the world and both achieve peace under a new political order. The heroic monarch surrounded by a religious aura and worshipped by once rebellious, now devoted subjects is a highpoint of political idealism on the Cornelian stage. The two ontologies are harmoniously fused.

In the middle period of Corneille's career (1643-59), things change once more. The world represented on stage, like Octave's Rome, is again in turmoil, but the monarch, usurper or hereditary king, is most often a weakling or a despot. The period opens with *La Mort de Pompée,* where King Ptolomée cowers in the midst of a crisis-ridden Egypt, and it ends with *Œdipe,* a play overlapping the middle and late periods. Here the king, Thebes's savior in the final moments, is, for much of the action, her tyrant.

Paradoxically, despite the decline in the image of the ruler in most of Corneille's works at this time, the sacred ontology flourishes here: being descends from above and monarchical religion captures the language. The passages cited earlier to illustrate the king's sacred nature and powers all come from plays of this period—*La Mort de Pompée, Pertharite,* and *Œdipe.* Royal legitimacy and the claims of the blood become an obsessive motif in this phase of Corneille's career. *Rodogune* (1645), for example, turns on the issue of primogeniture and princely blood rights. A widowed queen has borne twin sons, but clasping power to herself, refuses to identify her first born and yield him the throne. Providence intervenes to crush her and crown the sacred blood. A similar message emerges from *Héraclius* (1647) where a tyrant in the mould of Macbeth thinks he has eliminated the emperor's male line. But the emperor's son, Héraclius, lives on in the royal palace under an assumed name. Publicly exhibiting him to the people is enough to doom the tyrant: "Montrons Héraclius au Peuple qui l'attend," becomes the play's refrain (476, 1182, and 1916), with variations on "montrons," "montrez," "montrer," ringing out until the curtain falls. Corneille "corrects" history to engineer this triumph for sacred blood. According to the playwright's sources, Héraclius is no royal son, but himself a usurper. Faithful to the religion of monarchy in this phase of his career, Corneille makes the young man's enthronement proof of the magic of legitimacy.[8]

Interestingly, at the same time that Corneille embraces the religion of monarchy, he slips into melodrama. Throughout his middle period, there are not only villanous queens and violent tyrants to overthrow, but threats of incest and muffled *cris du sang.*[9] Phocas, the usurper in *Heraclius,* tries to force a marriage between the man he considers his son and the emperor's daughter, whom he takes to be the one surviving vessel of the sacred blood. But because of an exchange of infants at the time of the emperor's murder, the usurper has mistaken the emperor's son for his own. The marriage he wants, like those narrowly missed in so many romantic fictions, is a union of brother and sister. Carlos in *Don Sanche,* like Héraclius and other heroes of melodrama, is a sovereign's heir, separated in infancy from his royal kin. Along with all the other characters in the play, including his biological mother, Carlos believes that his blood is "base." ("Son sang que le Ciel n'a

formé que de boue" [I, 1, 46]). But late in the action, Queen Léonor de-
codes heaven's language in the young man's majestic brow and claims him
for the throne.

> Et le vrai sang des Rois, sous le Sort abattu,
> Peut cacher sa naissance, et non pas sa vertu.
>
> Il porte sur le front un luisant caractère,
> Qui parle malgré lui de tout ce qu'il veut taire.
>   (IV, 3, 1315-18)

Evidence is marshaled in the form of portraits, locks of hair, and a letter
from the dead king. By the curtain's fall, Carlos, bethrothed to a queen,
unites two thrones.

Corneille's middle period, full of this monarchical fantasmagoria,
does not coincide with esthetic success. Despite many stirring passages,
none of the dramas of the period, with the exception of *Nicomède* and
Rodogune, continue in performance. The two exceptional plays have ties
with Corneille's earlier works and with the heroic ethos. For if Nicomède
derives regal hauteur from a "vieux droit d'aînesse" (IV, 4, 1357), he also
recalls the Cornelian self-created hero, confident that his deeds, and not just
his "nature," prove his worth. The villainous queen gives life to *Rodogune;*
her murderous plots and driving energy monopolize the play. She recalls
Corneille's formidable and heroic Médée, but represents a more coherent
and electrifying version of that demonic type.

It is not the royal mystique itself that interferes with dramatic success. Many of Shakespeare's best plays resound with the worship of kings
and the cries of their sacred blood. But *le merveilleux royal* does not seem
to work for Corneille. He resorts to plot convolutions and melodramatic
devices to compensate for the loss of dynamism and dazzles his audience
with ingeniously contrived situations rather than heroic soul-searching.
Pertharite, in particular, is a disappointment. It reads like a repudiation of
the main thrust of *Cinna.* There is no heroic earning of the crown here.
The virtuous usurper Grimoald, having won power by his own hand and
proven his worth as a ruler, never becomes an Auguste. Instead he abdicates in obeisance to the principle of legitimacy. The sacred blood wins the
day and the defeated Pertharite resumes the throne merely by showing himself. Even though Grimoald's sudden defection at the sight of royal blood

accords with the worship of kings, the play as a whole lacks the fire of Corneille's earlier works and meets with an immediate failure.

Discouraged by the reception of *Pertharite,* Corneille withdraws from the theater in the middle of his career and meditates upon his craft. These are the years in which he writes *Examens* and three discourses on dramatic art. Perhaps during this interval of systematic study of previous work, he also considers the problem of how to accommodate two disparate ontologies reconciled only in *Cinna. Œdipe,* in this regard, both because of its mixture of features and its late date (1659), seems a transitional work. With its startling *dénouement*—Œdipe's blood working miracles—it belongs in Corneille's middle period and provides the last fulsome expression of monarchical religion that Corneille writes for the stage.[10] But there are other elements in the play's final moments that point to a different conception of the sacred king.

Given its conflicting images of the monarch, *Œdipe* contains an ill-aligned plot. In the first half of this free adaptation of *Oedipus rex,* the playwright composes in the vein of his later career—dramas concerned with the politics of monarchy, court maneuvers, and matrimonial alliances. Œdipe appears as the queen's husband, jealous of his authority. Dircé, a newly invented character, daughter of the dead king, Laïus, views Œdipe as a usurper and herself as the blood heir to the throne. She defiantly refuses the marriage by which Œdipe intends to dispose of her. In the second half of the play, Corneille switches to the traditional story of Oedipus and here he turns his protagonist into a sacred king, the shedding of whose blood ends the Theban plague and resurrects the dead.

But suddenly, in the recital of Œdipe's self-blinding, heroic notes resound. Corneille makes the king's self-punishment an impassioned choice, a moral exploit combining self-assertion and self-sacrifice which, along with the discovery of Œdipe's royal origin, legitimizes his kingship. When Œdipe tears out his eyes, he does so with characteristic Cornelian bravura, insisting upon his autonomy in the face of a fate he has not made. The passage describing his act and evoking his voice contains a cascade of belligerent imperatives as the king rebels against unjust gods.

> Son cœur semblait calmé, je le voyais sans armes,
> Quand soudain attachant ses deux mains sur ses yeux,
> 'Prévenons, a-t-il dit, l'injustice des Dieux,
> Commençons à mourir, avant qu'ils nous l'ordonnent.
> Qu'ainsi que mes forfaits, mes supplices étonnent.

Ne voyons plus le Ciel après sa cruauté,
Pour nous venger de lui, dédaignons sa clarté,
Refusons-lui nos yeux, et gardons quelque vie
Qui montre encore à tous quelle est sa tyrannie.'
                    (V, 9, 1986-94)

In effect Corneille is changing his representation of monarchical religion here by returning in spirit to the heroic vein of *Cinna*. Just as Œdipe
condemns the gods but accepts punishment for his crimes and becomes a
sacred king, Auguste, revulsed by the order of things that turns friends into
assassins, "sacrifices" his feelings and atones for his past. Immediately
thereafter he receives divine sanction. In both instances the reward for submission is an aura of grandeur. Œdipe's sacrificial act is physical, waged
against his body; Auguste's is moral. Each sacrifice brings an ending to the
competition for greatness. Cinna and Emilie humble themselves before
Auguste; Dircé expresses allegiance to Œdipe.

Sacrifice, as René Girard illuminates the concept in *La Violence et le
sacré,* is an act of violence that absorbs all the tensions within a community,
ending the need for further aggression, and solidifies the social order. On
the Cornelian stage, starting with *Œdipe,* the "true" monarch acts as both
victim and sacrificer, dealing with himself as if he were his own enemy. By
his act, and never again by dint of royal blood alone, he brings peace to
the community and achieves sacred kingship. After *Œdipe,* the require-
ment that a monarch commit an act of self-suppression to sanctify his rule
dominates Corneille's version of the religion of monarchy.[11]

Corneille's final period, which coincides with the first years of
Louis XIV's personal reign, contains several plays whose idealism and
heroic sentiments run counter to the moral skepticism prevalent in much of
the literature of the time. The religion of monarchy Corneille upholds here
is rule by supererogatory example. The splendor of sacred blood is now,
by itself, "la vaine splendeur du sang" (*Agésilas,* II, 5, 701), insufficient to
consecrate monarchs unless they sacrifice private desires to the state. And if
they do not, they risk personal shame and political chaos.

Agésilas, Tite et Bérénice, and *Pulchérie* all display monarchs embodying the theme of sacrifice foreshadowed in *Cinna.* They ensure their
rule by self-abnegation. Whereas in the plays of Corneille's middle period,
sacred blood is fetishized and legitimacy magically imposes order, in
Corneille's late career, only sacrifice of the monarch's personal happiness
and private desires will end the feuding that threatens the state. The

monarch's self-denial becomes necessary to the body politic's survival. Agésilas embraces the intimidating general he hates and denies himself the woman he loves in order to ensure Sparta's peace. The Roman emperor, Tite, weaker than Auguste ("Maître de l'univers sans l'être de moi-même" [II, 1, 407]), nevertheless renounces happiness with Bérénice to quell dissension in Rome and ensure his brother's untroubled succession. Privation is again the key in *Pulchérie*. The empress abandons Léon, the man she loves, for a union she will never consummate, suppressing the woman for the sake of the monarch. Her sacrifice, like Auguste's, averts civil war. A rivalrous nobility, contemptuous of Léon and unwilling to see him rise above them, is silenced at the price of the monarch's self-fulfillment. To sustain the state means disregarding the private self. "Je suis Impératrice, et j'étais Pulchérie" (III, 1, 754 and 794) rings out in this play and recalls from *Tite et Bérénice:* "J'ai des yeux d'empereur et n'ai plus ceux de Tite" (II, 2, 495). Shakespeare expresses the theme elegiacally in a king's meditation: "What infinite heart's ease must kings neglect that private men enjoy" (*Henry V,* IV, 1). The self-renunciation that Corneille depicts as the moral equivalent of an heroic exploit attaches in his late plays to royal heads.

But not uniformly. For the sacred blood has lost its magic in the last phase of Corneille's career, "sang" and "qualité" diverge and hereditary kings, more often than not, prove unequal to their task. Only one monarch meets the test of greatness in *Sophonisbe,* and she lacks the sacred blood. Queen by marriage and daughter of a Carthaginian general ("digne sang d'un tel père" [V, 7, 1793]), Sophonisbe struggles alone against Roman dominion. Rather than outlive Carthage's freedom, she takes her own life, whereas the two kings who love her, unable to resist Roman power, survive in shame.[12] The captive kings in *Attila* are similarly inglorious. ("Eux qui n'ont de leur trône ici que de vains titres" [I, 1, 6]). In *Sertorius* the queen of Spain prefers marriage to a heroic general over union with a descendant of Roman kings. "Mais parmi vos Romains je prends peu garde au sang, / Quand j'y vois la vertu prendre le plus haut rang" (II, 2, 575-76). The empress Pulchérie expresses the thought that is whispered in many of Corneille's late plays: the sacred blood "degenerates." As she remembers the ill-starred reign of her royal brother, Pulchérie shows no eagerness to perpetuate her "race."

> Qu'on ne prétende plus que ma gloire s'expose
> A laisser des Césars du sang de Théodose;

> Qu'ai-je affaire de race à me déshonorer,
> Moi qui n'ai que trop vu ce sang dégénérer.
> *(Pulchérie,* V, 3, 1533-36)

At the end of Corneille's career the climate of feeling has changed and much of the exaltation has gone. The late plays, even those peopled with heroic rulers, abound in talk of vanity and *amour-propre (Tite et Bérénice)*, degeneration of the blood, sexual deprivation, sterility, or suicide *(Pulchérie, Tite et Bérénice, Agésilas, Sophonisbe).* Comedies traditionally end on a celebratory note, with a marriage, never with the wear and tear of conjugal life. Corneille's late works—even those like *Agésilas,* labeled "comédies héroïques"—impart a sense of uneasiness, dwelling as they do on the wear and tear of royal power.

And Corneille's final play, *Suréna,* imbued with a dark vision, brings everything into question. The sacred blood has degenerated to such a degree that both king Orode and his heir are criminal "by nature." Suspicious of the hero who has saved the state, they take his life. The union of monarch and hero, achieved in *Agésilas* and assured by royal sacrifice in *Pulchérie* and *Tite et Bérénice* disintegrates in *Suréna.* But even before the monarch destroys Suréna, having undermined his belief in royal justice, he destroys Suréna's reason to live. Urged by Eurydice, whom he loves, to cling to the future and to pass on his blood, Suréna reveals that, like Pulchérie, he has lost the desire to perpetuate his line. Here even the mystique of noble blood comes into doubt. Suréna sees vanity in the aristocrat's obsession with immortality and speculates that his blood too "degenerates."

> Que tout meure avec moi, Madame. Que m'importe
> Qui foule après ma mort la Terre qui me porte?
> Sentiront-ils percer par un éclat nouveau,
> Ces illustres Aïeux, la nuit de leur tombeau?
> Respireront-ils l'air où les feront revivre
> Ces neveux, qui peut-être auront peine à les suivre,
> Peut-être ne feront que les déshonorer,
> Et n'en auront le sang que pour dégénérer?
>   (I, 3, 301-08)

In the midst of this despair, the religion of monarchy collapses in *Suréna,* sacrifice and the "healing touch" disappear; kings stand demystified. When Eurydice urges Suréna to save his life by abandoning her for the king's daughter, the hero insists that his union with the king will not prevent his death. Brute force, not sacred blood or morality, he declares, is the ultimate secret of power.

> Quoi, vous vous figurez que l'heureux nom de gendre,
> Si ma perte est jurée, a de quoi m'en défendre,
> Quand malgré la Nature, en dépit de ses lois,
> Le parricide a fait la moitié de nos Rois?
> Qu'un frère pour régner se baigne au sang d'un frère?
> Qu'un fils impatient prévient la mort d'un père?
>
> (V, 4, 1637-42)

In this passage Suréna is alluding both to monarchy as an institution founded upon an original violence and to Orode as its exemplar. For Orode has committed fratricide and after the curtain's fall, he is, in turn, killed by his own son. Before *Suréna* Corneille obscures the scandal of monarchical origins. But according to the sources he used, the noble Nicomède was a parricide; Héraclius a murderer; Antiochus, the gentle prince in *Rodogune,* poisoned his mother. In *Suréna* there is no blinking harsh truth.

Myths of the blood and of the divinity of kings provide a rationale for an order based on social and political inequality. They are part of a web of beliefs that hold culture together and conceal disruptive facts. The classic problem of legitimacy—how do some individuals come to be credited with the right to rule over others—seems to have troubled Corneille, firm monarchist and believer in Providence though he doubtless was. On stage, where he expresses himself through recurrent language and through the choice and handling of historical and legendary subjects, he works through several answers: some magical (mana and divine dispensation), some idealistic (the reconciliation of hero and king or their fusion in the selfsame individual by means of sacrifice), some despairing. According to Corneille's contemporary, Pascal, and to many of the age's thinkers as well, it is best to refrain from questioning the origins of monarchical power and privilege: to do so risks inciting civil disorder and the fall into anarchy. "C'est le fils aîné du roi; cela est net, il n'y a point de dispute. La raison ne peut mieux faire, car la guerre civile est le plus grand des maux" (*Pensées,* ed. Brunschvicq 320). But Corneille, the eulogist of heroic and sacred blood, explores the terrain and in the rich diversity of his theater communicates his ideals and questions his faith.

NOTES

1 See Marc Bloch, *Les Rois thaumaturges* (Paris: Armand Colin, 1961); Etienne Thuau, *Raison d'état et pensée politique à l'époque de Richelieu* (Paris: Armand Colin, 1966); Ernst Kantorowicz, *The King's Two Bodies: A Study in Medieval Political Theology* (Princeton: Princeton University Press, 1957).

2 Cited by Thuau, 22.

3 See Bloch for a full discussion of the persistence of this practice in seventeenth-century France as opposed to its steady decline in England. Henri IV began touching the scrofolous in 1594 (Bloch, 342). On Louis XIII and XIV, see Bloch, 360-68. Louis XV touched 2,000 at his coronation.

4 All my quotations of Corneille's works are from the three-volume Pléiade edition, edited and richly annotated by Georges Couton (Paris: Gallimard, I, 1980, II, 1984, and III, 1987).

5 A variety of beliefs and superstitions about the blood are discernible in texts of the Ancien Régime. Blood was commonly considered a mirror of clan ties and of social and sexual inequalities of all sorts. It testified to the abject station of commoners as well as to the sacred status of kings. Ambroise Paré wrote that female blood was more abundant than male blood but of an inferior quality. "On peut vrayement dire que la femme a beaucoup plus de sang que l'homme: mais nous retournerons le fueillet, et dirons qu'une drachme de sang d'un homme vaut mieux que deux livres de celuy d'une femme, parce qu'il est plus cuit et digeré, et plus spirituel" *Œuvres complètes,* ed. J.F. Baillière, 3 vol. 1840-41, reprint Genève: Slatkine, 1970, II, 764. Descartes held that animal spirits in the blood were the means by which the soul moves the body to act. Bleeding was considered a standard treatment for nearly all diseases.

6 For the concept of two ontologies in the theater of Corneille, I am indebted to Jean Starobinski, "Sur Corneille" in *L'Œil vivant* (Paris: Gallimard, 1961). I see no reason to invoke a "bourgeois attitude," as Starobinski does, to clarify the opposition between the two ontologies. I am also much indebted to Paul Bénichou, Octave Nadal, *Le Sentiment de l'amour dans l'œuvre de Pierre Corneille* (Paris: Gallimard, 1948) and Serge Doubrovsky, *Corneille et la dialectique du héros* (Paris: Gallimard, 1963) for their analyses of the Cornelian hero.

7 The king's name always appears at the head of the list of characters because of his social rank but this does not necessarily reflect his dramatic importance. In the *Examens* Corneille criticizes his early portrayal of kings. Of Don Fernand in *Le Cid* he writes, for example: "Il remplit assez mal la Dignité d'un si grand Titre, n'ayant part en l'action que celle qu'il veut prendre pour d'autres" (*Examen de Clitandre,* 103). And of the royal figures in *Clitandre,* he writes apologetically: "Le Roi et le Prince son fils y paraissent dans un emploi fort au-dessous de leur Dignité" (102). It is true that in *Horace* he reminds the audience, through Camille, of the early Roman belief that kings were divinely inspired and in direct communication with the gods (III, 3, 841-46).

8 For Corneille's discussion of how he changed his historical material, see his "Au lecteur," Couton, II, 354-56.

9 See the excellent treatment of this subject in Clifton Cherpack, *The Call of the Blood in French Classical Tragedy* (Baltimore: The Johns Hopkins Press, 1958).

10 There is one exception in *Attila* (II, 5, 555-89), but the passage is a description of a king (Mérovée) who never appears on stage. Ruler of the Franks, Mérovée is supposed to be Louis XIV's ancestor and thus the passage constitutes Corneille's hommage to the reigning king.

11 See the provocative discussion of Corneille, much influenced by Bloch, Kantorowicz and Girard, by Jean-Marie Apostolidès, *Le Prince sacrifié: théâtre et politique au temps de Louis XIV* (Paris: Minuit, 1985). Apostolidès does not consider *Œdipe* in connection with the theme of sacrifice.

12 Couton points out (III, 1467) that Corneille departs from Mairet in depicting the heroism of Sophonisbe. In Mairet's version the queen takes the poison Massinisse sends her; in Corneille's version she spurns all help and dies without moral debts: "Et quand il me plaira de sortir de la vie, / De montrer qu'une femme a plus de cœur que lui, / On ne me verra point emprunter rien d'autrui" (V, 2, 1612-14).

4

Sociological Aspects of "La Querelle du *Cid*"

Milorad R. Margitić

THE "QUERELLE DU *CID*" IS KNOWN mainly as a noisy literary controversy that was triggered and fueled by the vanity, the jealousy, and the personal animosity of, as well as the esthetic differences between the chief antagonists, most of whom were young, ambitious playwrights. Yet the violence of some attacks, the gratuitous excessiveness of some responses, the dogmatism of certain ideological positions, the extraordinary intervention of the country's highest public official, and the official muzzling of the principal adversaries, all point to a root cause deeper than the theoretical disagreements and the individual rivalries, however acrimonious these may have been. Indeed, a closer look at the famous *querelle* reveals a strong undercurrent of collective tensions and hostility, unmistakable signs of a larger conflict that goes beyond big ego clashes and doctrinal disputes.

Seventeenth-century France is undergoing fundamental political, social, economic, ideological, moral, and esthetic changes, which create tensions and conflicts. A major source of frictions and antagonism is a progressive shift in the socio-economic power. With the waning of the old aristocracy, the middle class is on the rise. The latter has already made and continues to make huge strides economically. Socially, however, its progress is at best slow and arduous. While, as can be expected, the bourgeois are trying to parlay their growing economic might into social prestige, their quest for respectability is encountering strong resistance. Resented for their wealth, they are decried for their alleged materialism, and ridiculed for their social ambitions. They are among the favorite targets of satire, in dramatic literature and elsewhere.[1]

Another sociological phenomenon marks seventeenth-century France: the emergence of the dramatist as a man of letters.[2] The establishment in Paris of three theaters, with permanent professional companies assuring regular performances thanks to a steady stream of new plays by gifted young authors, signals the growing professionalization of the dramatic art. Indeed, the latter is becoming both lucrative and respectable. Witness these lines from Corneille's *L'Illusion comique:*

> Le Theatre est un fief dont les rentes sont bonnes,
> . . . .
> L'entretien de Paris, le souhait des Provinces,
> Le divertissement le plus doux de nos Princes,
> Les delices du peuple, et le plaisir des grands.
> (V, 6, 1802, 1785-87)[3]

It goes without saying that the key contributor to this success is also one of its major beneficiaries: the playwright, who, in part because of the growing popularity of his art, the generosity of grateful patrons, and the official support, and in part due to his own business acumen, ceases more and more to be a *poète à gages,* be it in the manner of a Malherbe, or a Hardy, in order to become a professional writer. Yet here, too, there is evidence of strong resistance as well. Actors are routinely excommunicated, spectators threatened with excommunication, and major dramatists subjected to scathing attacks by various individual and collective enemies of the theater, powerful enough to have occasionally a play censored or its performance banned.[4]

* * *

With this general background in mind we should be better able to perceive the social overtones of the "Querelle du *Cid.*" They are already audible in the very first controversial statement of the *querelle,* the line that started it all, the famous "Je ne dois qu'à moy seul toute ma Renommée" by Corneille.[5] Only weeks after the triumphant première of *Le Cid,* its author has been conferred a nobiliary title. Thus, when in the *Excuse à Ariste,* which appears a month or two later, he talks of his "Renommée," the word alludes to his newly won nobility as well as his skyrocketing fame as a playwright. Whether or not the social allusion is made deliberately, or even consciously, it does not go unnoticed, as we can see from this comment by an anonymous contemporary observer:

[Corneille] tout freschement annobly, fait (comme il dit) esclatter sa renommée, non pas par des actes de vaillances [*sic*], mais par des Crieurs de Gazettes, fidels heros [hérauts?] de ses vertus heroïques . . . (Gasté, 199)

In this context the statement "Je ne dois qu'à moy seul toute ma Renommée" does not appear to allude, as is often assumed, to *Le Cid*'s originality. In fact, Corneille will publicly disclaim the latter by listing in the 1648 edition of his play all of its sources, including a large number of lines he admittedly borrowed from Guillen de Castro's *Las Mocedades del Cid*.[6] In the above statement he is simply proclaiming that both his stage success and the resulting social promotion are due entirely and exclusively to his poetry, which is to say that they are undeniable evidence of his personal merit. "[Mes] vers en tous lieux sont mes seuls partisans / Par leur seule beauté ma plume estimée," he says in the lines preceding "Je ne dois qu'à moy seul toute ma Renommée" (Gasté, 64), and twenty years later he will address the following verses to the young Louis XIV:

La noblesse, grand Roi, manquoit à ma naissance;
Ton père en a daigné gratifier mes vers,
Et mes vers anoblis . . .[7]

It is not difficult to grasp the social implications of the notion of personal merit. The aristocrat takes pride in his ancestry, his lineage, his family honor, and the purity of his noble blood. Not so the bourgeois (not yet, anyway!), whose only source of pride can be his own accomplishments. Thus, by bragging about his success, by glorifying his personal merit, Corneille is publicly displaying his pride in being a bourgeois. Such behavior in itself is scandalous enough in a highly hierarchic society such as that of seventeenth-century France, where commoners are expected to show modesty appropriate to their humble origins and their low social status. Yet Corneille goes a step further; he also proclaims his superiority over any and all of his rivals, some of whom are noble: "[Je] pense [. . .] n'avoir point de rival / A qui je fasse tort en le traittant d'égal" (Gasté, 64). While he is ostensibly talking about the literary rivalry, there is no denying that his claim contains social overtones as well, for only they can account for his adversaries' indignant and angry response: as if something had hit a raw collective nerve, they shout in chorus, "Rabattons cet orgueil!," which is to say, "Remettons ce bourgeois à sa place!" Of course, the loudest ones are

those most sensitive in such matters, that is, the socially most vulnerable: a
fellow bourgeois rival, who may resent being left behind by a more successful member of his own class; or rivals of petty or dubious nobility, who
are likely to perceive the success of a gifted and ambitious bourgeois as a
direct threat to their own uncertain or relatively low social status.

Though Corneille's assertions are provocative, the viciousness and
the violence of the attacks and counterattacks that follow are often surprising. Yet what really strikes about these is a certain orderliness. Like a well-
established ritual, they seem to be regulated by an unwritten code which
determines their aims, strategies, arguments, vocabulary, and tone. Thus,
there is no pulling punches in the socially inconsequential clashes between
commoners, and crude personal insults quickly turn into ugly social af-
fronts. On the other hand, and for reasons easy to imagine, contentions pitting commoners against the nobility, or against any higher authority, tend to
appear, on both sides, less personal, bitter, and violent, unless, of course,
they are carried out anonymously. Indeed, as I will attempt to show in the
following pages, much of the *querelle* can be linked to and explained by the
social background and standing of both the attacker and the attacked.

* * *

Take, for example, the dispute between Corneille and Claveret, both
bourgeois, both lawyers, both playwrights, though the former is the more
gifted and successful of the two. It starts with a scornful remark by
Corneille: "Il n'a pas tenu à vous," he tells Scudéry, "que du premier lieu
où beaucoup d'honnestes gens me placent, je ne sois descendu au dessoub
de Claveret" (Gasté, 149). Claveret retorts by calling Corneille "soy disant
Autheur du *Cid*," the "froideur" and the "stupidité" of whose mind make
him pitiful and ridiculous, and by accusing him of vanity, arrogance, jealousy, cowardly vindictiveness, and, worse yet, of crass bourgeois materialism (". . . vous avez vendu vos denrees Poëtiques"), thus, of being a
nouveau noble unworthy of his rank (Gasté, 187-92). "[V]os parens
[vous] ont laissé pour tout heritage la science de bien tirer les bottes,"
Corneille sneers at Claveret, then calls him a man "qui dans ses plus
grandes ambitions n'a jamais prétendu au delà de Sommelier dans une
mediocre maison" (Gasté, 193, 207). Claveret retaliates with an ethnic slur:
apparently, used to being jeered in his native Rouen, Corneille let the first
applause in Paris go to his head, just as his fellow Normans, "pour estre
accoustumez à ne boire que du Cidre, s'enyvrent lors qu'ils boivent du vin"

(Gasté, 307). But it is Corneille who has the last nasty word, all the more offensive as it is couched in a mock praise:

> Ce n'est pas que je veille [*sic*] mespriser Monsieur Claveret, au contraire, j'estime ceux, qui comme luy s'efforcent à se tirer de la bouë, et se veulent eslever au dessus de leur naissance. (Gasté, 316)

*   *   *

Unlike Claveret, Mairet is, or at least claims to be noble. Still, orphaned in infancy, he has a rather difficult start in life. Later, as an aspiring young writer, he enjoys the patronage and the protection of members of high nobility, in whose service he remains even after becoming one of the leading playwrights of his generation. Mairet attacks Corneille indirectly, borrowing the voice of "Don Baltazar de la Verdad," "l'Autheur du vray *Cid* Espagnol" (Gasté, 67-68). And while he does use personal insults ("vanteur," "fous Capitans," "froid d'esprit"), his argument is basically a literary one, with a slight social overtone: it deals with authorship and merit. Yes, he admits, *Le Cid*'s popularity is undeniable (". . . ce suject esclatant sur la Scene, / Puis qu'il ravit le Tage a pu ravir la Seine"), but its true author is "Don Baltazar de la Verdad"; Corneille is only its "Traducteur François," who, instead of getting credit for its success, should be exposed as an impostor; his vaunted "Renommée" is thus the result of his shameless plagiarism and not a sign of his "merite" (Gasté, 67-68). Though Corneille retorts in kind ("jeune jouvencel," "fou," "criminel"), and even more crudely so ("Paris entier ayant leu son cartel, / L'envoye au Diable, et sa muse au Bordel"), his basic argument, too, is literary: "Qu'il face mieux," he challenges his opponent (Gasté, 70). Yet the social insult proves, once again, irresistible. First, Corneille insinuates that Mairet's nobility is of questionable authenticity: "[I]l faut apporter de la foy quand il s'agit de son origine," he says, adding a cautious parenthesis ("j'ayme mieux parestre obscur que médisant") (Gasté, 207). This prompts Mairet to drop his initial mask, and to retaliate directly, and rather offensively. He claims to have "des domestiques d'aussi bonne condition que [Corneille]," whom he accuses of disloyalty and vindictiveness caused by greed, while comparing him to early travelling merchants, who became rich by tricking primitive peoples into exchanging gold and precious stones for trinkets (Gasté, 285-90). In other words he calls Corneille a greedy and unscrupulous commoner. Corneille now throws caution to the winds. "[V]ous n'estes pas de

meilleure maison que [mon] valet de chambre," he tells Mairet, reminding
him repeatedly and contemptuously of the "bassesse" of his birth, and of his
"pauvreté originelle," which allegedly explain his craving for social acceptance and his manipulative and obsequious behavior in high society (Gasté,
319-26). In addition, capitalizing on the fact that Mairet was a native of
Besançon, which at the time was under the Austrian crown, Corneille affirms that his adversary "n'est pas né François" (Gasté, 323), then, turning
to him, issues a warning with clear xenophobic overtones:

> . . . malgré vos impostures *Le Cid* sera tousjours *Le Cid,* et [. . .] tant
> qu'on fera des pieces de cette sorte, vous ne serez Prophete que parmy
> vos Allemands. (Gasté, 327)

This is followed by one of the seemingly most bizarre, and yet, in the sociological perspective, most revealing texts of the "Querelle du *Cid,*" a "petit
memoire genealogique" of Mairet's "maison" (nine pages of his family's
history covering several generations), intended to prove that he is French by
birth, and that he has "des tiltres [de noblesse] bien authentiques" (Gasté,
333-41).

* * *

Scudéry, for his part, does not have to prove anything of the sort,
for he *is* French and noble. Still, he behaves as if he did have something to
prove, and as if he were trying to ward off a threat. Having been born into
petty nobility of rather modest means, and having abandoned a relatively secure military career for the uncertainties of a literary vocation, he must feel
uncomfortable seeing his chief rival, a young and talented bourgeois, reap
the material and social benefits of a stage triumph that has suddenly pro-
pelled him into stardom; especially since this rival has the indelicateness to
publicly boast about his accomplishment, ostentatiously displayed as proof
of his allegedly superior personal merit. That is why Scudéry, in his
Observations sur le Cid, brandishes his own nobility (". . . estant ce que je
suis . . ."), while issuing a barely veiled threat of physical violence (". . . je
ne scaurois ny dire ny souffrir d'injures . . ."), a threat which is not to be
taken lightly, considering his notoriety as a swashbuckler, and the prospect
of which is made quite dreadful by the disdainful reminder that Corneille,
a commoner, "n'est pas homme d'esclaircissement" (Gasté, 110, 73, 88).
Scudéry's offensive / defensive waving of his social status transpires

elsewhere as well, though somewhat less obviously. For example when he denies envying his bourgeois rival's success, or even having any literary ambitions, by affirming that envy is too base a vice for a noble soul such as his, and that, if he had any ambition at all, "elle auroit un plus haut objet, que la renommée de cét Autheur" (Gasté, 110). Or when he states his motive in attacking Le Cid. "[J]'ay creu, he claims, que je ne pouvois sans injustice et sans lascheté, abandonner la cause commune," the latter being "la reputation de tous ceux qui font des vers" (Gasté, 72, 111). Which is presumably why he feels compelled to "faire voir à l'Autheur du CID, qu'il se doit contenter de l'honneur, d'estre Citoyen d'une si belle Republique, sans s'imaginer mal à propos, qu'il en peut devenir le Tiran" (Gasté, 111). Not unlike the feudal lord who would do some sabre-rattling in order do keep at bay a would-be tyrant threatening his vassals, Scudéry displays aggressively his self-righteousness and courage for the ostensible purpose of protecting helpless poets against the threat of one who "se deifioit d'authorité privée" (Gasté, 72). Actually, his aggressive behavior is self-protective, thus self-serving. The only threat to anyone comes, not from Corneille, but from Scudéry himself, who is, in fact, attempting to intimidate his bourgeois rival by menacingly asserting his own social and physical superiority over him.

"J'ataque Le Cid, et non pas son Autheur, Scudéry claims; j'en veux à son Ouvrage et non point à sa personne" (Gasté, 72). He sticks to his claim to the extent that he refrains from insulting Corneille the individual. However, he does not spare Corneille the member of the middle class, which he holds in utter contempt. In Scudéry's vocabulary "bourgeois" is synonymous with "ignorance" (Gasté, 71). Now, the most persistent argument in his critique of Le Cid is that the analysis of any and every aspect of it—whether it be its dramatic structure, or characterization, or versification, or syntax, or vocabulary—reveals Corneille's lack of judgment, which allegedly stems from his ignorance. Thus, Corneille is ignorant of Plato's and Aristotle's precepts, which is why his play "choque les principales regles du Poeme Dramatique" (Gasté, 73). His ignorance of Spanish history explains why, against all likelihood, no fewer than 500 noblemen come to avenge Don Diègue's honor (Gasté, 91). Relying on common opinion, a poor substitute for knowledge, he depicts all Spaniards as vain (Gasté, 85). Likewise, we are told, Don Fernand behaves like a buffoon, rather than the king he is; Chimène, "une fille bien née," says things worthy of a prostitute, and she commits a virtual parricide; l'Infante is given feelings unworthy of a princess, and le Comte, "un homme de valeur," is made to talk like "un Capitan ridicule" (Gasté, 93, 89, 94, 75, 86, 84). Why? Apparently because Corneille, a commoner, has no knowledge or understanding of the aristocracy. Nor, and for the same reason, does he know anything about duels, or warfare, and so on (Gasté, 88, 92-93). While the causal link between Corneille's alleged ignorance and his being a bourgeois is usually only implied, on at least one occasion Scudéry states it explicitly. In commenting on the play's line 1271 ("Tant à nous voir marcher en si bon esquipage"), he quips: "C'est encor parler de la guerre en bon bourgeois qui va à la garde" (Gasté, 102). In sum, the basic charge levelled at Corneille in the *Observations* concerns his social background. He is nothing but a bourgeois, we are told, and a mediocre one at that, that is, one without any particular merit, since his greatest personal accomplishment is *Le Cid,* an allegedly badly written play, whose success Scudéry explains away by attributing it to an optical illusion:

> Il est de certaines Pieces comme de certains animaux qui sont en la Nature, qui de loin semblent des Etoiles, et qui de pres ne sont que des vermisseaux. (Gasté, 71)

Corneille, of course, knows how to read between the lines. "[Je] ne doute ny de vostre Noblesse ny de vostre vaillance," he assures Scudéry, with a little ironic grin, while affirming proudly and defiantly that he will not be intimidated: "[Je] suis assé glorieux pour vous dire de porte à porte que je ne vous crains ny ne vous ayme" (Gasté, 147, 150). He dryly urges his critic to resist bringing into their literary argument considerations of their social status:

> . . . ne meslons point de pareilles difficultez parmi nos differends; il n'est pas question de sçavoir de combien vous estes Noble ou plus vaillant que moy, pour juger de combien *le Cid* est meilleur que *l'Amant liberal.* (Gasté, 147)

"Vous protestez de ne me dire point d'injures," Corneille continues, "et [. . .] incontinent apres vous m'accusez d'ignorance en mon mestier et de manque de jugement en la conduite de mon Chef-d'oeuvre" (Gasté, 148). Yet, though he feels offended, and though he says he could easily throw the same argument back at Scudéry ("[Je] n'aurois besoin que du texte de vostre Libelle, et des contradictions qui s'y rencontrent pour vous convaincre de l'un et de l'autre de ces deffaux . . ."), he will not retaliate; nor is there any danger of physical violence by him, he states cavalierly, while sarcastically feigning to believe that his accuser needs reassurance ("Je ne suis point homme d'esclaircissement, vous estes en seureté de ce costé là" [Gasté, 148, 150]). In short, Corneille's response is a refusal to respond. Which may be a sign of caution on his part, for, as proud and as defiant as he is, he never loses his bourgeois sense of reality: a public confrontation with a swashbuckling nobleman would be risky. Or does it rather point to his artfulness? For, by refusing to engage in a public debate with his attacker, he may be slyly—and safely—signifying his contempt of him. That is, at any rate, how he will privately interpret his own silence later on:

> ... d'ordinaire le silence d'un Autheur qu'on attaque est pris pour une marque de mépris qu'il fait de ses censeurs. J'en avois ainsi usé envers Monsieur de Scudéry. (Gasté, 487)

Publicly, however, Corneille justifies his refusal to respond on pragmatic grounds, that is, in an unmistakably bourgeois manner, by claiming that all charges against his play are rendered null and void by the reality of its success, which even its harshest critic cannot and does not deny:

> Je me contente pour toute Apologie, de ce que vous avouëz qu'il [Le Cid] a eu l'Approbation des Sçavans et de la Cour; Cest Eloge veritable par où vous commencez vos Censures, destruit tout ce que vous pouvez dire apres. (Gasté, 151)

And he pointedly reminds his adversary that "Le Cid a esté representé trois fois au Louvre, et deux fois à l'Hostel Richelieu," and that Chimène, whom his opponent calls "impudique," "prostituée," "parricide," and "monstre," has been "receuë et caressée en fille d'honneur" by "La Reyne, les Princesses, et les plus vertueuses Dames de la Cour et de Paris" (Gasté, 148).

* * *

Frustrated, Scudéry seeks arbitration by the recently founded French Academy, whose members accede to his request most reluctantly, and only after being told that their patron and master, the Cardinal, wants them to do so.[8] Now, Richelieu not only commissions a formal critique of Corneille's play, he also maintains a very active personal interest in the text being prepared by his protégés, as he examines its successive drafts, demands substantial revisions in it, suspends its first printing, and allows it to be published only when he is satisfied that it is consistent with his own thinking in the matter. Thus, while *Les Sentimens de l'Academie Françoise sur la Tragi-Comedie du Cid* are actually written by a panel of Academicians led by Chapelain, their true author, albeit by proxy, is the Cardinal himself.

Why would France's Prime Minister intervene in a private literary dispute, insisting that *Le Cid* be publicly subjected to a rather harsh critical review, which is all the more telling as it has the appearance of an official judgment?[9] Certainly not because he envies Corneille's success, or feels in any way uncomfortable about it. After all, he has contributed to it through his moral and financial support of the budding Norman playwright.[10] A generous patron though he may be, he is, however, also a demanding master, impatient of insubordination, quick to wield his authority, and intent on keeping in line those under his protection, that is, in his service. Corneille, who is one of these, obviously has stepped out of line by publicly behaving in a manner improper for a commoner. This gives Richelieu the opportunity to teach a bourgeois a lesson in social humility, while asserting and strengthening his growing control over France's cultural life. On the other hand, as an astute politician he also understands how useful to his cultural politics a gifted and popular writer can be. Thus, his instructions to the Academicians must be to both humble and encourage Corneille, to lecture him sternly on his play's flaws, while at the same time praising his talent as a dramatist. That is precisely what they do throughout their *Sentimens,* and what clearly transpires in their conclusion, which is as follows:

> Enfin nous conclüons qu'encore que le Sujet du *Cid* ne soit pas bon, qu'il peche dans son Desnoüement, qu'il soit chargé d'Episodes inutiles, que la bien-seance y manque en beaucoup de lieux, aussi bien que la bonne disposition du theatre, et qu'il y ait beaucoup de vers bas, et de façons de parler impures; Neantmoins la naïveté et la vehemence de ses passions, la force et la delicatesse de plusieurs de ses pensées, et cet agréement inexplicable qui se mesle dans tous ses defaux luy ont acquis un rang considerable entre les Poëmes François de ce genre qui ont le plus donné de satisfaction. Si son Autheur ne doit pas toute sa reputation à son merite, il ne la doit pas toute à son bonheur, et la Nature lui a esté assez liberale, pour excuser la Fortune si elle luy a esté prodigue. (Gasté, 416-17)

Obviously, the ultimate object of this critique of *Le Cid* is to pass a judgment on its author's claim to the superiority of his personal merit, a notion whose social implications we already know. Contrary to Mairet and Scudéry, who reject and even ridicule Corneille's claim, calling him a mediocre and dishonest bourgeois whose "Renommée" is based on a hoax, or an illusion, the Academy takes it seriously, but only to reduce its validity significantly, attributing his fame to his luck as much as to his talent. In other words, the Cardinal's message seems to be: "Not bad, Corneille, not bad at all . . . for a bourgeois; just don't have any delusions of grandeur!"

Only implied in the above passage, this patronizing is quite openly and self-righteously displayed elsewhere in the *Sentimens*. Commoners, according to the Academicians, are an ignorant "multitude" devoid of judgment, and defenseless against bad influences coming from anywhere, including the stage:

> Les mauvais exemples sont contagieux, mesme sur les theatres; les feintes representations ne causent que trop de veritables crimes, et il y a grand peril à divertir le Peuple par des plaisirs qui peuvent produire un jour des douleurs publiques. (Gasté, 360)

To protect the "Peuple," certain subjects, even if historically true, must be avoided by dramatists: "[N]ous maintenons que toutes les verités ne sont pas bonnes pour le theatre, et qu'il en est de quelques-unes comme de ces crimes enormes, dont les Juges font brusler le procés avec les criminels" (Gasté, 356-66). By putting on stage without altering it a scandalous historical event which was "de trop mauvais exemple pour l'exposer à la veuë du Peuple" (Gasté, 366), Corneille has thus failed his moral duty as a playwright. Such a failure can be explained either by the "goust depravé" typical of "les libertins et les vicieux," or by the lack of judgment characteristic of the bourgeoisie (Gasté, 360). Since the Academy does not impute it to the former of the two possible causes, it probably has to be attributed to the latter. In the last analysis, then, Corneille's "crime" appears to be, once again, that of being a bourgeois.

Corneille, of course, would like to defend himself against the French Academy's indictment. But he knows who is behind it, and understands what is at stake for him. He will thus refrain from responding for obvious reasons, which he explains to Boisrobert, with a mixture of solid bourgeois realism and a healthy dose of personal cynicism:

> Je m'estois résolu d'y répondre, [. . .] Mais maintenant que vous me
> conseillez de n'y répondre point, veu les personnes qui s'en sont
> mêlées, il ne me faut point d'interprète pour entendre cela; je suis un
> peu plus de ce monde qu'Héliodore, qui aima mieux perdre son Evesché
> que son livre, et j'aime mieux les bonnes grâces de mon Maistre que
> toutes les réputations de la terre. Je me tairay donc, non point par
> mépris, mais par respect. (Gasté, 487-88)

Yet, sure of being in the right, and indomitable as ever, he accepts the
Sentimens' verdict only under protest:

> Je me résous, puisque vous le voulez, he tells Boisrobert, à me laisser
> condamner par vostre Illustre Académie. [. . .] Mais je vous supplie de
> considerer qu'elle procède contre moy avec tant de violence, et qu'elle
> employe une authorité si souveraine pour me fermer la bouche, que
> ceux qui sauront son procédé auront sujet d'estimer que je ne serois
> point coupable si l'on m'avoit permis de me monstrer innocent.
> (Gasté, 485-86)

And once again he proudly points to that against which even an official
judgment is powerless, the success of *Le Cid:*

> J'ay remporté le témoignage de l'excellence de ma Pièce par le grand
> nombre de ses représentations, par la foule extraordinaire des personnes
> qui y sont venuës, et par les acclamations générales qu'on luy a faites.
> (Gasté, 468)

* * *

Lest we get the impression that Corneille is alone in his defense
against the socio-political and literary establishments and would-be authorities of the day, I hasten to add that, on the contrary, he has plenty of support. Some of his supporters, under the cover of anonymity, go boldly to
the heart of the issue, that is, far beyond the personal and literary disputes at
hand. Indeed, as if some long-held-in frustrations and pent-up hostilities
were just waiting for a signal to explode, the attacks against *Le Cid* trigger
an avalanche of pamphlets ranging from defiant assertions of the bourgeois
ways of thinking, to vehement denunciations of the aristocratic dogmatism and arrogance, as well as the official heavy-handedness and abuse of
authority.

Two such anonymous texts clearly stand out. One of them, *Le Jugement du Cid,* attacks Scudéry and his *Observations.* Its author, who indentifies himself as "un Bourgeois de Paris," claims to express "le sentiment des honnestes gens d'entre le peuple" (Gasté, 230, 231). Proudly asserting his low social status (". . . nous autres qui sommes du peuple . . ."), he undertakes to show an arrogant and narrow-minded nobleman such as Scudéry that "tout le peuple n'est pas composé de sots," that commoners, too, can competently judge the merit of a dramatic poem (Gasté, 239, 240, 235). Their judgment, however, is not rooted in the Aristotelian canon, he states, but in common sense:

> Je n'ay jamais leu Aristote, et ne sçay point les regles du theatre, mais
> je regle le merite des pieces selon le plaisir que j'en reçoy. (Gasté,
> 231)

The "merite" of a play, he continues, grows in direct proportion to the number of spectators it delights, in other words to the number of satisfied customers, whose rate of approval is a clear indication of its esthetic worth. Consequently, he declares, "je trouve [que *Le Cid*] est fort bon par ceste raison, qu'il a esté fort apprové" (Gasté, 233). And, pushing his bourgeois pragmatism to its logical extreme, he affirms that the financial success of Corneille's play transcends any and all esthetic flaws it may have:

> En fin je sçay qu'il y a [dans *Le Cid*] des fautes d'esprit et de jugement;
> mais ceste piece n'a pas laissé de valoir aux Comediens plus que les dix
> meilleures des autres Autheurs. (Gasté, 234)

The target of the other text in question, *Observations sur les Sentiments de l'Academie Françoise,* is none other than the French Academy. Its anonymous author, apparently unimpressed by the intimidating protection of the Academy's mighty patron, levels a stinging and sweeping indictment against the would-be official judges of the French Letters. As for the French language, he states, "nous n'avons point de loy certaine ny aucunes regles prescrites qui en puissent expressement decider," which is why "nos escrivains [. . .] ont convenu que l'authorité des bons autheurs et l'usage commun en seroient les juges," guiding principles that "nulle Academie contredisant [. . .] ne sçauroit esbranler" (Gasté, 442, 443). Neither, according to him, does the Academy have any jurisdiction over literature (Gasté, 418). Consequently, "elle n'avoit nulle puissance ny authorité publique pour se pouvoir rendre Juge [du] differend" between Scudéry and Corneille (Gasté, 429). Worse yet, by judging *Le Cid* "à la rigueur et par des regles severes et tyranniques," the Academicians not only are abusing their authority, but are indeed attempting to terrorize the French literary community: ". . . sans authorité ils exercent une espece d'inquisition sur les Lettres . . ." (Gasté, 419, 418). Then, arguing that "ceux qui font profession de pureté de langage ne doivent rien dire qui ne soit pur et net" (Gasté, 435), the author turns the tables: he subjects the Academy's *Sentimens* to the same harsh critical scrutiny to which it has subjected Corneille's play. What he finds is, of course, that the Academicians' text is marred by scores of linguistic and stylistic imperfections, one of which (their use of "estrange" for "mauvais") inspires him this indignant comment: "Si nostre Poëte [Corneille] en avoit usé en la mesme signification, il seroit censuré et mis à l'inquisition de l'Academie . . ." (Gasté, 422).

Among the remaining texts one often finds direct social and political statements, such as the following series of maxims combining an attack on the nobility with the praise of the bourgeoisie, contained in the authorless *Le Souhait du Cid en faveur de Scudéry:*

> . . . qui merite d'estre Gentilhomme par sa vertu est plus que celuy qui tient cette qualité de ses peres, il vaut mieux estre le premier noble de sa race que le dernier, et de Poëte devenir Gentilhomme plustost qu'estant né Gentilhomme faire le Poëte . . . (Gasté, 186)

Or such as the pamphlet that protests against treating sovereigns as divinities. Scudéry having said in speaking of the French queen, "Je parlerois plus clairement de cette divine Personne, si je ne craignois de prophaner son nom sacré, et si je n'avois peur de commettre un sacrilege, en pensant faire un acte d'adoration" (Gasté, 85-86), the author of this anonymous text, titled *La Deffense du Cid,* comments that these are "[p]aroles qui ne peuvent bien estre tolerees qu'en la bouche d'un Payen, qui tiendroit son Roy pour un Dieu, et qui l'adoreroit pour tel" (Gasté, 117).

* * *

In conclusion, what is "La Querelle du *Cid*"? A series of personal disputes between young, ambitious, vain, and envious rivals competing rudely and crudely for public attention and official honors? Of course, it is. A literary controversy pitting theoreticians against practitioners, doctrinaires against pragmatists, and signaling the powerful emergence of the soon-to-prevail rules of the Classical Doctrine? It is that, too, without a doubt, although this eventual outcome is, at the moment, far from a foregone conclusion. More significantly, however, though less obviously, it is an echo of a deeper and larger, socio-political conflict rumbling underneath the clashes between rivaling individuals and opposing ideals. The personal and the esthetic are inextricably linked to the socio-political, and are, indeed, a function of it. It is no accident that Scudéry, who so haughtily brandishes his nobiliary status, also professes his worship of both the divine monarchy and the almighty Aristotelian canon; or that the anonymous "Bourgeois de Paris," who is so defiantly proud of his plebeian background, is also the one to denounce the official abuse of power and attempts at intimidation, as well as to reject Aristotle and plead the cause of common sense and poetic license. Nor is it accidental that the French Academy, a tool of the government's cultural politics, patronizes the commoners, while abusively and intimidatingly asserting the rule of law, order, and morality in public entertainment.

In this underlying conflict, as we very well know, the forces of repression—be they in the form of esthetic dogmatism, or social intolerance, or political absolutism, or ideological orthodoxy—will have the upper hand, and will remain in control for quite some time. Still, it is worth noting that, as the "Querelle du *Cid*" reveals, the voices of dissent are many, strong, and clear, and that, though facing formidable odds, they refuse to be silenced.

NOTES

1 See Jean V. Alter, *L'Esprit antibourgeois sous l'Ancien Régime: Littérature et tensions sociales aux XVIIe et XVIIIe siècles* (Genève: Droz, 1970).

2 See Alain Viala, *Naissance de l'écrivain: sociologie de la littérature à l'âge classique* (Paris: Minuit, 1985), and Jacqueline de Jomaron [ed.], *Le Théâtre en France. I. Du Moyen Age à 1789* (Paris: Colin, 1988).

3 Ed. Robert Garapon (Paris: Didier, 1965).

4 See Jomaron.

5 "*Excuse à Ariste,*" in Armand Gasté, *La Querelle du Cid* (1898; Genève: Slatkine Reprints, 1970), 64.

6 See my edition of *Le Cid* (Amsterdam/Philadelphia: John Benjamins, 1989), 129-48.

7 "*Sonnet au Roi,*" in *Œuvres de P. Corneille,* ed. Ch. Marty-Laveaux, 10 (Paris: Hachette, 1862-68), 135-36.

8 About this episode of the *querelle* see Paul Pellisson-Fontanier, *Relation contenant l'histoire de l'Académie Françoise* (Paris: Pierre le Petit, 1653), 186-215.

9 This question, a stumbling block in the *querelle* scholarship, has produced a fairly large body of research (without settling the issue), of which the following is a partial list: Colbert Searles, "L'Académie française et *Le Cid,*" *Revue d'Histoire Littéraire de la France*, 21 (1914), 331-74; Henry Lyonnet, *"Le Cid" de Corneille* (Paris: Malfère, 1928), 67-97; Gustave Reynier, *"Le Cid" de Corneille* (Paris: Mellottée, 1929), 294-322; Henry Carrington Lancaster, *A History of French Dramatic Literature in the Seventeenth Century*. II. *The Period of Corneille (1635-1651)* (Baltimore: Johns Hopkins Press, 1932), I, 128-44; Louis Batiffol, *Richelieu et Corneille: La légende de la persécution de l'auteur du "Cid"* (Paris: Calman-Lévy, 1936); Georges Collas, "Richelieu et *Le Cid,*" *Revue d'Histoire Littéraire de la France*, 43 (1936), 568-72; Gerard Bauer, *"Le Cid* et Richelieu," *Conferencia*, 31, 2 (1937), 258-72; Joseph Hanse, *"Le Cid* et *Les Sentiments de l'Académie Française*," *Etudes Classiques*, 6 (1937), 171-202; Antoine Adam, "A travers la *Querelle du Cid,*" *Revue d'Histoire de la Philosophie et d'Histoire Générale de la Civilisation*, 6 (1938), 29-52; Sister M. Amelia Klenke, "The Richelieu-Corneille Rapport," *PMLA*, 64 (1949), 724-45; M. Sedgwick, "Richelieu and the *Querelle du Cid,*" *Modern Language Review*, 48 (1953), 143-50; Georges Mongrédien, "Corneille, *Le Cid* et l'Académie," *Revue Générale Belge*, 106, 2 (1970), 67-78; Edmund Roney, "La *Querelle du Cid:* Classical Rules or Political Expediency?," *Transactions of the Wisconsin Academy of Sciences, Arts, and Letters*, 61 (1973), 157-64; Georges Couton, *Richelieu et le théâtre* (Lyon: Presses Universitaires de Lyon, 1986).

10 In 1635 Richelieu had made Corneille a member of the "Société des cinq Auteurs" (a group of leading young playwrights whose task was to write plays based on plots outlined by the Cardinal himself), and the recipient of a sizable *pension*.

5

Strategies of Seduction in *Cinna*

Susan Read Baker

IN *CORNEILLE ET LA VERTU DE PRUDENCE*, Germain Poirier notes that the name Emilie derives from the Greek Aimylia, "celle qui séduit," "celle qui est habile dans l'art de tromper."[1] Many readings of *Cinna* view this "aimable Furie" as a potent seductress who misleads her lover into paths of ingratitude she herself has pursued, overwhelms by erotic charm the hapless Maxime, and "feminizes" both rivals to the detriment of heroic values in the play. Emilie would thus seem to provide the obvious focus for an exploration of seduction in *Cinna*. Cinna himself views her role in such a bittersweet fashion, thereby foregrounding seduction in its erotic form: "Mais l'empire inhumain qu'exercent vos beautés / Force jusqu'aux esprits et jusqu'aux volontés" (III, 4, 1055-56). Close scrutiny of the text reveals, however, that Emilie's employment of seduction is by no means isolated. Reinserted into the atmosphere of misrepresentation which prevails in the tragedy until its close, Emilie's example becomes one among many. In the present study, I shall argue that seduction as a sexual, political, and textual practice dominates the economy of *Cinna*. I shall propose further that beyond the abundant strategies of seduction which *Cinna* displays, a broader problematic emerges concerning the seductions of rhetoric and of theatrical spectacle in general. I shall conclude that the ultimate thrust of Corneille's tragedy is to bring under control the alluring powers of theater itself.

To seduce, from the Latin *seducere*, means to lead away from the proper path. In its broadest connotation, seduction is a form of persuasion. The *Dictionnaire de l'Académie* (1694) thus gives as one definition "toucher, plaire, persuader" (Article "Séduction"). Seduction can also, however, be deemed an offshoot of misrepresentation because persuasion may include some form of deception. Hence the first meaning of *séduire* listed by the same *Dictionnaire*: "Egarer, abuser, faire tomber dans l'erreur par ses insinuations, par ses écrits, par ses discours, par ses exemples, etc." To seduce, then, is to create misrepresentations and promote false values; to be seduced is to fall prey to such misrepresentations. In all of its meanings, the link between seduction and language, particularly rhetoric that aims to persuade, is readily apparent.

As an avatar of misrepresentation, seduction can be effected by a wide variety of strategies. The final goal of those who employ such strategies, however, is not seduction for its own sake. Rather, seduction is a practice in the service of existential projects which, in theater, will naturally attach to roles. Thus in *Cinna*, Auguste wants to be loved by his subjects; Emilie seeks revenge for her father's assassination; Maxime covets Emilie's love; Cinna desires both high political office and Emilie. As the action of the tragedy shows, these goals are not correctly formulated by any of the *dramatis personae*; they are rather seductive visions of happiness which produce inner turmoil. In Auguste, the radically subjective search for love conflicts with the exercise of supreme political authority; in Cinna, love struggles with political ambition; in Maxime, love is opposed by friendship, and in Emilie, love is put at risk by Republican ideals.[2]

One of the most fascinating aspects of *Cinna* is thus the extraordinary confusion of values which the tragedy generates prior to Act V. Just what the "proper path" to follow really is must ultimately be indicated by the values which the text itself promotes.[3] To anticipate, what finally triumphs in *Cinna* is an ideal of *générosité* embued with Christian and Stoic tints, which attains fruition in an absolute royal figure held forth as an *exemplum*. At the denouement, love for the monarch and devotion to his service will hold the key to all other loves and desires. Until this libidinal "monism" is fully established, various forms of seduction forcibly prevail.

These forms may be broadly categorized as sexual, political, and textual strategies of seduction. While these categories are arbitrary and evidently overlap, their chief virtue is to facilitate analysis of a very complex play. Apart from illuminating various facets of Corneille's dramaturgic practice, such an analysis underscores the Protean nature of seduction in *Cinna*. It is therefore useful to consider some narrower practices of seduction in the tragedy.

Sexual strategies dominate the uppermost layer of the play's action.[4] Because they entail an appeal to libidinal desire, they form a broad category which subsumes all personal dealings, including friendship, family, and marriage. In *Cinna*, according to Western cultural tradition, the roles most prone to strategies of sexual seduction are those of the younger players, Emilie, Cinna, and Maxime. Conventions of tragedy prevailing in the classical period further dictate, as in this play, that the seduced be a man; the agent of seduction, a woman.[5]

In *Cinna*, as elsewhere, the outcome of such gendering of the process of seduction is paradoxically unheroic. To be seduced is arguably to find oneself in a "feminized" posture; that is, passive and enslaved. When Maxime tries to seduce Emilie in IV, 5 by presenting himself as a surrogate Cinna, he reaches the bottom of his decline from heroic values. This is so not simply because he betrays his friend, but also because he aspires through such substitution to attain an idealized union with Cinna through Emilie. From this point of view, Cinna has seduced Maxime.[6] In addition, by asking Emilie to cherish him as she would Cinna himself, Maxime is effectively asking Emilie to seduce him. Because his plea discloses a loss of identity or proper sense of self, it signals a loss of honor.[7]

Although erotic power does not invariably produce degradation in Corneille's theater, it is frequently portrayed by its "victims" as a form of tyranny (as in Cinna's verses III, 4, 1055-56, quoted earlier). According to the *code des généreux* which informs Corneille's plays, persons wielding true power and authority presumably do not rely upon mere appearances to manipulate others. In line with the sexual ideology underlying that same *code des généreux*, however, such potent persons are invariably male. Hence the common view that Emilie uses her beauty and charms to corrupt otherwise upright individuals such as Cinna and Maxime (V, 2, 1622), a reading which overly privileges Emilie's role as seductress and promotes as the play's would-be lesson the somewhat banal admonition that women's erotic power poses a grave threat to political stability.

Indeed, critics have not failed to note that the tragedy gestures towards sexual seduction of Auguste by Emilie.[8] At issue is Emilie's stated willingness to marry the emperor: "Je recevrais de lui [d'Auguste] la place de Livie / Comme un moyen plus sûr d'attenter à sa vie" (I, 2, 81-82). Clearly, the fantasy of seducing Auguste in order to kill him denotes Emilie's recognition of the difficulty of successfully enacting her own revenge.[9] It is perhaps more important, however, to recognize in this verse Emilie's fantasy that she might usurp the mother/Livie's place, even though her putative motive would be murder. Emilie's desire thus assumes the form of an Electral fantasy which in fact matches Cinna's Oedipal fantasy: though wholly unimportant on his own (III, 3, 882; V, 1, 1509-40), he nevertheless aspires to assume the sovereign/father's role.[10] In this regard, the text of *Cinna* carefully maintains its pair of lovers on an even footing.

The basic difficulty with Cinna's and Emilie's fantasies is that they are prompted by a hatred which hitherto has remained hidden. Concealed hatred, unlike an overt *haine par devoir*, is not a heroic attribute. Emilie has seduced and continues to manipulate foster parents who love her, but are unloved in return.[11] This is doubtless the reason why Emilie never appears on stage with Livie or Auguste until the denouement. To show Emilie impersonating a loving adopted daughter would demean her. Cinna himself does not escape unscathed from such play-acting in the consultation scene of Act II.

Friendship, like family ties, is based upon the sublimation of erotic desire. For Auguste, Cinna and Maxime have become replacements for Mécène and Agrippe (II, 1, 393-96). Similarly, Emilie has assumed the place of his daughter Julie (II, 1, 637-38). Persons thus circulate like commodities in Auguste's libidinal network. On this account, his relationships assume an interchangeable, unstable quality. Auguste is an easy target for seduction because of his need to fill empty slots with seemingly fungible persons. Ironically, however, the text makes seduction inoperative in marriage. Livie attempts in IV, 3 to use her conjugal influence on Auguste to persuade him to show clemency out of political expediency. Her advice is scorned by her husband, who throws into question both her love for him and her desire for his well-being.

While the text presents sexual seduction as a menace to heroic values, political seduction actually poses in comparison a far more potent danger in *Cinna*. Here, a different, now anachronistic meaning of seduction as sedition comes into play. It is found in Auguste's reaction to Euphorbe's disclosure of Cinna's plot ("Lui seul les [the conspirators] encourage, et lui seul les séduit!" [IV, 1, 1095]) and again in Emilie's defiant retort: "Si j'ai séduit Cinna, j'en séduirai bien d'autres" (V, 3, 1622). In these verses, seduction induces disobedience of rightful authority. This particular usage reflects a specifically Cornelian context, where service to one's liege lord and the ties of community are major values. The entire action of *Cinna* is in fact predicated upon a case of seduction away from allegiance to the sovereign.

In the broadest sense, the chief political mirage which the tragedy presents is the Republican ideal of liberty which has apparently prompted such disloyalty. Rome as an entity has been seduced by Republican ideology (II, 1, 571-72; V, 3, 1765-70). Maxime and presumably some of the

conspirators—perhaps those whom Auguste deigns to mention by name in
V, 1, 1489-91—have also come under the sway of Republican ideals. The
seductress Emilie has herself been seduced in this regard. Insofar as her fidelity to her murdered father Toranius represents fidelity to history and the
past, Emilie is a daughter seduced by her father's values and a seductress
seduced by the warring abstractions of her own psychomachia. Despite her
implacable stance as upholder of patriarchal values, a wholly orthodox ideological position in Cornelian theater, she herself is led astray by an outdated
devotion to Republican ideals, which are arguably less compatible than
monarchy with her patriarchal values, and by a private passion for revenge,
according to Cinna's bitter accusation: "Vous faites des vertus au gré de
votre haine" (III, 4, 977).[12]

The case of Cinna is far murkier. Is he a true "neveu de Pompée" as

In Emilie's role, Republican rhetoric is confused with the *code des
généreux* and set against the discourse of love. Emilie's patriarchal values
may seem curious in a seductress whose regicidal plot threatens to subvert
the symbolic order. As the outcome shows, she mistakenly identifies her
private law of vengeance with the public good (*res publica*), an error which
results in autocracy or tyranny, as Cinna labels it. It is important to stress,
nonetheless, the deep significance of Emilie's vendetta. It is not the case, as
classic Freudian theory would have it, that she gives precedence to a private
passion merely because she is a woman and is thereby prone to be less
"just" than a man. Nor is it merely private (self-)interest which provokes
her plot, as Doubrovsky claims.[13] She seeks rather to uphold patriarchal
values which Auguste himself has violated with the murder of his symbolic
father/tutor Toranius. Because Auguste and Toranius are rivals in patriarchy, Emilie must in fact choose between paternal love objects. Like
Chimène, she is forced to oppose her murdered father to a father figure who
is also her king. Her conflict is thus not between values, but between persons. Emilie's strict adherence to a masculine code of honor is blurred by
the fact that, as a woman, she must operate covertly, from a position of
weakness.[14]

The case of Cinna is far murkier. Is he a true "neveu de Pompée" as
Emilie wants to believe (III, 4, 1030), or is he an opportunist who espouses
Republican ideology to further his own ambitions? In either case, he mas-
terfully plays the role of political seducer: first, in I, 3 where he conceals
his true motivation and emphasizes Auguste's cruelty to the detriment of the
emperor's generosity; second, in II, 1 where he reverses his political stance
and persuades Auguste to retain the throne by an appeal to "l'amour du

pays."[15] In *Cinna*, recourse to oratory is a weapon of choice for those bent on sedition.

In the anatomy of political seduction which Corneille's text performs, the preponderant role of discourse is further underscored by a related economy of signs signifying political favor. As sovereign, Auguste has dispensed all the tokens of royal largesse to win Emilie's affection, while she in turn has used his money and her influence to procure supporters for her own cause. Similarly, Auguste has secured the alliance of Cinna, a former enemy, and of Maxime, an ardent Republican. Like the abstractions of rhetorical speech, such counters of royal favor as money, gifts, and high political offices can function as commodities: they can be detached from individuals, values, and contexts, thereby becoming empty markers. As the analogy between rhetoric and money suggests, in *Cinna* the problem of political seduction must eventually be recast into the problem of textual seduction.

With its roles anchored in such powerful motivating passions as love and hatred, ambition, satiety, and fear, *Cinna* ultimately concerns the seductions of rhetoric and of theatrical spectacle itself. As befits a political tragedy, the whole text is infused with direct appeals to the hearts and minds of the spectator/listener.[16] More particularly, with its conflated representation of Cinna as both orator and interlocutor in Act I, scene 3, the tragedy enacts from the start the practice of rhetoric as seventeenth-century theoreticians conceived it: both a decorative "art de bien dire" and a functional "art de persuader."[17]

In I, 3, the spectator/reader of the tragedy is given two broad views of rhetoric, both of which are arguably ironic. First, rhetoric appears as a form of seduction through manipulation of its addressees. At the same time, however, the seductions of rhetoric are shown to recoil upon its practitioner. At best, rhetoric assumes a life of its own, turning an actor into a histrion. At worst, rhetoric has the power to entrap its purveyor, to fashion a linguistic prison out of artful discourse.[18] From the start of *Cinna*, these ambiguous powers of rhetoric are thrust into view.

The major problem posed by Cinna's great speech of I, 3 is the problem of reported speech. To quote Holquist and Clark on Bakhtin: "Reported speech, or quoting, . . . is 'speech within speech, utterance within utterance, and at the same time also *speech about speech, utterance about utterance.*'" The quality which characterizes reported speech is its highly reflexive nature: "'. . . once it becomes a constructional unit in the author's speech . . . the reported utterance concurrently becomes a theme of that speech. It enters into the latter's thematic design precisely as reported, an utterance with its own autonomous theme: the autonomous theme thus becomes a theme of a theme.' "[19] Following Bakhtin's logic, the "theme" of Cinna's reported speech is thus oratory itself, the theme of his tableau is painting, and the theme of his portrayal of audience reception is audience affectivity. Cinna's role in I, 3 thus contains a threefold *mise en abyme* of rhetoric itself as speech and spectacle combined; that is, it presents rhetoric as theater. It thereby functions to underscore the seductions of rhetoric and of theatrical spectacle itself.

In dramaturgic terms, the spectator/reader can discern three "voices" at work in Cinna's role in I, 3: the overarching voice of the dramatic poet which informs the text of the tragedy in its entirety; the voice of Cinna the lover whose attentive interlocutor onstage is his beloved; and the voice of Cinna the incendiary orator, whose interlocutors are his fellow conspirators. Analysis of the direct and indirect forms of speech which Cinna employs in his report to Emilie shows that these three voices do not wholly merge.

Cinna's speech onstage to Emilie purportedly offers an instant replay of his oration to the plotters. In it, Cinna re-presents both directly (in reported speech, I, 3, 163-72 and 215-40) and indirectly (in a summarizing *récit*, I, 3, 173-208) a speech which is already a representation, since it is both a historical account and an interpretation of Auguste's rise to power. The reported speech duplicates the *exordium* (I, 3, 163-72) and concluding portions (I, 3, 215-40) of the earlier oration.[20] Intercalated between the two is the summarizing *récit*, with its "tableaux" (I, 3, 177, 189) of internecine carnage.

The reported speech is accompanied by three rudimentary *mises-en-scène* (I, 3, 157-62, 209-14, 241-48) which describe the effect of the oration on Cinna's audience. These portrayals of Cinna's spectators/interlocutors are akin to stage directions insofar as they indicate how the conspirators would react if the scene were actually played. However, the setting of this imaginary spectacle is not described. While the verb "eussiez vu" in verses 157 and 160 does convey the idea of spectacle, the conditional mode suggests a certain unreality, as Catherine J. Spencer points out. On the other hand, verses 209-14 and 241-48 are purely psychological in tenor and signal above all Cinna's astute manipulation of his audience.[21]

Further complicating scene three's play of mirrors is the fact that all the component parts of Cinna's role in I, 3 are enunciated at shifting spatial and temporal removes (Spencer, "*Cinna*," 423). Assuming that it is not wholly a figment of Cinna's imagination, the reported speech is, at the very

least, at one temporal/spatial remove. Nor are its removes constant in nature, for in the first part of the reported speech (I, 3, 169-88), there is a
flashback to Auguste's crimes; in the second (I, 3, 229-40), a flashforward
to Auguste's assassination (in the future immediate and future tenses). As
word pictures, the accompanying *mises-en-scène* are forcibly at two removes because one of these removes is verbal. Finally, given that Cinna is
supposedly quoting himself, his words may well be at some verbal remove
from their so-called origin. This is necessarily the case when he relates in
indirect speech what he supposedly said earlier.

The temporal/spatial and verbal gaps implicit in I, 3 pose a grave
problem. Though Cinna's voices or roles as reporter and as orator are
seemingly the same, in actuality they cannot be. As Emile Benveniste has
shown, each discursive recourse to *je* is unique.[22] Such ordinary shifts in
the speaking subject are compounded in this instance by the fact that the
speaker is quoting. Quotation, as John D. Lyons emphasizes, is a distancing device that changes the enunciator by requiring a shift in enunciation.
Because the act of quotation is actually a form of silence on the part of the
person quoting, the relationship between Cinna and his (self-) quotation becomes forcibly ambiguous. It is unclear, in fact, just to whom the quotation
really belongs.[23] Finally, matching Cinna's own shifts as enunciator, one
finds a shift in Cinna's addressees from the conspirators to Emilie. This
changes the context, hence the content, of the earlier speech and its later reported version.

The presence of quotation marks in the printed text of *Cinna* would
seem to confer a *bona fide* ontological status upon the reported speech by
guaranteeing its accuracy, at least formally.[24] Yet, apart from the fact that
the spectator cannot view such graphics, their presence does not automati-
cally insure that Cinna actually made the oration which he reports in I, 3.
For the text's reader, quotation marks function to distance the speaker even
from words of his own (Lyons, *Exemplum*, 31). The ontological status of
the first unplayed oration to the conspirators thus remains necessarily ambiguous: it is a shimmering mirage of pure eloquence which floats at various removes before the spectator/reader.

It is crucial to underscore the effects of this indirect representation
of Cinna's speech to the conspirators.[25] Principal among them is the mistrust of Cinna's "sincerity" which the reported speech stirs in the specta-
tor/reader. This suspicion is especially fostered by textual signs that Cinna
is acting.[26] Because such distancing devices promote self-referential theatricality, the alert spectator/reader becomes aware that Cinna is playing a

part. Once this becomes clear, one must ponder why he is doing so, for the gap between actor and script makes it less than certain that this orator corresponds to the classical ideal of a *vir bonus dicendi peritus*.[27]

It is plausible to conclude that Cinna desires above all to persuade Emilie that her conspiracy is in worthy hands and that he is its fitting leader, even though he may not be the whole-hearted Republican he purports to be.[28] In fact, this is a misrepresentation, as subsequent disclosures concerning the group of conspirators make clear.[29] The more the reader/spectator learns about the plotters, the clearer it becomes that the closing challenge of Cinna's reported oration idealizes their true nature: "Faites voir après moi si vous vous souvenez / Des illustres aïeux de qui vous êtes nés" (I, 3, 239-40).

Whatever his motivation, however, Cinna's seduction of the reader/spectator in I, 3 must remain incomplete in order to provoke reflection concerning rhetoric itself. For this to occur, the speech to the conspirators must be accompanied by the commentary on its reception which Cinna makes to Emilie. Unlike Cinna's fellow plotters, including Maxime, who are genuinely seduced by the speech because the orator's real motivation is concealed from them, the reader/spectator is carefully led to perceive a possible gap between Cinna's love for Emilie and the "sincerity" of his Republicanism.[30]

The chief function of the speech is therefore to seduce fully the spectator/listener onstage, Emilie, and to seduce at least partially, but not fully, the audience. The naive reader/spectator may of course believe, like Emilie, that Republican ardor prompts both Cinna and the conspirators to assassinate Auguste. Emilie is fully persuaded—and fully seduced, since Cinna has embellished the character of her father's avengers—because she hears precisely what she self-admittedly wants to hear (I, 3, 153-6): Cinna speaking like the "neveu de Pompée."

In this regard, Cinna's reported oration functions like a generic representative of the speeches which instigated ten earlier plots against Auguste (II, 1, 491). This function in and of itself does not harm Cinna's "authorship" of his reported speech. From the point of view of his interlocutors both onstage and off, both real and imaginary, however, the problem of ownership of Cinna's reported oration again arises. For, by rights as instigator of the conspiracy, Emilie should make this speech. She cannot, of course, owing to the seventeenth-century rule of decorum. This impossibility leads to the necessity of having Cinna make the oration. He is speaking for Emilie, and though she has not dictated the text, the reader/

spectator may well ask once more to whom the speech belongs.[31] It is, in fact, impossible to determine to what extent Cinna speaks for himself, either in the reported speech, or in the direct speech onstage to Emilie, whom he wants to impress.

It is equally impossible to determine whether Cinna himself is seduced by his own oratory.[32] Obviously, he is transported by his own skill at public speaking.[33] As inheritor of "le grand Pompée," Cinna knows how to speak the language which both the plotters and Emilie want to hear. Just as he serves in the reported oration of I, 3 as Emilie's spokesman, so also is he the permanent conduit of inimical blood, according to Auguste: "Tu fus mon ennemi même avant que de naître, / Et tu le fus encor quand tu me pus connaître, / Et l'inclination jamais n'a démenti / Ce sang qui t'avait fait du contraire parti" (V, 1, 1441-44). In *Cinna*, the power of ancestral rhetoric is thus shown to be greater than the speaker himself. Such inherited eloquence works against what its speaker really knows or even cares about; like Emilie, Cinna is a victim of the Father's discourse. Thus seduction can become self-deception. Cinna is aware that he has little value in and of himself, and that sovereign rule best serves the interests of Rome; Maxime recognizes the extent of his own self-betrayal in IV, 6. In this tragedy, rhetoric nonetheless assumes a life of its own. All speech, and not just sworn oaths alone, ensnares its speakers.

The seductions of rhetoric are freighted in *Cinna* by a thematics of *éblouissement*, which details the artifices of misrepresentation. They range from flattery and self-illusion (II, 2, 649; IV, 3, 1229; IV, 5, 1362; IV, 6, 1395-96) to outright deception: "la fourbe" (IV, 6, 1416); "l'artifice" (III, 1, 782-83; IV, 6, 1394; V, 2, 1637; V, 3, 1685); "grossières amorces" (V, 3, 1681); "parjures" (IV, 5, 1386); "une fausse adresse" (IV, 6, 1401); "un faux rapport" (IV, 5, 1316); and "feindre" (III, 1, 718). In the end, this thematics, which orchestrates those verbal activities that captivate and mislead, is linked to unheroic themes which make a surprising appearance in *Cinna*: *la lâcheté* (III, 1, 744; III, 2, 839, 852; III, 4, 1040) and *la traîtrise* (I, 1, 28; I, 3, 186; I, 4, 290, 306, 311). All misrepresentation which literally bedazzles is intimately related to theatricality, and it profoundly threatens the Cornelian *code des généreux*.[34]

As an analysis of Cinna's reported oration in I, 3 makes clear, rhetoric, in order to be wholly convincing, must at the very least not seem histrionic, that is, capable of being separated like a mere script from its speaker. If it appears detachable, it runs the risk of becoming demagoguery. By an ultimate paradox, however, in classical French tragedy, rhetorical language itself must convey the distinction between eloquence and demagoguery, between "good" and "bad" rhetoric. Cinna's speeches in I, 3 and II, 1 demonstrate that rhetoric is a problematic skill whose use and abuse lie in dangerous proximity.

Rhetoric's ambiguous power is not the prerogative of the actor/orator alone; it is notably that of the dramatist as well.[35] In a broad sense, every player of *Cinna* who resorts to grandiloquence to attain a goal is a dramatist *in petto*. It is Auguste, however, who fully assumes the dramatist's role at the denouement.[36] Earlier the victim of sated ambition, Auguste is tempted to abdicate rather than master his power—a temptation that the original text of *Cinna* presented as a seduction: "Si vous laissant séduire à ces impressions / Vous-même condamnez toutes vos actions" (II, 1, 411-12). Portions of the script of Octave, the original "nature" of Auguste (IV, 2, 1130), have also made themselves heard in passages which reveal that Auguste has yet to assimilate this historic part of his role.

Confronted by his failure to seduce others in Acts IV and V, the emperor uncovers the role of destiny, a figure both of metaphysical and of metatextual seduction. He perceives that his very relationship to reality functions like a text which he has refused to write. So buffeted, Auguste transcends his fate by asserting his individual power against it. This is the power of will, which allows him to assume sovereignty: "En est-ce assez, ô ciel, et le sort, pour me nuire, / A-t-il quelqu'un des miens qu'il veuille encor séduire? / Qu'il joigne à ses efforts le secours des enfers: / Je suis maître de moi comme de l'univers; / Je le suis, je veux l'être" (V, 3, 1693-96). If nothing else, these famous verses indicate that Auguste becomes, albeit by sleight-of-hand, the self-proclaimed master of his word (*sa parole*)—its origin, source and author—and thereby, master of the symbolic order ("ô vertu sans exemple!" [V, 3, 1731]). Auguste's wholly self-referential verses constitute an enactment of imperial truth, for *imperium* as the right to exercise supreme authority here becomes a truth that language itself performs. As a result, Auguste finally appears to write his own script, a mastery which gives him the power to write the scripts of others, to guide them by emulation into new, better roles.[37] Thanks to this supremely theatrical moment of self-pronounced self-transcendence, in which he paradoxically does not appear to be acting, Auguste becomes what he claims to be. Laying the cornerstone of a union of words and deeds that shines forth in the royal *exemplum*, he assures the realm of proper representation by assuming his proper place at the apex of the symbolic order.

Auguste thus reabsorbs the power of seduction by garnering all power, including that of language and spectacle, into himself alone. To quote Baudrillard: "... *la séduction représente la maîtrise de l'univers symbolique, alors que le pouvoir ne représente que la maîtrise de l'univers réel.* La souveraineté de la séduction est sans commune mesure avec la détention du pouvoir politique ou sexuel."[38] Or, as Livie puts it in seventeenth-century terms: "Vous avez trouvé l'art d'être maître des cœurs" (1764). This art, which assimilates the art of seduction, insures the triumph of the actor over the histrion, the triumph of imperial over Republican rhetoric, and the "cure" of Emilie's Electra complex with Auguste's second gift of Cinna ("plus qu'un père," 1713-14) to Emilie. Absolute monarchy becomes the proper path, Republicanism an outmoded political ideal. But these triumphs can only occur subsequent to Auguste's recuperation of all powers, including those of language and seduction, for himself.[39]

It is this reintegration that allows Auguste to overcome a racial and national curse—the parricide of Romulus, founder of Rome—and to close an unending cycle of violence. It produces the apotheosis with which the tragedy concludes. And in so doing, it effects the ultimate seduction of the spectator/reader, according to an eroticized royal ideology: "The fusion between politics and aesthetics in the *libido dominandi* of the sovereign makes of the latter a subject of erotic interest for the spectator in an experience that moves from submission—of the subject to the king and of the king to the state—to fascination and pleasure" (Ferrier-Caveriviere, "Raison d'Etat," 90-91).

NOTES

[1] Germain Poirier, *Corneille et la vertu de prudence* (Genève: Droz, 1984), 193.

[2] According to Serge Doubrovsky, *Cinna* takes up anew the grave problem first posed in *Horace*: "Si tout héroïsme doit passer par la lutte à mort des consciences, voilà la société des héros vouée à s'entre-déchirer et, en fin de compte, à se détruire. La tension entre les visées subjectives et les besoins objectifs de la Maîtrise . . . risquent d'aboutir à un éclatement fatal" (187). Doubrovsky presents Auguste's project as a form of seduction: "La séduction et la fascination d'autrui par l'amour est un rêve, un projet inauthentique pour un empereur, qui doit choisir entre les valeurs de la Maîtrise et celles du Sentiment. Pour un Maître, en effet, le seul rapport véritable à autrui ne saurait être que le combat en vue de la domination" (207). See *Corneille et la dialectique du héros* (Paris: Editions Gallimard, 1964).

3 In opposition to G. Poirier's narrowly allegorical reading, I subscribe to Gordon Pocock's conviction concerning the conflict of values in *Cinna*: "The play creates its own meaning. . . . This, by its nature, goes beyond any conscious intention of the author, and is not expressible by any means other than the play." See *Corneille and Racine, Problems of Tragic Form* (Cambridge, England: Cambridge University Press, 1973), 59.

4 The erotic connotations which a modern reader attaches to seduction do not appear explicitly in dictionary definitions of the classical period. In Furetière's *Dictionnaire universel* (1684), the notion of religious error predominates in the definition of "séduction" ("Tromperie, engagement dans l'erreur ou dans le péché) and of "séduire" ("Abuser quelqu'un, lui persuader de faire le mal, ou lui mettre dans l'esprit quelque mauvaise doctrine"). In the *Dictionnaire de l'Académie,* sexual seduction is merely implied by the second meaning noted for the verb "séduire": ". . . Faire tomber en faute, suborner, corrompre, débaucher." As the evolution of the word's use suggests, however, seduction inevitably sollicits unruly desire.

5 Emilie is joined by Sophonisbe, Cléopâtre, and Bérénice in Corneille, and by Roxane and Phèdre in Racine. Don Juan, on the other hand, is notably a protagonist of comedy.

6 Antoine Soare notes the libidinal sway which Cinna exercises over Maxime: "Quant à Maxime, il est républicain de toute son âme, mais par l'intermédiaire de l'amitié qui le lie à Cinna. Déçu par cette amitié, et la jalousie aidant, il rendra des services insignes au camp adverse" ("*Cinna* ou la clémence au deuxième degré," *Actes de Wake Forest, PFSCL,* 37 (Paris, Seattle, Tübingen: Biblio 17, 1987), 115.

7 The argument that seduction casts the seduced into a feminine posture is borne out by Cinna's reaction to Emilie's claim in V, 2, 1619-22 that she is the true instigator of the plot against him. Denying that she seduced him, Cinna claims to have seduced her (V, 2, 1625-38); moreover, he seasons his reprimand with two references to his *bras* (V, 2, 1632, 1636). All subsequent quotations from the play will be drawn from Corneille's *Œuvres complètes,* ed. Georges Couton (Paris: Bibliothèque de la Pléiade, 1980-87) and indicated in parentheses in the text.

8 Following Doubrovsky and Marie Tastevin, Susan Tiefenbrun comments: "The nature of their relationship is purposely left unclear in order to enhance the irony of Emilie's heroic sacrifice in instigating the murder of Auguste and to establish an identity and exchange between Livie and Emilie, on the one hand, and Auguste and Emilie's father on the other hand." See *Signs of the Hidden,* chapter 8, "The Big Switch: A Study of *Cinna*'s Reversals" (Rodopi: Amsterdam, 1980), 184.

9 As a woman, she must entrust such a deed to a man, and this necessity leads to a further difficulty: the emperor must know that he dies to avenge Emilie's father (I, 2, 101-02). This is why Cinna must be the first to attack Auguste. The modern reader/spectator may compare *Cinna* to *Andromaque,* where Hermione's vengeance is thwarted by Pyrrhus's final ignorance of the true cause of his death.

10 Although he does not use the term, Roger Zuber stresses Emilie's Electra complex; he speaks of "monomanie" (273), "fantasmes" (274), and the cure of Emilie's "traumatisme d'enfance" (275) in "La conversion d'Emilie," *Héroïsme et création littéraire sous les règnes d'Henri IV et de Louis XIII, Actes du Colloque de Strasbourg*, éd. Noémi Hepp et Georges Livet (Paris: Klincksieck, 1974), 261-76.

11 Zuber comments: "Au moment où se lève le rideau, la santé morale d'Emilie est forcément compromise par les années de mensonges et de faux-semblants" ("La Conversion," 266).

12 As Juliet Mitchell reminds her reader: "It is quite specifically the importance of the *father* [rather than of men in general] that *patriarchy* signifies" ("On Freud and the Distinction Between the Sexes," 1974; rpt. in Mitchell, *Women: The Longest Revolution* (New York: Pantheon, 1984), 232, italics in text. Quoted by Gail Finney, *Women in Modern Drama* (Ithaca and London: Cornell University Press, 1989), 103.

13 Commenting on Emilie's "vengeance," Doubrovsky declares: "Sous l'apparence de l'attachement sentimental au père immolé se cache la révolte orgueilleuse du Maître qui ne veut se tenir que de lui-même la source de sa richesse ou de sa puissance . . ." (*Corneille et la dialectique*, 201).

14 Tiefenbrun subtly analyzes the dialectics of masculinity and femininity in *Cinna*, pointing out that both qualities, like heroism itself, "remain in a dynamic state of becoming until the end of the play" (*Signs*, 186).

15 Reviewing the opposing interpretations of Doubrovsky, who argues that Cinna is a convinced monarchist whose defense of absolutism in II, 1 is sincere, and Tiefenbrun, who emphasizes the strength of Cinna's arguments in II, 1 and the sincerity of his hatred of Auguste in I, 3, Odette de Mourgues concludes that one need not choose between them. See "Coherence and Incoherence in *Cinna*, Form and Meaning" in *Aesthetic Coherence in Seventeenth-Century French Drama*, eds. W. D. Howarth, Ian McFarlane, Margaret McGowan (Amersham, England: Avebury Publishing Company, 1982), 57. I shall shortly return to the question of Cinna's opportunism from the point of view of rhetoric, and shall confirm de Mourgues's proposal that both commentaries are appropriate.

16 For a general study of rhetoric in *Cinna*, see Sharon Harwood, *Rhetoric in the Tragedies of Corneille* (New Orleans: Tulane Studies in Romance Languages and Literatures, 8 (1977), 77-86, and Pocock, *Corneille and Racine*, 40-63.

17 A. Khibédi-Varga notes that treatises of the period indiscriminately define rhetoric both ways. See *Rhétorique et littérature. Etudes de structures classiques* (Paris, Montréal, Bruxelles: Didier, 1970), 8-9. As Jacqueline Lichtenstein observes, a similar syncretism in Quintilian's thought produces contradictions which reappear in the classical period: "Elle [la pensée de Quintilien] révèle en effet l'ampleur des difficultés que la rhétorique doit affronter en voulant réaliser l'alliance peut-être impossible de la vertu et du plaisir, de la vérité et de la séduction, de la connaissance et de la beauté, du langage et de l'image." See *La Couleur éloquente* (Paris: Flammarion, 1989), 110.

18 These perspectives on rhetoric can be related to Marc Fumaroli's analysis of the choice of role which *dramatis personae* of classical theater must ultimately make. See "Rhétorique et dramaturgie: le statut du personnage dans la tragédie classique," *Revue d'Histoire du Théâtre* 3 (1972), 250.

19 Katerina Clark and Michael Holquist, *Mikhail Bakhtin* (Cambridge, Mass. and London, England: Harvard University Press, 1984), 233, italics in text.

20 More specifically, the concluding portion contains part of the *narratio* (I, 3, 215-20), the *amplificatio* (I, 3, 221-26), and the *peroratio* (I, 3, 237-40) of the reported oration. See Harwood, *Rhetoric*, 81.

21 Catherine J. Spencer, "*Cinna*: 'Un crayon imparfait . . . ?'" *Romanic Review*, 78 (1987), 420-31.

22 Benveniste declares: ". . . les instances d'emploi de *je* ne constituent pas une classe de référence, puisqu'il n'y a pas d'objet définissable comme *je* auquel puissent renvoyer identiquement ces instances. Chaque *je* a sa référence propre, et correspond chaque fois à un être unique, posé comme tel." See *Problèmes de linguistique générale* (Paris: Gallimard, 1966), 252.

23 As Lyons observes: "Because of the shift in enunciation, the quotation is a kind of common property, since neither the speaker nor the audience is 'saying' it, but is only repeating it. Even self-quotation refers to something the speaker said, not to something he might now say." See *Exemplum* (Princeton, New Jersey: Princeton University Press, 1989), 30 and 23 note 50. Lyons's analysis thus highlights a problem of "ownership" which is equally raised by Bakhtin: "The problem in reported speech is how to handle the borders, how to demarcate the places where one person's speech ends and the other person's speech begins, and ends. . . . The problem . . . is to find the true author, the person answerable for the words in question" (Clark and Holquist, *Bakhtin*, 234).

24 See again Lyons's analysis: "The quotation is hearsay evidence, but unlike most hearsay evidence, the quotation has a specific weight derived from the very form of the utterance reported. Unlike a paraphrase, a quotation must not be altered in its form (or form of expression, in Hjelmslev's terms), and in this way the form is emphasized" (*Exemplum*, 30).

25 If Cinna's imaginary oration were staged, the tragedy's subject would be a failed conspiracy, rather than Auguste's clemency. Compare Spencer's point that it is precisely in I, 3 that the conspiracy fails and ceases to be the principal subject of the tragedy ("*Cinna*," 430-31).

26 See Pocock, who dwells on ironic elements in the speech (*Corneille and Racine*, 44-46) and Spencer, who stresses Cinna's complacent self-congratulation ("*Cinna*," 421-24).

27 This is Cato's definition of the orator, adopted by Quintilian, *Institution oratoire* (Paris: Les Belles Lettres, 1975), 2, livre 2, "Notice"). Fumaroli asserts that the seventeenth century pursued in all its genres this Roman ideal ("Rhétorique et dramaturgie," 247).

28 In "Plénitude et théâtralité dans l'œuvre de Corneille," *PFSCL*, 32 (1990), J. D. Hubert thus writes: ". . . c'est surtout pour éblouir Emilie que Cinna a recours aux plus belles ruses de la théâtralité, notamment en lui faisant le récit si riche en discours de sa réunion avec les conjurés et en l'informant d'avance de tout ce que sa conduite manifestera d'héroïque et de spectaculaire si par malheur l'empereur découvre la conspiration en train de se tramer contre lui" (63).

29 In I, 3, Cinna presents his fellow conspirators as fervently Republican aristocrats. When Maxime upbraids Cinna in III, 1 for betraying their cause, he speaks of "Ceux qu'engage avec nous le seul bien du pays" (760). His verse implies that all the plotters are worthy Republicans, as do Auguste's subsequent verses IV, 2, 1171-74, which allude to "tant de gens de cœur" and "tout ce que Rome a d'illustre jeunesse." Yet such passages mislead the spectator/reader, for Livie states in IV, 3 that the plotters generally come from the dregs of Roman society (1207-08)—a statement Auguste confirms in V, 1, 1492-96: "Le reste ne vaut pas l'honneur d'être nommé: / Un tas d'hommes perdus de dettes et de crimes, / Que pressent de mes lois les ordres légitimes, / Et qui, désespérant de les plus éviter, / Si tout n'est renversé, ne sauraient subsister." Apart from the fact that it tarnishes the image of Republicanism in *Cinna*, such intermittent and contradictory information concerning the plotters allows the reader/spectator to grasp in retrospect the seductive aspects of Cinna's reported oration in I, 3.

30 Spencer finds the description of the conspirators' reactions highly contradictory and argues that the text thereby signals their own "insincerity" or opportunism ("*Cinna*," 426). Even if the plotters are deceivers, however, the fact remains that they are themselves deceived by Cinna.

31 This is the problem of the actor as mouthpiece. See Vincent Descombes on linguistic slavery in *L'Inconscient malgré lui* (Paris: Les Editions de Minuit, 1977), 106-07.

32 According to classical theories of rhetoric, and principally Cicero, the listener can feel no emotions unless the orator himself is stirred by them. Brian Vickers terms this phenomenon "auto-arousal, or self-persuasion." See *In Defence of Rhetoric* (Oxford: Clarendon Press, 1988), 311-12.

33 J. D. Hubert also analyzes how Cinna becomes "an admirer, so to speak, of his own discourse" in "A Theatrical Reading of *Cinna*," *Convergences. Rhetoric and Poetic an Seventeenth-Century France*, eds. David L. Rubin and Mary B. McKinley (Columbus, Ohio: Ohio State University Press, 1989), 105-07.

34 See my study "Personation and Impersonation in the Theater of Pierre Corneille" in "Rethinking Classicism. Textual Explorations" *Continuum* 2 (New York: AMS Press, 1990), 41-63. It is precisely for this reason that although Cinna views his oath to Emilie as a snare, it is crucially important to his heroic stature that he not go back on his promise: the given word is bedrock.

35 Brian Vickers declares: ". . . in this [the sixteenth] and the following century, the poet's power to influence the passions was reiterated untiringly" (*In Defence*, 279-81).

36 See J. D. Hubert, "A Theatrical Reading," 102 and "Plenitude," 64.

[37] See Jacques Erhmann, "Structures of Exchange in *Cinna*," *Structuralism* (New York: Doubleday & Company, Inc., 1970), 182-84 and Antoine Soare, "*Cinna* ou la clémence," 113.

[38] Jean Baudrillard, *De la séduction* (Paris: Editions Galilée, 1979), 17. Italics in text. A later comment of Baudrillard further elucidates Auguste's recuperation of the seductive nature of power: "Le pouvoir n'est séduisant que lorsqu'il redevient une sorte de défi pour lui-même, sinon il n'est qu'un exercice et ne satisfait qu'une logique hégémonique de la raison." In Auguste's case, this occurs in that moment of divine illumination which marks V, 3, 1693-1714.

[39] See Nicole Ferrier-Caveriviere's analysis of this transcendent act in "Raison d'Etat et rois de tragédie de 1600 à 1660," *Actes de Wake Forest*, PFSCL, 37 (1987), 88-90.

6

La *Bérénice* de Pierre Corneille: *Pulchérie*

Eléonore M. Zimmermann

Commençons par quelques faits[1]: la première représenta-
tion de la *Bérénice* de Racine eut lieu le 21 novembre 1670, sur le théâtre de
l'Hôtel de Bourgogne. Huit jours plus tard, le 28 novembre, la troupe du
Palais-Royal que dirigeait Molière présentait *Tite et Bérénice* de Corneille.
Corneille demande le privilège pour l'impression de la pièce le 31 décembre.
Racine fait imprimer la sienne en janvier 1671 alors qu'elle tenait encore
l'affiche. Comme la coutume était de n'imprimer une pièce que lorsqu'elle
n'était plus jouée, cette suite d'événements indique, selon Georges Couton,
que Corneille a vu bientôt que sa pièce qui, dès le 5 décembre, était jouée en
alternance avec *Le Bourgeois gentilhomme,* n'aurait pas le succès espéré.
La pièce de Racine, qui aura trente représentations, aurait pu être imprimée
parce que son libraire voulait profiter de la rivalité qui avait opposé les deux
pièces. Couton note que Racine écrit sa préface sur un ton de vainqueur et
que les considérations sur l'art dramatique qu'il y présente vont à l'encontre
de quelques-unes des notions les plus chères à Corneille selon ses *Discours*.
Corneille, en revanche, ne fait précéder sa pièce que de deux citations latines
qui justifient les personnages de Domitie et de Domitian.

On a beaucoup écrit sur la parution simultanée de ces deux pièces.[2]
La coïncidence ne saurait être due au hasard. La rivalité entre les deux
auteurs, malgré leur différence d'âge (Corneille a 64 ans, Racine, débutant,
en a 30) est clairement établie. Après environ huit ans de silence, Corneille
était revenu au théâtre avec *Œdipe* en 1659 et avait écrit assez régulièrement
jusqu'en 1666-67, dates d'*Agésilas* et d'*Attila*, qui furent mal reçus du
public. Il se tait dans les années qui suivent, jusqu'à *Tite et Bérénice*.
Racine cependant faisait jouer une pièce par an depuis *Andromaque* en
1667. En 1669, soit l'année qui précède *Bérénice,* son *Britannicus*

remplace sur les planches de l'Hôtel de Bourgogne la *Mort d'Hannibal* de Thomas Corneille qui n'a duré que du 25 novembre au 13 décembre. *Britannicus,* on l'a souvent noté, envahit le domaine que Pierre Corneille avait fait sien. La tradition veut qu'il ait assisté à la première représentation et ait manifesté hautement sa désapprobation. En tous les cas Racine se sent persécuté par les partisans de Corneille et, dans sa première préface à la pièce, publiée en janvier 1670, attaque durement, avec toute la fougue de la jeunesse, ce rival qui semble lui barrer le chemin.

Corneille, qui s'était tu depuis 1667, semble alors prêt à rentrer en lice. L'explication que Henriette d'Angleterre l'y aurait encouragé pour établir un concours entre les deux poètes ne surgit que près de cinquante ans plus tard et ne saurait être retenue telle quelle. Couton a montré dans quel sens il pouvait être désirable à cette époque de présenter un empereur capable de renoncer à l'amour en faveur de ses devoirs de souverain, alors que les infidélités de Louis XIV inquiétaient et que Henriette d'Angleterre elle-même n'était pas à l'abri des libelles. Un Titus glorifié pour avoir renoncé à Bérénice pouvait rappeler que Louis XIV avait renoncé jadis à épouser la nièce de Mazarin pour conclure un mariage qui assurait la paix avec l'Espagne. J'ai moi-même jadis émis l'hypothèse que le sujet avait pu être suggéré à Racine qui l'aurait adopté, que Corneille en aurait eu vent et aurait décidé de se mesurer à ce jeune rival. Celui-ci, ayant appris à son tour que Corneille travaillait sur ce sujet, aurait alors poussé la note pseudo-cornélienne de son texte.[3]

Cette interprétation qui me semble toujours possible, est liée à un examen de l'œuvre des deux poètes, chacune vue dans sa cohérence intérieure. *Bérénice,* mon essai visait à le montrer a, toute racinienne qu'elle soit, des traits étrangers aux tragédies qui la précèdent et qui la suivent, alors que la pièce parallèle de Corneille me semble particulièrement maladroite. Comme dans *Œdipe,* dont le sujet avait également été choisi par un autre, Corneille détourne notre attention du conflit de Tite et Bérénice et d'Œdipe et nous ramène aux tragédies dites matrimoniales typiques de son théâtre à cette époque. *Tite et Bérénice* est autant une tragédie de l'orgueil, de l'ambition déçue de Domitie, que d'un noble renoncement. Quoiqu'il en soit, la pièce ne réussit pas alors que celle de Racine connut un succès dont il put se vanter dans sa préface.

Pulchérie est datée de 1672, deux ans après *Tite et Bérénice.* Lettres et journaux de l'époque nous permettent cependant de rapprocher leurs dates: *Tite et Bérénice* se jouait encore au mois de mars 1671. Dès le 15 janvier 1672 Mme de Sévigné rapporte à sa fille que Corneille avait lu

Pulchérie chez M. de la Rochefoucauld. On voit donc que les deux pièces ne sont séparées que d'un an environ. Leur sous-titre, "comédie héroïque," que Corneille n'avait utilisé qu'une fois auparavant, en 1650, pour *Don Sanche d'Aragon,* les rapproche aussi.

Ma thèse, le titre de cet essai l'indique, est que l'insuccès de *Tite et Bérénice,* survenu à la suite de plusieurs autres échecs, a amené Corneille à méditer sur son art, à repenser sa pièce, et que *Pulchérie* est le fruit de cette méditation.

Affirmer que *Bérénice* a influencé *Pulchérie* serait trop simplifier les choses. Bénichou l'a bien dit: "Il n'est rien de plus obscur que les cheminements de l'esprit créateur, en littérature comme ailleurs. L'étude des sources, au sens précis de ce terme, c'est-à-dire des créations antérieures que l'auteur a dû connaître et qui ont pu l'influencer, se révèle bien vite insuffisante."[4] Mais s'il y a eu, chez Corneille, une "méditation sur son art," elle ne s'est pas faite dans le vide: il a certainement passé mentalement en revue les réactions qu'avaient suscitées ses pièces, réexaminé en esprit le théâtre contemporain et réfléchi notamment aux raisons du succès de la pièce de Racine. *Pulchérie* en porte les traces.

Corneille, en effet, a toujours attaqué ses détracteurs, mais a aussi su s'adapter et tenir compte de leurs critiques—il suffit de comparer la première et la dernière version du *Cid* pour s'en convaincre.[5] Les "Sentiments de l'Académie" ce sont, pour le Corneille des années 70, moins les attaques de l'Abbé d'Aubignac, que les préfaces de Racine à *Britannicus* (janvier 1670) et à *Bérénice* (janvier 1671). Racine s'y vante de ne pas "trahir le bon sens," de ne pas "s'écarter du naturel," d'avoir su mettre en œuvre une "action simple, chargée de peu de matière," sans "quantité d'incidents qui ne se pourraient passer qu'en un mois" ni "infinité de déclamations." Autant d'allusions à ce qu'était devenu le théâtre de Corneille. Pour Racine "toute l'invention consiste à faire quelque chose de rien" et non à accumuler des incidents.

Ce sont donc les complications, inutiles selon lui pour soutenir l'attention du public, que Racine ridiculise avant tout chez Corneille. Ce faisant, il touchait au cœur de la conception du théâtre prônée par son rival, les *Examens* de 1660 en font foi. Déjà à propos de *Rodogune* Corneille se vantait des "incidents surprenants qui sont purement de mon invention et n'avaient jamais été vus au théâtre" et notamment de la "nouveauté de l'invention" qui fait que Rodogune demande à ses prétendants de tuer leur mère pour obtenir sa main. *Héraclius,* dont Corneille avoue que les complications ont échappé à la représentation, a "encore plus d'effort d'invention" que *Rodogune*. De même pour son *Œdipe* Corneille ne se contente pas de ce que lui fournit la pièce de Sophocle dont Racine louera la relative simplicité dans sa préface à *Bérénice*. Enfin *Tite et Bérénice* se distingue d'abord de *Bérénice* par tous les détours que l'intervention de Domitie apporte à l'intrigue.

Dans *Pulchérie* Corneille semble changer de cap et, sans aller jusqu'au dépouillement de Racine, trop étranger à son génie, viser à une plus grande simplicité. On note d'abord que la liste des acteurs est réduite à six, la plus courte du théâtre de Corneille. Même *Bérénice* en avait davantage, quoique l'action, Corneille en était sûrement conscient, se jouât entièrement entre trois personnages. Dans *Pulchérie* Corneille supprime en outre les confidents et, avec eux, les longs discours moralisateurs de *Tite et Bérénice*. Les confidences qu'il peut y avoir font partie de l'action, et cette action est dépouillée d'incidents secondaires: tout dépend des décisions de Pulchérie.

S'il y a quelques rappels de *Tite et Bérénice,* la situation de *Pulchérie* semble plus nettement calquée sur celle de *Bérénice*.[6] Nous sommes au lendemain de la mort d'un souverain. Titus a déjà été couronné empereur; Pulchérie, qui a régné quinze ans pour son frère, sera élue impératrice avant le second acte. Les deux nouveaux souverains étaient sur le point de conclure un mariage que leur nouvelle dignité met en question. Alors que le Tite de Corneille était prêt à abandonner le trône pour suivre Bérénice, Titus a pris dès le début de la pièce la décision douloureuse de renoncer à son amour. Pulchérie fera de même. Tite, Titus et Pulchérie se sentent tous les trois transformés par leur accession au trône,[7] mais Tite oublie bientôt sa déclaration hautaine. D'autre part dans *Tite et Bérénice* le sénat et le peuple adoptent la reine étrangère, ce qui rendrait son mariage avec Tite possible. Dans *Bérénice,* par contre, le peuple ne se prononce jamais et Titus doit prendre lui-même la pénible décision de renvoyer Bérénice, convaincu que s'il enfreint la coutume qui s'oppose à ce qu'un empereur romain épouse une reine, il invite le désordre dans l'état. C'est la même situation ambiguë qui se retrouve dans *Pulchérie;* nul n'empêche l'impératrice d'épouser le jeune Léon qui n'a pas encore su s'imposer au point de mériter l'empire, mais d'obscures menaces confirment ce qu'elle sait, que les grands du royaume se ligueront contre lui et provoqueront la guerre civile. Enfin, en un dernier parallélisme, on pourrait rapprocher Martian dans *Pulchérie* de l'Antiochus de *Bérénice*. Tous deux sont estimés, tous deux sont valeureux et nourrissent un amour secret, l'un pour Pulchérie, l'autre pour Bérénice, les soutenant de leur amitié et de leurs conseils. Tous deux sont prêts à s'exiler du moment où celle qu'ils aiment en épouse un autre.

Si la pièce de Racine a pu, sans doute inconsciemment, influencer celle de Corneille non seulement par les principes qu'elle reflète mais dans son action même, cela pourrait être parce qu'elle contenait, toute racinienne qu'elle fût, une note cornélienne, peut-être incluse par Racine qui tenait à battre son rival sur son propre terrain. Aucune autre pièce de Racine ne s'intéresse à ce point au combat de l'amour et d'un devoir qu'impose la société et l'état, aucune autre n'utilise si souvent le terme "gloire." Comme si souvent chez Corneille, Titus et Bérénice se trouvent sur un théâtre dont le public est l'univers et les générations à venir. Comme dans le premier Corneille, les obligations qu'impose la société jouent dans *Bérénice* le rôle d'un destin antique, et les personnages atteignent leur stature de héros en l'acceptant volontairement au prix du sacrifice de leurs désirs individuels. A le faire ils acquièrent cette gloire qui les rend exemplaires. Chimène veut ". . . que la voix de la plus noire envie, / Elève au ciel [sa] gloire et plaigne [ses] ennuis" (*Le Cid* III, 4, 970-71) et Rodrigue lui fait écho (V, 1), comme Tite proclame:

> Du Levant au Couchant, du More jusqu'au Scythe
> Les Peuples vanteront et Bérénice, et Tite,
> Et l'histoire à l'envi forcera l'avenir
> D'en garder à jamais l'illustre souvenir
> (*Tite et Bérénice* V, 5, 1755-58)

Bérénice semble, du moins à première vue, s'exprimer en des termes semblables à la conclusion de la pièce de Racine quand elle prononce les vers justement célèbres:

> Adieu. Servons tous trois d'exemple à l'univers
> De l'amour la plus tendre et la plus malheureuse
> Dont il puisse garder l'histoire douloureuse.
> (*Bérénice*, V, 7, 1502-04)

Mais si le vocabulaire est comparable, le ton est moins exalté. La douleur n'est pas infléchie, comme chez Corneille, par cette ouverture sur le monde et sur l'avenir. Racine n'est pas Corneille et ne tient pas à l'être.

Et Corneille n'est pas davantage Racine ni ne désire l'être. *Pulchérie* n'imite pas Racine: elle s'enrichit de l'apport de *Bérénice* au théâtre mais reste profondément cornélienne. Le renoncement amènera de nouveau l'exaltation et l'amour, quoique omniprésent, ne forme pas vraiment le corps de la pièce. Les thèmes même de *Pulchérie* préoccupaient Corneille depuis longtemps. Ainsi Martian, on l'a souvent dit, peut se ranger parmi plusieurs "vieillards amoureux."[8] Pulchérie, c'est dans un sens l'Infante du *Cid,* grandie, aimée. Elle semble annoncée dans un autre sens par Domitie qui déclare à son amant que si son père avait été empereur, son amour "en [ses] mains eût mis, sans balancer / Le sceptre qu'en la mienne il aurait dû laisser" (*Tite et Bérénice* I, 2, 253-54). D'autre part la jalousie est un thème fréquent chez Corneille, le "don" de l'amant auquel elle doit renoncer par la femme aimée de même (*OC* III, 1626). Le besoin pour un souverain de renoncer à l'être aimé, d'"épurer" (le terme est de Corneille) son amour est tout aussi caractéristique de ce théâtre.[9] Enfin d'autres pièces avaient fait une certaine place à l'amour entre frères et sœurs, notamment *La Mort de Pompée, Rodogune, Nicomède* et, plus récemment, *Agésilas.* On pourrait continuer. *Pulchérie* n'en demeure pas moins unique par la façon dont ces thèmes sont mis en œuvre et, si je puis dire, "mis en tragédie."[10]

Aussi voudrais-je faire ressortir l'intérêt—et cela en tant que pièce de théâtre, non comme stade dans le développement de sa psychologie—de cette pénultième pièce de Corneille qui me semble très injustement négligée.[11] Rappelons brièvement son intrigue.

Pulchérie, sœur de l'empereur Théodose, a régné quinze ans pour lui. Au début de la pièce celui-ci vient de mourir et le sénat doit élire un nouvel empereur. Pulchérie espère que ce sera Léon, qu'elle aime, tout en craignant que le sénat ne rejette ce candidat valeureux qui, à cause de son jeune âge, n'a pas encore eu l'occasion de se distinguer suffisamment. Elle veut toutefois être impératrice et ne l'épousera que s'il est élu. Léon, au désespoir, suit le conseil de sa sœur Irène: pour que Pulchérie l'épouse et soit impératrice il faut la faire élire elle-même. Le sénat le fait sans hésitation mais lui impose de choisir un mari. Elle prévoit que si elle choisit Léon les nobles qui ne veulent pas se voir donner des ordres par lui se révolteront. Aspar, l'un d'entre eux, qui voudrait que Pulchérie l'épouse pour le faire empereur bien qu'il soit l'amant d'Irène, confirme ses soupçons. Aux considérations politiques vient s'ajouter l'hésitation de Pulchérie qui voit tout à coup que se donner un mari, c'est inévitablement se donner un maître. Comme le sénat, sollicité une seconde fois, refuse à nouveau de désigner un mari pour elle aussi bien que de la laisser régner seule, elle décide, à la surprise de tous, d'épouser Martian, un chef réputé de la noblesse, vieux déjà, qui la sert depuis longtemps fidèlement et à qui elle fait avouer qu'il l'aime en secret. Ce sera un mariage blanc qui assurera son trône et la paix de l'état. Cependant elle donne Léon à la fille de Martian, Justine, dont seul le père (et les spectateurs!) savent qu'elle aime Léon. Quant à l'ambitieux et intrigant Aspar, il doit se décider dans les deux jours à épouser Irène ou à renoncer à elle.

Ce résumé ne communique naturellement rien de la richesse ni du charme de la pièce. Les rares critiques qui examinent brièvement *Pulchérie* ont tendance à ne le faire, peut-être parce que ce sont en général des hommes, que du point de vue du sort des personnages masculins. Ils s'intéressent à Martian comme figure d'un Corneille vieillissant, amoureux sans espoir de la Marquise, ils déplorent la faiblesse de Léon qui ne ferait que se lamenter sur son sort, victime d'une Pulchérie virilisée. Ils ne voient pas que cette pièce appartient aux femmes et que c'est sur elles que doit surtout se porter notre attention. Mais—les critiques se sentent-ils menacés par le fait que les hommes ne tiennent pas ici le premier rôle et que le sort des personnages n'est pas entre leurs mains?—[12] même les hommes sont bien plus que les stéréotypes auxquels on les réduit. Arrêtons-nous un instant à examiner leur représentation avant de porter notre attention sur les femmes.

Martian insiste, il est vrai, sur son âge et sur cet amour pour Pulchérie qu'il juge déshonorant. Les vers où il décrit la naissance de cet amour, mûri en lui à son insu, sont d'une grande perspicacité psychologique. Quand sa fille, à qui il l'avoue, s'étonne qu'il n'ait pu se défendre d'aimer, il répond:

> Et l'ai-je regardé comme tu le [l'amour] regardes [?],
> ....
> Je m'attachais sans crainte à servir la princesse,
> Fier de mes cheveux blancs et fort de ma faiblesse,
> Et, quand je ne pensais qu'à remplir mon devoir,
> Je devenais amant sans m'en apercevoir.
>   (II, 1, 454-60)

Cet amour, il "ne l'a point reconnu que par [sa] jalousie" (II, 1, 463) jalousie dont il sait, dans les vers qui suivent, nous communiquer les tourments. Proust aurait compris ces sentiments et on se demande si Victor Hugo qui, si jeune encore, sut créer Don Ruy Gomès, jaloux de tout "jeune pâtre" (*Hernani* III, 1), les connaissait. Toute la scène entre Martian et Irène mérite d'être relue, de même que celle où Pulchérie force Martian à avouer son amour (V, 3).

Cependant Martian n'est pas seulement le "vieillard amoureux." Si Aspar le dit "tout vieil et tout cassé" (V, 5, 1587), c'est qu'il est jaloux de lui, et si Léon insiste sur cet aspect, c'est parce qu'il est très jeune. Son désir de mourir, ". . . la langueur qu'on voit sur [son] visage / Est encore plus l'effet de l'amour que de l'âge" dit-il (V, 3, 1509-10). Martian n'est pas Don Diègue. De nombreux vers nous le montrent général encore actif.[13] Il a le respect de tous, mais surtout de Pulchérie qui reconnaît ses services sans détours (II, 1, 804, 818; V, 6, 1548) et laisse échapper un "cri du cœur" éloquent par sa simplicité, quand Martian lui apprend qu'il compte la quitter après son mariage: "Quoi! Martian m'abandonne!" (III, 1, 817).

Mais Martian existe aussi en soi. Nous le voyons politique avisé: il connaît les humeurs du sénat et sait le manipuler (II, 1) et il perce les intentions traîtresses d'Aspar (II, 3). En outre, et c'est peut-être son aspect le plus attachant, il est un père attentif aux sentiments, même inexprimés, de sa fille ("Pour l'intérêt public rarement on soupire . . . / Et jamais, à ton âge, on ne plaignit l'Etat" [II, 1, 393, 396]). Il la comprend, sait se confier à son tour sans égoïsme, garde les secrets qu'il lui fait avouer et sait qu'elle gardera les siens. Il la dirige de ses conseils (II, 3; II, 5) selon sa conception de la droiture et du désintéressement, même en amour.[14] Dans *Pulchérie,* j'aurai à y revenir, Corneille sait présenter des rapports humains autres qu'amoureux. Nulle scène n'est plus touchante que celle où père et fille se consolent l'un l'autre à écouter l'histoire de leurs amours secrètes, de leurs rêves et de leur souffrance.

Il est tentant de ranger Léon, d'un haussement d'épaule, parmi les "soupirants humiliés aux pieds de leurs princesses."[15] Corneille a eu le courage d'explorer avec ce personnage les réactions d'un homme dans la position où se trouvent en général les femmes lorsqu'elles dépendent de celui qui a le pouvoir absolu de disposer d'elles. Selon Domna Stanton, les réactions de Léon rappellent les réactions stéréotypées des femmes.[16] En fait, les femmes de Corneille montrent en général plus de soumission ou plus de révolte que lui. Corneille n'a pas simplement interverti les sexes, et un acteur de talent pourrait trouver assez de matière dans le texte pour donner à ce jeune Chevalier à la Rose d'un autre siècle une personnalité distincte. Doubrovsky a bien vu que Léon était "une sorte de Rodrigue . . . à qui le destin a dénié l'occasion de transformer ses 'coups d'essai' en 'coups de maître'."[17] Tous reconnaissent ses exploits et sa valeur. Il est aussi plein de promesse que le prétendant de Chimène (*Le Cid,* I, 1).

Malheureusement la situation dans laquelle il se trouve le rend impuissant et quand il s'en plaint, il le fait la plupart du temps dans un langage galant qui nous est devenu étranger et qui peut nous irriter autant que celui d'Alexandre, de Pyrrhus ou de Britannicus. Mais Corneille donne aussi à Léon la capacité de s'exprimer avec plus de force simple. Lorsqu'Irène annonce qu'elle sait un moyen de surmonter les hésitations qu'a Pulchérie de l'épouser, l'alexandrin se désarticule. Au "Croyez-moi, Seigneur, et l'empire est à vous" il répond par un seul cri: "Ma sœur!" Peu après les mots se bousculent: "N'y perdons aucun temps: hâtez-vous de m'instruire; / Hâtez-vous de m'ouvrir la route à m'y conduire" (I, 3, 211-14). Quand, repoussé par Pulchérie, il vient se réfugier auprès de Martian et de Justine pour implorer leur aide, son langage se fait à nouveau pressant: "Seigneur, parlez pour moi; parlez pour moi, madame"; "Allez, seigneur, allez empêcher son parjure" (II, 4, 669; 686). Tout respire son impatience juvénile.

Sa jeunesse est plus qu'un attribut abstrait qui l'empêche d'accéder au trône: elle colore tout ce qu'il fait et dit. Il s'y associe une grande naïveté: les complexités machiavéliques de la politique lui échappent. Aspar s'est dit son ami, il le croit (I, 3); le sénat a élu Pulchérie et lui a imposé de se marier sachant qu'elle l'aime, c'est que le sénat voulait l'élire empereur (II, 3, 681-84). Il est entier, aveugle, tout à son amour, mais franc et modeste. Il reconnaît qu'il n'est pas prêt pour le trône (I, 4) avec d'autant plus de simplicité que la politique ne l'intéresse pas. Le politique Aspar est prêt à changer de maîtresse pour servir son ambition. Léon se rebiffe non seulement à l'idée de changer d'amour (V, 6), mais même à la suggestion qu'il fasse semblant de se tourner vers une autre afin de reconquérir Pulchérie par le biais de la jalousie (III, 4).

Cependant son désespoir, que Corneille nous présente dans toutes ses phases, appréhension, jalousie, rage, ne le rend pas insensible. Face à Irène il se montre attentif à ne pas bousculer sa sœur, à ne pas exiger qu'elle subordonne ses espoirs aux siens (I, 3). Une fois de plus Corneille a su mettre en scène des rapports autres qu'amoureux. Face à Pulchérie, une seule exclamation de douleur de son amante, "Ah, Léon!" arrête son flot de récriminations (V, 6, 1637). Des situations diverses révèlent ainsi des aspects divers de son caractère, montrant qu'il n'est pas indigne de l'amour-estime qu'il a éveillé en Pulchérie.

Le troisième personnage masculin de la pièce, Aspar, est plus difficile à saisir, même si on retrouve en lui des traits de bien d'autres héros et héroïnes cornéliens, comme Honorie d'*Attila* et plus encore Domitie de *Tite et Bérénice* qui implore son amant de l'aider à se faire épouser par Tite

prétextant, alors même qu'elle l'assure de son amour, qu'il doit tout faire
pour qu'elle devienne impératrice s'il l'aime vraiment. Cette façon de
concevoir l'amour ne semble pas avoir paru incongrue à Corneille dans le
contexte de son temps, mais peut nous laisser perplexes alors que Aspar
nous paraît vil, fourbe et menteur. Il y a quelques indications cependant
qu'il l'était pour Corneille aussi. Vaillant, bon général, mais prêt à tout
sacrifier à son ambition, il est le seul qui n'hésite pas devant "la honte du
change," et tous lui en font grief.[18] Pulchérie le malmène fort, et on se
demande pourquoi Irène continue à l'aimer. Sans doute pour le jouer
faudrait-il un acteur d'un "sex appeal" marqué qui nous fascinerait suffisamment pour nous faire oublier ses manigances.

Si on juxtapose ces trois hommes on comprend qu'à un certain
niveau ils ne font qu'un. Ils incarnent les trois stades de l'homme: jeune et
idéaliste (Léon); adulte, orgueilleux, cherchant à s'établir dans le monde
(Aspar); et vieux, ayant renoncé aux ambitions, doué d'une certaine sagesse
désabusée, paternel et essentiellement observateur d'un monde qu'il
s'apprête à quitter (Martian).

Au trio des hommes correspond un trio de femmes où l'on reconnaît des aspects divers de la condition féminine. Toutes trois sont soumises
à certaines contraintes inhérentes à la structure de la société.[19] Mais grâce à
la création de Pulchérie, elles ne représentent pas seulement des formes
variées de la soumission, comme les femmes d'*Attila* par exemple. Irène est
la femme mal aimée et trahie dont le sort reste incertain à la fin de la pièce;
Justine, la non aimée, soumise en apparence, nourrit un rêve qui se
réalisera; Pulchérie est la seule aimée et amoureuse. Elle devra renoncer à
son amant mais son autre rêve, celui de régner, sera comblé sans qu'elle ait
à sacrifier, comme Aspar, son intégrité.

Ce schéma invite à spéculer sur les raisons profondes qui ont mené
Corneille, dans une pièce qui n'est pas une tragédie, à ne laisser aucun
rapport amoureux trouver sa satisfaction dans la réciprocité. Toutefois la
vie affective de ces femmes ne se limite pas à l'amour. Irène est maltraitée
par son amant, mais elle est sœur aimante et chérie (I, 3; 5). Justine n'a pas
d'amant, mais elle protège son père et est protégée par lui (II, 5; III, 2).
Enfin Pulchérie se repose sur toutes les deux, mais veille aussi sur elles
pour sauver leur dignité et assurer, dans la mesure du possible, leur
bonheur. Corneille semble avoir senti quel rôle peut jouer l'amitié féminine
pour les femmes. Il a éliminé les confidentes, et a représenté trois amies.
On voit leur tact, et leur sensibilité à l'autre, que ce soit lorsqu'Irène devine
l'amour secret de Justine (IV, 1, 1137), qu'elle défend la noblesse et la

sincérité de Pulchérie contre les attaques d'Aspar (III, 4, 1358; 1425-30), lorsque Justine lui rapporte les infidélités d'Aspar (III, 4), ou quand Pulchérie cherche à établir les sentiments véritables d'Irène pour celui-ci (IV, 2, 1243-1251).

Le climat de confiance qui règne entre ces femmes donne son ton aux scènes, si importantes pour l'action, où Pulchérie leur confie son amour pour Léon. Elue impératrice et sommée de choisir elle-même son époux, elle vient d'expliquer à Martian que jamais elle ne choisira Léon contre qui, elle le sait, tous les grands se ligueront (III, 1). Restée seule avec Justine, elle lui révèle le prix de cette décision en des vers qui rappellent parfois *Bérénice:*

> Léon seul est ma joie, il est mon seul désir;
> Je n'en puis choisir d'autre, et n'ose le choisir:
> Depuis trois ans unie à cette chère idée,
> J'en ai l'âme à toute heure en tous lieux obsédée;
> Rien n'en détachera mon cœur que le trépas,
> Encore après ma mort n'en répondrais-je pas;
> Et si dans le tombeau le ciel permet qu'on aime,
> Dans le fond du tombeau je l'aimerai de même.
>
> (III, 2, 847-854)

Elle confiera à la même amie que jamais elle ne prendra un autre époux et lui demande enfin d'essayer de conquérir Léon car

> Je le crains, je me crains, s'il n'engage sa foi,
> Et je suis trop à lui tant qu'il est tout à moi.
>
> (III, 2, 867-68)

Justine s'y essayera en vain (III, 4). Quand Pulchérie reparaît sur scène, c'est pour chercher du réconfort auprès d'Irène et de Justine auxquelles elle fait subir un interrogatoire serré: que fait Léon? L'aurait-il déjà oubliée? Elle ne saurait le supporter. Et à nouveau elle confie son trouble aux deux jeunes femmes:

> Fais-lui, fais-lui plutôt soulager son ennui
> A croire que je souffre autant et plus que lui.
> C'est une vérité que j'ai besoin qu'il croie
> Pour mêler à mes maux quelqu'inutile joie.
>
> (IV, 2, 1163-66)

Mais elle leur explique aussi les considérations politiques qui la contraignent à agir comme elle le fait:

> Epargne à mon amour la douleur de te dire
> A quels troubles ce choix hasarderait l'empire:
> ....
> Ton frère a l'âme grande, intrépide, sublime;
> Mais d'un peu de jeunesse on lui fait un tel crime,
> Que si tant de vertus n'ont que moi pour appui,
> En faire un empereur, c'est me perdre avec lui.
>
> (IV, 2, 1185-92)

Ces vers, et le long développement qui suit, expliquent l'action mais servent en outre à nous faire voir qui est Pulchérie. Ayant régné quinze ans déjà, elle connaît les complexités de la politique. Dans *Bérénice* seuls les hommes, Titus et Paulin, s'adonnaient à des considérations politiques. Les questions que posent Irène et Léon sont celles mêmes de Bérénice (*Bérénice* IV, 5, 1081-85): Vous êtes tout(e)-puissant(e), pourquoi ne pas imposer votre volonté? Si les réponses sont semblables (ce faisant, j'introduirais le désordre dans l'état dont je suis responsable), Corneille nous propose un canevas beaucoup plus vaste. Dès la première tirade il nous a montré les hordes barbares aux portes (I, 1, 27-28), l'état en danger et risquant d'être déchiré intérieurement par les intrigues "des partis et des ligues" (29-30). Aspar apporte ces intrigues sur scène, Martian même n'y échappe pas et le sénat, consulté trois fois, est une autorité et une menace omniprésentes.

Pulchérie appartient à ce monde et, à voir l'aise avec lequel elle s'y meut, on comprend qu'elle ne soit pas prête à le quitter pour quelque exil amoureux. On a reproché à Corneille d'embrasser une conception phallocentrique de la société pour ne pas lui permettre de posséder amour et pouvoir à la fois.[20] Mais Titus et Louis XIV, ce dernier amoureux de la nièce de Mazarin, ce dont *Bérénice* s'est peut-être fait en partie l'écho, ont-ils été plus heureux? Corneille n'écrivait pas d'utopies mais des pièces où les spectateurs pouvaient reconnaître la réalité qui les entourait et ils savaient qu'il fallait faire certains choix. La situation ici comme dans *Bérénice* peut sembler arbitraire, mais c'était le douloureux dilemme qui intéressait les dramaturges.[21]

Admirons plutôt que Corneille ait osé donner à une femme le rôle de Titus, qu'il ait osé créer une femme qui n'est pas condamnée à attendre qu'un homme dispose d'elle et n'a de choix, comme Camille, Emilie et tant d'autres grandes révoltées de ce théâtre, qu'entre la soumission et la mort. Le choix de Pulchérie est limité, mais elle obtient le pouvoir. Corneille a repris le thème du renoncement de *Bérénice,* mais sa pièce n'est pas une longue élégie, expression d'une passivité impuissante. Elle présente des étapes nettement marquées au cours desquelles Pulchérie doit se définir pour devenir pleinement impératrice, pour conquérir le titre qu'on lui a conféré.

Au départ nous savons qu'elle a gouverné sagement, mais l'a fait au nom de son frère. Le sénat agira maintenant *in loco parentis:* elle attend sa décision au premier acte, prête à lui voir élire un homme et à jouer son rôle de femme en l'épousant. Cet homme l'élèvera jusqu'à lui (I, 1, 11-12; III, 1, 775-76). Mais quand le sénat renverse les rôles, la nomme impératrice, lui impose de se marier mais refuse de lui choisir un mari c'est, du point de vue politique, lui enlever son soutien pour le choix qu'elle fera (III, 1, 732-44), mais d'un point de vue psychologique, la pousser vers l'indépendance, vers la responsabilité pour son sort. Cependant sa conception de soi, de son destin, subit une modification et, se confiant de nouveau à Justine, elle avoue, toute surprise et quelque peu honteuse: "Je crains de n'avoir plus une amour si parfaite." A la réflexion elle a compris "qu'on n'épouse pas l'amant le plus chéri / Qu'on ne se fasse un maître aussitôt qu'un mari" (V, 1, 1437, 1442-44).[22] Elle voudrait "régner avec l'indépendance . . . des vrais souverains" (1445-46).

Mais si elle est désormais prête pour l'indépendance, la société ne l'est pas, et elle se heurte à la réalité de sa condition féminine, muraille que sa volonté même ne peut abattre: il est inadmissible qu'elle soit impératrice et célibataire (IV, 3, 1305). La révolte est futile:

> Sexe, ton sort en moi ne peut se démentir:
> Pour être souveraine il faut m'assujettir,
> En montant sur le trône entrer dans l'esclavage,
> Et recevoir des lois de qui me rend hommage.
> (V, 2, 1475-78)

Pour sauvegarder son indépendance réelle, elle contournera donc la
barrière érigée par les conventions sociales: que Martian soit son époux en
nom et "dispense [ses] lois" (V, 3, 1548). Il n'y a aucun dédain pour lui
dans cette décision. Elle profitera de ses clartés comme par le passé (III, 1,
804).[23]

Poussée vers l'indépendance, puis l'assumant, Pulchérie reconnaît
sa nature profonde qui est d'être souveraine, et agit en conséquence. Ce
n'est pas sans combat. Elle avait proclamé dès le vers 3 que son amour
n'était pas conçu "par les sens en tumulte," mais le vocabulaire de joie, de
bonheur est lié tout au long de la pièce au vocabulaire de "désirs." C'est
ainsi que, très consciemment, elle sacrifie ce qui est pour elle joie et bonheur
au devoir d'être fidèle à soi.

Chez Léon aussi "aimer" doit être remplacé par "régner."
Pulchérie n'a pas voulu s'assujettir à Léon, mais elle n'a pas renoncé à son
projet initial de le faire empereur.[24]

Léon

Il faut aimer ailleurs!

Pulchérie

Il faut être empereur,
Et le sceptre à la main, justifier mon cœur,
Montrer à l'univers, dans le héros que j'aime,
Tout ce qui rend un front digne du diadème,
Vous mettre, à mon exemple, au-dessus de l'amour
Et par mon ordre enfin régner à votre tour.

(V, 6, 1691-96)

Le vocabulaire ("montrer à l'univers," "digne," "exemple") peut
rappeler l'adieu de Bérénice. Le ton est tout autre. Il n'est pas dénué de
tendresse ("Croyez-en votre amante, et votre impératrice," 1725) mais ce qui
domine, c'est une exaltation, née de l'immensité du sacrifice et de la vision
de l'avenir.

Peut-on parler de la stérilité de Pulchérie? Quoiqu'elle ait renoncé
à avoir des enfants elle semble plutôt, comme le dit une médaille que
Corneille connaissait sans doute, "vierge très féconde."[25] Elle renonce à
une descendance biologique, mais elle se crée un descendant, fils de son
choix et de sa volonté. Léon, beaucoup plus jeune et se comportant souvent
en enfant, déjà formé par elle (I, 1, 19-24) comme Titus l'avait été par

Bérénice, va devenir son fils et celui de Martian qu'il doit "[suivre] pas à pas" (V, 3, 1681).[26]

Pulchérie, dans les dernières scènes de la pièce, agit en impératrice. Mais tout en exerçant son pouvoir absolu sur ses sujets, elle se montre bienveillante, tenant compte des besoins et des désirs de chacun. Comme Auguste à la fin de *Cinna,* elle dispose de tous, de Martian, de Léon, de Justine, d'Irène, récompensant les bons et punissant les méchants (Aspar). Le spectateur ne peut avoir aucun doute sur sa capacité de régner.

De même que Pulchérie cherche et trouve sa voie dans le cadre étroit des contraintes sociales, Corneille se débat une fois de plus avec les lois qui régissent son art. Les vers par lesquels Pulchérie s'exprime ont été justement célébrés par Benedetto Croce dans un essai enthousiaste.[27] Moins denses que ceux de Racine, moins éclatants que ceux du premier Corneille, ils mériteraient une étude en soi qui montre le dramaturge libre et esclave dans les chaînes de l'alexandrin.

Sertorius, oublié pendant des siècles, a été repris à la Comédie Française en 1981 dans une remarquable mise en scène de Jean-Pierre Miquel avec des acteurs—M. Etcheverry, Mlles Vernet et Ferran dans les rôles principaux—qui ont su faire revivre ces personnages et même leur donner une certaine actualité. *Pulchérie* mérite un sort aussi heureux. Il faudrait des acteurs qui ne se sentiraient pas humiliés dans leur orgueil à se soumettre aux décisions d'une femme; il faudrait une Pulchérie sincèrement amoureuse et qui l'avoue franchement,[28] qui laisse entrevoir des faiblesses possibles, qui se cherche et se trouve et, de passive qu'elle était, devient active, mais sans crispation. Enfin il faudrait un metteur en scène qui sache donner leur importance aux scènes d'intimité entre amies, père et fille, frère et sœur, et qui les contraste avec les forces menaçantes du monde extérieur à la scène. Ainsi ressusciteraient devant nos yeux ces "ressources de nouveauté et même de fraîcheur"[29] dont Corneille, riche de sa longue expérience dramatique, pouvait faire don au théâtre.

BIBLIOGRAPHY

Allentuch, Harriet. "Reflections on Women in the Theatre of Corneille," *Kentucky Romance Quarterly* 20 (1974), 97-111.

Bénichou, Paul. *L'Ecrivain et ses travaux*. Paris: Corti, 1967.

Corneille, Pierre. *Œuvres complètes*. Paris: Gallimard, 1980-87. *Le Cid: Tragi-Comédie*, ed. Milorad R. Margitić. Amsterdam and Philadelphia: John Benjamins, 1989. *Le Cid*, ed. Peter H. Nurse. London: Harrap, 1978.

Couton, Georges. *La Vieillesse de Corneille*. Paris: Librairie Maloine, 1949.

Croce, Benedetto. *Ariosto, Shakespeare, and Corneille*. New York: Holt, Rinehart & Winston, 1920.

Doubrovsky, Serge. *Corneille et la dialectique du héros*. Paris: Gallimard, 1963.

Guichemerre, Roger. "Le Renoncement à la personne aimée en faveur d'un/une autre dans le théâtre de Pierre Corneille." *Actes du Colloque de Rouen, Octobre 1984: Corneille*. Paris: PUF, 1985, 581-92.

Knight, Roy C. "Que devient l'héroïsme dans les tragédies 'matrimoniales'?" *Actes du Colloque de Rouen, octobre 1984: Corneille*. Paris: PUF, 1985, 626-31.

Marthan, Joseph. *Le Vieillard amoureux dans l'œuvre de Corneille*. Paris: Nizet, 1979.

Michaut, Guy. *La Bérénice de Racine*. Paris: Société française d'imprimerie et de libraire, 1907.

Nadal, Octave. *Le Sentiment de l'amour dans l'œuvre de Pierre Corneille*. Paris: Gallimard, 1948.

Rousset, Jean. *La Littérature de l'âge baroque en France. Circé et le Paon*. Paris: Corti, 1954.

Stanton, Domna. "Power or Sexuality: the Bind of Corneille's Pulchérie," *Women and Literature*, vol. 1, *Gender and Literary Voices*, ed. Janet Todd. N.Y.: Holmes and Meier, 1980, 236-45.

Sweetser, Marie-Odile. *La Dramaturgie de Pierre Corneille*. Paris and Geneva: Droz, 1977.

Zimmermann, Eléonore M. "L'Innocence et la tragédie chez Racine. Le Problème de *Bérénice*," Papers on French Seventeenth Century Literature, 12 (1979-80), 109-27, reprinted in *La Liberté et le destin dans le théâtre de Jean Racine*. Saratoga: Anma Libri, 1982, Appendix II.

NOTES

1 Pour tous ces renseignements voir Georges Couton, *La Vieillesse de Corneille* et les notes du même auteur dans Corneille, *Œuvres complètes* III. Toutes les citations de Corneille proviennent de cette édition.

2 Voir notamment Guy Michaut, *La Bérénice de Racine*, mais aussi tous les commentateurs et biographes des deux auteurs!

3 Voir "L'Innocence et la tragédie chez Racine; Le Problème de Bérénice."

4 *L'Écrivain et ses travaux*, 167.

5 La version de 1637 nous est devenue plus accessible par l'édition de 1980 des *Œuvres complètes* par G. Couton, et par les éditions du *Cid* de Peter Nurse et de M. R. Margitić.

6 Un certain nombre de critiques ont rapproché en passant les deux pièces. Voir notamment Marie-Odile Sweetser, *La Dramaturgie de Corneille*, 235 et Serge Doubrovsky, *Corneille et la dialectique du héros*, 415. Toutefois, selon lui, c'est *Suréna* qui représente "la revanche de *Tite et Bérénice*." Je me hâte d'ajouter que rien ne nous permet d'établir si les coïncidences notées sont conscientes ou inconscientes.

7 "J'ai des yeux d'Empereur et n'ai plus ceux de Tite" (*Tite et Bérénice* II, 2, 495;); "Dès que ma triste main eut fermé sa paupière [de son père] . . . Je sentis le fardeau qui m'était imposé" (*Bérénice* II, 2, 460-62—voir aussi IV, 5, 1095-98); "Je suis impératrice et j'étais Pulchérie" (*Pulchérie* III, 2, 754 et 794).

8 Voir en particulier Couton, *La Vieillesse de Corneille* et Marthan, *Le Vieillard amoureux dans l'œuvre de Corneille.*

9 Voir en particulier Guichemerre, "Le Renoncement à la femme aimée."

10 Ces liens semblent avoir été perçus par S. Doubrovsky qui n'a pas vu, cependant, l'orginalité de la pièce et peut écrire dédaigneusement: "Après *Tite et Bérénice*, le théâtre de Corneille demeurera l'art d'accommoder les restes" (*Corneille et la dialectique du héros*, 415).

11 On a parfois l'impression que l'attention des critiques se lasse à lire les nombreuses pièces que Corneille écrit encore après *La Mort de Pompée* et *Nicomède*, ce que suggèrent des remarques comme celle de R. C. Knight qui, après avoir consacré une seule phrase à *Pulchérie* conclut: "il y aurait mille autres choses à dire sur toutes ces pièces" (630), ou Couton qui ne mentionne même pas *Pulchérie* dans la préface de *La Vieillesse de Corneille.* Dans le corps de son texte il se contente de la résumer et d'ajouter qu'elle "mérite qu'on fasse cas d'elle. Il y avait encore bien des ressources de nouveautés et même de fraîcheur dans l'âme de Corneille" (206). Aussi est-ce un plaisir de lire les cinq pages pleines d'enthousiasme sur la pièce dans le court essai de Croce sur Corneille dans *Ariosto, Shakespeare, and Corneille.*

12 Voir Doubrovsky: "*Pulchérie* porte à son point culminant l'inversion des sexes cornélienne" (*Corneille*, 425).

13 Voir à ce propos Marthan, *Le Vieillard amoureux*, 161.

14   Servons-les en amis, en amants véritables;
    Le véritable amour n'est point intéressé.

    ....

    Suis l'exemple, et fais voir qu'une âme généreuse
    Trouve dans sa vertu de quoi se rendre heureuse,
    D'un sincère devoir fait son unique bien,
    Et jamais ne s'expose à se reprocher rien.
                                                 (III, 5, 718-24)

15 Nadal, *Le Sentiment de l'amour*, 240.

16 "His emotional outbursts and ready tears all provide Léon with more than minimal stereotypes of femininity." ("Power or Sexuality," 241).

17 *Corneille et la dialectique*, 417.

18 Rousset voit "l'affirmation solitaire et véhémente d'un moi autonome" comme unité de l'être cornélien qui se fait autour du noyau de gloire. "Ce bel orgueil que [les personnages] appellent devoir" est, selon lui "le roc durable qui résiste au flux de l'inconstance" (*La Littérature de l'âge baroque*, 212). On voit combien, dans ce sens, la constance est plus qu'une simple fidélité amoureuse, et comment Aspar se sépare de tous les autres personnages qui y adhèrent.

19 Corneille n'écrit pas une utopie, et son public n'aurait pas compris qu'il le fasse. C'est ce que Harriet Allentuch fait ressortir clairement: sans doute les femmes de Corneille sont-elles dans un contexte social réel, limitées par les coutumes patriarcales, empêchées d'agir directement et par la force physique. Cela ne les empêche pas de vouloir ce que veulent les hommes, et de l'atteindre souvent. ("Reflections on Women in the Theatre of Corneille," 97, 103, 109).

20 Voir l'article de Domna Stanton.

21 Rappelons la réponse de Titus à Bérénice qui lui propose de rester à Rome sans l'épouser: "Hélas! vous pouvez tout, Madame. / Demeurez: Je n'y résiste point. Mais je sens ma faiblesse. / Il faudra vous combattre et vous craindre sans cesse, / Et sans cesse veiller à retenir mes pas / Que vers vous à toute heure entraînent vos appas." (IV, 5, 1130-34).

22 "Corneille a vécu l'histoire de la préciosité dans sa quasi-totalité" écrit Nadal (*Le Sentiment de l'amour*, 43; voir aussi 50-53). Or "mariage" rime avec "esclavage" dans la pensée précieuse, pour de bonnes raisons sociales et légales qui font que ces notions sont très répandues. Même l'auteur des *Précieuses ridicules* fait constater à sa Princesse d'Elide que les amants acceptés comme mari deviennent des tyrans (*La Princesse d'Elide* II, 1). A sa propre femme il fait dire "le mariage change bien les gens et vous ne m'auriez pas dit [vous êtes une bête] il y a dix-huit mois" (*L'Impromptu de Versailles*, scène 1).

23 "Où vos conseils régnaient autant, et plus que moi", formule polie, ne me semble pas justifier l'assertion que Martian aurait manipulé Pulchérie et garderait tout le pouvoir, selon la thèse de D. Stanton ("Power or Sexuality" 243). Certes, il a encouragé l'amour de Pulchérie pour Léon (II, 1, 476) et l'a dissuadée de l'épouser jusqu'à ce qu'il fût plus

digne de l'empire. Maritan dit avoir choisi Léon en fonction de son âge, espérant ainsi repousser l'hymen qu'il craignait. Mais il a toujours voulu "servir la princesse" et "remplir [son] devoir" (457, 459). Il est prêt, dans la pièce, à servir loyalement Léon. La fin de la pièce, où Pulchérie dispose de sa fille sans son consentement, illustre bien qu'elle compte prendre ses propres décisions.

24 "She would desire to raise her youthful beloved to the level of her intent, by removing him from the sphere of weak lamentations and assuring his union with herself in a mystic marriage of superior will" écrit Croce (*Ariosto, Shakespeare, and Corneille*, 418).

25 Couton nous apprend que *Cour sainte* de Caussin qui décrivait Pulchérie comme étant "faite pour gouverner les hommes et les Empires" et faisait état du mariage blanc de Pulchérie et de son vœu de virginité, s'ornait d'une médaille avec l'inscription "Femme stérile et Vierge très féconde" (*OC* 3, 1661). Les hommes aussi, Tite, Suréna, à cette époque du théâtre de Corneille renoncent à leur descendance (*La Vieillesse*, 221). Les accuse-t-on de stérilité?

26 Les critiques présentent souvent Martian comme impuissant, ce qui rendrait futile la longue tirade où Pulchérie assigne de strictes limites à leur intimité. Ainsi Doubrovsky voit dans le mariage de Pulchérie et son renoncement à avoir des enfants une fixation obsessionnelle sur son aïeul, son père et son frère impotent, ce qui l'empêcherait de se tourner vers l'avenir (*Corneille*, 422). Stanton interpète ces mêmes données et le désir de préparer Léon à l'empire comme une abdication de Pulchérie qui renoncerait à la victoire du principe féminin pour aider à rétablir l'ordre masculin. Il s'agit chez ces critiques d'une interprétation psychanalytique mettant en cause la psychologie profonde de Corneille autant que celle de ses personnages. Ma lecture se place au niveau de ce qu'à mon sens, Corneille communique à son public par le ton exalté et confiant des dernières scènes.

Citons à propos du rôle que Pulchérie donne à Martian une lettre de Saint-Evremond, que Corneille connaissait, où il exprime le souhait que celui-ci "avant sa mort adoptât [Racine] pour former avec la tendresse d'un père son vrai successeur" et notamment qu'il l'instruise dans "le goût de l'Antiquité." Il est amusant de penser que Léon, tout à l'amour, pourrait représenter le jeune Racine que son rival en amour "adopte" pour le former dans l'art militaire et l'art de régner.

27 "Pulchérie is the last and one of the most marvellous Cornelian condensations of force in deliberation. . . . Here we have clearly the lyricism of a soul which has achieved complete possession of itself, of a soul overflowing with affection . . ." (*Ariosto, Shakespeare, and Corneille*, 415).

28 Pulchérie, contrairement aux normes de l'époque, prononce sans hésitation devant son amant le "mot si rude" (*Attila* II, 6, 653). Le premier vers de la pièce est "Je vous aime, Léon, et n'en fais point mystère."

29 Nadal, *Le Sentiment de l'amour*, 206.

7

Banditry, Madness, and Sovereign Authority: *Alexandre le Grand*

Timothy J. Reiss

"Tout beau", dira quelqu'un, "raillez plus à propos;
Ce vice fut toûjours la vertu des Heros.
Quoi donc? A vostre avis, fut-ce un fou qu'Alexandre?
Qui? cet écervelé qui mis l'Asie en cendre?
Ce fougueux l'Angely qui de sang altéré,
Maistre du monde entier, s'y trouvait trop serré?
L'enragé qu'il estoit, né Roi d'une province
Qu'il pouvoit gouverner en bon et sage prince,
S'en alla follement, et pensant estre Dieu,
Courir comme un Bandit qui n'a ni feu ni lieu,
Et traînant avec soi les horreurs de la guerre,
De sa vaste folie emplir toute la terre."
—Nicolas Boileau-Despréaux, *Satire* viii, 1667

IN 1664, RACINE BROUGHT his *Thébaïde* to what all contemporary theories of sovereignty would have judged the inevitable conclusion of its ongoing violence and divided authority. It gave a terrifying vision of a "society" at its zero point: lacking a head, lacking authority, prey to what could only seem unlimited warfare. It more nearly resembled Hobbes's state of nature than any recognizable form of civil society. Such was the end of Racine's first dramatic "experiment" with theories of sovereignty familiar to all cultured spectators and readers of his day.[1]

The experiment had not dramatized these issues only in their political dimension. It also made room for concerns we would call psychological, although Racine and his fellows, after Aristotelian tradition, would think of them as about "the passions of the soul," as had Descartes just fifteen years before. *La Thébaïde* had shown the loss of political order to be matched by that of rational control in individuals. Political writers themselves explored the issue, arguing that a prince's legitimacy came in part from (was manifest in) an ability to control passion by Reason. Commanding Reason was the psychological equivalent of political sovereignty—the physiological equivalent even, for the passions arose from changes in the humors. Both Le Bret and Richelieu in fact claimed a lack of controlling Reason as one reason why women were unsuited to wear a crown: it was, they assured their readers, most rare to find women with such ability. Like Corneille before him, Racine doubted the claim. *La Thébaïde* presented three male protagonists, Etéocle, Polynice, and Créon, in thrall to passions of love, hate, and ambition. Its women protagonists, Jocaste and especially Antigone, spent the play in vain urging the men toward a rational peace.[2] These women were not alone in Racine's theatre.

Most of these issues would remain constant points of reference for Racine throughout his dramatic career. What interests me is how the political elements and practices with which he experimented in his plays record a development in many ways echoing theoretical and practical problems of policy and politics more broadly. The matter of sovereignty itself was an old issue, dating (as an urgent question in France) from the Civil Wars. It remained vital a century or so later due to recent memories of regency and Frondes, and of alliance between Spain and Condé (diplomatically and legally plausible only if that prince was sovereign); and no doubt because the declaration of Louis XIV's majority and personal rule was as recent as 1661. If Racine was to choose political issues at all, it was no surprise that he should experiment with sovereignty in his first three plays. *La Thébaïde* analyzed the consequences of divided sovereignty, showing (in the bounds of staged experiment) the need for that unique sovereignty which Le Bret had called "non plus diuisible que le poinct en la Geometrie."[3] *Alexandre* (1665) warned of the perils of unlimited sovereignty. *Andromaque* (1667) explored its legitimate establishment and depicted a foundation.[4]

Not unexpectedly, the most appealing solution to the disasters wrought by divided sovereignty seemed at first a total authority. This matched, across the Channel, the patriarchal claim of Robert Filmer, whose *Patriarcha* had been circulating for thirty or forty years by the time Racine was writing *Alexandre*.[5] In this play, the dramatist staged a monarch on his way to "remplir tout l'univers," and loved by a queen (Cléofile) just because she saw him as such a "maître de l'univers."[6] Racine's use of this phrase, we will see, did not by chance recall the earlier performance of another storied emperor: "Je suis maître de moi comme de l'univers," Corneille's Auguste had exulted in 1642, at a time, in play and in real life, when it did seem as if the virtues of absolute sovereignty might be confirmed (*Cinna,* V, 5, 1696). But that did not end matters. Five years after *Alexandre,* Corneille used the phrase again, now to query the certainty of such authority: "Maître de l'univers," lamented Tite, "sans l'être de moi-même" (*Tite et Bérénice* [1670], II, 1, 407). This time the older playwright may have taken his cue from the younger. For in *Alexandre* the first use of the phrase in fact questioned its validity. Do you see any prince, Taxile asked his sister,

> qui, sans rien entreprendre,
> Se laisse terrasser au seul nom d'Alexandre;
> Et, le croyant déjà maître de l'univers,
> Aille, esclave empressé, lui demander des fers?
> Loin de s'épouvanter à l'aspect de sa gloire,
> Ils l'attaqueront même au sein de sa victoire.

(I, 1, 17-21)

Racine might easily have been drawing a warning from Louis XIV's own mentor, to the effect that "periculosum in communitate est, si unus sit nimium potens" (it is dangerous in a community if one individual becomes overweeningly powerful).[7]

If Racine did, then, follow *La Thébaïde*'s exploration of the absence of unique sovereignty with a study of its presence, he did not thereby assume a straightforward solution. In the second case, as his sources forcefully observed and we now see hinted, a surfeit of strength was likely as perilous as division or weakness. Abuse of untrammeled power, of a *maîtrise* too overweening, became a principal threat. Indeed, it marked a passion for glory no less irrational than love or hate. As usual, it was Racine himself who guided his reader to these concerns, framed their critical understanding, and set them in their immediate political context (as he had, for example, by dedicating *La Thébaïde* to the Duc de Saint-Aignan, Colbert's strong political ally). Again, he did this in the dedication and prefaces placed before the published play, at once limning a general commentary and implying a more particular application: an admonition of sorts against possibilities of abuse.

It may not be instantly clear that in 1665 Louis's activities justified any such warning. Despite what Racine stated in his *Dédicace* to the king, Louis XIV was no "glorious conqueror," the equal of Alexander, before whom "tous les peuples se taisent" (85). True, he seemed on his way to some central position in European politics. Certainly he had long been deeply conscious of his gloire (85), though his old minister and political guide had counselled against it: "viam ludicram," Mazarin had advised, "aliis concede, ut applausum, gloriam, &c. . . . Gloriam, & nomen habere sine aliis, tu solidam potentiam quaere" (cede to others such trifling matter as plaudits and glory. . . . Let others have glory and renown, you seek real power: *Breviarium,* 121-22; *Bréviaire,* 90). But Racine was also correct in writing that such respectful admiration as Louis was beginning to attract was due less to military prowess than to other *vertus,* although we might understand these to refer to a rather Machiavellian *virtù.* Richelieu had praised such ability as a determined will to act in one's own interest, whether for sovereign power or glory (denying Mazarin's distinction). He urged "une mâle vertu," that overcame "Passion" and let "Raison" function with a clarity whose desired effect Racine caught in his wistful proposal that even in youth Louis "ait répandu sa lumière jusqu'au bout du monde" (86).[8] In *Alexandre,* Porus echoed Richelieu's phrase: "une mâle assurance" (I, 2, 126). There, however, violence, not reason, was its outcome.

The young king's first actions of international policy all involved the demand that foreign powers recognize French diplomatic preeminence, a precedence that was a wholly symbolic mark of glory. This started (and for years continued) with disputes between the navies of France and other countries, but in the first year of his personal rule a more precise excuse was provided by a brouhaha with the Spanish in London over ambassadorial precedence. It ended the following year with a Spanish apology. Toward the end of that year, a spat at Rome in which Louis felt his ambassador had been slighted, provoked him to demand similar reparations. When the curia delayed into 1663, Louis occupied the papal territory of Avignon and the Comptat Venaissin, claiming them to be "terre française."[9] One saw the "glory" might have more material—violent—uses.

By the end of 1665, if Louis was not the conquering hero some would think him two (and surely seven) years later, such straws had begun to gather. He did give evidence of seizing or manufacturing occasions "de se signaler dans un âge où Alexandre ne faisait encore que pleurer sur les victoires de son père" (85).[10] In 1662, by the no doubt disappointingly commercial deal of paying off a penniless Charles II, Louis recovered

Dunkirk from the English (to whom it had been ceded in 1658 in return for aid against Spain). Later than year, in a clever bit of diplomatic legerdemain known as the Treaty of Montmartre, he got Charles IV of Lorraine to cede to the French crown the duchies of Lorraine and Bar in his will. When Charles reneged the next year, Louis grabbed the excuse to occupy the fortified town of Marsal. Because Lorraine was an Imperial duchy, the action was the first of many in which Louis chose to beard the emperor, foreshadowing a policy of provocation that the king's *Mémoires* suggest was linked to his idea that France was the rightful imperial power of Europe.[11] This putative claim was assuredly not foreign to the staged experiment of *Alexandre*.

Nonetheless, and still in 1663, the emperor was not deterred from including Louis in an appeal for help when the Turks invaded Austrian territory. The king responded by sending 6,000 men across southern Germany; they participated in the rout of the Turks on the Raab River, near the St. Gothard monastery (about fifty miles east of Graz, just inside the border of modern Hungary, some 750 miles from Paris). For Louis's adversaries, the speed and success of this mobilization had its disquieting side, emphasized in 1664 when he sent a like detachment of soldiers to subdue Erfurt in Thuringia, a dependency of the Imperial electoral city of Mainz (not so far away as before, but still some 400 miles). He did so at a moment when France had persuaded Brandenburg and Saxony to join the Rhenish League of Trier, Mainz, and Cologne—with France as guiding spirit. This was a much more serious provocation of the Empire than the rather slight events of 1663.

Louis was moreover showing how he could at the same time use the navy in the Mediterranean to counter a Barbary threat against the Marseille trade, eventually (in 1666) forcing both Algiers and Tunis to accept treaties. In 1663, Louis had signed an agreement with Frederick III of Denmark, by which settled payments assured a regular supply of material for Colbert's navy. The similar foresight of the accord with the Imperial cities made it safe in 1665 to send 6,000 French soldiers to guard the Netherlands against any attack through Westphalia (from England and her allies). As early as 1662, while such minor but often provocative incidents were occurring or being prepared and amid divers diplomatic skirmishes between France and the other powers, Louis began to examine the issue of Maria-Teresa's southern Netherlands inheritance. Their marriage agreement had included renouncing all claims to Spanish lands in return for payment of a dowry within eighteen months. When this went unpaid, Louis was not slow to

dream of new territory. The project was to culminate in the 1667 War of
Devolution, when the king could at last satisfy his yearning for military
activity. Yet from at least 1664, it was becoming ever clearer that a Spanish
war was likely and even probable.[12] Even more was this so after Philip III
died in September 1665 (barely three months before the première of
Alexandre).

Louis was not yet some heroic conqueror, then, but nor was it
mere flattery to describe him as coming to "se rendre redoutable à toute
l'Europe." It was not farfetched to picture his majesty as likely soon to acquire "une gloire toute nouvelle" (not, we have seen, wholly to be admired),
and, marching "à la tête d'une armée, achever la comparaison qu'on peut
faire d'elle et d'Alexandre, et ajouter le titre de conquérant à celui du plus
sage roi de la terre" (86). Precisely there, Racine further—cautiously—
implied, lay the danger of glory and power.

The portrait drawn of Alexander in the ancient sources was by no
means universally favorable. Among these Racine insisted in both Prefaces
on the eighth book of Quintus Curtius, an author whose remarks could be
fairly damning.[13] The dramatist was more coy about another undoubted
source, of far greater overall importance in his (and everyone's else's) education and general culture, and especially in his dramatic writing. I mean
Plutarch, who was if anything even less enamored of Alexander than was
Quintus Curtius.

Apart from the plays' common preoccupation with sovereignty, this
perhaps less evident bond created a fascinating interplay between Racine's
first three tragedies. It is especially important for understanding *Alexandre,*
helping to explain among other things the powerfully pacific tone and argument of the play. The tragedy became a warning that I have sought to suggest was in fact both appropriate and timely.

Racine was imbued with Plutarch since his schooldays at Port-
Royal. At that time he had annotated a copy of the 1517 edition and had
since owned and marked Amyot's translation.[14] At work on *La Thébaïde,*
Racine would surely have recalled a passage where one of the sons of a
much-married king, asking his father to which of the half-brothers "he
would leave the kingdom," received the reply: "to him that had the sharpest
sword." Of this, Plutarch remarked that it "was much like that tragical curse
of Oedipus to his sons: 'Not by the lot decide, / But within the sword the
heritage divide.' So unsocial and wild-beast-like is the nature of ambition
and cupidity." One cannot help feeling the passage could well have had a

share even in the idea for a play on the subject of Thebes, one that would—did—explore the chaos caused by divided sovereignty.[15] The author of this brutal reply was Pyrrhus of Epirus, namesake and perhaps descendent of *Andromaque*'s protagonist. Plutarch's genealogy is not clear, but certainly implies he was descended from "Neoptolemus, Achilles's son" (Racine's protagonist). For his part, Alexander was descended "from Æacus by Neoptolemus on the mother's side."[16] The putative kinship could hardly escape Racine, even had the *Life of Pyrrhus* not constantly emphasized it. We are told how Pyrrhus's sister Deidamia, "while she was but a child, had been the wife of Alexander, son of Roxana" (and Alexander the Great: *Lives,* 2. 43, 505). We are informed how the Macedonians, defeated by Pyrrhus, "thought his countenance, his swiftness, and his motions expressed those of the great Alexander, and that they beheld here an image and resemblance of his rapidity and strength in fight; other kings merely by their purple and their guards, by the formal bending of their necks and lofty tone of their speech, Pyrrhus only by arms and in action, represented Alexander." Later, insulted by young men in their cups, Pyrrhus just laughs, changing but recalling the notorious occasion when Alexander killed his general (and earlier savior) Clitus for insulting him in like circumstances. Clitus had pushed the king's fury to its peak, as Racine would likewise not have failed to notice, by quoting from Euripides' *Andromache:* "In Greece, alas? how ill things ordered are?" (*Lives,* 2. 47-48, 507-10).

As if this were not enough, Plutarch next related how Pyrrhus, campaigning in lower Macedonia, had a dream in which Alexander on his sickbed promised to help him. How could he, in such condition? Pyrrhus asked. " 'With my name,' said he, and mounting Nisæan horse, seemed to lead the way." In victory, Pyrrhus was "declared King of the Macedonians." He was, however, soon forced back to Epirus, where he accepted an appeal from the Tarentines to lead them against the Romans. In a first battle he was so successful that it seemed the Senators would agree to terms. But the aged Appius Claudius shamed them by recalling a famous speech in which they had said, "if he, the great Alexander, had come into Italy, and dared to attack us when we were young men . . . , he had not now been celebrated as invincible, but either flying hence, or falling here, had left Rome more glorious." The outcome once again made Pyrrhus the stand-in for that Alexander.[17] One is tempted to assert that Racine's reading of Plutarch's *Pyrrhus* predetermined the matter of his first three plays once he had chosen one of them—and even his attitude toward that matter: an emphasis on the limits and abuse of power, the fury and passion of "gloire," the desirability of peace, and the proper application of authority.

The *Andromache* quotation that provoked Alexander to Clitus's murder got its full savor and insult from its being the first line of a longer attack on Menelaus. Peleus accused him of taking the "glory" of victory at Troy for himself, gaining "great renown" and "majesty" although doing no more—and maybe less—than others. The increasing envy with which Alexander was regarded, and accumulating examples of the self-glorification that provoked it, are common elements in almost all the surviving histories. Clitus's murder was presented as a kind of crux. Among extant sources for Alexander's exploits, only Plutarch mentioned Euripides. But Arrian also used Clitus's death as more explicit evidence of Alexander's growing violence, barbarity, and arrogance. So too did Quintus Curtius, who drew an increasingly savage, hard-drinking, and vainglorious Alexander: "immodicus æstimator sui."[18] The last was, we saw, the source Racine claimed he had most followed in writing *Alexandre*.

Doing so, the dramatist had not chosen the most noncommittal source. This would have been Arrian, who concentrated mostly on military and logistical detail. Comments of the sort that Alexander was "always more illustrious in war than after a victory" (when drunkenly and violently carousing, for example) or that his first action in India was to "butcher" the population of a beaten city, "even venting his anger on its buildings," although its people were "wholly unknown to him," were far more usual in Quintus Curtius (*History,* 2. 303 [VIII. ix. 1], 315 [VIII. x. 7]). Plutarch surely had a moral goal in depicting the degeneracy suscitated by war and self-regard. Alexander thus "lost his tenderness of heart, and gave credit to those also that were false; and especially when anybody spoke ill of him, he would be transported out of his reason, and show himself cruel and inexorable, valuing his glory and reputation beyond his life or kingdom." In his mourning after Clitus's death, instead of the gentle commiseration offered by Aristotle's friend Callisthenes, he accepted the philosopher Anaxarchus's consolation, that "all the actions of a conqueror are lawful and just." Thereby, added Plutarch, he calmed Alexander, but withall corrupted his character, rendering him more audacious and lawless than he had been."[19] Indicating the political and personal decay brought on by unleashing such passion, Racine had annotated the *Life* ten years before: "c'est une chose plus digne d'un roi de surmonter ses passions que de vaincre ses ennemis" (ed. Picard, 2. 940-41).

Alexander's loss of reason echoed that criticized in a prince by Richelieu, Le Bret, and so many others. Mazarin, too, had urged that one should try to avoid "erga quod maximo affectu & appetitu traheris" (what you are drawn to with greatest passion and desire). Indeed, he couched his advice in vehement terms: "If you are drawn violently [*violenter obtrudaris*] to gambling, hunting, or love, or torn by other passions [*ab affectibus abripiaris*], give them up once and for all, you would otherwise comit many imprudent acts." He ended: "mistrust what passion impels [*quo te affectus abripit, id suspectum habe*]."[20] In 1638, Rohan had begun his little work on the "interests" of European princes, some of which were France's expansive ones, by asserting reason to be the basic and excellent particular of humans, whose first task was to control the passions and appetites.[21] Modern theory thus wholly agreed with the ancient sources.

For Plutarch and Quintus Curtius, the aim of world conquest was by its very nature and idea fraught with unreason. In *Pyrrhus,* the former had provided a much-celebrated commentary on the matter. At Epirus, between the two failures of Macedonia and Rome, Pyrrhus and his friend and counsellor, Cineas, engaged in a debate. It was to be mined by Montaigne (*Essais,* 1. 42) and Rabelais (*Gargantua,* 33), and in 1668-70 became a main source of Boileau's Epître 1, part of which almost directly translated Plutarch (11. 61-90).[22] Cineas sought to persuade Pyrrhus that by constant conquest one finally gained nothing. Once the whole Mediterranean was won, Pyrrhus at last explained, they could: "live at our ease, my dear friend, and drink all day, and divert ourselves with pleasant conversation." What, asked Cineas, stops us doing so now? "Since we have at hand without trouble all those necessary things, to which through much blood and great labour, and infinite hazards and mischief done to ourselves and to others, we design at last to arrive" (*Lives,* 2. 53). "Hé! Seigneur," echoed Boileau, "dès ce jour, sans sortir de l'Épire, / Du matin jusqu'au soir qui vous défend de rire?" (11. 85-86). Furthermore, the Epître clearly recalled another French work, wistfully admired long since by Naudé, familiar to Boileau and his contemporaries—especially perhaps since Charles Sorel had just now listed it among important political writings in his *Bibliothèque françoise* (1664).[23]

In this 1623 *Nouveau Cynée,* Eméric Crucé laid out a system of international peace and explained why it was essential. But he began and ended by deploring the futility and the horror of war: "les guerres estrangeres s'entreprennent pour l'honneur, ou pour le proffit, ou pour reparation de quelque tort, ou bien pour l'exercice. On pourroit adiouster la religion,

si l'experience n'eut fait cognoistre qu'elle sert le plus souvent de pretexte."
To glory in war and esteem those successful in it was to glorify and esteem
precisely that by which we are least human, "ce que les plus imbecilles animaux peuuent executer."[24] The four excuses for war were all equally fatuous and false. If one just wanted to keep people busy, one could do so—
profitably—by industry and commerce (Crucé's full title was "Le nouveau
Cynée ou discours des occasions et moyens d'establir vne paix generale, &
la liberté du commerce par tout le monde"). The view hardly differed from
that now held by Colbert (whose rivals for Louis's ear, Le Tellier and his
son, Louvois, took an entirely more belligerent stance). War, Crucé had
written, leads only to barbarism, butchery, disease, famine, and death
(Cynée, 19-83, 345-47). While still at school, Racine had marked his
margin of Plutarch's Coriolanus: "Il est bien plus louable de bien manier
l'argent que de bien manier les armes" (ed. Picard, 2. 936). Small wonder
if he later chose the Colbert/Saint-Aignan faction at Court.

Halfway through his work, Crucé called for a royal edict to end
war, adding a ringing appeal:

> Qu'on publie seulement la paix De par le Roy. Ces paroles leur feront
> tomber les armes des mains. . . . Il n'est plus temps de s'imaginer des
> trophées. Il faut quitter ces meurs barbares, & monstrer au peuple le
> chemin d'humanité & vray honneur, afin qu'on ne viue plus d'une façon
> brutale. Il faut faire regner la raison & la iustice, & non pas la vio-
> lence, qui ne conuient qu'aux bestes. On a esté par le passé prodigue de
> la vie des hommes. On a veu vn deluge vniuersel de leur sang, capable
> d'empourprer la mer & la terre. Baste.[25]

Plutarch ended his Life of Pyrrhus by describing its protagonist's notably
unpleasant death, his head inefficiently hacked off. Both Racine's chief
sources for Alexandre described the emperor's habits and behavior degen-
erating under the pressure of constant war. Both showed how his efforts
did not only not lead to a life of ease and pleasant conversation, but brought
his poisoning. When, two years later, in his eighth Satire Boileau wrote of
Alexander's madness ("l'enragé qu'il estoit"), his lack of wisdom, and mere
"banditry," he was surely reflecting his future friend's views. For Racine
had certainly these matters and texts in mind while fashioning a play that
brought them to a focus—and at least as to its moral tone he was not at all
unjustified in claiming "il n'y a guère de tragédie où l'histoire soit plus
fidèlement suivie que celle-ci" (86).

The play opened, however, on a dialogue between the only two characters he had in fact changed: between Cléofile and Taxile.[26] She is urging her brother that it is useless to fight Alexandre, whose power ("puissance") has "forced the heavens to protect him," has made Asia "*see*" her kings fall, and has enabled him to keep "la fortune attachée à ses lois." Taxile must "*open his eyes* to know Alexandre," to "*see*" the thrones burned, the peoples enslaved, the kings captured (I, 1, 1-7). He opposed her wish (*vouloir*) on the grounds of treachery, but mainly because so to yield would be to admit his rival Porus the better man and let him win the beautiful Axiane (I, 1, 34-36, 104). Cléofile is free to love Alexandre, but his own fate is bound to that of the state: "je tiens avec mon sort sa fortune enchaînée" (I, 1, 61-62). Yet, he must pursue his love for Axiane (66-68). It is not a just defense, but "les beaux yeux d'Axiane" that are "ennemis de la paix" (67).

In this exchange the very terms of reason, sovereignty, and reason of state are set down (together with the material conditions of conquest and quarrels between sovereigns giving their context). The terms Cléofile uses (or that are used of her or Alexandre), of power, knowledge, *vouloir,* are those by which Le Bret, Richelieu, Mazarin, and others always defined sovereign Reason: of which the principal and wholly clichéd metaphor was that of sight and seeing. Against this her brother sets his fear that Alexandre only seeks him as a friend because his "vertu" (I, 1, 35) is less resistant than Porus's, his wish to be able to emulate those princes, and his competitive love for Axiane. Worse yet, he confuses the personal interest of these passions—fear, ambition, love—with his duties to his state: which is secondary. For Taxile the fight is personal, and its goal is to satisfy passions whose interests are indifferent to those of state. Cléofile's concern is from the first far wider: "le ciel," "toute l'Asie," "les trônes," "les peuples," "les rois."

When we then learn that Alexandre loves Cléofile (and later that maybe she returns his love), the effect of this order is to subordinate *their* passion to reason, even to make it serve reason. The more is this so as Cléofile's role is always to urge the others toward peace. Racine's wish to emphasize this role explains both a notable change in Cléofile and the more interesting fact that he drew attention to it (on grounds of justifying her relation with Alexandre). Noting her appearance in Quintus Curtius, Racine added that she was also in Justin, whom he quoted. This is intriguing, to say no more, for if the first was bland the second was downright rude, as even Racine's expurgated citation showed (87). Justin condemned the morality of Cleofis's behavior in crude terms.[27] *Bienséance* gave ample cause to alter it, but neither needed nor received justification. Why should Racine emphasize for Cléofile a pejorative source whence he otherwise got nothing? Was it not that he wanted to draw readers' attention to the change, to signal what is peculiar in her role? Like Antigone, Cléofile takes reason to guide passion. Like Antigone, she seeks rational peace and quiet community of states: "quae possunt componi pace, aut quiete, bello, aut liti non committenda," Mazarin had doubtless advised Louis.[28]

Nor are reason and passion, peace and war the only oppositions set up in Cléofile's opening lines. When she describes Alexandre forcing the heavens and "keeping *fortune bound to his laws*," in the background was a celebrated work:

> I hold strongly to this [wrote Machiavelli]: that it is better to be impetuous than respectful; for fortune is a woman, and if you want to keep her quiet you must beat and force her. And we see that she is more easily subdued by those who do this than by those who act coldly; and always, since she is a woman, she is a friend to young men, because they are less respectful, and command her more fiercely and with greater audacity.[29]

Coming at the start, I take this reference as comment on an action culminating in Cléofile's anguished cry to Alexandre: "Mais quoi, seigneur, toujours guerre sur guerre!" (V, i, 1325)—a reminiscence of Hobbes's state of nature surely also deliberate.[30] Even in the Prince, the rape of fortune gives the greater shock because of how Machiavelli ordered his text: the sentence before the quoted text explained that humans "sono felici mentre concordano insieme, e, come discordano, infelici [prosper while they agree together and are miserable when they are in discord]." The assault on fortune, one would think, is hardly an image of concord. The peace urged by Cléofile is flawed from the outset. Alexandre may combine *virtù* and *fortuna*, indeed he may even be creating thereby a single sovereign order. But in the way those issues were thought there remained a violent ghost in the machine: one still begetting war upon war, the peril of excessive power against which we saw Mazarin warn.

Throughout *Alexandre,* sovereign authority lies in individual power (indeed, political thinkers were only beginning to separate the idea of sovereignty from its concrete embodiment—almost always monarchical). The demonstrated result is twofold. Firstly it always brings strife, because power is (was) thought of in terms of extent of possessions.[31] Secondly its wider interests are readily confused with the individual's interests and desires (passions). Indeed, the idea of "glory," constantly and repetitively flourished by Taxile, by Porus, by Axiane, by Alexandre, and held the shining proof of power, easily changed from such a symbol of sovereignty to just another misguided passion among others. Such are the confusions emphasized in the opening scene and pursued in the next.

When Taxile suggests they wait to see if Alexandre may not propose peace, Porus does not hesitate: "La paix! ah! de sa main pourriez-vous l'accepter?" (I, 2, 140). Such a reply is, of course, utterly to confuse the general interest with individual "glory." Porus is aware of it: "Je veux, à mon tour, mériter les tributs / Que je me sens forcé à rendre à ses vertus" (155-56). And Taxile is right to observe (though it falls with ill grace from his lips) that this is the "pride," false glory, exhibited by Darius, and directly responsible for his defeat and death. Should I count for nothing "la perte de ma gloire?" Porus insists, adding: "Quand la gloire parle, il n'écoute plus rien" (198, 216). Foolhardiness and scorn are weak guides, responds his rival, before passing to wider interests: "Le peuple aime les rois qui savent l'épargner." They respect more those "qui savent régner," ripostes Porus. Taxile's reply that this is mere arrogance draws from Porus the barb that certain queens may admire it. Would you "expose your subjects" to such danger on account of your love? Not only that, ends Porus, but "ma juste colère" which "aime la guerre," my wish to "éprouver ma valeur" against Alexandre's, my "orgueil inquiet" at the tales of his achievements (221-39). The scene is remarkable for its almost textbook recounting of total confusion (on both sides, for Taxile's accusations are equally motivated by passion) between general interest and individual passion.

Such then is the idea of glory making Porus exclaim that these are the reasons why he has hoped to see Alexandre in India, envious of all others who have already had a chance to fight him, and why, if the Macedonian sought not to compose the issue: "Vous me verriez moi-même, armé pour l'arrêter, / Lui refuser la paix qu'il nous veux présenter" (248). But, of course, it is not only glory. As Porus will later say to Axiane:

Je vais, dans l'ardeur qui m'entraîne,
Victorieux ou mort, mériter votre chaîne;
Et puisque mes soupirs s'expliquaient vainement
A ce cœur que la gloire occupe seulement,
Je m'en vais, par l'éclat qu'une victoire donne,

> Attacher de si près la gloire à ma personne,
> Que je pourrais peut-être amener votre cœur
> De l'amour de la gloire à l'amour du vainqueur.
> (II, 5, 649-56)

She had given the excuse, earlier exclaiming that she would not prevent a hero running to victory, "jalouse," as she put it, "de sa gloire" (I, 3, 333).

Such exchanges again recalled a famous play. Porus's proposal to refuse proferred peace echoes Cinna's rejection, in conversation with Maxime, of Auguste's proposed abdication: both events would stop the protagonist from proving his valor and winning his beloved (Émilie, in Cinna's case). Racine followed Corneille in emphasizing these reasons, and even gave Taxile and Porus a further brief scene to recall, perhaps, the dialogue between Maxime and Cinna (II, 3). He did so, indeed, just before Porus emphasized the similarity of the role played by Émilie and Axiane as instigators of violence: "C'est vous, je m'en souviens, dont les puissants appas / Excitaient tous nos rois, les traînaient aux combats" (II, 5, 643-44).

In Racine's play, the reminiscence acquires a quite particular force from the moment when Alexandre's ambassador Éphestion leaves Porus in some anger, having sought to persuade him to accept the emperor's rule. As he does so, he recalls Porus's proposed refusal of amnesty: "puisque votre orgueil ose lui disputer / La gloire du pardon qu'il vous fait présenter" (II, 2, 591-92). By the end, this cue will have been many times repeated: "Je veux bien toutefois," Alexandre will say to Porus, "Vous offrir un pardon refusé tant de fois" (V, 3, 1411-12), and when the Indian prince still refuses, Alexandre glories in giving him back his kingdom: "c'est ainsi," he explains to Cléofile, "que se venge Alexandre" (1510). So Porus finally yields:

> Je me rends; je vous cède une pleine victoire:
> Vos vertus, je l'avoue, égalent votre gloire.
> Allez, seigneur, rangez l'univers sous vos lois;
> Il me verra moi-même appuyer vos exploits:
> Je vous suis; et je crois devoir tout entreprendre
> Pour lui donner un maître aussi grand qu'Alexandre.
> (V, 3, 1533-38)

Axiane had already shown Cléofile her changed view: "et souffrez que moi-même / J'admire le grand cœur d'un héros qui vous aime" (1525-26). Both take the stance of Cinna and Émilie after Auguste's concluding pardon, persuaded by Livie as Alexandre has perhaps been by Cléofile's constant pleas.

In his *Dédicace,* Racine drew attention to this relation by proposing that "on n'a point vu de roi qui, à l'âge d'Alexandre, ait fait paraître la conduite d'Auguste" (85-86). The background presence of Cinna is rather over- than underdetermined for Racine. Plutarch's *Life of Caesar,* meant for immediate comparison with that of Alexander (*Lives,* 2, 463), had no fewer than three men by the name of Corneille's protagonist. One is met right away: Cornelia's father, "late sole ruler of the commonwealth," Caesar's father-in-law. He was also, Cicero recorded in his first *Philippic,* killer of Antony's grandfather.[32] Two appear at the end. One, a friend of Caesar, was torn apart by a crowd in the forum after the dictator's murder. They had mistaken him for a third Cinna, who was indeed one of the conspirators (Corneille's character: *Lives,* 2. 579-80). Nor do I idly recall the *Philippic,* occasioned by Antony's attack on Cicero's absence from a Senate meeting called to discuss a public thanksgiving and maybe Octavian whose behavior was worrying Antony. Next day Cicero noted that the meeting was not such as when "a peace with Pyrrhus was at issue, [to which] debate history informs us that even Appius was carried when both blind and old." Appius brought Alexander and Pyrrhus together in Plutarch. We may add now Octavian (Augustus), whose activities were as much a part of the context of the Philippics as he was a protagonist of them. Indeed, Cicero was soon urging that the Senate hurry to honor Octavian, though yet a youth, for "did not Alexander of Macedon, when he had begun the greatest exploits in opening manhood, die in his thirty-third year . . . ?[33]

Racine surely found much more in the first Philippic. He had annotated the *Epistulae ad familiares* with remarks on Cicero's son-in-law, P. Cornelius Dolabella.[34] It was he whom Cicero addressed in the Senate about true "glory" as "praise won by honorable deeds, and grave services towards the State, a thing that is approved alike by the testimony of every honest person, and also by that of the multitude" (*Philippics,* 49: I. xii. 30). He went on to instruct Antony in the difference between true and false glory:

> What I more fear is this—that blind to glory's true path you may think
> it glorious to possess in your single self more power than all, and to be
> feared by your fellow citizens. If you think so, you are totally blind to
> the true way of glory. To be a citizen dear to all, to deserve well of the

State, to be praised, courted, loved, is glorious; but to be feared and an
object of hatred in invidious, detestable, a proof of weakness and decay.

(*Philippics*, 53: I. xiv. 33)

In the Tusculan Disputations (another standard school text and
certainly equally familiar to Racine), Cicero had linked confusion of true
and false glory directly to reason's blinding by passions, to "civil office"
and "military command," to the fall of states. False glory was an illusion by
which "human beings . . . are blinded and, as they do not know where to
look or what to find, some of them bring about the utter ruin of their country and others their own downfall." They are misled, carried away by desire, ambition of glory, lust, or other disorders (*perturbationes*) of the
soul.[35] Alexander was again exemplary, especially by his murder of Clitus
and the gentle philosopher, Callisthenes. Roman reason against the on-
slaughts of Pyrrhus was thrice recalled, once by Decimus Mus's supposed
victory, once by Caecilius's refusal of his bribes, and once by reference to
the virtues of Cineas, Pyrrhus's ambassador to the Senate.[36] Reason
against passion, vision against blindness, Rome against Alexander, Cineas
against Pyrrhus, the true excellence of civil office against the vain phantom
of empire, formed a set of oppositions whose association Racine, his spectators, and his readers would have found wholly expected.[37]

Glory is the overwhelming desire of most of the protagonists in
Alexandre, as it was, we are told, of Louis XIV himself: whose "principal
motive . . . during the whole of his reign was the search for 'glory' " And
if this was attained "only by victories, and therefore by war," then Racine's
call to make Louis an Augustan Alexander was at least problematic.[38] As
the examples show, Racine's classical sources opposed the two figures.
Corneille's example was similarly unpropitious. In *Cinna*, it was not war
that brought glory. On the contrary, it was the successful refusal of more
strife. Further, where Auguste's pardon was just that (his life being threatened by Cinna's conspiracy), Alexandre's is not. Mazarin may have advised a prince to show himself "natum qvidem ad clementiam (inclined to
clemency: *Breviarum*, 109; *Bréviaire*, 82), as had Le Bret and others—
clementia being the virtue of princes—but his own aggression cannot become clemency. As Cicero scornfully observed to Antony regarding the
latter's claim to have granted him some benefit: "how are brigands
'benefactors,' except in being able to assert that they have granted life to
those from whom they have not taken it?" (*Philippics*, 69: II. iii. 5).
Alexandre's representative Éphestion comes close to echoing Cicero: "Il

[Alexandre] suspend aujourd'hui la terreur de ses armes; / Il présente la paix à des rois aveuglés, / Et retire la main qui les eût accablés" (II, 1, 410-12). Racine's point may be that both the glory and the clemency are false.

Indeed, when speaking to the princes, rather than to Cléofile as in the passage just cited, Éphestion does not mince matters. Alexandre has raised his "grandeur" on the "tombs of kings," their "espoir de gloire" is wholly vain, and they must wait no longer "à lui rendre hommage." As conquered satellites they should accept "l'appui que vous offre son bras," and allow their states to be honored "d'un si grand défenseur" (II, 2, 460-69). There is not the slightest doubt here but that the sovereignty in question is that of the conqueror, of a questor after expansive empire. And Taxile's question, however motivated, is no bad one. It observed one of the perennial justifications for clemency:

> N'est-il pas temps, seigneur, qu'il cherche des amis?
> Tout ce peuple captif, qui tremble au nom d'un maître,
> Soutient mal un pouvoir qui ne fait que de naître.
> Ils ont, pour s'affranchir, les yeux toujours ouverts;
> Votre empire n'est plein que d'ennemis couverts;
> Ils pleurent en secret leurs rois sans diadèmes. . . .
> (II, 2, 488-93)

The question was regularly asked of conquerors of course: how does such a one make his rule secure? Machiavelli had answered that he should rid himself of all who pose such a threat. Others had other ideas, from colonies to forts, from gentleness to violence. Crucé had proposed that the only answer was to give up conquest. Scathingly rejecting the appeaser Taxile, Porus approaches this view, as he too takes up Cicero's scornful line:

> Que vient chercher ici le roi qui vous [Éphestion] envoie?
> Quel est ce ce grand secours que son bras nous octroie?
> De quel front ose-t-il prendre sous son appui
> Des peuples qui n'ont point d'autre ennemi que lui?
> Avant que sa fureur ravageât tout le monde,
> L'Inde se reposait dans une paix profonde;
> . . . .
> Quelle étrange valeur, qui, ne cherchant qu'à nuire,
> Embrase tout sitôt qu'elle commence à luire!

Qui n'a que son orgueil pour règle et pour raison:
Qui veut que l'univers ne soit qu'une prison,
Et que, maître absolu de tous tant que nous sommes,
Ses esclaves en nombre égalent tous les hommes;
Plus d'états, plus de rois: ses sacrilèges mains
Dessous un même joug rangent tous les humains. (II, 2, 513-18, 529-36)

This is total and unique sovereignty with a vengeance: that of Cicero's brigand (*latro*), of Boileau's bandit, whose "pardon" and "glory" are both wholly false.

When Axiane later adds her voice to the chorus, she once more emphasizes the wholly personal desire behind this quest for empire. Indeed, Alexandre has admitted as much to Cléofile, speaking of his heart yearning for renown, his passion for vast dominion, his love for glory (III, 6, 886-88, 893), and of how only Porus was offered as a worthy opponent (937-38). So Axiane is quite right in asking Alexandre, both believing Porus dead, why, if he thought so highly of Porus's valor and virtue, he needed to fight him: "Par quelle loi faut-il qu'aux deux bouts de la terre / Vous cherchiez la vertu pour lui faire la guerre? / Le mérite à vos yeux ne peut-il éclater / Sans pousser votre orgueil à le persécuter? (IV, 2, 1017-20). She has rightly reduced Porus's question to its personal dimension. From it, repeating Porus, she draws the only possible conclusion:

Je crois tout. Je vous crois invincible:
Mais, seigneur, suffit-il que tout vous soit possible?
Ne tient-il qu'à jeter tant de rois dans les fers?
Qu'à faire impunément gémir tout l'univers?
Et que vous avaient fait tant de ville captives,
Tant de morts dont l'Hydaspe a vu couvrir ses rives?
Qu'ai-je fait pour venir accabler en ces lieux
Un Héros sur qui seul j'ai pu tourner les yeux?
A-t-il de votre Grèce inondé les frontières?
Avons-nous soulevé des nations entières,
Et contre votre gloire excité leur courroux?
Hélas! nous l'admirions sans en être jaloux.

....

Non, de quelque douceur que se flatte votre âme,
Vous n'êtes qu'un tyran.
                    (IV, 2, 1073-84; 1093-4)

For the definition of a tyrant is surely of one who willfully confuses the general interest with the personal; rather, who makes the first serve the second. And the lust for individual glory and power can never be assuaged. The wish for total personal authority never ends. In the *Tusculans*, the *Philippics*, and elsewhere, such was Cicero's constant point, who, we may usefully recall, always argued tooth and nail against any hint of monarchic authority. As Alexandre soon allows, there must always be one more victory, one more conquest, until the world itself is one (1317-24). The desire of glory and quest for empire—of "power after power," as Hobbes had put it—were endless. Not so many years before, referring to the stability of the very Empire that Louis XIV was to covet, the Spanish diplomat Diego Saavedra Fajardo had generalized the same case with the same example. He lamented that no defence sufficed to defeat "el apetito insaciable de dominar, porque la ambición es tan poderosa en el corazón humano, que juzga por estrechas las cinco zonas de la tierra. Alexandro Magno lloraba porque no podía conquistar muchos mundos."[39]

Racine, we saw, managed to praise Louis by citing Alexander's earlier, equally lacrimose, fear lest his father not leave him even one world to conquer. From one world to many. . . . All agreed that growth in desire was inevitable: a boundless expansion of ambition neatly caught by Saavedra Fajardo in a Tacitean maxim rounding off the passage just quoted. It depicted a passion that would echo the Hobbesian hunger for power were it not that in Hobbes, civil society ended that hunger's freedom. The more a victor has, wrote Saavedra, the more he wants: "crece con el imperio la ambición de aumentalle" (*Empresas*, 577). The Spanish torrent of which Daniel Priézac wrote in the 1630s when defending French involvement in the Low Countries had been just such a murderous passion for conquest.[40] And both the watery metaphor and many of the references we have been seeing had been taken up as recently as 1661 by Jean-François Senault, clearly warning Louis XIV against adopting the earlier Spanish role:

Alexandre qu'on produit toûjours pour Exemple, quand on veut faire connoistre les perfections et les defauts des Souverains & des Conquerans, a passé toute sa vie dans l'exercice de la Guerre; Il a couru comme vn Torrent qui désole toutes les Terres qu'il inonde; Il a éclaté comme vn Tonnerre, qui renverse tout ce qui s'oppose à sa fureur; Il a porté l'étonnement & la crainte dans tous les Estats qu'il a conquis: Mais il n'a jamais pensé à se rendre absolu dans sa Personne, ni à vaincre son Ambition ou sa Colere; Et le Victorieux des Nations s'est veü

l'Esclave des vices, dont sa raison ne s'éstoit pas défenduë. Ce malheur, dit le Philosophe Seneque, n'est procédé que de la honteuse negli-
gence de ce Monarque & de ce qu'il avait eü plus de soin de domter les
hommes, que de vaincre ses passions.[41]

Senault dedicated his volume to Louis XIV. The passage just
cited occurs in the "Second Discours" of the "Quatriesme Traité," which
discussion is titled: "Que les rois doivent commander à leurs passions"
(*Monarque*, 190-97). At the same time, my reference to Priézac is not, I
think, indifferent, because in his "Epistre au Roi," Senault had lauded Louis
XIV for, among other things, having put an end to France's longest war:
the one, that is to say, with Spain—a preoccupation much in the wind. In
the mid-1660s, with Louis's lust for conquest increasingly taking aim—
precisely—at Spanish dominions, these references could hardly be missed.

Such were the demands of passion, dangers of conquest, and terrors
of imperial expansionism provoking Cléofile's agonized "Mais quoi,
seigneur, toujours guerre sur guerre!" She proposes the very contradiction
just implied: that so violent a passion for the glories of conquest and power
ruins, as Cicero wrote, the very state and society they claim to establish.
She evokes a reminiscence of Hobbes's state of nature as the inevitable only
outcome of such conquering glory—adding, too, something more:

Qu'espérez-vous en des climats si rudes?
Ils vous opposeront de vastes solitudes,
Des déserts que le ciel refuse d'éclaircir,
Où la nature semble elle-même expirer.
Et peut-être le sort, dont la secrète envie
N'a pu cacher le cours d'une si belle vie,
Vous attend dans ces lieux, et veut que dans l'oubli
Votre tombeau du moins demeure enseveli.
(V, 1, 1325-36)

This (too) recalls a text no less familiar (surely to Racine) than those
others we have seen lying more than in the background. I mean the moment
at the end of chapter 30 of *Agricola* when Tacitus showed a soon-to-be-
defeated Briton (Calgacus) urging his soldiers against the conquering
Romans: "To plunder, to butcher, to ravage they misname empire, and
where they make a desert [a desolation: *solitudinem*], they call it peace."[42]
Death, slaughter, had been the immediate outcome for the Britons. Roman

victory itself was to lead directly to Agricola's own death at Domitian's envious hands. For, of course, Cléofile was right not only through such allusions. The outcome for Alexander himself would indeed be his death— not told by Racine, but known to all his spectators and readers. And what should we make of the fact that while Porus survives in the play, Diodorus Siculus had him being "treacherously slain after the death of Alexander" by a satrap, Eudaemon (also in Quintus Curtius)?[43] Or what of the analogous fact that while Taxiles survives in all the sources, Racine kills him off? The dramatist makes sure that all his violent and vainglorious male protagonists will die, during or after the play. He was making a point emphasized in the lines just quoted, equating the arena of the lust for conquest with the Hobbesian state of nature where human life is "solitary, poore, nasty, brutish, and short." Not for nothing perhaps did Sorel name together the *Nouveau Cynée*, Hobbes's *Foundations*, and a *Politique des conquérans* (see note 30).

Unique and total sovereignty could *only* be gained by imperial conquest. As Cléofile ever implored, that meant constant terror and final desolation: a sovereignty over the dead, where even nature expired. So Crucé had concluded, depicting at length the horrors of war: "quand il n'y auroit autre consideration que la brieueté de nostre vie, & la certitude de la mort, qui nous menace à tous momens, nous deurions auoir honte de nous tant tourmenter par vn honneur imaginaire" (*Cynée*, 347). A more considerable personage than even a Senault had in fact summed up much of the matter drawn together by Racine in *Alexandre*, offering the playwright's own people and drawing his conclusion in similar terms:

> S'il y a quelque chose qui doiue apparemment esloigner un Prince victo-rieux de faire ioüir ses Sujets du bon-heur de la paix, c'est le desir d'accumuler conqueste sur conqueste . . . & d'estendre ses trophées iusques aux extremitez du monde, ou au delà. si son ambition esgale celle d'Alexandre. Il faut opposer à des desirs si violens & si déreglez, les sages considerations de Cineas au Roy Pyrrhus qui estoit de cette humeur, & à qui ce sage Ministre fit voir accortement la vanité de ses pensées, puis qu'elles alloient à vn bien fort difficile & fort esloigné, qu'il se pouuoit donner sans peine & sans retardement, en se contentant du present.[44]

François de La Mothe Le Vayer had offered this advice in 1640 to the future Louis XIV in hope of becoming his tutor. By the late 1640s, into the 1650s, he was tutor to the King's brother, helping complete Louis's own education, a councillor, colleague of Mazarin, whose views he was echoing. In 1665, though very old, he was still writing and publishing. The *Instruction* containing this passage was constantly reprinted during these years in editions of his works.[45] One is almost tempted to believe Racine had simply dramatized them (echoed as they so recently had been by Senault), furthering views of a group at court, of which Colbert was a chief representative, and which, while still powerful, had now rather lost the ear of a youthful king aching to prove his military prowess and expand the boundaries of his kingdom.

Much later, Racine and Boileau returned to these glorious imperial hopes imagined by Louis, though only by tactful allusion. In the "Éloge historique du roi sur ses conquêtes depuis l'année 1672 jusqu'en 1678," they proposed that the thought had been but a mistaken apprehension on the part of the Emperor, who, in 1673, "publie partout que le roi de France veut usurper la couronne impériale et aspirer à la monarchie universelle."[46] The Emperor's view, we saw, was not unfounded. And when the historians insist that such an accusation and fear could only imply forgetfulness that just a few years before, on the banks of the Raab, the French "avaient sauvé l'Empire de la fureur des infidèles," they actually recall that the troops sent across Germany against the Turks in 1663 had been one element in a generally growing sense of French menace (ed. Picard, 2. 213). By the time of the 1684 *Éloge,* not only had fears of French expansionism been fully justified, but so had those of its image in *Alexandre*, simultaneously examining and criticizing the possibility of unique sovereignty as a response to the chaos of *La Thébaïde.*

A later Colbertian, Archbishop Fénelon, was to draw a similar picture of desolation both directly to the king and in *Télémaque*, the novel meant for Louis's grandson. In his view imperial conquest led only to catastrophe, whose single solution could be some sort of perpetual peace. A king whose eyes were fixed on the general interest, who saw sovereignty not in terms of personal glory but in those of "great services towards the State," might achieve so illustrious a result: as Auguste seemed to have done at the end of *Cinna.* Such kings however, as Boileau had said, were more than just rare. They and poets alike could easily bind "Alexander and Caesar" to the war chariot. They found less glory in the tranquillity of peace (*Épitre*, 1, 11. 7ff.). And yet, as he wrote:

On peut être héros sans ravager la terre.
Il est plus d'une gloire. En vain aux Conquérans
L'erreur parmi les rois donne les premiers rangs

....

Mais un roi vraiment roi, qui sage en ses projets
Sçache en un calme heureux maintenir ses Sujets,
Qui du bonheur public ayt cimenté sa gloire,
Il faut, pour le trouver, courir toute l'histoire.
La Terre conte peu de ces rois bienfaisants. (11. 94-6, 103-107)

Such was Racine's apparent desire a few years earlier. It was satisfied by none of the princes to whom he alluded in one way or another in *Alexandre* and its printed text. His fear was that it would be no more satisfied by Louis XIV. The difficulty was that ideas of glory, of unique monarchical sovereignty, of empire, of individual rational control and authoritative order seemed none of them bound to produce—in any inevitable way—a stable polity and society. In fact they created an *im*balance of power, foreseen by Mazarin and so many others, that presaged unlimited war: furiously endless torrent of selfish passion and general disaster, Senault had deplored; "conqueste sur conqueste," La Mothe Le Vayer had warned: "guerre sur guerre," Cléofile accused. Racine's was a voice in chorus.

Innumerable classical sources had depicted such a catastrophic outcome via the linked figures of Pyrrhus and Alexander. Racine's "discovery" of such consequences of absolute power would lead to his exploring what sort of sovereignty might theoretically be legitimized, and how. *Alexandre* raised both issues in the form of an external menace to a "community" of *other* states. *Andromaque* would transform such an external threat (symbolized by the Trojan presence at Epirus) into a debate internal to a single state.[47] In the meantime *Alexandre* stood as a strong and complex warning on the dangers of excessive force and imperial pretension, on the nature of power and of passion. It did so through a complicated interplay between classical and modern writings on history, politics, and psychology, with its many commentators, its public and privy debates (within the Royal Council itself, as we know), and—above all—its steadily mounting tensions.

NOTES

1 See my *"La Thébaïde* ou la souveraineté à la question," in *L'âge du théâtre en France/The Age of Theater in France,* ed. David Trott and Nicole Boursier (Edmonton: Academic Printing and Publishing, 1988): 197-205. Theories of sovereignty were drawn from Bodin's *République* (1576), Le Bret's *Souveraineté* (1632), Richelieu's *Testament politique* (in ms. since 1638), Hobbes's *De cive* (1642, French trans. Samuel Sorbière, 1648) and *Leviathan* (1653).

2 On Corneille especially and debate over Reason and gender more generally, see Chs. 4 and 7 of my *Meaning of Literature* (Ithaca: Cornell University Press, 1992). Neo-scholastic *summae* always examined *animi passiones.* Typical in French before Descartes were: Nicolas Coëffeteau, *Tableau des passions humaines,* 1615; Eustache du Refuge, *Traité de la cour,* 1617 (in 1631 ed. 46-118 treat will, reason, and passions); Pierre Le Moyne, *Les peintures morales,* 1640; and Jean-François Senault, *De l'usage des passions,* 1641. No simply psychological treatment seemed to distinguish on grounds of sex or gender (although in his 1659 *Art de connoistre les hommes,* Marin Cureau de la Chambre, who in 1640 had written "descriptively" on the passions, did so). One unusual work, unique or not, was Oliva Sabuca de Nantes Barrera's 1623 *Nueva filosofía de la naturaleza del hombre.* In her opening "coloquio de el conocimiento de si mismo," exploring "los afectos, y passiones del alma," she made "el afecto del enojo, y pesar" (anger and grief) the principal passion—or at least cause of most harm (*daño* being the product of all passions, just as the Stoics had held). Did this reflect a frustration whose justification is further confirmed by claims that Sabuca's father must have written her work?

3 Cardin Le Bret, *De la souveraineté du Roy* (Paris: Toussaincts du Bray, 1632), 71. This work of constitutional law became a kind of manual of the French monarchy.

4 Molière's Palais-Royal premiered *Alexandre* on Dec. 4, 1665. From whatever causes, Racine unprecedentedly gave the play to the rival Hôtel de Bourgogne, which opened on the 19th. Molière was forced to close a week later. His anger was natural.

5 Sir Robert Filmer, *Patriarcha and Other Writings,* ed. Johann P. Sommerville (Cambridge: Cambridge University Press, 1991), xxxii-iv. The Stuart Restoration of 1660 gave Filmer's arguments added plausibility. Less than twenty years later, John Locke would be writing his *First Treatise on Government* against *Patriarcha.*

6 Jean Racine, *Œuvres complètes,* pref. Pierre Clarac (Paris: Seuil, "l'Intégrale," 1962), I, 3, 192; II, 1, 399. All refs. are to this edition, by page for front matter.

7 Cardinal Jules Mazarin, *Brevarium politicorum secundum rubricas mazarinicas* (Cologne: Ioannes Selliba, 1684), 136. Drawn from the *carnets* Mazarin had kept, this work had much success. In a *postface* to a modern translation, G. Macchia cites this maxim more vividly: "Il est dangereux pour le bien commun que la puissance d'un seul homme soit trop écrasante." This form seems to come from a 1698 Italian edition: *Bréviaire des politiciens,* trans. Florence Dupont (Langres: Café Clima, 1984), 90.

8 Armand-Jean du Plessis, Cardinal-Duc de Richelieu, *Testament politique,* éd. Louis André (Paris: Laffont, 1947), 276, 327, 329. "Nacen con nosotros los afectos, y la razón llega despues de muchos años, cuando ya los halla apoderados de la voluntad," wrote Diego Saavedra Fajardo in 1640. A prince's masters had to train his reason to win *imperio,* "undeceive his judgment, and let him know his errors of will and vanity of apprehension, that he may judge truly of things and act *libre y desapasionado*" (*Empresas políticas: Idea de un príncipe político-cristiano,* ed. Quintín Aldea Vaquero, 2 vols. [Madrid: Editora Nacional, 1976], 117, 120). Twenty years before, in a work on the size, glory, and permanence of the Spanish monarchy, Juan de Salazar wrote that a chief pillar was its kings' ability to defeat, "con grandísima entereza," the eight passions: "pesar y contento, el aborrecimiento y amor, la esperanza confiada y demasiado temor, la ira y misericordia" (*Política española,* 1619, ed. Miguel Herrera García [Madrid: Instituto de Estudios Políticos, 1945], 133-41).

9 G. Zeller, "French Diplomacy and Foreign Policy in Their European Setting," in *The New Cambridge Modern History,* vol. 5: *The Ascendancy of France 1648-88,* et. F. L. Carsten (Cambridge: Cambridge University Press, 1961), 210; Robert Mandrou, *Louis XIV et son temps 1661-1715* (Paris: PUF, 1973), 231-32.

10 The reference was to Alexandre's unhappy fear in Plutarch that Philip would leave him nowhere to conquer. Justified by flattery, it recalled here that Louis XIII (and Richelieu) had indeed been personally present at military engagements.

11 The claim was not only the king's. When Richelieu was taking France to war in 1634, Jacques de Cassan published a treatise, *La Recherche des droicts du roy . . . ,* on the French monarch's right to European empire by history, genealogy, treaty, conquest, and purchase. In 1638, Henri de Rohan noted less expansive rights in a work on the "interests" of all Christian princes: *De l'interest des princes et estats de la chretienté.* Richelieu commissioned a work on the matter, although Pierre Dupuy did not have it ready until 1655: *Traité touchant les droits du roy. . . .* In 1649, right after Westphalia, Antoine Aubéry wrote *De la preeminence de nos roys, et de leur preseance sur l'empereur et le roy d'Espagne,* repeating part of his claim in time for Louis' 1667 War of Devolution: *Des justes prétentions du Roy sur l'Empire.* Aubéry was unrestrained. Even in a 1660 biography of Richelieu, the story of the Catalan revolt elicited pages on Louis XIII's rights to Catalonia, justified by ancient dominion and confirmed by its people's appeal and submission to the French king: *L'histoire du Cardinal Duc de Richelieu . . .* (Paris: Antoine Bertier, 1660), 450-58.

12 My main sources for all these matters are Zeller, "Diplomacy, " 201-16, and Mandrou, *Louis XIV,* 231-37.

13 "Le sujet en est tiré de plusieurs auteurs, mais surtout du huitième livre de Quinte Curce," wrote Racine (86, second Préface). In his first Préface, Racine virtually told readers to go to Q. Curtius: "il faudrait copier tout le huitième livre . . . " (86). The play was published (with the first preface) a month after Molière's first performance: guidance on how to understand was fast.

14 Racine, *Œuvres complètes,* éd. Raymond Picard, 2 vols. (Paris: Gallimard, 1964-66), 2. 1140 (941 note 1).

15 Plutarch, *Lives: The Dryden Plutarch,* revised by Arthur Hugh Clough, 3 vols. (London and Toronto: Dent; New York: Dutton, 1910), 2. 48. Was this the passage (as its last sentence might suggest) that Racine annotated with "princes avares ne peuvent demeurer en paix" (éd. Picard, 2. 937)? This would confirm that his attention had long since been drawn to it.

16 *Lives,* 2. 41, 463. As a baby, furthermore, this Pyrrhus was once rescued by a man "named Achilles" (42).

17 *Lives,* 2. 49-50, 58. This part of Pyrrhus's story had been retold by Scipion Dupleix, *Histoire romaine . . . ,* 2 vols. (Paris: Sonnius, 1638), 1. 655-66 (the history was reissued in 1643 with a third volume). One more "Alexandre" was linked to Pyrrhus—"Roy d'Epire son oncle paternel" (1. 655)—and Appius's speech was given at length (1. 659-60). The Appius story was commonplace, and Racine would have known it from many familiar texts: "On the other hand will it be denied," asked Quintilian, "that it was by his gift of speech that Appius the Blind broke off the dishonorable peace which was on the point of being concluded with Pyrrhus?" (Marcus Fabius Quintilianus, *Institutio oratoria,* trans, and ed. H. E. Butler, 4 vols. (1920; rpt. London: Heinemann; Cambridge, MA: Harvard UP, 1963), 1. 321 (II. xvi. 7). For other such references, see page 127 (and notes 33 and 36).

18 Lucius Flavius Arrianus, *Anabasis,* in *Anabasis Alexandri; Indica,* ed. and trans. P. A. Brunt, 2 vols. (Cambridge, Mass.: Harvard University Press; London: Heinemann, 1976-83), 1. 362 (IV. 8. 2. For the full story, see 1. 362-71: IV. 8. 1-9. 8); Quintus Curtius Rufus, *History of Alexander,* ed. and trans. John C. Rolfe, 2 vols. (London: Heinemann; Cambridge, Mass.: Harvard University Press, 1946), 2. 238-39 (VIII. i. 23. See 2. 236-47: VIII. i. 20-ii. 2 for the whole). Of the two last sources, only an index title remains to a lost section in Diodorus Siculus (*Library of History,* ed. and trans. C. H. Oldfather et al., 12 vols. [London: Heinemann; New York: Putnam; Cambridge, Mass.: Harvard University Press, 1933-67], 8. 111), while Justin, the second and only other source Racine actually named (87), ignored the affair.

19 *Lives,* 2. 501, 510. The emphasis, here and in Q. Curtius, on Alexander's progressive degeneracy may have stirred Racine further. For of whom is this decline more reminiscent than of Nero, subject of *Britannicus* in 1669?

20 Mazarin, *Breviarum,* 69, 73, 137; *Bréviaire,* 59, 60-61, 100. For the synonymity of *affectus* and *passio,* see Sabuca and Saavedra Fajardo in nn. 2 and 8. Noting books that "décriuent naïuement des Passions, pour les faire haïr," Charles Sorel continued: "outre les affections . . . " (*La bibliothèque françoise . . .* [Paris: Compagnie des Libraires du Palais, 1664], 51).

21 Duc Henri de Rohan, *De l'interest des princes et estats de la chrestienté.* A Monsieur le Cardinal de Richelieu (Iouxte la copie imprimée à Paris [Leiden]: n. p., 1639), 9-11. The bond between control of passions and political stability was a cliché. Recent history

showed the savagery coming from their mutual failure, while ethics and politics had always been allied—so Nicolas Faret: "la Politique et la Morale sont les vrayes sciences, et
l'Histoire qui de tout temps a esté nommée l'estude des Roys, n'est gueres moins neces-
saire" (*L'honneste homme ou l'art de plaire a la court* [*1630*], ed. M. Magendie [Paris:
PUF, 1925], 27). That Du Refuge devoted so much of his 1617 work on the court to the
passions was no wonder (see n. 2), nor that Salazar in 1619 and Saavedra Fajardo in 1640
did likewise (see n. 8). The latter's work was in many ways wholly about training
princes to defeat their passions (1. 117-51: mainly those of *gloria y fama*) thence to embody the state as "instrumentos de la felicidad política y de la salud pública" (1. 83). The
view came from neo-Stoic debate: "le vouloir bien reglé ne veut que ce qu'il peut . . . "
(Guillaume Du Vair, "La philosophie morale des stoïques," in *Les oevvres . . . comprises
en cinq parties,* derniere edition reueuë & corrigée [Paris: Iacques Bessin, 1619], 518).

22 On the matter of connections (nn. 17, 19, 37, etc.), I may note that Boileau was pol-
ishing this Epître while Racine was finishing *Bérénice:* its lines 109-10 did not by
chance praise pacific Titus.

23 Naudé found its project, "quo Principes omnes inter se convenire possent, & pacem
universalem stabilire," some "animi potius exercendi gratia," than an idea capable of ful-
filment (*Bibliographia politica . . .* [Wittebergae: For Balthasar Mevius by Johannes
Röhner, 1641], 69), but Sorel listed the work among those "qui traitent de choses solides
& faisables," admitting that while its success might need a little extra (such as a better
humanity), "le dessein en est tousiours beau & hardy" (*Bibliothèque,* 62).

24 Eméric Crucé, *Le nouveau Cynée; The New Cyneas,* ed. with original French text of
1623, and trans. Thomas Willing Balch (Philadelphia: Allen, Lane and Scott, 1909), 17-
19, 21.

25 *Cynée,* 133. Crucé's view of sovereignty was largely Bodin's, one in many ways criticized in *Alexandre.* The prince was sole font of authority and subsumed the *rempubli-
cam: Cynée* addressed "Monarques & Princes Souverains," ignored the "vulgaire" because
it "ne vit qu'à patron, & n'a aucune reigle en ses actions" (15), and let republics vote in
the proposed international assembly at Venice only to break a deadlock between monarchical states (101-03).

26 Racine invented Axiane. His major changes of fact concerned Taxiles. When
Alexander came to India, this ruler had long been Porus's enemy. Some texts imply lack
of courage. Plutarch (2. 515) wrote that he just saw no point to a fight over plenty.
When he and his army joined the Macedonians (allied against Porus), a confused moment
did occur when Alexander thought they were to fight. Racine combined him and Abisares,
an ally of Porus who surrendered instead of aiding him. Diodorus and Q. Curtius mention
this prince, the second recording his later natural death. He also told of Taxiles's brother,
slain by Porus while urging surrender (*History,* 2. 354-56: VIII. xiv). All sources show
Taxiles living on as an important ruler. In both Arrian and Q. Curtius, he and Porus become friends. It was Racine who made him and Cléofile brother and sister.

27 "Thence he attacked the Daedalos Mountain and Queen Cleofis's realms," wrote Justin. "She regained her kingdom from Alexander by bedding him [*concubitu redemptum regnum Alexandro recepit*], getting by lascivious tricks [*illecebris*] what she could not by virtue. The son born by him she named Alexander, who later acquired rule over the Indians. Queen Cleofis, due to her prostituted chastity, was thereafter called the royal whore of the Indies [*propter prostatam pudicitiam, scortum regium ab Indis exinde appellata est*]" (Justin, *Historiae, Philippicae,* ex nova recensione Ioannis Georgii Graevii . . . , 4th ed. [Leiden: C. Boutesteyn, J. du Vivie, J. Severinus, A. de Swart, 1701], 268: XII.vii). Racine cited the d of the genitive "Cleofidis" as an l. He left out "concubitu redemptum" and the last sentence. Of Porus, Justin wrote only that he fought, was captured when "multis vulneribus obrutus," and got his kingdom back "ob honorem virtutis." Of Taxiles he wrote one sentence to say he too regained his lands (268-69: XII.viii; 300-1: XIII.iv:). No third source mention Cleofis.

28 "Things able to be composed peacefully and calmly must not be committed to war or legal action" (*Breviarum,* 136; *Bréviaire,* 99).

29 Niccolò Machiavelli, *Il principe; Scritti politici,* ed. L. Fiorentino (Milan: Mursia, 1969), 115 (Principe, I. 25).

30 With *Le nouveau Cynée,* Sorel named as realistic political works (see n. 23) books by Monchrestien, de Lucinge, and La Noüe; adding four more, among them Hobbes's *Fondements de la politique* and this: "Depuis peu on a imprimé, *la Politique des Conquérans,* de laquelle on attend de belles choses, comme on croit que le Liure répond au titre" *Bibliothèque,* 62-63). Given my argument here, it may be fortunate that I can find no trace of it.

31 "In the annexation of a new province [the *ancien régime*] saw only an accretion of power for the kingdom and for the king" (Zeller, "Diplomacy," 206).

32 *Lives,* 2. 530; Marcus Tullius Cicero, *Philippics,* ed. and trans. Walter C. A. Ker (London: Heinemann; New York: Putnam, 1926), 55 (I. xiv. 34). Cicero, of course, took the name Philippics from Demosthenes's orations against Alexander's father.

33 Cicero, *Philippics,* 31 (I. v. 12), 305 (V. xvii. 48). Was Racine recalling *this* identification of Alexander and Augustus, and its gloomy prognostication, when he linked them in his *Dédicace*?

34 Ed. Picard, 2. 981-82. Given Racine's education, not to mention his interests, he certainly knew these and other Cicero texts well.

35 Marcus Tullius Cicero, *Tusculan Disputations,* ed. and trans. J. E. King (London: Heinemann; New York: Putnam, 1927), 226-29 (III .ii 3-4). Books III and IV of this work discuss the *habitus* and *adfectiones* of the soul. Of the term *perturbations,* François de La Mothe Le Vayer had written: "les passions sont nommées, perturbations par les Philosophes Latins " (*La morale du prince,* in *Œuvres,* 2nd ed., 2 vols. [Paris: Augustin Courbé, 1656], I. 849).

36 *Tusculan Disputations,* 251 (III. ix. 21) and 419 (IV. xxxvii. 79) for the first two; 107 (I. xxxvii. 89), 293 (III. xxiii. 56), and 71 (I. xxiv. 59) for the others. These were among

Cicero's favored references. In *De senectute*, yet another school text, he evoked both Appius's appeal about Pyrrhus and Cineas's tale of Epicurus, who thought pleasure the aim of life. If only Pyrrhus agreed, said the Romans, his defeat would be easy: unfortunately, his disordered passion was not joy or lust, but glory and renown (*De senectute, De amicitia, De divinatione*, ed. and trans. William Armistead Falconer (1923; rpt. Cambridge, MA: Harvard UP; London: Heinemann, 1971), 25 (vi. 16), 53 (xiii. 43). Cineas's wisdom was a byword, his bearing gifts to Rome as Pyrrhus's ambassador a constant story (Livy, XXXIV. 4; Dupleix, *Histoire*, I. 658-59).

37 In the *Tusculans*, discussing the nature of glory and analyzing the passions, Cicero also recalled Andromache. He cited lines from a play by Euphorion, in which she bewailed Hector's death, Troy's fall, the horrors of murder and sack, her loss of hope (*Tusculan Disputations*, 277-79 [III, xix. 44-46]). Cicero was arguing that Epicurean pleasures could not help such grief. Beyond the overt contrast of material and spiritual goods lay an implied contrast of passionate Greek violence and reasoned Roman virtue: for Troy was, of course, the legendary origin of Rome. Racine had annotated a page in the first book of *Tusculans*: "avantage des Romains sur les Grecs en toutes choses. — Excepté dans les Lettres" (ed. Picard, 2. 982). The poet was to make profound use of the contrast and of the Trojan "foundation" of Rome in *Andromaque*. He would know, as well, the famous (and controversial) set-piece in Livy's *History*, again when Pyrrhic wars were in question, where Livy inserted an aside comparing Rome and Alexander (IX. 17-19).

38 Zeller, "Diplomacy," 207. The view is something of a cliché.

39 Saavedra Fajardo, *Empresas*, 2. 576: "the insatiable desire for domination, because ambition is so strong in the human breast that it finds even the five regions of the earth constricting. Alexander the Great wept because he could not conquer many worlds. . . ."

40 Daniel Priézac, *Vindiciae gallicae, adversus Alexandrvm Patricivm Armacanvm* [i.e. Cornelium Jansenium] (Iuxta exemplum Parisiis: n. p., 1638), 15-16: where he writes of the Spanish in the Low Countries as a ruinous river flood.

41 Jean-François Senault, *Le monarque, ou les devoirs du sovverain* (Paris: Pierre Le Petit, 1661), 191-92.

42 Publius Cornelius Tacitus, *Agricola*, ed. and trans. Maurice Hutton, in Tacitus, *Dialogus; Agricola; Germania* (1914; rpt. London: Heinemann; Cambridge, MA: Harvard UP, 1946), 220/221: "Auferre trucidare rapere falsis nominibus imperium, atque ubi solitudinem faciunt, pacem appellant."

43 Diodorus Siculus, *Library*, 9. 268-69 (XIX. 14. 8); Quintus Curtius, *History*, 2. 472-73 (X. i. 20).

44 La Mothe Le Vayer, *De l'instruction de Monseigneur le Dauphin*, in *Œuvres*, 1. 59.

45 Richelieu had chose La Mothe Le Vayer "comme futur précepteur de l'enfant royal; destitué par Anne d'Autriche de cette fonction promise, et prié de reporter ses soins sur le frère cadet du jeune Roi, La Mothe Le Vayer ne nous a pas moins laissé tout un recueil de travaux rapides, construits par matières qui définissent le 'métier du roi' en des termes pré-

cis qui ne laissent guère place à l'ambiguïté. Pas question du 'bon sens', dont Louis XIV a usé et abusé dans ses *Mémoires*. Tout tient, selon le précepteur déchu, dans un certain nombre de connaissances nécessaires à celui qui veut gouverner les hommes: finances, armes, rhétorique, morale, logique, physique, 'arts mécaniques', agriculture, géographie, morale [sic], etc."; Robert Mandrou, *La raison du prince: l'Europe absolutiste 1649-1775* (1977; rpt. Verviers: Maribout, 1980), 38.

[46] Ed. Picard, 2. 213. According to Dangeau's *Journal*, the work was bound and given to the king by Madame de Montespan on Dec. 31, 1684 (ed. Picard, 2. 1046, note 1 to page 207); there is no clue as to when it was actually written.

[47] The complexity of issues raised, their artful mixture with the show of individual passion, and the rest, may explain why Marie de Sévigné found the two plays Racine's best (not to mention the one's pointing to Corneille): "jamais il n'ira plus loin qu'*Alexandre* et *qu'Andromaque*" (letter of 16 March 1672, *Correspondance*, 3 vols., ed. Roger Duchêne (Paris: Gallimard, 1972-78), I. 459. She often wrote of Racine and others of his plays, but never changed this opinion. The two early works, of course, dealt with issues familiar from Corneille—than whom, for her, none could be greater.

8

Sacrifice and Truth in Racine's *Iphigénie*

Sylvie Romanowski

IN THE VERY FIRST SENTENCE of the *Preface* to *Iphigénie,* Racine states that the play is about a sacrifice. Yet his preface and the play suggest that the focus was not so much the concept itself but how to *represent* it. Racine enumerates the possibilities that were open to him, in light of the rules of seventeenth-century classical theater forbidding showing an actual death on stage: Eschylus, Sophocles, Lucretius, and Horace had shown Iphigénie herself being killed, while others had substituted a doe; still others had opted for the existence of a second character named Iphigénie, which is of course the solution that Racine seized on eagerly:

> Je puis donc dire que j'ai été très heureux de trouver dans les Anciens
> cette autre Iphigénie, que j'ai pu représenter telle qu'il m'a plu et
> qui . . . mérite en quelque façon d'être punie . . .[1]

Thus what seemed like a constraint for playwrights, Racine turned into an opportunity: he focuses on representation—taking representation in a basic sense as explained by Benveniste: "la faculté de représenter le réel par un 'signe' et de comprendre le 'signe' comme représentant le réel, donc d'établir un rapport de 'signification' entre quelque chose et quelque chose d'autre."[2] In the seventeenth century, there was a debate about the value of the sign and whether it could be also considered as a means of knowledge about the thing represented, of cognition by the mind. For a seventeenth-century audience the sacrifice of an innocent young woman for her country probably spoke very directly (witness the "succès de larmes" it enjoyed at that time); no less a concern of that time was also the question of knowledge and of the mind's access to it. For Descartes and for Pascal, for

Malebranche and for the Port-Royal logicians, this was a crucial philosophical issue, one to which we are still heirs. The philosophers Arnauld and
Malebranche debated on the nature and status of ideas: are ideas mirrors of
the external world, resembling the world and having independent existence
(Malebranche), or are they cognitions different from the external world and
giving direct access to it (Arnauld)?[3]

Though Racine is writing plays and not taking part in the philosophical debate, these concerns form a background to a play where identities are
problematic, where questions of representation and truth become crucial in
certain exemplary situations: the sacrifice of a person, the ability of the king
to be the ruler, the veracity of divine oracles. Representation and knowledge
are at the center of this play more than in any other play of Racine.[4] How to
find knowledge amidst the ambiguous signs, in a play where displacements,
redoublings, and splits abound: there are two Iphigénies, two oracles, two
rulers (the king and the priest), two persons within the king (father and
monarch), and a sacrifice that masks a suicide, or is it the reverse? The play
is resolved through a sacrifice, which, being itself referred to as a spectacle,
adds a self-referential strand to the play and indicates that a dramatic representation conveys another type of knowledge.

Exposition: Names, Split Identity, and Truth

The play opens with a statement startling someone out of his sleep,
"Oui, c'est Agamemnon, c'est ton roi," containing a proper name and a
common noun joined by the basic indicator of equivalence "c'est." The
equation Agamemnon = king is then restated in the barest of tautologies,
"C'est vous-même, Seigneur!" (I, 1, 3) by the person whom we know to be
of inferior rank since he is addressed with the pronoun "tu." Why does the
king have to state his identity in an exceptional time (the middle of the night)
and place (a subordinate's quarters), if not because his identity is doubtful?
In his next speech, he undermines the equation Agamemnon = king = himself with nostalgic verses on the life of humble people:

> Heureux qui satisfait de son humble fortune,
> Libre du joug superbe où je suis attaché,
> Vit dans l'état obscur où les Dieux l'ont caché!
>
> (I, 1, 10-12)

Since extolling the virtues of simple life is a commonplace of anti-court literature,[5] the subordinate, Arcas, is understandably surprised: "Et depuis
quand, Seigneur, tenez-vous ce langage?" (I, 1, 13). For the king represents himself as longing for the simple life of a humble man, while having
just reminded Arcas—and the spectators—that he is the king. The disjunction between the self-representation (Agamemnon longing for the humble
life) and self-reference (I am your king and can command you to wake up in
the middle of the night) is further emphasized by the speech (I, 1, 15-28)
where Arcas paints a picture of the king as kingly through his affiliations
and possessions:

> Roi, père, époux heureux, fils du puissant Atrée,
> Vous possédez des Grecs la plus riche contrée.
> Du sang de Jupiter issu de tous côtés,
> L'hymen vous lie encore aux Dieux dont vous sortez.
>
> (I, 1, 17-20)

But such possessions are not a sure means of creating an identity: they define Agamemnon's social standing in an external manner, but cannot make
him feel like a ruler from the inside. The king's simple words "c'est ton roi"
are not so easily understood. After all (as Arnauld had discussed at length in
the *Logique,* Part I, chapter 15), the entire quarrel between the Protestant
ministers and the Catholic Church had turned on the exact impact of the also
apparently simple words "ceci est" in the Eucharistic proposition "Ceci est
mon corps," and on the possible confusion occasioned by the deceptively
simple term "ceci."[6]

The opening of *Iphigénie* highlights the disjunction between referring by name on the one hand, and self-representation through descriptive
language on the other, a split between the king as monarch and the king as
father caused by the oracle asking him to sacrifice Iphigénie: already he declares himself conquered and defeated by Ulysses' reprimands, and reduced
to tears (71-90). Ambiguity and confusion hold the characters in their grip,
preventing them from motion while creating incessant movement on the
stage, just as the winds, whose function is to blow and propel, are suddenly
stilled and, in an oxymoron, solidified, "enchaînés sur nos têtes" (I, 1, 30).
While referring to the necessity for clarity and unequivocal reference, the
play is one long representation of confusion and ambiguity. This exposition
points to the need for names to have clear meaning (Agamemnon = king,
Iphigénie = Iphigénie), but it shows the opposite: Agamemnon is king in

name only, not kingly, and "Iphigénie" will have two referents (the king's daughter, and Ériphile). The tragedy will be the moment of passage out of ambiguity and confusion, though whether univocity and clarity are achieved remains to be seen.

Oracles: Revelations of Truth or Confusion?

What made the king lose his desire to be kingly was the oracle demanding Iphigénie's death. That the oracle will prove to be ambiguous seems a cruel joke indeed. But the name "Iphigénie" refers so evidently to his daughter that both he and Arcas concur without a trace of doubt.[7] In the oracle, an inspired priest, Calchas, is speaking in the name of a divinity. Surely the guarantees of truth seem amply present: yet the oracle is misunderstood, even though it contains a paraphrase, " 'Une fille du sang d'Hélène,' " (I, 1, 59) followed by the name in the last verse " 'Sacrifiez Iphigénie,' " (62) in the only two eight-syllable verses of the play.

"Iphigénie" will turn out to have two referents, namely the two young women, Iphigénie and Ériphile, as does indeed the supposed clarification. The phrase "une fille du sang d'Hélène" was thought to be, in the terms of the Port-Royal *Logique* (with which Racine might be familiar as he was the product of an education at the Port-Royal school) both an "explanation" and a "determination." Explanation expands: "elle ne fait que développer . . . ce qui lui [le terme] convient comme un de ces accidents," just as "Prince of Philosophers" is an explanation of the name Aristotle. Determination has a restrictive function: "ce qu'on ajoute à un mot général en restreint la signification," just as the word "Pope" refers to the person of Alexander VII.[8] Both as an explanation and as a determination, "une fille du sang d'Hélène" is true, yet not specific enough to differentiate between the two daughters of Helena's lineage. Racine presents on stage an oracle which seems to have all the guarantees of clarity and univocity, whereas it produces confusion and "équivoque." Only further explanations in the form of historical facts will clarify the reference in Act V: as the *Logique* states, such a term "a besoin d'être encore déterminé par diverses circonstances ou par la suite du discours."[9] The problem here is one of excessive confidence in names as vehicles of truth, a tendency of the human mind to judge too quickly: "Une grande partie des faux jugements des hommes . . . n'est causée que par la précipitation de l'esprit, et le défaut d'attention, qui fait que l'on juge témérairement de ce que l'on ne connaît que confusément et obscurément."[10] Language is both necessary for knowledge, and insufficient to convey the whole truth, for which history is needed.

At the beginning of Act II there is a second oracle summarized by Eriphile:

> J'ignore qui je suis; et pour comble d'horreur,
> Un oracle effrayant m'attache à mon erreur,
> Et quand je veux chercher le sang qui m'a fait naître,
> Me dit que sans périr je ne me puis connaître.
>
> (II, 1, 427-30)

Certainly Racine had a purpose in putting two contrasting oracles in the play, not so much to compare them, as to show very different examples of problematic speech. While the first oracle calling for the sacrifice of Iphigénie, quoted verbatim, seems clear and reliable, the second oracle, in indirect speech, telling Eriphile she must die to learn her identity, is vague and puzzling. The first seems immediately intelligible like a proper name, but is not understood correctly; the second seems unclear, but will be true exactly as stated: here, language turns out to be more reliable than seemed possible.

Both these oracles focus on the proper name and its problems. Doris's commentary on the second oracle (432-37) emphasizing the link between self-knowledge and one's name, is a mixture of error and insight. There is prophetic insight on the possible double meaning of the oracle (432-34), but this double meaning will apply instead to the first oracle requiring the sacrifice of "Iphigénie," not to the second oracle concerning Eriphile. There is almost complete error (she does hedge with "peut-être" [436]) as Doris minimizes the risk in losing or acquiring one's name, suggesting that Eriphile will not perish literally, but only in her old identity, as she finds out her true name:

> En perdant un faux nom vous reprendrez le vôtre.
> C'est là tout le danger que vous pouvez courir,
> Et c'est peut-être ainsi que vous devez périr.
>
> (II, 1, 434-36)

Her interpretation is an immediate demonstration of the kind of precipitous judgment that also wrongly interpreted the first oracle. Here the crucial link of name and identity is augmented by the relation between a name and life, or between a name and death.

Up till now, Eriphile has lived with a substitute name, and substitute parents (424), or more precisely, a substitute father, Doris's father, who alone knew her identity but would not reveal it (439-40). If in patriarchal societies one of the main functions of the father is to provide his name, his rank, and his legitimacy to his offspring, then Eriphile is completely deprived of identity and social rank, while Iphigénie is fully endowed with father, mother, and fiancé. Eriphile, being "à moi-même inconnue," (449) is reduced to being a "vile esclave des Grecs" (451). Furthermore, when she falls in love with Achille, the very man who deprived her of the only source of meaning in society (he was responsible for her imprisonment and for her substitute father's death [474]) she commits perhaps the most reprehensible and destructive act possible: it undermines the foundations of society as she links herself with her substitute father's murderer.

The positive imperative of fathering children and providing clear blood lines, along with the negative interdiction of incest, constitute the very foundations of culture and society as we understand them.[11] Later in this essay, Eriphile's crime will be connected with sacrifice, the means by which men "maintain through time, not only social structures whose continuity flows through fathers and sons but also other forms of male to male succession that transcend dependence on childbearing women."[12] In this play, Racine treats the infraction committed against the first imperative, surely one that was taken very seriously in a hierarchical society based on inherited rank. Interestingly, he will deal with the other major prohibition, that of incest, in his very next play, *Phèdre*. The quasi rape aspect of the scene described by Eriphile—Achille seizing her in his bloody arms—is, I suggest, not the most profound source of her horror, or rather it is a representation of her truly unspeakable crime, which is her finding an identity in the person responsible for her non-identity: witness the six verses (II, 1, 497-502) which all begin with "Je." Her new identity as the lover of Achille is a prohibited identity added to her previous one which was false. It is not surprising that terms of dishonor and shame abound in this and in her next speech, which concludes with a clear reference to her crime: by identifying and falling in love with Achille, she has placed herself on the side on the killer of the only link with her parents and of her substitute father:

Je périrai, Doris, et par une mort prompte
Dans la nuit du tombeau j'enfermerai ma honte,
Sans chercher des parents si longtemps ignorés,
Et que ma folle amour a trop déshonorés.

                              (II, 1, 525-28)

Eriphile's oracle, which links her true self-knowledge with her
death, is everything that Iphigénie's was not: vague and unclear, where the
first was precise and clear. Iphigénie's oracle appeared to refer to one person, and will refer to another; Eriphile's oracle refers to the impossibility of
knowing one's name and living with that knowledge. Both oracles represent
the imperative of searching for truth and self-knowledge, and the link of this
search with the proper name, the signifier of one's existence in society.
Both indicate the need for a sacrifice: the sacrifice of Iphigénie at the hands
of the priest, which Iphigénie fears but accepts, or the self-sacrifice of
Eriphile, which she wants to avoid but does not escape. The first sacrifice
will be avoided, but the second one, taking the place of, that is, representing
the first, will take place. But for that event to happen, the king must first ac-
quiesce to the demands of Calchas for the sacrifice.

The stage is set for the crux of the play, Agamemnon's dilemma: as
king he must carry out the demands of the oracle requiring his daughter's
death, while as father he does everything to avoid that duty. He too lives in
the danger zone of ambiguity and split identity; he too must sacrifice his
identity either as monarch, or as father. From Act III on, the play shows
how split identity threatens society, as represented by the king. For a sacrifice to be successful, as well as for a ruler to be effective, it is essential to
know one's identity. However, both the victim and the ruler show divisions
of identity: the name "Iphigénie" will apply to two persons, Eriphile has
two names, and the king has two roles within himself, as parent and as
ruler. Before Agamemnon can carry out the sacrifice which brings the play
to a close, he must resolve the split between his role as king and his role as
father, an inner split doubled by the external threat of the emergence of another ruler in the Greek camp, the priest Calchas.

The Knot: Conflicts of the Monarch(s)

In order to understand the king's roles in the play, a brief plot analysis will be useful. I will use Thomas Pavel's method of syntactic narrative analysis while partially modifying his analysis of this play.[13]

The initial situation (the first Narrative Structure, NS 1) is that the Greeks want to leave Troy but are prevented by lack of wind, and Calchas as spokesman for the Gods is given the role of mediator. He in turn asks Agamemnon to be the mediator; since the latter is not willing at first to perform the sacrifice, he is therefore a Transgressor in the Universe of Calchas and the Gods (NS 2). The first two Narrative Structures are therefore as follows:

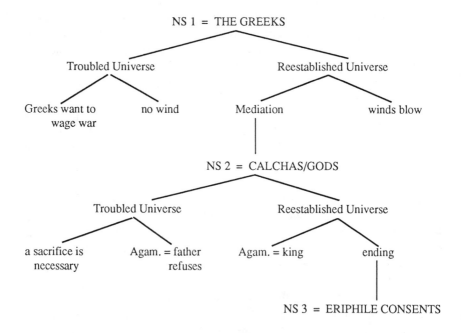

Here I have modified Pavel's schema which placed Agamemnon as a mediator in NS 2. Agamemnon is split into two sub-roles, those of father and monarch, both within the universe of Calchas. However, it is not his grudging consent which furnishes the play's resolution, nor is it his daughter's sacrifice, but Eriphile's, whose Narrative Structure NS 3 completes the schema as follows:

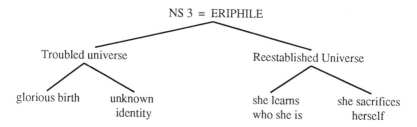

This plot analysis points out, first, the rivalry of Agamemnon and Calchas, and the latter's dominant role in the structure of the play, even though he is invisible;[14] and, second, Eriphile's significance, and the relative insignificance of the other characters in the course of the action. Adding the actions of Clytemnestre, Achille, and Ulysse to the schema—not to mention Iphigénie, a mere pawn in the action—would not alter the main schema as I have shown it. Their actions merely postpone or hasten the inevitable outcome and have no effect on the narrative structure, though they occupy the major part of the play.[15]

This plot analysis emphasizes Agamemnon's weakness: not only is he split into two roles, as king and father, but he is a player in another person's narrative (Calchas's). As king, he represents himself as weak and reluctant to exercise his office; as loving father, he is also powerless.[16] As both king and father, he loses control of his capacity to tell the truth, disintegrating into an abundance of lies, subterfuges, and double entendres (his deceptive use of the word "autel" as altar of marriage or altar of sacrifice). He becomes entrapped in a web of desperate efforts to save his daughter— but he must, in the end, sacrifice her according to Calchas's demands. From the beginning he knows he ought to appear strong, and not "Par des larmes . . . soulager ma douleur!" (I, 5, 364), but in the very next lines he yields to his grief:

> Triste destin des rois! Esclaves que nous sommes
> Et des rigueurs du sort, et des discours des hommes!
> Nous nous voyons sans cesse assiégés de témoins;
> Et les plus malheureux osent pleurer le moins!
> (I, 5, 365-68)

At the end of the play, at the moment of truth, he literally cannot bear to watch and dissolves into tears:

Le triste Agamemnon, qui n'ose l'avouer,
Pour détourner ses yeux des meurtres qu'il présage,
Ou pour cacher ses pleurs, s'est voilé le visage.

(V, 5, 1708-10)

His final appearance on the stage occurs in Act IV, scene 10, when in a last attempt to save Iphigénie, he again seeks refuge in evasive action, in flight and postponement, after having wreaked his last vengeance on Achille by denying him his daughter (IV, 8, 1458-60)—at her expense and without the least empathy for her. For Racine's spectators, living under an absolute monarch, such a portrait must have been shocking, a clear counter-example of how not to be king.[17] Since the head of state is concerned, this creates a gap at the very center of power: he may refer to himself as king, but this is erroneous if he cannot also be powerful.

Iphigénie belongs to the type of Racinian play where the monarch is absent: *Mithridate, Bajazet,* and *Phèdre,* rather than to the category of plays where the monarch is dominant, this in spite of Agamemnon's presence (along with Clytemnestre, he appears in fifteen scenes, the most scenes for any character in this play). This hiatus in power is just as crucial, though more paradoxical, in a play where the monarch is both present on stage and absent as an effective ruler, where he is represented, though not actually ruling.[18]

In the space opened up at the center of power, when the monarch—the one who represents the nation—is no longer trustworthy and no longer master of his own discourse, several other personages want to fill this vacuum, each of whom emits a partial truth and possesses some power. But none of them can be the monarch and say the whole truth; indeed, the closer they are to the center of power, the less insight they have. Moving outward from the ruler, one finds that the person closest to him, the queen, is also the most powerless and perhaps the least perceptive. His daughter is extremely deluded about her father, though very insightful about Eriphile. Achille, a potential member of the royal family, is less deprived of power, but nevertheless lacks insight into the king's mind. Ulysse, who is not a member of the royal family, and is on stage for the fewest number of scenes (5), proves to be the most perceptive and able to persuade Agamemnon to have the sacrifice conducted. Finally, the most minor characters, Arcas and Eurybate, tell the hardest truths of all, especially in the last act.

Clytemnestre, the queen, who is on stage for as many scenes as Agamemnon (15), seems to have all the strength and willpower that her husband lacks. She is a portrait of a "femme forte"[19] and like Arcas in the first scene of the play, she speaks the kingly language that her husband does not. But she is powerless to act: "je me consume en impuissants efforts" (V, 4, 1671). Her vision of Agamemnon as powerful is completely off the mark, when she attributes his willingness to carry out the sacrifice to his thirst for power:

> Cette soif de régner, que rien ne peut éteindre,
> L'orgueil de voir vingt rois vous servir et vous craindre,
> Tous les droits de l'empire en vos mains confiés,
> . . . .
> Trop jaloux d'un pouvoir qu'on peut vous envier.
>   (IV, 4, 1289-91, 1295)

She cannot imagine how uninterested in power he really is, while on the contrary she herself is quite willing to give up her queenly dignity in order to save her daughter's life, and even plead for help on bended knee (III, 5, 930-32), a gesture which scandalizes Achille (III, 6, 951-52). While her speech represents strength, this representation is erroneous, as she is ultimately ineffectual and weak because of her political position.

Like her mother, Iphigénie is extremely wrong about her father whom she portrays as happy in his exercise of power over the Greeks (II, 2, 539-46), then appeals to him to be her father (558-567) precisely when that hurts him the most. But her lucidity, which enables her to pierce Eriphile's secret love for Achille, foreshadows her prophetic vision of glory for Greece's historic destiny.

One might imagine that the reason for the weakness of the two women, the fact that they are women in a patriarchal world, might be special to them, but the same pattern holds for another powerful man in the play, Achille. In the moment immediately preceding the sacrifice, Eurybate uses the same argument to underscore both the queen's and his powerlessness. To Clytemnestre: "Mais de nos faibles mains que pouvez-vous attendre?" (V, 3, 1621); about Achille: "Que fera-t-il, Madame? et qui peut dissiper / Tous les flots d'ennemis prêts à l'envelopper?" (1631-32).

Achille's view of Agamemnon is also skewed by his own interest in Iphigénie as his future bride. He was eager to have the sacrifice performed as long as he did not know the identity of the victim, but he becomes furious when he learns that the king must, and will reluctantly, sacrifice his daughter. He accuses Agamemnon of being "barbare" (III, 6, 964, IV, 6,

1382), "sanguinaire, parjure" (III, 6, 973), "cruel" (III, 6, 991, 1023), and "assassin" (1000), and his last words on stage contain even a threat to kill him and Calchas (V, 2, 1605-06, 1609-10). These harsh epithets hardly fit the weak, irresolute, and susceptible king who is doing all he can to avoid shedding his daughter's blood.

In order to reinforce his claim to Iphigénie, Achille uses contractual language: "Je voulais votre fille, et ne pars qu'à ce prix" (IV, 6, 1400), and he reminds Agamemnon that the latter is in his debt: "Pour vous, à qui des Grecs moi seul je ne dois rien, / Vous, que j'ai fait nommer et leur chef et le mien" (1383-84). The king answers in equally commercial terms: "J'entrevois vos mépris, et juge à vos discours / Combien j'achèterais vos superbes secours" (1407-08). The significance of contractual language has been discussed by critics who point out its newness and its association with commercial transactions and the increasingly important new trading class, the bourgeoisie.[20] The descent of royal prestige into the language of an inferior class will continue, as we will see shortly.

Achille's position is weak, being that of an individual pitted against a collectivity of kings united against Troy. Finding for a moment the language of power, Agamemnon renounces his pact with Achille ("Je vous rends le serment qui nous lie" [1402]) and sends him back with contempt to where he came from: "Retournez dans votre Thessalie" (1401). Achille's image as glorious and impetuous hero belies his weakness: he is alone against the united Greek kings, and while he is not as helpless as Clytemnestre, he is just as angry, possessing only limited power and very little of the truth about the ruler.

Ulysse, a general of the Greek armies, speaks a more moderate language than either the tempestuous queen or the passionate Achille. His is the language of reason and duty, employing also the concept of contractual obligation, but in a context so different from Achille that it makes a crucial impact on the king: namely the fact that the king's contract is with a nation who made him supreme commander, and not with an individual. In Act I, scene 1, he uses this language to convince Agamemnon, according to the king's own testimony, and the king even uses it himself:

> AGAMEMNON
> Il me représenta l'honneur et la patrie,
> Tout ce peuple, ces rois à mes ordres soumis
> Et l'empire d'Asie à la Grèce promis.
>
> (I, 1, 74-76)

ULYSSE
... Vous devez votre fille à la Grèce,
Vous nous l'avez promise: et sur cette promesse (I, 3, 285-86)
. . . .
Nous jurâmes dès lors de défendre ses droits. (304)
Nos mains du ravisseur lui promirent la tête. (306)

Of course, loyalty oaths and promises are at the center of any cohesive social class, but the commercial, mercantile nature of Ulysse's mind-set can
hardly be doubted: "Le seul Agamemnon, refusant la victoire / N'ose d'un
peu de sang acheter tant de gloire?" (II, 3, 317-18). The complete reductive-
ness of a human being to "un peu de sang," and the reification of "acheter"
seem both inglorious and inhuman; but that is not the ground on which
Agamemnon opposes Ulysse. Instead, he uses an "ad hominem" argument,
tinged with sarcasm, that is also in the same mind-set: if Ulysse had to sacrifice his own son, he too would hesitate (321-28). The argument must have
registered, for later Ulysse admits: "Je suis père, Seigneur, et faible comme
un autre" (I, 5, 369). Ulysse will find a better argument at the end of his
speech that will end this type of wrangling:

Considérez l'honneur qui doit en rejaillir.
Voyez tout l'Hellespont blanchissant sous nos rames,
. . . .
Voyez de vos vaisseaux les poupes couronnées
. . . .
Et ce triomphe heureux qui s'en va devenir
L'éternel entretien des siècles à venir.
(I, 5, 380-81; 385; 387-88)

This is an important shift away from contractual *quid pro quo* language, which cannot accomplish what this prophetic vision does: Ulysse
appeals to history, and to honor and triumph for society. History is seen not
as a process, but as a static essence to be achieved, a discourse of eternal
glory that will happen (for them) and has happened (for us later readers)—a
kind of future and past at the same time.[21] It is as if the characters already
possess foreknowledge of Homer's epic poem[22] and can see what has already happened and will be told after their deaths.[23] Iphigénie uses the same
argument in her final appeal to Achille in Act V:

> J'espère que du moins un heureux avenir
> A vos faits immortels joindra mon souvenir;
> Et qu'un jour mon trépas, source de votre gloire,
> Ouvrira le récit d'une si belle histoire.
> (V, 2, 1559-62)

Ulysse also foresees the formation of an alliance between Calchas, the gods and the Greek people who will unify and seize power in order to wage war:

> Pensez-vous que Calchas continue à se taire;
> . . . .
> Gardez-vous de réduire un peuple furieux,
> Seigneur, à prononcer entre vous et les Dieux.
> (I, 3, 290, 295-96)

Clytemnestre and Achille spoke as individuals, as did indeed Agamemnon, who, as it was pointed out earlier, is king in name only. His very limited power fades before the power of the collectivity, and only Ulysse understands this. No single individual can stand in the way of the conquest of Troy and immortal glory.

While history is a representation of a future essence that individuals must coincide with, there is another kind of future in the play: the threatening and necessary sacrificial act. Unlike the static vision of pure and eternal glory, this coming act is likely to be violent, action-filled, and bloody. Clytemnestre's depiction of her daughter as an animal victim (IV, 4, 1301-4) and Achille's prediction of generalized carnage (V, 2, 1606-12) are not visions of essential, grandeur, but the opposite—hectic moments filled with cruel events. In these moments, history will be made in a very different, dynamic process that will create the eternal truth of history. Racine thus represents not only the essence of history but the becoming of history, the binding together of the collective forces into their appointed roles. It is time to analyze the sacrifice which initially sets the action into motion and furnishes its dénouement.

Resolution, Part 1:   The Sacrifice

As expressed by Calchas's words, quoted verbatim by Agamemnon in Act I, the sacrifice is presented as an exchange, a *quid pro quo,* blood for wind: a contractual arrangement, as Ulysse also emphasized (I, 3, 318), between the gods and men[24] who must buy the gods' favor in order to wage war. The human nature of these arrangements is further emphasized by the fact that the gods speak only through Calchas, a representative that is human rather than divine—as R. Barthes states: *Iphigénie* is "la plus séculière des tragédies de Racine."[25] One of the distinguishing features of the play is the repeated juxtaposition of Calchas's name and the references to the "dieux."[26] But this close relationship neither divinizes Calchas nor humanizes the gods: rather it gives Calchas effective power over all the Greeks, including the king who, as was shown, is only a player in the priest's plot line. By the end of the play, Calchas acquires so much power that something like a coup d'état is suggested by the lucid Eurybate (and also by Iphigénie who warns the queen against going into "Un camp rebelle à votre époux" [V, 3, 1644]):

> Calchas seul règne, seul commande:
> La piété sévère exige son offrande.
> Le Roi de son pouvoir se voit déposséder,
> Et lui-même au torrent nous contraint de céder.
>
> (V, 3, 1625-28)

Confusion blurs roles and identities: a priest resembles and even threatens to overthrow a king,[27] and gods with human, mercantile natures are not remote beings but involved intimately in the course of human history.

The means for Calchas's take-over is, of course, his demand for a sacrifice which unites a rather fractious group of rulers, "ses [of Greece] rois, qui pouvaient vous disputer ce rang" (I, 3, 315), into a unified force. The servant Eurybate, the most perspicacious, warns that Calchas reigns not over "un vain peuple en désordre assemblé" (V, 3, 1623), but over a people now united by a common purpose: "C'est d'un zèle fatal tout le camp aveuglé" (1624), just as Iphigénie also warns against a single-minded people bent on war, the "Grecs contre moi [Iphigénie] conjurés" (V, 2, 1547). The effect of the demand for a sacrifice is to cement an alliance better than Agamemnon ever could.

At this moment, the sacrifice thus fulfills not so much a psychological function of expulsing violence and guilt via a scapegoat (René Girard),[28] but a positive, political function (Walter Burkert) that binds human society together and makes group killing possible through the unification around a ritual killing: "Among the Greeks, a military expedition was prepared and ended by sacrificial ritual."[29] The ritual killing represents, by means of a "displaced referent,"[30] the social, communal killing that will follow during the war. Without this cohesiveness, there would be internal dissension, even civil war: "The only . . . historic groups obviously able to assert themselves were those held together by the ritual power to kill."[31] Eriphile correctly perceives this (her name means the "lover of discord"[32] and as such she understands its mechanism):

> Que d'encens brûlerait dans les temples de Troie,
> Si, troublant tous les Grecs, et vengeant ma prison,
> Je pouvais contre Achille armer Agamemnon;
> Si leur haine, de Troie oubliant la querelle,
> Tournait contre eux le fer qu'ils aiguisent contre elle,
> Et si de tout le camp mes avis dangereux
> Faisaient à ma patrie un sacrifice heureux!
>
> (IV, 1, 1134-40)

Here she suggests the reverse of the needed sacrifice, one in which disunity impedes common action and saves Troy by default. But when she is declared to be the "Iphigénie" demanded by the gods, unity of the people takes shape around her: "L'armée à haute voix se déclare contre elle" (V, 6, 1769), and she is the cause of the alliance between Agamemnon and Achille: "désormais tous deux d'intelligence, / Sont prêts à confirmer leur auguste alliance" (1793-94).

Sacrifice, however, is not only a ritual which achieves political unity around a common goal, it is also a representation affirming certain values. Here the scapegoating aspect of the sacrifice is indicated. Eriphile replaces the innocent Iphigénie since she is deserving of death according to the system of Christian values which declares that the sinner must repent or die, at least metaphorically. The woman who sinned sexually and socially, and who was herself the product of Thésée's sexual sins, replaces the pure maiden who, in Greek times, was sacrificed on the eve of war. The maiden sacrifice was a "sign that is exaggerated and heightened . . . a symbol" of "the strongest expression of the attempt to renounce sexuality."[33] Whereas the Greeks sacrificed the innocent for the sake of creating guilt and inhibitions and exacting compensatory reparation afterwards,[34] Racine represents a deserved death, thus reshaping the function and meaning of sacrifice.

Eriphile's suicide is a complex sign containing many strands of reality and meaning. She eliminates herself as the illegitimate descent of Thésée

and Hélène, and as the social sinner who dared to love her (substitute) father's killer. She seems the designated expiatory victim, but the situation is
more complex. Since she is a woman, she is not capable of making a sacrifice, as only men fulfill this function in society. She is a substitute victim,
killing herself in a suicide which is a substitute for the sacrifice, and which a
priest, a stand-in for the gods, or rather for the king, wants to carry out;
but, in a sacrifice which substitutes for a suicide, the priest is pre-empted by
a woman, in the place of the king, the one person who should rightfully
commit the sacrifice but cannot. In addition to these multiple layers of representation and substitution, there is the final layer of the drama itself, to
which we now turn.

Resolution, Part 2:   The Play As Representation and Knowledge

For the characters in the play and for the audience, the sacrifice represents certain values held by society, and that representation allows society
to move forward and fulfill its historical destiny. Both the play and the sacrifice act upon, and confirm beliefs in their audiences. The sacrifice unites
the characters around a symbol of what must be eliminated—sexual and social sin—and the play too represents what must be eliminated: not only
these sins, but also disorder caused by weakness at the center of political
power. The sacrifice is referred to as a spectacle: "un spectacle . . . plus
cruel que la mort" (V, 3, 1648), and Ulysse's long speech (V, 6, 1731-94)
depicts it as a small drama played out in front of an audience, the Greek
camp, and the play's audience. Indeed it is structured like a miniature play,
with five parts: exposition (1734-45), the action (second part, 1746-60,
third part, 1761-67, fourth part, 1768-76), and the dénouement (1777-90).
Sacrifice is dramatic in nature, and drama is similiar to sacrifice in its effect.
The resolution of problems with certainty of knowledge and identity
is not perfect, indeed only partially successful. The sacrifice does eliminate
the lack of knowledge of Eriphile's identity, and her identification with the
enemy Achille, but she cannot live with that truth and dies immediately. The
name "Iphigénie" again has a single clear referent, but the remaining
Iphigénie is left with a less than clear sense of her own identity, as is suggested by the fact that she weeps over her rival's death.[35] The sacrifice re-
stores the king to his position, but does it restore his inner unity and

strength? It enables the Greeks to sail on to conquer Troy, and so makes the question moot.

Like the sacrifice, the play does not provide knowledge nor resolve questions of ambiguity and identity, it only points to the necessity for doing some action to move on and achieve society's historical destiny. The play's representation of disorder caused by weakness and uncertainty opens out onto the necessity for order based on strength and action. Indeed, the inner spectacle of the sacrifice of a sinful maiden uniting all the characters in a common action parallels the play itself, which gives up claims to knowledge of truth and unitary identity. The form of knowledge conveyed by the play, and by the sacrifice, is based upon a different principle, that of action. The play *shows* the problems caused for society by sin, ambiguity of names, language, and identity, weakness at the top of the social hierarchy, and it resolves these problems, as a sacrifice *does,* by eliminating the counter-examples.[36] In both play and sacrifice, error is represented and overcome through action, not through new knowledge. The less than successful search for truth and certainty yields to the power of the play and theatrical representation to move a nation toward its historical destiny.[37]

NOTES

[1] Jean Racine, *Préface,* in *Œuvres complètes,* vol. 1 (Paris: Gallimard, Pléiade, 1950), 670. Quotes from the *Préface* and the play are taken from this edition and references to the pages or the verses will be given in the text.

[2] Emile Benveniste, *Problèmes de linguistique générale* (Paris: Gallimard, 1966), 26.

[3] The Arnauld-Malebranche debate is referred to, and mirrored by, the debate between Richard Rorty and John W. Yolton. See Rorty's *Philosophy and the Mirror of Nature,* (Princeton: Princeton University Press, 1979) and Yolton's *Perceptual Acquaintance from Descartes to Read* (Minneapolis: University of Minnesota Press, 1984) and his "Ideas and Knowledge in Seventeenth Century Philosophy," *Journal of the History of Philosophy,* 14 (1975), 145-65. Barbara Woshinsky examines in detail the philosophical background and the relation to Racine's play in her article "Image, Representation, Idea" in *Actes de Baton Rouge,* ed. Selma A. Zebouni, *Papers on French Seventeenth Century Literature,* 25 (1986), 227-42.

[4] Bernard Weinberg summarizes the plot of *Iphigénie* as the "movement away from igno-rance and toward knowledge," in *The Art of Jean Racine* (Chicago: University of Chicago Press, 1963), 217, and Judd Hubert also points out the role of identity and dual identities

in his *Essai d'exégèse racinienne: les secrets témoins* (Paris: Nizet, 1956), 187, 191-92, 196.

5 See for example Pauline Smith, *The Anti-Courtier Trend in Sixteenth Century French Literature* (Geneva: Droz, 1966).

6 Antoine Arnauld and Pierre Nicole, *La logique ou l'art de penser,* which I quote in the recent edition prefaced by Louis Marin (Paris: Flammarion, 1970), 136-39. I have modernized the spelling in the quotes. On the debate regarding the Eucharistic formula, see Louis Marin, *La critique du discours* (Paris: Minuit, 1975), especially 181-90. For an application of the *Logique* and Marin's analysis to literature, see for example John Lyons, "Speaking in Pictures, Speaking of Pictures: Problems of Representation in the Seventeenth Century," in *Mimesis: from Mirror to Method, Augustine to Descartes* (Hanover: University Press of New England, 1982), 166-87.

7 This is one of the many ironies of the play, which have been analyzed with precision by Bernard Magné, "L'ironie dans *Iphigénie* de Racine," *Papers on French Seventeenth Century Literature,* 9 (1982), 237-52. I suggest that this ambiguity goes beyond mere irony and that it is at the center of the play's significance.

8 *Logique,* I, 8, 95-96.

9 *Logique,* I, 8, 97.

10 *Logique,* Premier Discours, 37.

11 The interdiction of incest being also the means of establishing clear blood lines: see C. Lévi-Strauss, *Anthropologie structurale* (Paris: Plon, 1958), 56-62.

12 Nancy Jay, *Throughout Your Generations Forever: Sacrifice, Religion, and Paternity* (Chicago: University of Chicago Press, 1992), 37.

13 Thomas G. Pavel, *La syntaxe narrative des tragédies de Corneille* (Paris: Klincksieck, 1976). See his analysis of *Iphigénie,* 32. Philip Lewis in "Sacrifice and Suicide: Some Afterthoughts on the Career of Jean Racine," *Actes de Baton Rouge, Papers on French Seventeenth Century Literature,* 25 (1986), 53-74, also gives a narrative analysis of the play according to Pavel's method, which is more detailed and different in some ways from Pavel's and mine. I lack the space here to go into further detail on this topic.

14 See Jean-Pierre Collinet's analysis in "Racine et ses personnages invisibles," in *The Equilibrium of Wit: Essays for Odette de Mourgues,* eds. P. Bayley and D. G. Coleman (Lexington: French Forum, 1982), 176-90, which suggests the existence of an imaginary shadow universe of gods and mythical figures, though I think they are more secular than mythical; this also indicates the importance of the off-stage priest, Calchas.

15 Pavel, following Greimas, calls these sequences without effect on the plot "séquences au mode déceptif," *Syntaxe,* 50.

16 The King is divided into two aspects, as E. H. Kantorowicz describes them in *The King's Two Bodies* (Princeton: Princeton University Press, 1957). The King must either be a father, as an individual, and give up being King, or be King, embodying the essence of Kinghood, and kill his daughter. Racine suggests rather daringly that the theory of the

"two bodies" is perhaps impossible to carry out. This will be echoed in Eriphile's impossibility of living with her true identity.

[17] As P. Bénichou states, this "démolition du héros" (the title of one of his chapters) was bold for his time: "Pendant près de deux siècles, personne n'a senti la violence ou l'audace de Racine." *Morales du grand siècle,* (Paris: Gallimard, 1948), 146.

[18] I have studied the notion of hiatus of the monarch's power in the action of one of those plays, *Bajazet* in "The Circuits of Power and Discourse in Racine's *Bajazet,*" *Papers on French Seventeenth Century Literature,* 10 (1983), 849-67.

[19] On the "femme forte" type, see Ian Maclean, *Woman Triumphant: Feminism in French Literature, 1610-52* (Oxford: Clarendon Press, 1977), especially Chapter III. This book probably gives much too positive a portrait of women's situation in the seventeenth century, making them seem more triumphant than they were in reality. But the stereotype of the "femme forte" was indeed current, especially in the first half of the century, and it lingered on as a memory in the later part of the century.

[20] See, for example, Walter Ong's essay "Ramist Method and the Commercial Mind," in *Rhetoric, Romance and Technology* (Ithaca: Cornell University Press, 1971), 186-89 especially; Erica Harth, *Ideology and Culture in Seventeenth-Century France* (Ithaca: Cornell University Press, 1983), particularly Chapter 1. I have analyzed the problems posed by the coexistence of the generous and the mercantile codes of exchange in my study of *Bajazet.*

[21] On this particular concept of history, see Richard E. Goodkin, "The Death(s) of Mithridate(s): Racine and the Double Play of History," *PMLA,* 101 (1986), 203-17: history is "taken not as a process of becoming but rather as a state into which the tragic hero and the name that is meant to represent him become fixed" (203). Anticipation, and the contrast between the brevity of individual lives and the eternity of glory is mentioned by J. Hubert, *Essai,* 181-84 and 198.

[22] Marcel Gutwirth points this out in his *Jean Racine: Un itinéraire poétique* (Montréal: Presses de l'Université de Montréal, 1970), 71.

[23] In "Image, Representation, Idea," Barbara R. Woshinsky argues that "the soul of the play is contained not in what happens, but in the characters' *ideas* (her emphasis) of what will happen: each one creates a different image of Iphigénie's sacrifice, according to an intimate internal model" (236).

[24] I am using the word "men" literally, since both war and offering sacrifice were principally male functions, as they are in this play. See Marcel Détienne, "Violentes 'eugénies' " in M. Détienne and J.-P. Vernant, *La Cuisine du sacrifice en pays grec,* (Paris: Gallimard, 1979). See also Nancy Jay, *Throughout Your Generations,* especially the Introduction and Chapters 2 and 3.

[25] *Sur Racine* (Paris: Seuil, 1963), 109. This secular interpretation of Calchas will correspond with a secular interpretation of Eriphile, who, though a sinner in Christian terms, does not represent so much, in my opinion, a separate, divine universe, as Reiss says in

Tragedy and Truth, 249-55; she does represent a threat to, and a negation of social order, and hence must be eliminated.

[26] Examples of this juxtaposition are numerous: I, 3, 287-92; I, 5, 374-76, 390-92; II, 1, 455-58; II, 2, 571-73; III, 3, 837; III, 5, 917-19; III, 7, 1083-84; IV, 6, 1358-59; V, 2, 1545-46, V, 6, 1743-45.

[27] See Collinet's suggestive analysis of a potential revolution, too threatening to occur anywhere else but in the wings, along with the invisible characters (1472-78). Barthes calls Calchas "an ecclésiastique habile" (*Sur Racine,* 111), of which *ancien régime* France had known a few.

[28] René Girard, *La violence et le sacré* (Paris: Grasset, 1972).

[29] Walter Burkert, *Homo necans: the Anthropology of Ancient Greek Sacrificial Ritual and Myth,* trans. Peter Bing (1972; Berkeley: University of California Press, 1983), 48. See especially section I.

[30] *Homo necans,* 34.

[31] *Homo necans,* 35.

[32] Whereas *Mithridate,* the play immediately preceding *Iphigénie,* has names that exhibit "*orthonomia* or right naming," according to Goodkin (203), the "mysterious consonance of words and things or of names and people" (203) is absent in *Iphigénie.* Only one person is "right-named": Eriphile = lover of discord, as R.-C. Knight has pointed out in *Racine et la Grèce* (Paris: Boivin, 1950), 318, and even that name turns out not to be her real name—though it is representative of her being.

[33] *Homo necans,* 41 and 64.

[34] *Homo necans,* 63. Without immersing myself into the debate between Burkert and Girard over the origin and nature of sacrificial violence, I suggest that Racine shows the coalescing of the two aspects: scapegoating (Eriphile) and functionality (unification around a common goal of war). See the discussion between Girard and Burkert in *Violent Origins: Ritual Killing and Cultural Formations,* with W. Burkert, R. Girard, and J. Z. Smith, ed. R. G. Hamerton-Kelly (Stanford: Stanford University Press, 1987), 177-79.

[35] Goodkin has suggested in *"Killing Order(s):* Iphigenia and the Detection of Tragic Intertextuality," *Yale French Studies,* no. 76 (1989), 81-107, that Iphigénie's tears at the end indicate the Eriphile within her, pointing to her internal split between virtuous acquiescence to fulfill her duty, and her own revolt (98-102). Though I would not emphasize quite so much Iphigénie's inner revolt, I agree that indeed she is not a completely unified person at the end. Russell Pfohl reaches the same conclusion in his *Racine's* Iphigénie: *Literary Rehearsal and Tragic Recognition* (Geneva: Droz, 1976), 225.

[36] This tragedy does catalog error, as Barbara Woshinsky says in "Image, Representation, Idea," but I believe that the purpose of the play is not "to delight in showing us how little we know" (239); rather, as T. J. Reiss maintains, it "creates order and makes it possible to ascribe meaning to that order," *Tragedy and Truth* (17). On terror and suffering caused by knowledge of the truth, see Russell Pfohl, 199-200.

[37] I am indebted to John D. Lyons for his helpful reading of this essay.

BIBLIOGRAPHY

Arnauld, Antoine and Pierre Nicole. *La Logique ou l'art de penser,* préf. Louis Marin. Paris: Flammarion, 1970.

Barthes, Roland, *Sur Racine.* Paris: Seuil, 1963.

Benveniste, Emile. *Problèmes de linguistique générale.* Paris: Gallimard, 1966.

Bénichou, Paul. *Morales du grand siècle.* Paris: Gallimard, 1948.

Burkert, Walter. *Homo necans: the Anthropology of Ancient Greek Sacrificial Ritual and Myth,* trans Peter Bing. 1972; Berkeley: University of California Press, 1983.

Collinet, Jean-Pierre. *"Racine et ses personnages invisibles,"* in *The Equilibrium of Wit: Essays for Odette de Mourgues,* eds. P. Bayley and D G. Coleman. Lexington: French Forum, 1982, 176-90.

Détienne, Marcel. "Violentes 'eugénies' " in M. Détienne and J.-P. Vernant, *La Cuisine du sacrifice en pays grec.* Paris: Gallimard, 1979.

Girard, René. *La Violence et le sacré.* Paris: Grasset, 1972.

Goodkin, Richard E. "The Death(s) of Mithridate(s): Racine and the Double Play of History," *PMLA* 101 (1986), 203-17.

—————. *"Killing Order(s):* Iphigenia and the Detection of Tragic Intertextuality," *Yale French Studies* 76 (1989), 81-107.

Gutwirth, Marcel. *Jean Racine: Un itinéraire poétique.* Montréal: Presses de l'Université de Montréal, 1970.

Harth, Erica. *Ideology and Culture in Seventeenth-Century France.* Ithaca: Cornell University Press, 1983.

Hubert, Judd. *Essai d'exégèse racinienne: les secrets témoins.* Paris: Nizet, 1956.

Jay, Nancy. *Throughout Your Generations Forever: Sacrifice, Religion, and Paternity.* Chicago: University of Chicago Press, 1992.

Kantorowicz, E. H. *The King's Two Bodies.* Princeton: Princeton University Press, 1957.

Knight, R.-C. *Racine et la Grèce.* Paris: Boivin, 1950.

Lewis, Philip. "Sacrifice and Suicide: Some Afterthoughts on the Career of Jean Racine," *Actes de Baton Rouge,* ed. Selma A. Zebouni, *Papers on French Seventeenth Century Literature* 25 (1986), 53-74.

Lévi-Strauss, Claude. *Anthropologie structurale.* Paris: Plon, 1958.

Lyons, John. "Speaking in Pictures, Speaking of Pictures: Problems of Representation in the Seventeenth Century," in *Mimesis: from Mirror to Method, Augustine to Descartes.* Hanover: University Press of New England, 1982, 166-87.

Maclean, Ian. *Woman Triumphant: Feminism in French Literature, 1610-52.* Oxford: Clarendon Press, 1977.

Magné, Bernard. "L'Ironie dans *Iphigénie* de Racine," *Papers on French Seventeenth Century Literature* 9 (1982), 237-52.

Marin, Louis. *La Critique du discours.* Paris: Minuit, 1975.

Ong, Walter. "Ramist Method and the Commercial Mind," in *Rhetoric, Romance and Technology*. Ithaca: Cornell University Press, 1971.

Pavel, Thomas G. *La Syntaxe narrative des tragédies de Corneille*. Paris: Klincksieck, 1976.

Pfohl, Russell. *Racine's* Iphigénie: *Literary Rehearsal and Tragic Recognition*. Geneva: Droz, 1976.

Racine, Jean. *Préface*, and *Iphigénie*, in *Œuvres complètes*, vol. 1. Paris: Gallimard, Pléiade, 1950.

Reiss, Timothy J. *Tragedy and Truth: Studies in the Development of a Renaissance and Neoclassical Discourse*. New Haven: Yale University Press, 1980.

Rorty, Richard. *Philosophy and the Mirror of Nature*. Princeton: Princeton University Press, 1979.

Romanowski, Sylvie. "The Circuits of Power and Discourse in Racine's *Bajazet*," *Papers on French Seventeenth Century Literature* 10 (1983), 849-67.

Smith, Pauline. *The Anti-Courtier Trend in Sixteenth Century French Literature*. Geneva: Droz, 1966.

Violent Origins: Ritual Killing and Cultural Formations, with W. Burkert, R. Girard, and J. Z. SMith, ed. R. G. Hamerton-Kelly. Stanford: Stanford University Press, 1987, 177-79.

Weinberg, Bernard. *The Art of Jean Racine*. Chicago: University of Chicago Press, 1963.

Woshinsky, Barbara. "Image, Representation, Idea" in *Actes de Baton Rouge*, ed. Selma A. Zebouni, *Papers on French Seventeenth Century Literature* 25 (1986), 227-42.

Yolton, John W. *Perceptual Acquaintance from Descartes to Read*. Minneapolis: University of Minnesota Press, 1984.

———. "Ideas and Knowledge in Seventeenth Century Philosophy," *Journal of the History of Philosophy* 14 (1975), 145-65.

9

Render unto Caesar: Historical and Sacred Representation in *Esther*

Barbara R. Woshinsky

IN THE PROLOGUE TO *ESTHER,* La Piété declares that the play is
being performed in a privileged place. This is not the "legitimate" theater,
frequented by "Profanes amateurs de spectacles frivoles," but St-Cyr,
refuge of innocent young girls living under the protection of the King. But
almost at once, the ironies begin to proliferate: this alleged place of retreat
has become the center of a royal spectacle, and a simple school theatrical has
been elevated into a most exclusive event which nobles vie with one another
to attend. Mme de Lafayette, always a cool observer of Louis XIV's court
rituals, remarked severely: "Ce qui devait être considéré comme une comédie de couvent devint l'affaire la plus sérieuse de la Cour. Les ministres,
pour faire leur cour en allant à cette comédie, quittaient leurs affaires les plus
pressées."[1] Thus, it is not difficult to understand why some critics, including Racine's editor Maurice Rat, have labelled *Esther* a simple *pièce de
circonstance.*[2] Constant Venesoen, less categorical in his judgment, nevertheless asserts that "La poésie spirituelle de Racine a surtout été écrite à la
suite d'une sollicitation extérieure," and therefore its religious significance is
open to question.[3]

No one was more aware of the conflicts and contradictions inherent
in this theatrical enterprise than Racine himself. As he writes in his Preface,
the subject of *Esther* interested the St-Cyr authorities because it offered "de
grandes leçons . . . de détachement du monde au milieu du monde même"
(601). Being in the world and yet not of it: a challenge faced not only by
classical moralists and novelists, but by Louis XIV's courtiers themselves
in their daily lives. For Nicole as for the Princesse de Clèves, the object is
to find a place where the sacred, the private, and the political might coexist.

Does *Esther* contain, or create, such a place? I will approach this question
from both a historical and a textual perspective—from outside and in, as it
were. I concur with René Jasinski that Racine's plays are "une synthèse
féconde" of the circumstantial and the artistic.[4] However, I do not seek to
uncover specific historical allusions or to treat *Esther* as a *pièce à clé*.
Rather, I will analyze the general relationships existing between drama and
society—their "intertextuality," so to speak. Since this topic is too large to
develop fully in a short article, I will only give a general overview here. My
analysis comprises three parts. First, I will briefly examine the social status
of seventeenth-century convents in general and St-Cyr in particular: what is
the "place" of the convent in the aristocratic world, and what can be inferred
about the place of women in that world? Then I will describe the play's
immediate reception: the invasion of the St-Cyr space by Louis's assiduous
courtiers. Finally, through a reading of *Esther,* I will attempt to show how
the sacred and the monarchical realms find their place within Racine's poetic
geography.

I

Like many other aspects of seventeenth century French society,
the convent reflects an uneasy alliance of the sacred and the secular. In
the Middle Ages, the word *couvent* referred to any religious community,
whether of men or women, living together and apart from the world. By
the seventeenth century, the convent had taken on both a gender differentiation and a secular function: it was the place of last resort for unwanted or
unmarriageable girls. Françoise d'Aubigné, later to become Mme de Maintenon, Louis XIV's morganatic wife and founder of St-Cyr, herself experienced the realities of convent life. Lacking family support or economic
resources, she was twice boarded out with the Ursuline sisters and finally
obliged to choose between the convent and marriage to the aged poet Paul
Scarron. She chose Scarron who, fortunately for Françoise's future career,
did not live very long.

Within the context of the court, the convent played a more specialized but analogous role to the one it performed in the larger world. It was a
place of exile, or refuge, for a class of women who had no other place:
Louis XIV's ex-favorites. In fact, the traditional mark of the end of royal
intimacy was the King informing the lady in question of the place to which
she should retire. Thus, Mlle de La Vallière, who had five illegitimate

children by the King, entered the Carmelite convent when Louis threw her over for Mme de Montespan. Mme de Maintenon, who first came to court as the governess of Mme de Montespan's illegitimate children, long feared a similar rejection and exile. She anticipated this eventuality by creating a retreat for herself, first at her property at Noisy, then at St-Cyr. She called Noisy "un petit couvent," praising its country setting and the simplicity of life there which she found a refreshing change from the stifling political atmosphere at court.

As Mme de Maintenon's remarks reveal, the classical image of the convent is a profoundly ambivalent one: it is both prison and refuge, retreat and exile. This ambivalence is not surprising, for the convent or, in a larger sense, the conventual space, finds its place within the overall dialectic of Versailles life, a dialectic comprised of entry and withdrawal, access and expulsion, all motivated by the presence or absence of the King. Within this pattern, it is necessary to distinguish between entry and access. It was surprisingly easy to gain entrance to Versailles. In fact, according to Jacques Levron, "The royal palace of Versailles was far more open to the public than the presidential palace of the Elysée is today."[5] For the ladies, all that was required was proper court attire; for the gentlemen, a sword (which the *concierge* would willingly rent out). So the grounds of Versailles were constantly filled with sightseers from Paris. But acquiring an apartment there was very difficult, catching sight of the monarch himself harder still, and actually speaking to him, almost impossible: "The restrictions that the king imposed upon himself hedged his presence with awe and made his glance more majestic" (Hatton, 132). Most important, these restrictions furthered Louis's aim of attaching the nobility to himself. " 'I would rather die than go two months without seeing the King,' the duc de Richelieu once confessed to Mme de Maintenon" (Hatton, 148). The courtiers would do anything, endure all humiliations, to remain at Versailles within Louis's presence. Thus, one could say that Louis's nobility underwent a kind of feminization; they could only live within the royal space, as women could only live within their husbands' establishments; and exile from court for men, like retreat into a convent for women, constituted a kind of social death.

The role played by physical space in this power dialectic is dramatically demonstrated by Narbonne's account of Louis's own last hours. When the King's state appeared hopeless, his antechambers would empty themselves of courtiers who all went to wait on the duc d'Orléans. But as soon as Louis seemed better, the current would flow back from the ducal apartments into the King's, leaving the future regent's space deserted. Finally, at the moment of Louis's death, his courtiers had totally abandoned the royal chambers, just as they would abandon Versailles itself in the ensuing years.

What specific role did St-Cyr play in this royal mechanics of approach and retreat, favor and disfavor? Mme de Maintenon first spoke to the King of her plans for founding a girls school in 1684. She already was educating 180 girls at Noisy. Her ambition was to expand this number and to take in only young ladies (*demoiselles*) of the nobility. They would be given an education designed to make them good Christians, certainly, but also good wives and mothers rather than *couventines*. For the late seventeenth century, Mme de Maintenon's project was both innovative and anomalous. It would be the first time the French royal family had ever concerned itself with the education of girls; moreover, by the King's wishes, their education would be a partly secularized one. Louis was generally hostile to religious houses which he viewed as parasitic bodies, enriching themselves for the benefit of "persons useless to the State." Thus the superior of the School, Mme de Brinon, would be an Ursuline nun, but none of the teachers had taken orders. Later controversies, partly growing out of the *Esther* performances, forced St-Cyr to undergo changes. In 1692, it became a regular convent of the order of St-Augustine, and its teachers were obliged to take holy vows or leave. But in 1686, the year of *Esther,* St-Cyr was not yet a convent in the strict sense. In fact, Mme de Maintenon's goal for St-Cyr, which she hoped would serve as a model for hundreds of schools throughout France, was to provide girls with a Christian education within a secular context. This vision would be realized in the eighteenth century, when the word *couvent* came to be almost synonymous with a girl's boarding school (*une pension*).

At this point, it should be easier to understand the fascination exerted by *Esther* on the court population. St-Cyr, as Mme de Maintenon's favorite project, supported by the King, was part of the royal territory and drew the courtiers with the same inexorable magnetism as Versailles. And given Louis's quasi-divinity,[6] it was a sacred territory as well, to which the King alone controlled access. To return to Mme de Lafayette's criticisms quoted above, though they give a useful indication of contemporary views, they also reveal a misapprehension, or perhaps a refusal, of certain court realities. First, the ministers deserted their apartments for St-Cyr because paying court to the King *was,* in fact, "l'affaire la plus sérieuse de la cour." Moreover, *Esther* was never a simple *comédie de couvent* in the sense

La Fayette appears to give the expression, since St-Cyr was anything but an ordinary convent. As we will now see, Jean-Marie Apostolidès's definition of classical drama—"spectacle sacré dans un espace partiellement laïcisé"[7]—applies particularly well to *Esther* at St-Cyr.

II

The worldly, or courtly, significance of *Esther* is well documented. Letters and chronicles of the period reveal how its production crowned Racine's court success and cemented his personal favor with the King. As official historiographer, he had already become, with Boileau, "le coryphée du culte royal" (Picard, 365). And as an unusually adept courtier, he had been able to ingratiate himself with the nobility at a time when most poets were regarded as the next thing to pedants, and not very far removed from shopkeepers. The commission for *Esther* consecrated Racine's position *vis-à-vis* Louis XIV. The King viewed the rehearsals and, pleased with the spectacle, invited favored members of the court to attend the performances. The run had to be extended to five nights because the whole court was clamoring for a seat. In her letters, Mme de Sévigné describes her disappointment at not getting a seat for the first performances, and her elation when, on the last night, the King actually came up and spoke to her:

> Le roi vint vers nos places, et après avoir tourné, il s'adressa à moi, et me dit, "Madame, je suis assuré que vous avez été contente." Moi, sans m'étonner, je répondis: "Je suis charmée: ce que je sens est au-dessus des paroles." Le Roi me dit: "Racine a bien de l'esprit." Je lui dis: "Sire, il en a beaucoup, mais en verité, ces jeunes personnes en ont beaucoup aussi." Il me dit: "Ah! pour cela, il est vrai!" Sa majesté s'en alla, et me laissa l'objet de l'envie. . . .

Picard, who quotes this conversation in *La carrière de Jean Racine,* comments ironically on its high intellectual level (*cette conversation d'une haute intellectualité,* 402). But intellectuality is obviously not the point here. What is at issue is rather the position of "ces jeunes personnes" in the political geography of the court and the poetic geography of Racine.

III

Esther, in its text and staging, re-presents many of the historical complexities described above. In this play, contrary to his usual theatrical practice, Racine violates unity of place both literally and figuratively. The play constitutes an intersection, or rather a co-location, of many real and symbolic places. In the *Prologue,* the figure of Piety situates the theater in a separate, sacralized space, "Un Lieu par la Grâce habité" and a refuge (*asile*) for *innocence . . . dispersée* (603). But she also alludes to its real geographic location: in a palace near Versailles (*à la porte . . . du roi*). This duality is immediately carried forward into the play itself. The first act takes place in Esther's apartment, which is presented as a place of retreat and sanctuary: "un lieu séparé de profanes témoins" (I, 1, 105). This wording almost duplicates Robert's dictionary definition not of a convent, but a cloister: "partie d'un monastère interdite aux profanes et fermée par une enceinte (clôture)." Thus when Mardochée approaches unrecognized, Esther challenges him: "Quel profane en ce lieu s'ose avancer vers nous?" (I, 3, 155).

At the same time, like the "lieu par la grâce habité" of the Prologue, Esther's forbidden, cloistered space is contained within the secular architecture of a palace, with its antechambers, doors and corridors filled with petitioners seeking entrance. In her first speech, Elise proudly says to Esther: "De ce palais j'ai su trouver l'entrée" (I, 1, 24). And like Versailles, the Persian palace makes access to kings extremely arduous: "Au fond de leur palais leur majesté terrible / Affecte à leurs sujets de se rendre invisible" (I, 3, 193-94). In Act II, Assuérus will ask Hydaspe what noble happens to be waiting outside the throne room door: "Regarde à cette porte, / Vois s'il s'offre à tes yeux quelque grand de ma cour" (II, 4, 574-75). The King supposes someone will be there; in fact, it is Aman: "Aman à votre porte a dévancé le jour" (II, 4, 476). Only Mardochée disdains to enter the palace, sitting by the door like a modern-day political demonstrator. Aman remarks, "Du palais cependant il assiège la porte" (II, 1, 433). But Mardochée's siege is an act of protest, not an attempt to gain access to the King.

Esther's cloistered retreat is counterbalanced by another sacred, forbidden place: the throne room, scene of Act II. If anyone enters "ce lieu redoutable" without the express consent of the King, his or her life is forfeit. When Assuérus upbraids Esther for daring to come in without his permission, she faints in holy terror: "Sur ce trône sacré qu'environne la foudre / J'ai cru vous voir tout prêt à me réduire en poudre" (II, 4, 649-50).

But as the scene progresses, the chorus of young girls enters this forbidden space and literally surrounds the throne, transferring the place of sanctuary from Esther's apartments to the King's. This transference is affirmed when, before leaving the stage, Esther tells the girls to wait there: "Sans craindre ici les yeux d'une *profane* cour, *à l'abri de ce trône* attendez mon retour" (II, 8, 711-12, my underlining).

The third act again takes place in the Queen's apartments, which are successively entered by the King, Esther's entourage, and finally the whole court. In the end, "unity of place" is recovered as the separation between cloister and royal sanctuary is abolished. This movement of integration reenacts the historical subtext of the play, drawn from the Bible. The temple at Jerusalem is replaced by the Persian palace as the center of spiritual life when the dispersed exiles find a home at Assuérus's court and their captivity is transformed into asylum.

In conclusion, *Esther* enacts a movement of convergence (*conversion* in the spatial sense) on at least three levels. On stage, there is the influx of the court into Esther's apartment; within the dramatic narration Jerusalem is transferred to Babylon; and at St-Cyr itself, Mme de Maintenon's unconventional convent seeks to create a Christian, feminine environment under the aegis of the divine monarch (*à l'abri du trône*) rather than of the church. The actual reception of the play adds a final, somewhat ironic, level to this structure. To cope with the unexpected popularity of the performances, Louis XIV himself acted as doorkeeper, barring the way with his cane when the theater was filled. In this way, *Esther* at St-Cyr constitutes both a utopian resolution of the secular/sacred duality and an exposé of its continuing contradictions.

NOTES

[1] Jean Picard, *La Carrière de Jean Racine* (Paris: Gallimard, 1956), 399.

[2] Racine, *Théâtre complet,* ed. Maurice Rat (Paris: Garnier, 1960), 596. Further references to this edition will appear in the text.

[3] Constant Venesoen, "Athalie ou le demi-échec de la théologie tragique," in *Racine: Mythes et réalités,* (London, Canada: University of Western Ontario Press, 1976), 28.

[4] "Sur un thème d'*Esther,*" *Littératures* 9-10 (Spring, 1984), 75.

[5] *Louis XIV and Absolutism* (Columbus: Ohio State University Press, 1976), 130.

[6] According to Marc Bloch in *Les Rois thaumaturges* (Paris: Gallimard, 1983), "Jamais époque n'a plus nettement et, peut-on dire, plus crûment que le XVIIe siècle, accentué la nature quasi-divine de l'institution et même de la personne royales" (351ff.).

[7] *Le Prince sacrifié* (Paris: Editions de Minuit, 1985), 53.

10

The World Turned Upside Down: Desire and Rivalry in *Amphitryon*

Michael S. Koppisch

MOLIERE'S THEATER IS FILLED WITH CHARACTERS who contend for recognition by setting themselves apart from others. To have the only wife whose faithfulness is guaranteed, to live a life purged of all that is "du dernier bourgeois," is to be sick, to be more devout, richer, or more clever than others—these are but some of the poses struck by characters who strive for superiority by making a show of difference. In *Amphitryon*, however, both distinction and superiority are given. Not only is Jupiter a god, he is also the greatest among the Olympians. There can be no question of equating or, for that matter, even comparing him with a mere mortal like Amphitryon. Jupiter represents power; his might is recognized by gods and by men. What Alceste and Monsieur Jourdain want Jupiter has. Rivalry between him and Amphitryon would seem, therefore, to be unthinkable. The god's higher position in the universe is securely established, as is his superiority to all humankind. There is certainly no need for Jupiter to prove that he is stronger, more ingenious, more masterly than Amphitryon. And yet, that is precisely what he does, for the god is not without desire. He falls head-over-heels in love with Amphitryon's new wife Alcmène, whom he will at whatever cost possess.

The world has been turned upside down in *Amphitryon,* more dramatically even than in *Dom Juan.* It is one thing for a noble to be attracted physically to a pretty peasant girl but quite another for a god to be so smitten with a mortal that he must play the jealous lover to the husband she continues to adore. As Jupiter admits in the last scene,

> Et c'est moi, dans cette aventure,
> Qui tout dieu que je suis, dois être le jaloux.[1]

By putting a jealous god on stage, Molière pushes to the limit the situation
he had created in *Dom Juan,* that of a character whose superiority is be-
trayed by his desire. If Dom Juan loses something of his nobility by his
shameless and mean-spirited pursuit of Charlotte, his brief rivalry with
Pierrot is, nevertheless, structured in the most normal of ways. The Don
woos Charlotte by emphasizing the difference between himself and his rival:
"Quoi?" he asks her, "une personne comme vous seroit la femme d'un
simple paysan! Non, non: c'est profaner tant de beautés . . . Vous méritez
sans doute une meilleure fortune, et le Ciel, qui le connoît bien, m'a conduit
ici tout exprès pour empêcher ce mariage, et rendre justice à vos charmes"
(II, 2). Charlotte is but too aware of Dom Juan's distinction and its potential benefits to her. She reproaches Pierrot for not wanting her to have the
very best: "Si tu m'aimes, ne dois-tu pas estre bien aise que je devienne
Madame?" (II, 3). Jupiter's approach is diametrically opposed to that of
Dom Juan. Rather than flatter Alcmène by courting her as the god he is,
Jupiter disguises himself as her husband. The rivalry between Amphitryon
and Jupiter is as intense as any in Molière's theater, but in this play,
difference between the rivals is immediately replaced as the central problem
by their similarity. When Jupiter first appears on stage, he is disguised as
his rival, and only at the very end does he divulge his true identity.

Critics have proposed a number of reasons for which Molière might
have chosen to write a play based on Plautus's *Amphitryon.* The most col-
orful—and fanciful—is that of Roederer, the first to suggest that Molière
saw in the story of Jupiter's love for the wife of Amphitryon a parallel with
the attachment of Louis XIV to Madame de Montespan, whose husband re-
acted badly to her infidelity (cited in *Œuvres,* 6, 316-17). Despois and
Mesnard, at pains to disprove Roederer's hypothesis, believe that Molière
may simply have reached a stage in his career at which Plautus appealed to
his creative sensibilities. Within months of *Amphitryon,* he writes *L'Avare*
under the influence of the Latin master. The editors of the Grands Ecrivains
de la France edition add to this supposition a more substantial explanation
of the playwright's affinity to Plautus's subject: its theatrical durability
(*Œuvres,* 6, 313-16). For Georges Couton, *Amphitryon,* written during
the War of Devolution, is an example of the kind of light-hearted works often inspired by the events associated with wars and produced "à côté des
discours aux morts."[2] Gérard Defaux prefers to see in the play a continua-
tion of Molière's pondering over "le problème des apparences du vice et
de la vertu, une méditation bien évidemment déclenchée par *Tartuffe.*"[3]
Whatever the reason for Molière's choice of his subject, one thing is certain.

The story Plautus tells touches directly upon preoccupations at the heart of Molière's comic vision. Jupiter, first among the gods and, therefore, responsible for the order of the universe, threatens that very order as his desire leads him into rivalry with Amphitryon.[4] Moreover, this rivalry reduces the world of mortals to chaos not as a result of the difference separating the rivals, but rather because they are so much alike. As he confronts the story of Amphitryon, Molière comes to grips with both the dynamics of rivalry and the danger inherent in it. Rivalry is a form of human behavior central to most of his greatest comedy.[5] And the French playwright's instinct is to be even more radical than his Roman predecessor. In Plautus's play, the audience can distinguish Jupiter from Amphitryon by the gold tassel the god wears on his hat. Mercury has a plume on his, lest he resemble too completely his human counterpart.[6] In Molière play, Amphitryon and Jupiter are supposed to look exactly alike, as are Sosie and Mercure.

At the origin of Jupiter's ambivalent relations with humans is, of course, his desire.[7] As he asks her to delay the onset of daylight so that Jupiter can prolong his tryst with Alcmène, Mercury reminds La Nuit that "ce maître des Dieux"

> Aime à s'humaniser pour des beautés mortelles,
>   Et sait cent tours ingénieux,
>   Pour mettre à bout les plus cruelles.
>   (Prologue, 56-58)

In fact, Jupiter is well known for disguising himself to conquer beautiful women. La Nuit, aware of the god's propensity to masquerade as someone other than himself, cannot, despite her admiration for Jupiter, understand why he does this. Mercure's explanation, in both its language and its substance, is richly suggestive. He speaks in an overly familiar way of his master's disguises as gestures of a "Dieu qui n'est pas bête" (Prologue, 79). Mercure would consider Jupiter "fort misérable" were the god never to abandon his formidable mien "et qu'au faîte des cieux il fût toujours guindé" (Prologue, 83). As Robert Jouanny points out, the word "guinder" is disrespectful and ought not, therefore, be used in reference to Jupiter.[8] Nor would one normally think of the greatest of the gods as "emprisonné toujours dans sa grandeur" (Prologue, 85). The esteem in which the "souverain des Dieux" (Prologue, 34) ought to be held is lowered by Mercure's deprecating talk. Jupiter's godliness, according to Mercure, is a hindrance when it comes to love, and he congratulates his master for coming down from the heights of glory for the sake of dalliance. Amorous desire in *Amphitryon* functions much as the desire for power in Corneille's *Cinna,* where Auguste feels trapped in his absolute authority:

> L'ambition déplaît quand elle est assouvie,
> D'une contraire ardeur son ardeur est suivie;
> Et comme notre esprit, jusqu'au dernier soupir,
> Toujours vers quelque objet pousse quelque désir,
> Il se ramène en soi, n'ayant plus où se prendre,
> Et monté sur le faîte, il aspire à descendre.[9]

The absence of limits itself becomes a limitation to be overcome for both the king and the god driven by desire.

Omnipotent though he be, Jupiter derives little personal gratification from the identity bestowed upon him by his exalted rank. His disguises, as Mercure tells La Nuit, are a way for the god to "goûter . . . toutes sortes d'états" (Prologue, 78). But why should a god need or want to share the experience of a mortal like Amphitryon? The truth is that the only difference between Molière's Jupiter and his other characters is that the king of the gods has at his disposal more efficacious means for achieving his ends, which are not altogether different from those of humans. Monsieur Jourdain cannot transform himself into a nobleman to conquer Dorimène, but Jupiter is quite capable of becoming Amphitryon, if that is what is needed to win the heart of Alcmène. Built into this very power, however, is the disadvantage that Jupiter cannot assuage his desire by indulging it, because his mask, which gives him entrée to Alcmène's bed, also makes it impossible for her to love him for himself. Whence Jupiter's jealousy of a rival who is clearly inferior to the god. Mercure's description of Jupiter once the god has transformed himself into a mortal is very much to the point:

> Et pour entrer dans tout ce qu'il lui plaît
> Il sort tout à fait de lui-même,
> Et ce n'est plus alors Jupiter qui paraît.
> (Prologue, 90-92)

The god neither appears to be nor, in fact, is any longer himself. In his imitation of Amphitryon, Jupiter loses a firm grip on his own being. His desire is, in a sense, fulfilled. On the other hand, he enjoys Alcmène's love only in the person of the mortal he is imitating. Alcmène remains faithful in spirit to her husband. Jupiter succeeds, as a god must, but at the same time he fails.

The contradiction is symptomatic of a disease that is epidemic in Molière's theater: a desire that characters try to placate by imitating others. What is particularly interesting about *Amphitryon* is that the identity between rivals does not emerge gradually as characters move to distinguish themselves from each other. It is, rather, the central feature of the play's action. The profound singularity between Alceste and his rivals—they all seek personal validation in the eyes of others—is initially hidden by the protagonist's insistence on his higher principles. Likewise, the *femmes savantes* at first look to be very different from their opponents. Only little by little does it become apparent that Philaminte and company hunger after power just as surely as the oppressive dullards they so abhor. In *Amphitryon,* this similarity, which is, finally, more dangerous than the struggle of seeming opposites that often hides it, rivets the attention of the audience. By imitating Amphitryon, Jupiter brings the community of mortals to the brink of chaos. The family, social order, even the integrity of the individual self are threatened by Jupiter's charade and the momentary elimination of difference caused by the god's behavior. Jupiter himself sums up the dilemma when, in the third act, he promises to clarify the mystifying confusion:

> Alcmène attend de moi ce public témoignage:
> Sa vertu, que l'éclat de ce désordre outrage,
> Veut qu'on la justifie, et j'en vais prendre soin.
>   (III, 5, 1691-93)

The word "désordre" describes perfectly the state of the community infected by Jupiter's virus. That he becomes a man reveals both the god's own frailty—he is no less subject to the whims of desire than mortals—and the highly contingent character of the order on which humans found their existence. Plautus and Rotrou, in his *Sosies,* conclude their plays by recalling the legendary tale of how Hercules, the son born of Jupiter's affair with Alcmène, strangles the serpents who attack him in the cradle. Molière drops this story from his plot, thus bringing into prominence the human.[10] When god and man can no longer be told apart, the ensuing problem is man's.

Jupiter descends into the company of mortals and brings with him a linguistic precept that disrupts human discourse and throws the community

into disarray. As Mercure explains to La Nuit, whose modesty is offended
by his request that she conspire, even indirectly, in Jupiter's escapade,

> Un tel emploi n'est bassesse
> Que chez les petites gens.
> Lorsque dans un haut rang on a l'heur de paroître,
> Tout ce qu'on fait est toujours bel et bon;
> Et suivant ce qu'on peut être,
> Les choses changent de nom.
> (Prologue, 126-31)

Meaning, according to this formula, is determined by the identity of the
speaker rather than by the language he uses or the nature of the object he
talks about: depending upon who one is, "les choses changent de nom."
On the surface, of course, there is nothing very complicated about what
Mercure says. His is just another cynical declaration of the ageless verity
that power imposes itself on every aspect of human existence, including
language. It is, however, also literally true in this play that the stability of
names—what a person is called, how one is identified—cannot be counted
upon. Mercure, for example, assumes the role of Sosie by stealing from the
servant both his looks and his name—"En lui volant son nom, avec sa
ressemblance" (I, 2, 281).[11] Once Sosie's name is gone, he does not know
who he is, he is adrift in a world in which the name Sosie no longer situates
him. The undermining of human language is a major component of the
turmoil that results from Jupiter's perfect imitation of his rival.

Shortly after Mercure forbids Sosie to be Sosie, the servant has his
first encounter in the play with his master Amphitryon, who wants to get to
the bottom of "cette confusion" (II, 1, 703). Sosie has learned the lesson of
servitude at the violent hand of Mercure. Seeing that Amphitryon is angry,
Sosie assures him that ". . . vous aurez toujours raison" (II, 1, 695).
Before his anxious master questions him about events in the household,
Sosie wants to be sure that he understands how the interrogation is to
proceed:

> Parlerai-je, Monsieur, selon ma conscience,
> Ou comme auprès des grands on le voit usité?
> Faut-il dire la vérité,
> Ou bien user de complaisance?
> (II, 1, 709-12)

Sosie, it seems, is nimble enough to adjust either to a language in which words represent the truth or to one in which what is said is dictated by the interlocutors' relations of power. But he must first ascertain the rules by which the game is to be played. Amphitryon claims to want nothing but the truth from his servant, but when Sosie, understandably, begins to sound confused, his master accuses him of being drunk and orders him to be silent. As if he had overheard Mercure's words to La Nuit, Sosie responds to Amphitryon's contention that he has been speaking nonsense:

> Tous les discours sont des sottises,
> Partant d'un homme sans éclat;
> Ce seroit paroles exquises
> Si c'étoit un grand qui parlât.
> (II, 1, 839-42)

Seen in context, Sosie's conclusion is more than a recognition of the power of a "grand." Sosie has just been told by Mercure that he is not Sosie, and now Amphitryon says that the truth Sosie speaks is meaningless gibberish. The solid underpinnings of Sosie's existence are giving way to utter confusion.

The gods' assault against the world of Amphitryon and Sosie does violence to meaning and, therefore, to human communication. When Sosie talks about "himself," he is incomprehensible to anyone not aware of his encounter with his "other self," Mercure; and Sosie can never assume that the words of Amphitryon or Mercure really mean what they seem to mean. Here as elsewhere in Molière's theater, the corrosive effects of power gone awry take their toll on the characters' ability to resolve problems by using language. Mercure, even as he unmasks himself at the play's conclusion, would have Sosie believe that the violence of the gods does not really hurt:

> Et les coups de bâton d'un Dieu
> Font honneur à qui les endure.
> (III, 9, 1878-79)

"Coups de bâton," obviously intended to inflict pain, suddenly become harmless. Like words, they lose their real meaning in Mercure's description of them. Sosie, who has suffered too often from Mercure's indulgence in gratuitous violence, replies with appropriate irony:

> Ma foi! Monsieur le Dieu, je suis votre valet:
> Je me serois passé de votre courtoisie.
>   (III, 9, 1880-81)

Similarly, Jupiter, revealing his true identity, flies in the face of the legitimate outrage that has been at the root of Amphitryon's behavior:

> Un partage avec Jupiter
> N'a rien du tout qui déshonore;
> Et sans doute il ne peut être que glorieux
> De se voir le rival du souverain des Dieux.
>   (III, 10, 1898-1901)

Jupiter tries to have his cake and eat it too. In the process, he contributes to the erosion of the important distinction between gods and men. The words and deeds of gods are qualitatively different from those of mortals, who should, therefore, be honored by the deities' intervention. On the other hand, these same gods, who claim to be so different in nature, act like men, take on the looks of men, and even admit to such human feelings as jealousy. To accept Jupiter's vision is to embrace chaos, to reject it is futile. Once again, nothing has changed fundamentally at the end of a Molière play. Mercure's flippant retort to La Nuit in the Prologue—"Et suivant ce qu'on peut être, / Les choses changent de nom"—returns to haunt the characters in the play's final lines. The silence of Amphitryon and his wife and Sosie's last words, bringing the play to its end—"Sur de telles affaires, toujours / Le meilleur est de ne rien dire" (III, 10, 1942-43)—signal the suspended status of the momentary return to order expected by the audience after Jupiter divulges the truth that had so confounded his human victims. Order is, indeed, restored, but it seems unlikely to endure beyond the point at which silence gives way to language.

Not by chance did Molière assign to himself the role of Amphitryon's servant, Sosie. The master experiences the chaos that comes from rivalry and the elimination of difference. No intellectual, however, Amphitryon lives an incomprehensible dilemma. His lot is to contend with the crisis rather than to understand it. He does not and, indeed, cannot know what is happening around him because he is not confronted by his double until the end of the play. The truth dawns on Amphitryon slowly. Sosie, on the other hand, meets his double almost immediately and is more than once called upon to explain his own behavior. If his explanations often bewilder his interlocutor and amuse the audience, what Sosie says is revealing about the structure and inherent danger of imitative rivalry. The rivalry between Sosie and Mercure is also more elemental than that of Amphitryon and Jupiter. The king of the gods wants to seduce Amphitryon's wife. Mercure has no interest at all in Cléanthis. He is after the very being of Sosie, who, therefore, has more at stake than his master. It is clear that the battle between Jupiter and Amphitryon engages the self of both combatants. Were Jupiter to succeed, Amphitryon would suffer the loss of both his wife and his self-esteem. Still, Amphitryon's experience of the rivalry is centered on the object of the two rivals' desire, Alcmène. In the case of Sosie, that object is the servant's name, his *moi*. When Sosie talks about his rivalry with Mercure, that is precisely what he talks about. No ordinary rival, Mercure becomes "ce moi plutôt que moi" (II, 1,741) who would replace Sosie in his entire person, rather than in the bed of Cléanthis. A victorious Mercure would swallow up the identity of Sosie.

The instability of Sosie's identity becomes apparent as soon as he steps on stage. In the first scene of Act I, the servant has returned home to deliver to Amphitryon's wife news of her husband's victory in battle. Sosie complains of being sent off to do this errand on the darkest of nights—La Nuit has obliged Mercure—and bemoans the fate of those who, like himself, are subjected to the will of "les grands," for whose benefit everyone else must "s'immoler" (I, 1, 169, 171). His musings imply that Sosie thinks he would do well to quit the service of Amphitryon. What keeps him on the job is neither fidelity to his master nor pride in his work. The servant is seduced by this master's "vue," by "la moindre faveur d'un coup d'œil caressant" (I, 1, 184, 186). Sosie's first thought is not to himself, but to the opinion of others:

> Cependant notre âme insensée
> S'acharne au vain honneur de demeurer près d'eux,
> Et s'y veut contenter de la fausse pensée
> Qu'ont tous les autres gens que nous sommes heureux.
>
> (I, 1, 178-81)

Being seen by others as happy is more important to Sosie than being happy. He lives under the gaze of others and allows it to determine his situation, despite certain knowledge that what others think is dead wrong, a "fausse pensée."

Sosie, however, is more than just another seventeenth-century fop worried about his appearance. His preoccupation with appearances is, above all, an expression of his will to be seen by others. It is that which determines how Sosie views himself. His identity has, in effect, been decentered; it has lost its place at the core of his being. He lives, in Pascalian terms, a diffused, imaginary existence over which he no longer retains control. Although discontented with his lot, Sosie carries on because others believe he is lucky to be able to keep company with the likes of his master. Pascal explains this kind of behavior well: "Nous ne nous contentons pas de la vie que nous avons en nous et en notre propre être: nous voulons vivre dans l'idée des autres d'une vie imaginaire, et nous nous efforçons pour cela de paraître."[12] Appearance becomes a metaphor, in the *Pensées* as in *Amphitryon,* for the dissipation of individual identity, which is replaced by the need for the recognition of others. It is impossible to answer the question "Who is Sosie?" by looking at the character himself. To the extent that he molds himself to fit the view of others, Sosie has no fixed identity. The appearance of Mercure disguised as Sosie defies realism but is a logical dramatic development in the portrayal of Sosie's protean nature. It forces the servant, as nothing else could, to face the question of his identity.

Even before Mercure dispossesses Sosie of his identity, Molière has Amphitryon's servant freely step outside himself to take on the roles of others. In a long monologue, Sosie rehearses what he will tell Alcmène. As the scene progresses, he plays the role of Alcmène, receiving news of her husband and responding to it. Sosie also pretends to be himself recounting Amphitryon's adventures and, finally, comments favorably on his own ability to play himself. Sosie surprises himself by the aplomb with which he answers Alcmène's questions:

> "Que dit-il? que fait-il? contente un peu mon âme."
> "Il dit moins qu'il ne fait, Madame,
> Et fait trembler les ennemis."
> (Peste! où prend mon esprit toutes ces gentillesses?)
>   (I, 1, 223-26)

The point of this scene, which foreshadows Sosie's unhappy fate, is to demonstrate the primordial instability of his character. Nothing here is firmly grounded in reality. Sosie is split between the imaginary Sosie and the actor who stands back and comments on his own acting. Alcmène, who is not present, is represented by a lantern with the voice of Sosie. And much that Sosie says is invented, for he had not been on the field of battle with his master. The actual meeting between Sosie and Alcmène, if it were to take place as planned, would be no more real than the rehearsal. Sosie puts on this little drama to prepare for that future encounter, in which he will once again only play at being Sosie:

> Pour jouer mon rôle sans peine,
> Je le veux un peu repasser.
>
> (I, 1, 200-01)

At Mercure's first appearance in the guise of Sosie, the servant calls up his limited courage in order to mount a defense of his own individual identity. Responding to Mercure's question "Qui va là?," Sosie identifies himself simply as "Moi" (I, 2, 309). Sosie may well be a coward, but he is, nonetheless, Sosie. On the other hand, he relies only upon appearances to defend himself—"Si je ne suis hardi, tâchons de le paraître" (I, 2, 305)—and conjures up an image of the brave Amphitryon to give substance to his false claim: "Il [Mercure] est seul, comme moi; je suis fort, j'ai bon maître" (I, 2, 307). Moments later, Sosie tries to solidify an otherwise playful description of himself by telling Mercure that "j'appartiens à mon maître" (I, 2, 319). Sosie's assertion of his own identity ties it closely to that of his master. There is in the servant an emptiness that can be filled only by reference to others. Since what distinguishes Sosie from Mercure is appearances or relatively insignificant and superficial facts about his past—his meal while Amphitryon was on the battlefield or the contents of the box containing Amphitryon's gift to Alcmène—Mercure can, with a good disguise and a bit of knowledge, easily replace him. Sosie clings to his individuality but neither experiences nor articulates it in ways that secure it against the incursions of his double.

The affirmation, in his first encounter with Mercure, that he is Sosie, albeit "Sosie battu" (I, 2, 382), gives way to the servant's recognition that he cannot prevail in the struggle for his identity against the odds of his double's violent pugnacity:

> Hélas! je suis ce que tu veux;
> Dispose de mon sort tout au gré de tes vœux:
> Ton bras t'en a fait le maître.
>
> (I, 2, 389-91)

Alarming though the prospect be, Sosie may have to "renoncer à moi-même" (I, 2, 399) and give up his name. The only questions that remain are whether Sosie can really erase his own identity and whether Mercure can assume it:

> Être ce que je suis est-il en ta puissance?
> Et puis-je cesser d'être moi?
>
> (I, 2, 426-27)

Furthermore, Sosie wonders, even if this is possible, where does it leave him? For he has to be something:

> Mais si tu l'es [Sosie], dis-moi qui tu veux que je sois?
> Car encore faut-il bien que je sois quelque chose.
>
> (I, 2, 511-12)

What is funny in all this is that Sosie, standing there on the stage being Sosie, talks as if he might evaporate into thin air, only to be drawn up short by the realization that he is still something. He seems, as servants at times do in Molière's theater, to be talking nonsense. In fact, Sosie's prattle, if taken seriously for a moment, exposes to view what Lionel Gossman calls the play's two major themes: "the nature of the self and the nature of relations with others."[13] Sosie must solve the puzzle of his own identity.

More perspicacious than literary critics and psychologists, Sosie recognizes instinctively what has happened to him. The difference between himself and others, which had once constituted his identity as an individual, has, in his contact with Mercure, disappeared. Resemblance has replaced difference, and Molière returns to an image from the work of Plautus to call attention to the dangerous collapse of difference:

> Des pieds jusqu'à la tête, il est comme moi fait,
> Beau, l'air noble, bien pris, les manières charmantes;
> Enfin deux gouttes de lait
> Ne sont pas plus ressemblantes.
>
> (II, 1, 783-86)[14]

The audience is amused by the confusion that this doubling causes; the participants in the story witness the breakdown of the order that lent a measure of meaning to their lives. Sosie earlier imitated others without losing a

sense of who he was. Now uncertainty confounds him. Violence sup-
plants reason as the guiding principle of human behavior. Sosie finally suc-
cumbs, beaten into submission by Mercure:

> Je me suis d'être deux senti l'esprit blessé,
> Et longtemps d'imposteur j'ai traité ce moi-même.
> Mais à me reconnoître enfin il m'a forcé:
> J'ai vu que c'étoit moi, sans aucun stratagème.
>
> (II, 1, 779-82)

To survive in any sense, Sosie must accept "ce moi plutôt que moi" (II,
1,741) who rules by force.

Sosie's acquiescence to the uncanny resemblance between himself
and Mercure has the effect of establishing a new perspective from which to
view the servant's dilemma. Thematically, *Amphitryon* does not differ
greatly from others of Molière's comedies. What is both novel and radical
about this play is the context—that of resemblance—in which the themes
appear. This illuminates them in a revealing way. Jealousy is a particularly
interesting case in point, because as he wrote *Amphitryon,* Molière evidently had in mind *Dom Garcie de Navarre ou le prince jaloux,* from which
he borrowed extensively. Babbling on to Amphitryon about Mercure, Sosie
goes right to the root of the relationship between the doubles when he calls
the god "Sosie, un moi, de vos ordres jaloux" (II, 1, 736). Shortly thereafter, Sosie refers to himself and Mercure as "ces deux moi, piqués de
jalousie" (II, 1, 755). Amphitryon's inability to understand why Sosie did
not see Alcmène as he had been ordered to do so frustrates the servant that
he assails his master with a hilarious litany of descriptions of Mercure, each
beginning with the words "ce moi." Among these is "ce moi de moi-même
jaloux" (II, 1, 815). Mercure, according to Sosie, is jealous of him.
Unaware of the true identity of his adversary, Sosie quite naturally assumes
that "ce moi" wants to usurp his place in Amphitryon's household.
Jealousy and rivalry here, as elsewhere, are one, Sosie jealously clings to
his threatened identity, and Mercure jealously covets it. They are in rivalry,
as Sosie comically supposes, for the position of servant to Amphitryon,
whose orders—"vos ordres"—each would like to have barked at him.
What disappears as the two combatants vie with each other is the very real
difference between them. One is a human servant and the other a god.
Mercure, however, uses his godly powers to make himself identical to

Sosie. This is precisely what Sosie's words reveal. The physical resemblance between Mercure and himself gives substance to a metaphysical dimension of their relationship that Sosie calls jealousy. What seems to distinguish the two ultimately has the opposite effect. Sosie and Mercure are the same; jealousy makes them identical and leads to chaos. Sosie loses any firm sense of who he is, as the god Mercure struggles to become a human servant.

Amphitryon, the successful warrior and happy bridegroom, is no less a victim of the gods' shenanigans than his servant. The master's attention is centered on his wife rather than on his identity, but the sentiment aroused in him is the same—jealousy:

> Ma jalousie, à tout propos,
> Me promène sur ma disgrâce;
> Et plus mon esprit y repasse,
> Moins j'en puis débrouiller le funeste chaos.
>   (III, 1, 1462-65)

Amphitryon knows for certain that he has been replaced in his wife's bed by another man, for she herself told him that "nous nous fûmes couchés" (II, 2, 1019) during the period when he was still off at war. He has also begun to understand that his rival bears a physical resemblance to him. What he cannot fathom is the complete breakdown of difference that has caused the dilemma he so rightly characterizes as chaotic:

> La nature parfois produit des ressemblances
> Dont quelques imposteurs ont pris droit d'abuser;
> Mais il est hors de sens que sous ces apparences
> Un homme pour époux se puisse supposer,
> Et dans tous ces rapports sont mille différences
> Dont se peut une femme aisément aviser.
>   (III, 1, 1470-75)

Difference orders Amphitryon's thought and makes his world comprehensible to him. If nature permits resemblance to intrude on this order, it is only in the form of appearances, which are, by definition, superficial, subject to penetration. Beyond appearances lie hard realities, the truth. That mere appearances based on resemblance might erase the difference in the eyes of his wife between her husband and another man is, quite simply, "hors de sens." The only possible explanations Amphitryon can imagine for the strange phenomenon confronting him are that some sort of magic has taken place, which he believes unlikely, or that Alcmène has lost her mind. Rational understanding of the events requires that difference remain intact. Its absence leads to distraction—"Je ne sais plus que croire, ni que dire" (III, 4, 1604), Amphitryon finally declares—and signals the reign of chaos.[15]

Mercure, in a particularly nasty bit of fun at Amphitryon's expense, locks the valiant soldier out of his own house and taunts him with a warning not to disturb the "douces privautés" (III, 2, 1556) that are going on inside between Alcmène and her "real" husband. Mistaking Mercure for Sosie— they do look exactly alike, after all—Amphitryon threatens "his servant" with the violent consequences of such insubordination: "Quels orages de coups vont fondre sur ton dos" (III, 2, 1530). Although this scene is, in one sense, nothing more than a comic elaboration of Mercure's malicious urge to harass Amphitryon, it is also a microcosm of what happens in the play before the mystery of resemblance between gods and men is unraveled. Mercure is neither fully a god nor totally human, for at the same time he teases Amphitryon unmercifully, and with impunity, he must hear himself threatened by a mere mortal. Amphitryon, on the other hand, both thinks of himself as Sosie's master and is mystified by his supposed servant's disobedience. Mercure accuses Amphitryon of drunkenness—"Dis-nous un peu: quel est le cabaret honnête / Où tu t'es coiffé le cerveau?" (III, 2, 1539-40)—just as Amphitryon had earlier blamed Sosie's double talk on drink (II, 1, 821-22). Roles are reversed all around: a god lowers himself to the level of bickering with a mortal, a master is mistreated by his servant, a man would give a god a sound thrashing. The danger of violence is imminent with god and man ready to attack each other and Amphitryon crying out for vengeance: "Et toute mon inquiétude / Ne doit aller qu'à me venger" (III, 3, 1569-70). Amphitryon's fear of chaos is not, it would seem, misplaced. Impending physical violence and its psychological counterpart have reduced the world to a state of confusion.

Jupiter himself is not untouched by the mischief he has wrought. First among the gods though he be, loving Alcmène quickly leads him to experience very human feelings. He is not satisfied, for example, that Alcmène think of him as the husband to whom she owes her love. Jupiter draws a neat line between the role of husband and that of lover, and even though he has disguised himself as Alcmène's husband, he wants her to desire him as she would a lover. As her lover, "Il veut de pure source obtenir vos ardeurs, / Et ne veut rien tenir des nœuds de l'hyménée" (I, 3, 597-98). Her love and his person must be sufficient for Jupiter to obtain the physical and metaphysical favors he wants from Alcmène (I, 3, 571-76). For physical desire alone cannot explain Jupiter's quest. He is, in fact, jealous of Alcmène's human husband and says so himself:

> Cet amant, de vos vœux jaloux au dernier point,
> Souhaite qu'à lui seul votre cœur s'abandonne,
>   Et sa passion ne veut point
>   De ce que le mari lui donne.
>   (I, 3, 593-96)

So manifestly superior is the god to Amphitryon that Alcmène is Jupiter's for the asking. He insists, however, that she choose him over her real husband, thereby demonstrating that his rivalry with Amphitryon is not just a squabble over sexual favors, which he has, in any event, already won. Jupiter's jealousy overpowers the god just as it does mortals. He will later, like Dom Garcie de Navarre, threaten to commit suicide if Alcmène rejects his love. Not only does Jupiter's jealousy reveal his personal insecurity and, thereby, undermine his claim to power, to mastery over the world. It also dooms him to ultimate failure. The only way Jupiter can possibly succeed with Alcmène is by being disguised as her husband. But the mask itself makes it unnecessary for Alcmène to take seriously Jupiter's distinction between lover and husband.

His insistence on the difference between *amant* and *époux* is a clear indication of how Jupiter sees the universe. Like the mortals whom he imitates, he too thinks along the lines of difference. Since Jupiter is a god, he permits himself to take liberties with Amphitryon's wife without ever a second thought about his own behavior. For Jupiter is fundamentally different from the mortals whose world he has invaded. What Jupiter has done in this play is to use his superiority, upon which the essential difference between himself and the likes of Amphitryon is founded, to overcome an impediment concomitant with that very difference. Difference is at once a blessing—it makes Jupiter omnipotent—and a curse, because it also isolates him from the object of his desire. To have what he wants—Alcmène—Jupiter violates the godly status that separates him from mortals by taking on all the attributes of a man, even as he continues to think of himself as a god. This disruption of the organizing principle of difference, however, is dangerous, even for a god. By becoming the rival of Amphitryon, Jupiter momentarily surrenders to his desire and abdicates his prerogatives as chief among the gods. He is ineluctably drawn into the snare of jealous rivalry that levels all difference. Taking up the dichotomy between *ressemblance* and *différence* enunciated earlier by Amphitryon, Jupiter tells Naucratès:

> Oui, vous avez raison; et cette ressemblance
> A douter de tous deux vous peut autoriser.
> Je ne m'offense point de vous voir en balance:
> Je suis plus raisonnable, et sais vous excuser.
> L'œil ne peut entre nous faire de différence,
> Et je vois qu'aisément on s'y peut abuser.
>
> (III, 5, 1669-74)

Like his rival, Jupiter stands fast by the existence of a real difference between the jealous lovers. Unlike Amphitryon, Jupiter understands what is happening, but even the god is obliged to admit that to the naked eye, the difference between himself and his rival has disappeared, with the result that general consternation ensues. In fact, his rivalry with a human being has made Jupiter behave as a mortal would and share the same feelings.

Alcmène is the only major character in *Amphitryon* who stays above the fray engendered by jealous rivalry. Recently married to Amphitryon, she loves him and believes that she has remained faithful to her husband. Alcmène is victimized by both Jupiter, with whom she unwittingly violates her vow of marital fidelity, and Amphitryon, who, initially at least, blames her for occurrences that he cannot understand. As the object of desire of the two rivals, Alcmène becomes an innocent victim of both men. Her role in the play is to stand outside the action dictated by the rivalry between Jupiter and Amphitryon and shed light by her innocence on the flaw in their thinking. During her first encounter with Jupiter, disguised as her husband, she rejects his attempt to distinguish between a husband and a lover:

> Je ne sépare point ce qu'unissent les Dieux,
> Et l'époux et l'amant me sont fort précieux.
>
> (I, 3, 620-21)

Later, she will have an opposite reaction to both lover and husband, but will, nevertheless, continue to reject the dichotomy urged upon her by Jupiter:

Je ne distingue rien en celui qui m'offense,
            Tout y devient l'objet de mon courroux,
                    Et dans sa juste violence
            Sont confondus et l'amant et l'époux,
    Tous deux de même sorte occupent ma pensée,
    Et des mêmes couleurs, par mon âme blessée,
            Tous deux ils sont peints à mes yeux:
    Tous deux sont criminels, tous deux m'ont offensée,
            Et tous deux me sont odieux.
                    (II, 6, 1332-40)

Needless to say, Alcmène is unaware that the person to whom she speaks in these scenes is not her husband. She simply reacts to people and events as they appear to her.

Alcmène is neither blind to differences among men nor foolish in her encounters with them. She would know perfectly well how to deal with a man other than her husband who made unacceptable advances to her. What she does not possess is any of the traits that induce Molière's characters to exaggerate the difference between themselves and others and, in the process, reduce themselves to being just like those from whom they feel most distant. Alcmène loves Amphitryon but has not the slightest concern about how others see either him or herself. She has no desire to be superior to anyone, and she has no rivals. She is, above all, devoid of jealousy. The motives for her actions are straightforward; she is never calculating. This is the reason for which she goes so far as to tell Jupiter that a jealous lover, if his feelings are spontaneous, can be forgiven:

        Des véritables traits d'un mouvement jaloux
                Je me trouverois moins blessée.
        . . . .
        De semblables transports contre un ressentiment
        Pour défense toujours ont ce qui les fait naître,
                Et l'on donne grâce aisément
                A ce dont on n'est pas le maître.
                    (II, 6, 1274-75, 1286-89)

"Véritables traits," even though they are associated with jealousy, are what Alcmène looks for and accepts instinctively. Her freedom from desire and her self-assuredness hold out a possibility for resolving the kinds of conflicts that plague the other characters.

Why, then, does Alcmène leave the stage at the end of Act II, never to reappear? The play's comic denouement is brought about by Jupiter's revelation of his true identity and his declaration that having had him as a rival carries with it a certain honor. Furthermore, the outcome, he admits, leaves him—"tout dieu que je suis" (III, 10, 1904)—as the jealous party, not Amphitryon. Moreover, Amphitryon's house is about to be glorified by the birth of Hercules, fathered by Jupiter during his affair with Alcmène:

> L'éclat d'une fortune en mille biens féconde
> Fera connoître à tous que je suis ton support,
> > Et je mettrai tout le monde
> > Au point d'envier ton sort.
> > (III, 10, 1918-21)

If, as the god proclaims, "Les paroles de Jupiter / Sont des arrêts des destinées," (III, 10, 1925-26), what is the meaning of what he has just told Amphitryon? Chaos has been averted and order restored by the voluntary unmasking of Jupiter and Mercure. On the other hand, the play's final moments hold out no promise of the elimination of the rivalry and jealousy on which the work's action has centered. On the contrary, Jupiter has simply arranged for everyone else to envy Amphitryon. The cuckoldry that might have turned him into a social pariah has redounded to Amphitryon's glory. The ending is a happy one, but it is a conclusion in which nothing is concluded. Rather, everything starts all over again. The restoration of difference between gods and humans re-establishes order, but the envy of Amphitryon that Jupiter predicts foretells a re-enactment, perhaps with different characters, of what has just happened in the play. Alcmène's absence is a sign that desire, rivalry, and jealousy have not been rooted out and banished once and for all. For Molière, it is difficult to imagine an order that will be permanent. The quest for order will always eventually have to be renewed.[16]

NOTES

[1] Molière, *Amphitryon,* in *Œuvres,* eds. Eugène Despois and Paul Mesnard, 14 vols. (Paris: Hachette, 1873-1900), 6, 470 (1903-04). All future references to this and other plays of Molière will be cited from this edition. Citations from plays in verse will be

followed by an indication in the text of the act, scene, and verses quoted. For prose plays, act and scene will be indicated.

2 Molière, *Œuvres complètes,* ed. Georges Couton, 2 vols. (Paris: Gallimard, 1971), 2, 351.

3 Gérard Defaux, *Molière, ou les métamorphoses du comique: De la comédie morale au triomphe de la folie* (Lexington, Kentucky: French Forum, Publishers, 1980), 213.

4 See Charles Daremberg and Edmond Saglio, *Dictionnaire des antiquités grecques et romanes,* 5 vols. (Paris: Hachette, 1881-1918), for a discussion of Jupiter's role as the guarantor of order in the universe: "Zeus, principe de tout ordre et de toute règle, est en particulier le dieu de l'ordre social; il préside aux multiples rapports qui existent entre les hommes, à la vie de la famille et à la vie publique, à l'hospitalité, aux traités" (3, pt. 1, 694). Ironically, he also presides over "naissances légitimes" and "protège avec Héra, déesse des justes noces, la sainteté du lien conjugal" (3, pt. 1, 694-95).

5 Paisley Livingston, "Comic Treatment: Molière and the Farce of Medicine, " *Modern Language Notes,* 94 (1979), 676-87, is right that "as Molière's career progresses the conflictual situations become more and more intricate, yet the disease is always a disruption of social mechanisms brought by rivalry" (678).

6 Plautus, *Amphitryon,* in *Plautus,* trans. Paul Nixon, 5 vols. (London and Cambridge, Mass.: William Heinemann and Harvard University Press, 1916-38), 1, 14. Mercury specifies that these distinguishing marks will be visible only to the audience, not to members of the household. My colleague Wm. Blake Tyrrell has suggested to me that the typical audience of Plautus's time required this kind of concession in order to be able to follow the action of the play. By making his gods indistinguishable from the humans they imitate, Molière engages his audience in the dilemma of his characters.

7 In a fascinating essay, "Comedies of Errors: Plautus—Shakespeare—Molière," in *American Criticism in the Poststructuralist Age,* ed. Ira Konigsberg (Ann Arbor: Michigan Studies in the Humanities, 1981), 66-86, René Girard discusses the literary use of twins to represent mimetic desire. The myth of the doubles Amphitryon and Jupiter, for Girard, has the advantage over stories of twins that it attributes to desire its rightful importance, whereas in tales about twins, problems of identity are more often than not caused by an accident of birth.

8 Molière, *Œuvres complètes,* ed. Robert Jouanny, 2 vols. (Paris: Garnier, 1962), 2, 887, n. 1186.

9 Pierre Corneille, *Œuvres,* ed. Charles Marty-Laveaux, 12 vols. (Paris: Hachette, 1862-68), 3, 402. What Auguste is talking about here is not the kind of *recueillement en soi* for which Montaigne would have humankind reserve and nurture a personal "arrière boutique." In Auguste's speech, desire is always—"toujours"—there and having reached a summit, the "esprit . . . aspire à descendre."

10 Despois and Mesnard believe that the omission would have been incomprehensible to the ancients—"la légende des deux serpents omise, la pièce, pour eux, eût été décapitée"— but "sur notre théâtre, le point de vue s'est déplacé" (*Œuvres,* 6, 337).

---

[11] See Jacques Scherer, "Dualités d'*Amphitryon*," in *Molière: Stage and Study*, ed. W. D. Howarth and Merlin Thomas (Oxford: Clarendon Press, 1973), 185-97. Professor Scherer cites this same verse and points out that to steal Sosie's name is to steal his very being: "Or le nom, c'est l'être. Si Sosie n'est plus Sosie, que peut-il bien être? . . . Un vide métaphysique est à la racine de ce comique qui, sous une autre plume que celle de Molière, risquerait de devenir angoissant" (193).

[12] Blaise Pascal, *Pensées et opuscules,* ed. Léon Brunschvicg (Paris: Hachette, 1963), 400 (pensée no. 147).

[13] Lionel Gossman, *Men and Masks* (Baltimore: The Johns Hopkins Press, 1963), 3.

[14] Cf. Plautus, *Amphitryon:* "neque lac lactis magis est simile quam ille ego similest mei" (I, 62).

[15] In his delightful and elegant book, *Tarte à la crème. Comedy and Gastronomy in Molière's Theater* (Columbus: Ohio State University Press, 1990), Ronald W. Tobin points out that at the play's end, Amphitryon—to no avail—calls for justice: "The supposition that the gods will render an eye for an eye is, of course, ironic and, in fact, refuted by the context; that is, integrity, truth, and faithfulness have no special power to attract the protection of the gods. Morality . . . disintegrates at this point" (80). This is yet another indication of the breakdown of order and good sense in the play.

[16] Frieda S. Brown and Paula B. Koppisch both read the penultimate version of this essay. I am grateful for their helpful suggestions.

II

Values in Process

11

Réécriture et transvalorisation dans les nouvelles de Sorel

Gabrielle Verdier

IL EST ASSEZ PEU D'ŒUVRES DE FICTION au dix-septième siècle qui permettent l'étude de la réécriture "de soi" dans des rééditions corrigées, remaniées, amplifiées.[1] Alors que cette pratique est fréquente— et combien révélatrice!—chez les auteurs dramatiques, les moralistes et les poètes, elle semble assez rare chez les romanciers, comme s'il y avait de la gêne à montrer qu'on parfaisait un écrit appartenant à ce genre méprisé. Certes, la "réécriture" au sens plus large, la reprise de thèmes obsédants, de personnages, de scènes d'une œuvre à l'autre, d'un romancier à l'autre est fréquente et même trop courante à en juger par les critiques de l'époque et de nos jours qui dénoncent les poncifs du genre. Mais les ouvrages romanesques réécrits et réédités par leur auteur se limitent à quelques titres, parmi lesquels les quatre versions du *Polexandre* de Gomberville (entre 1619 et 1637) et les histoires comiques de Charles Sorel. Cette pratique est riche d'instructions; les changements au niveau du lexique renseignent sur l'évolution de la langue, mais tout changement, même aussi insignifiant en apparence que le remplacement d'un adjectif évaluatif par un autre n'est pas indifférent et peut trahir des modifications plus profondes au niveau de l'esthétique et des valeurs. Lorsque ces variantes s'accumulent et qu'il s'y ajoute des modifications et des additions importantes, le travail de l'écrivain peut fournir des exemples probants non seulement de l'évolution du goût mais de celui des "morales du grand siècle."

Que Sorel, "l'ennemi" des fables et des romans comme il se plaisait à le proclamer, figure parmi les romanciers qui s'adonnent à la réécriture peut sembler surprenant. Tout en affichant son mépris de la fiction, il ne s'empêcha pas de produire trois versions de son chef-d'œuvre, l'*Histoire comique de Francion* (1623, 1626, 1633) et de refondre complètement *Le Berger extravagant* (1627-28) qu'il rebaptisa *L'Anti-roman* (1633-34). Cet acharnement s'explique en partie par le fait que les histoires comiques contestent par définition le roman officiel. Mais il est plus paradoxal que Sorel, nommé historiographe en 1629 et se consacrant depuis 1634 à son immense *Science Universelle*, reprenne dans les années quarante un ouvrage de facture plus conventionnelle, en apparence dépassé par ses propres expériences anti-romanesques. En 1623 à l'âge de 22 ou 23 ans, Sorel avait publié *Les Nouvelles françoises, où se trouvent les divers effets de l'amour et de la fortune*, composé de cinq récits d'une centaine de pages. Après un intervalle de vingt années, il réécrit le recueil, y ajoute deux nouvelles et un récit cadre, et le publie en 1645 sous le titre *Les Nouvelles Choisies, où se trouvent divers accidents d'Amour et de Fortune*.[2] Si les histoires comiques jouissent d'un grand succès et suscitent assez d'imitateurs pour constituer un nouveau genre, les deux recueils de nouvelles, par contre, ne seront édités chacun qu'une fois et semblent paraître à contre courant. Car en 1623, le roman sentimental et le roman d'aventure sont en vogue, et en 1645, le roman héroïque.

De nos jours les historiens de la littérature, notamment Georges Hainsworth, Frédéric Deloffre et René Godenne,[3] ont reconnu le rôle de pionnier joué par Sorel en introduisant en France la nouvelle relativement longue, à la fois romanesque, "réaliste" et morale, inspirée de la *novela* cervantine. Cette orientation rompait avec la tradition des recueils de nouvelles "à l'italienne," récits courts, amusants et souvent licencieux, mais elle n'allait attirer les suffrages du public que dans les années cinquante, avec la publication des nouvelles adaptées de l'espagnol de Scarron (*Nouvelles Tragi-comiques*, 1656) et des *Nouvelles françoises* de Segrais (1656). Si les "vérités destructrices" du premier recueil de Sorel ont été bien mises en lumière par Judd D. Hubert et la nouveauté de son style par Romeo Arbour,[4] le bilan des études consacrées à une œuvre dont l'importance est avérée, reste mince. Quant aux *Nouvelles choisies*, elles sont encore plus méconnues, la plupart des critiques se contentant de signaler l'existence d'une "seconde édition" avec quelques changements jugés facheux.[5] Sur cet ouvrage, qui est en réalité un nouveau recueil plutôt qu'une réédition, il existe peu d'études: un article de R. Godenne qui signale la nouveauté de la septième nouvelle, "Les Respects nuisibles," le premier récit à la première personne dans l'histoire du genre;[6] une thèse inédite sur les nouvelles de Sorel qui compare les deux recueils[7] et les articles récents de Daniela Dalla Valle et de Hervé Béchade. Leurs études relèvent des différences importantes entre les deux recueils, sans toutefois les épuiser ni en mesurer toutes les conséquences.[8]

Pourquoi Sorel, parmi les plus conscients des romanciers, aurait-il modifié tel aspect, plutôt qu'un autre? Les changements sont-ils systématiques et manifestent-ils une tendance générale? Quels en sont les effets narratologiques, partant idéologiques? Semblent-ils correspondre à une autre perception de "l'horizon d'attente" du public? M'inspirant d'études théoriques récentes dans le domaine de la poétique et de la sémiotique textuelles, en particulier des travaux de Gérard Genette et de Philippe Hamon,[9] je me propose d'identifier et d'analyser les changements qui se trouvent à des points textuels privilégiés, ce que Philippe Hamon nomme "points névralgiques" ou "foyers normatifs" du texte, lieux d'évaluation ou de modalisation (20). Dans *Les Nouvelles choisies*, les foyers normatifs les plus modifiés par rapport au premier recueil (qui correspond à "l'hypotexte" dans la terminologie de Genette) se situent à des lieux stratégiques: le paratexte, les instances de l'énonciation, les descriptions qui introduisent les personnages principaux, et dans un cas le dénouement. Outre cela, les deux nouveaux récits, placés en première et en dernière position, encadrent les cinq nouvelles originales, elles-mêmes disposées différemment, et ces récits réécrivent "en mineur" certains thèmes essentiels des *Nouvelles françoises*.

Afin d'apprécier la portée des changements, rappelons ces thèmes et leurs aspects contestataires. La "nouveauté" du recueil de 1623 ne se limite pas au décor "français," varié et contemporain, réplique aux nouvelles espagnoles; elle consiste surtout en la "naïveté"—le naturel des sujets et du style, des détails vrais.[10] Chacune des histoires développe une situation quelque peu paradoxale et dénonce des préjugés qui se traduisaient en lieux communs romanesques. Rejetant la convention qui faisait de l'amour sérieux l'apanage de l'aristocratie, Sorel représente une variété de conditions sociales, de la noblesse jusqu'à la paysannerie. (Il n'y manque que la bourgeoisie marchande et les artisans). Les amants franchissent les distances sociales et les différences de fortune qui devraient les séparer: les héros se montrent plus "généreux" que leurs supérieurs et le proclament ouvertement; les héroïnes, violant les bienséances, "franchi[ssent] les limites où [leur] sexe était enfermé" (NF, 17) pour satisfaire leurs désirs. Sorel dissocie la noblesse d'âme de la condition sociale. Il transforme la générosité, le courage propre aux âmes bien nées, "en qualité universelle" (Hubert, 34). Et qui plus est, ses "généreux" se distinguent autant, sinon plus par "l'esprit" et "les bonnes études"—talents bourgeois—que par la bravoure.[11]

1. "Le Pauvre Généreux" (près de Toulouse, la mer Méditerranée). La noble Elidore ose aimer Floran, fils d'un "sergent de village," pour sa valeur et son esprit. Celui-ci se montre plus généreux que l'arrogant Baron, son rival, qui le persécute. Grâce à ses actions héroïques le "pauvre" obtient la main d'Elidore.

2. "Les Mal Mariez" (la mer "germanique," la France, l'Angleterre et l'Ecosse). Deux "mal-mariés" de la noblesse se révoltent contre la servitude qui les assujettit: Orize, une Française, lutte contre un mari brutal et le "malheureux lien" du mariage tandis que l'Anglais, Alério, dénonce le Roi pour avoir séduit sa femme et par défi se fait corsaire. Ils finissent par s'unir après avoir échappé à leurs ennemis qui trouvent la mort.

3. "La Sœur jalouse" (un village aux alentours de Paris). Albert, paysan devenu valet de chambre et Francine, paysanne, s'aiment mais leur amour est contrarié par la jalousie d'une sœur et d'un rival éconduits. Cette histoire d'amour chez des paysans—et non des bergers de pastorale—représentés de manière sérieuse et naturelle conteste le préjugé qui réservait cette passion aux gens de qualité.

4. "Les Trois Amants" (Paris). Clerarque, un pauvre intellectuel, secrétaire d'un grand seigneur, finit par obtenir la main d'Hermiane, fille d'un trésorier, après lui avoir rendu de plus grands services que ses rivaux, un homme d'épée et un financier.

5. "La Reconnaissance d'un fils" (Tours et Rouen). Meligene, appartenant à la noblesse de robe, tombe amoureux d'un bel adolescent qui se trouve être une suivante déguisée, pauvre mais spirituelle. Elle lui cède et l'histoire de leurs amours, de leur séparation et de leurs retrouvailles sert à révéler l'identité de leur fils, jeune inconnu trahi par son ami dans l'histoire-cadre.

La "naïveté" qui exige la représentation de l'amour parmi toutes les conditions donne lieu à des résultats paradoxaux, tant au niveau de l'intrigue qu'à celui de la caractérisation. L'écart social crée des obstacles qui rendent souvent nécessaires des aventures bien romanesques pour parvenir à la fin heureuse. En même temps, le triomphe du héros supérieur par son intelligence est dû aussi souvent à la ruse qu'aux armes; celui de l'héroïne lui fait transgresser dangereusement les bornes de sa condition féminine. Enfin, les différences sociales risquent de contaminer le pur amour par des mobiles plus intéressés. Ces ambiguïtés contribuent à la richesse thématique du premier recueil.

A première vue, le changement le plus frappant dans les *Nouvelles choisies* consiste à banaliser le dénouement du "Pauvre généreux" en renversant le statut social du héros et de son rival: on découvre au roturier des ancêtres nobles tandis que l'aïeul du Baron se révèle avoir été "un vendeur de sabots" (NC, 346). Cependant, cette modification, qui a été souvent reprochée à Sorel, fait partie de toute une stratégie de réécriture qui vise à "normaliser" le récit, à en atténuer les contrastes "baroques," à le rendre plus conforme aux normes esthétiques et sociales.

Cet effort est sensible dès l'intitulé. Tandis que *Les Nouvelles françoises* proclamait le caractère unique du recueil dans la production nationale et l'article du sous-titre—"*les* divers effets de l'amour et de la fortune"—son caractère définitif et exhaustif, *Les Nouvelles choisies* et adjectif indéfini—"ou se trouvent *divers* accidents d'Amour et de Fortune"—suggèrent, tant sur le plan rhématique que thématique,[12] une sélection dans un ensemble plus vaste. Le ton modeste de bonne compagnie se prolonge dans la courte préface "Aux Lecteurs," qui se distingue fortement de l'ostentation des deux textes liminaires du premier recueil. Dans l' "Au lecteur" de 1623, l'auteur, bien qu'il reste anonyme, occupe l'avant-scène: "L'Auteur des Nouvelles françoises ne reconnaissant rien presque du sien excepté le titre, en leur impression faite en son absence, ne *veut pas* y mettre son nom. . . ." S'il dénigre l'ouvrage, c'est pour mieux vanter son talent: bien que "n'étant pas moindre que beaucoup d'autres ouvrages qui traitent ainsi d'amour," et "remplie en tous endroits de diverses raisons judicieuses," "cette manière d'écrire . . . n'est pas encore digne de son courage qui ne le porte naturellement qu'à des choses infiniment élevées au dessus de cela, & et de ce que tous les écrivains du monde ont pu faire" (NF, aij-aiij).[13] L'hyperbole et l'exhibitionnisme ambitieux font bien reconnaître l'auteur de "Avertissement d'importance aux lecteurs" du *Francion*. La dédicace, sans titre, aux "Belles Dames" nuance le panache de galanterie tant soit peu condescendante. Le sujet reste le "moi" de l'auteur qui se manifeste sans vergogne à la première personne dès la première phrase, tandis que les destinatrices—public traditionnel depuis Boccace—sont nommées dans une parenthèse: "Je ne désire pas m'acquitter ici des inviolables promesses que je vous ai faites autrefois (Belles Dames pour qui je voudrais souffrir une infinité de peines). . . ." Dans la suite ce "je" réapparaît insolemment encore treize fois. Cette épître reprend les arguments de la préface: les nouvelles ne sont même pas un "échantillon de ce que je me suis délibéré de vous offrir" (1). Leur valeur est bien inférieure à ce qu'il est capable de produire: "Je ne les ai mises par écrit que pour charmer les ennuis que la longueur du temps apporte quelquefois" (2). Même le compliment aux dames sert à rehausser le mérite de l'auteur: "dès que je commencerai à travailler pour un si glorieux sujet, le ciel qui montre n'avoir aucune influence qui ne s'observe à perpetuer la gloire de vos perfections rendra mon esprit pourvu d'une puissance extraordinaire" (2). Suit un commentaire du titre (elles sont "françaises" parce qu'elles contiennent des aventures de personnes de notre nation) et l'annonce de certains thèmes risqués, justifiés de manière plus galante que morale: "Et si vous y voyez de mauvaises actions de quelques personnes de votre sexe, ne vous en offensez aucunement. La perfection ne se peut pas trouver en toutes de même qu'en vous?" (2-3).

Tout autre est la stratégie de présentation de la préface de 1645, où le "vous" des destinataires prédomine. L'auteur s'efface presque complètement (un seul adjectif à la première personne plurielle "notre frontispice") pour au contraire, faire valoir la société de lecteurs, honnêtes gens sans distinction de sexe. "Le choix de ces sept nouvelles vous est offert pour vous faire participer au divertissement de ceux qui les ont racontées." Eliminant toute mention d'un contenu choquant, le préfacier discret développe l'explication du titre et commente l'utilité de l'ouvrage. Les sept nouvelles "choisies," chacune remplissant une journée, correspondent aux sept planètes (de Jupiter à la Lune) qui président aux jours de la semaine, représentées sur le frontispice avec leur attributs mythologiques.[14] Le livre est utile pour sa fonction récréative et sa fonction sociale: "vous trouverez dans ce livre une agréable matière d'entretien avec de beaux sujets pour des pièces de théâtre & le tout assez accommodé à la façon de vivre d'aujourd'hui" (NC, aiij). Ce qui est donc souligné, ce n'est plus la supériorité de l'auteur mais la parfaite adaptation du livre au public, la société d'honnêtes gens, dont il est le miroir et en quelque sorte le produit. Certes, la comparaison astronomique suggère l'excellence du "choix" de nouvelles, qui, semblables aux sept planètes connues à l'époque, représentent la diversité du monde et suffisent à nourrir la conversation. L'éloge, cependant, s'exprime au collectif et non au singulier et sera repris dans "Avant-propos" qui présente le groupe de devisants.

A première vue, le récit cadre de huit pages que Sorel ajoute aux *Nouvelles choisies* semble retrograde, un retour à la tradition rejetée en 1623. Mais comme le fait remarquer Hervé Béchade, la fiction de Sorel diffère considérablement du modèle italien, repris dans les recueils français de la Renaissance (Béchade, 66). Aucune catastrophe naturelle ne réunit les devisants, l'ambiance est toute de fête. La société de narrateurs/auditeurs se retrouve à la cour du Prince Polynice, "l'un des grands princes de notre siècle" qui visite la province de son apanage avec sa nouvelle épouse, la princesse Eromène. "L'Avant-propos" décrit son magnifique "château de plaisance," les banquets et les divertissements que le Prince offre à sa cour.

Un incident amusant mais source de réflexion morale fournit le prétexte de la narration de nouvelles. Hermiane, une demoiselle de la princesse, voit un vieillard faire la cour à une jeune fille au bal, et pour montrer que cette conduite est ridicule et condamnable, elle rapporte une histoire "véritable et moderne" qu'elle tient de Béronte. La princesse demande à celui-ci d'en faire le récit détaillé et invite aussi les autres cavaliers de son entourage à raconter "des Histoires ou Nouvelles les plus intriguées et le plus agréables dont ils eussent jamais eu connaissance" (8). Les nouvelles sont donc conçues comme un divertissement supplémentaire qui délasse des réjouissances de la journée. Ce rapport entre fêtes et narrations sera renforcé par la description des "entrées" en tête de la sixième et la septième journées et la remarque qu'elles "ne plairont possible pas tant que la nouvelle de Cléobule" qui fut récitée après "la collation" et "des autres passetemps" (NC, 669).

Bien que les discussions des devisants encadrant les récits soient peut-être "la partie la plus négligée par Sorel,"[15] elles remplissent plusieurs fonctions qui orientent sensiblement la lecture. Contrairement aux *Nouvelles françoises* qui se présentent sans aucun préambule, les commentaires d'introduction servent à annoncer le thème et le problème moral— tout comme Hermiane dans "l'Avant-propos" avait anticipé l'histoire de Béronte—et à atténuer ainsi l'effet de surprise. A la fin les devisants commentent l'agrément du récit et portent des jugements sur la conduite des protagonistes, la ramenant aux motivations et aux principes moraux admis par le groupe. Voici par exemple, la discussion qui sert de transition entre la deuxième nouvelle du recueil, "l'Heureuse recognoissance" (NF "La Recognoissance d'un fils") et la suivante, "La Vertu recompensée" (NF "Le Pauvre généreux"):

> les uns s'étonnèrent de l'infidélité de Julian, et les autres admirèrent
> surtout la fidélité que Meligène et Uralie s'étaient gardée jusqu'à ce
> qu'ils s'étaient retrouvés, et leur fils semblablement, par une heureuse
> reconnaissance. Une Dame sévère dit qu'Uranie avoit bien mérité une
> longue pénitence durant l'absence de son Amant, d'autant qu'elle avait
> témoigné trop peu de modestie et de continence, en se laissant si tôt
> vaincre par ses poursuites. Dynaste repartit qu'elle avait été surprise par
> l'espérance de se voir mariée à un homme qui était de plus grande condi-
> tion qu'elle, et que l'ambition faisait faire ainsi des choses hardies à
> plusieurs, lorsque l'amour n'y estoit point, vu que l'Amour étant tout
> seul se faisait même assez respecter, contraignant des filles de bon lieu

d'aimer les hommes de basse condition, lors qu'ils étaient à leur gré, de quoi il s'offrit de donner un bon exemple. . . . (NC, 203-4)

Malgré quelques critiques de la "Dame sévère" qui condamne surtout le manque de retenue des héroïnes, les différences d'opinion sont peu marquées et le jugement collectif s'exprime le plus souvent par l'emploi du pronom "on." Les devisants tombent tous d'accord sur "la vertu" qui mérite la récompense au "pauvre généreux," qui n'est plus désigné par cet oxymore mais reconnu par des parents nobles dans l'histoire telle que la raconte Dinaste.

> Plusieurs blamèrent Angélique [NF Elidore], non seulement de s'être laissée si facilement surprendre à l'Amour, mais encore d'avoir eu si peu de retenue que d'en avoir fait sa déclaration sans y être incitée. Les Dames disaient que Dinaste en avait falsifié la vérité, et qu'il était bien raisonnable que son Amant y contribuât quelque chose de sa part. Mais il remontra que la crainte qu'elle eut de la modestie de Belair [NF Floran] ne fut trop longue, lui donna cette hardiesse qu'elle avait assez excusée par les feintes qu'elle avait faites après. D'ailleurs le mérite du personnage fut examiné; l'on loua toutes ses vertus, comme l'humilité dans sa condition, la constance dans la prison et ses tourments, et sa valeur dans les combats, tellement que l'on jugea que d'épouser Angélique, c'était une récompense qu'on ne pouvait lui refuser. Alcidon se vanta de savoir une autre histoire d'un Amant qui pour avoir fidèlement aimé se montra digne de posséder l'objet de ses affections, malgré la concurrence de beaucoup d'autres plus relevés en condition et en biens de fortune et de dire cela, c'était témoigner qu'il avait envie d'être le successeur de Dinaste. . . . (NC, 346-48)

La dernière phrase sert non seulement à introduire le narrateur suivant et à annoncer le thème de sa nouvelle mais aussi à anticiper son dénouement. Aucun mystère donc quant à l'issue des "Divers amants" (NF "Les Trois amants").

L'attribution des nouvelles à des narrateurs diégétiques, même s'ils sont faiblement personnifiés, constitue une tranformation radicale de l'instance énonciative. Dans le deuxième recueil, ce sont Dinaste, Alcidon, etc., qui prononcent les "vérités destructrices" que proclamait le narrateur-auteur intraitable des *Nouvelles françoises*. En déléguant ainsi la responsabilité des histoires, l'auteur réussit deux effets: il se distancie des thèses contestataires, stratégie de défense déjà essayée dans les remaniements du *Francion*; mais en même temps il les fait partager, même si elles sont quelque peu assagies, à la compagnie de devisants qui représente si bien la société d'honnêtes gens. Cette universalisation des thèses est d'ailleurs renforcée par la modification des titres qui, dans *Les Nouvelles choisies* insistent sur soit le jugement moral soit une vérité générale plutôt que le cas singulier et extraordinaire[16]: ainsi "Le Pauvre généreux" devient "La Vertu recompensée," "La Sœur jalouse," "La jalousie cruelle," etc. La transformation énonciative permet aussi de soulever le problème de la véracité du narrateur, ce qui peut fonctionner à atténuer le récit: choquées par les actions d'Angélique, "Les Dames disaient que Dinaste en avait falsifié la vérité" (NC, 346).

Enfin le procédé dramatise une question plus générale, celle du rapport qui existe entre le narrateur et son histoire. Sorel l'exploite habilement, comme l'a montré René Godenne, pour créer la nouvelle à la première personne, faisant faire la déclaration suivante à Pamphile, narrateur de la dernière histoire:

> Il me semble, Madame, que la plupart de ceux qui m'ont précédé se sont acquittés de leur devoir assez légèrement, et au moins ont-ils parlé de plusieurs choses qu'ils ne savaient que par le rapport d'autrui, de sorte qu'ils ont pu nous débiter plusieurs mensonges sur la bonne foi de leurs amis. Pour moi je veux me comporter d'autre façon, et ne vous dire que les choses que j'ai vues, et que pour m'être connues sont celles où j'ai eu plus de part. Bref, les autres ne vous ont raconté que des amours étrangères, et je veux vous raconter les miennes. . . . (NC, 812-13)

Ce "pacte autobiographique" et le récit qui le suit mènent à son terme la thèse amorcée dans les propos d'Hermiane (Avant-Discours) et développée par le premier narrateur, Béronte—que la proximité entre le narrateur, son sujet et ses auditeurs est non seulement garant de crédibilité mais aussi source de plaisir. En introduisant l'histoire d'une fille dans son quartier, Béronte reprend le discours du narrateur qui figurait en tête de la quatrième nouvelle ("Les Trois amants") pour justifier le décor parisien aux "Belles Dames" qui s'attendaient à une histoire plus exotique (NF, 358-59):

> Si l'on veut trouver des exemples sur toutes sortes de sujets, il n'est presque aucun besoin d'en aller chercher ailleurs qu'à Paris. Comme cette ville est un abrégé du monde, l'on y remarque des incidents de

toutes les manières imaginables, et quiconque a connaissance des intrigues qui s'y passent n'a pas besoin d'inventer des fictions pour entretenir les compagnies, et n'a qu'à raconter naïvement ce qu'il a vu de ses
yeux, ou ce qu'il croit sur la foi de ses amis. Je tirerai donc de ce lieu-
là ma première narration, et je pense que le peu d'artifice que j'ai pour
controuver des mensonges vous la rendra d'autant plus recevable. (NC,
1-2)

Encadrées par les histoires d'un narrateur-témoin et un narrateur-héros, les
nouvelles originales semblent réorientées vers la familiarité par une disposition nouvelle. Alors qu'en 1623 les nouvelles les plus contestataires, "Le
Pauvre généreux" et "La Sœur jalouse" (la tragédie d'amour chez les
paysans) étaient placées en première position et au centre du recueil, la
position centrale est occupée en 1645 par la nouvelle dans laquelle Béronte
avait puisé sa thèse et qui se déroule entièrement à Paris, "l'abrégé du
monde." Cet ancrage des *Nouvelles choisies* modère l'impact des nouvelles
romanesques et tragiques qui détonnent tout en assurant une variété
agréable.[17]
    La nouvelle orientation du recueil vers les agréments de la bonne
société est renforcée par un élément paratextuel non verbal mais
iconographique. En signalant l'illustration des planètes—"C'est ce que la
figure de notre frontispice vous enseigne, afin qu'il n'y ait rien ici qui ne
serve à quelque chose" (NC, aiij)—le préfacier attire l'attention aux autres
gravures qui agrémentent *Les Nouvelles choisies*, et qui elles aussi
devraient "servir à quelque chose." A une exception près, elles représentent
les activités des personnages du récit cadre, les princes et leur cour: un
banquet avec divertissement ("Avant propos"), un ballet allégorique représentant des personnages mythologiques dans des chars (666), l'entrée de la
Princesse Eromène dans la ville capitale de la Province (809). Cette dernière
gravure pourrait également illustrer l'épisode qui ouvre la septième nouvelle, la rencontre de Pamphile et sa Maîtresse qui a lieu le jour de "l'entrée
de la princesse Alcidiane dans la ville de Persepolis" (813). Seule la troisième image (202), représentant des fortifications et des canons, correspond
à un épisode de la "La Vertu recompensée." Mais il s'agit d'un épisode
ajouté, dans lequel Belair (NF Floran) monte une campagne militaire en
miniature "pour donner plus de satisfaction à la compagnie":

lorsque la nappe fut levée, il fit apporter plusieurs cartes, et d'ordres
militaires. Ayant même tracé un petit fort dans le champ assez près de

la maison, l'on s'y alla promener sur le soir; il en fit en peu de temps
ouvrir les tranchées par tous les gens du village qu'il mit en besogne,
et auxquels il fit prendre un équipage militaire. Il fit tirer des petits
canons que l'on avait déjà chargés pour les réjouissances du jour. Surtout les dames prirent plaisir à ce spectacle qui leur représentait la guerre
qu'elles n'avaient jamais vue qu'en peinture. Belair, qui était l'inven-
teur de ceci, en fut beaucoup estimé. (NC, 211-12)

Cette mise en scène, qui amplifie une phrase des *Nouvelles
françoises* —"il conta les sièges, les escarmouches et les batailles rangées
où il s'était trouvé" (NF 10)—est typique des additions dans le deuxième recueil. Elle remplit plusieurs fonctions, la plus évidente, celle de "motiver"[18]
un moment capital du récit. Elle rend plus vraisemblable la réaction de
l'héroïne au fils d'un sergent de village. "Elidore [NC "Angelique"] qui ne
l'avoit jamais vu, admire sa bonne mine & ses propos bien arrangés [NC
"son adresse"], & le prend plutôt pour un grand Capitaine que pour un
simple soldat" (NF, 10; NC, 212). La motivation psychologique s'appuie
sur une autre stratégie de réécriture, la valorisation.[19] La campagne militaire
feinte rend visible—"adresse" remplace "propos"—la valeur de "Belair" (le
nouveau nom est valorisant également.) Elle le porte bien au-dessus des
gens du village auxquels il commande et lui mérite l'estime de tous, non
seulement d'Angélique, mais des dames, des devisants et des lecteurs qui
admirent la belle gravure dans *Les Nouvelles choisies*. Enfin le choix de
l'action et sa localisation dans le texte sont significatifs et correspondent tout
à fait à un de ces "points névralgiques" analysés par Philippe Hamon. Cette
première action du héros, dont le narrateur vient de résumer le passé (ses
basses origines, les bonnes études qu'il fit tout en étant domestique, ses
prouesses militaires et la fortune qui s'oppose à son avancement) met en
évidence son savoir-faire, son savoir-dire, son savoir-vivre et son savoir-
jouir.[20] La version de 1623 soulignait sa manipulation de signes linguistiques, fruit de ses bonnes études: il "conte" les batailles et ensuite ses
termes "infiniment courtois et infiniment élégants" (NF, 13) lui font gagner
le prix au "jeu des parfaits Amants" et l'amour de la fière Elidore. La
réécriture, faisant précéder le "jeu" de société du "spectacle" de guerre met
l'accent sur sa manipulation des outils militaires, son autorité de chef[21] et
ses talents de metteur en scène. Il est non seulement celui qui se distingue au
jeu mais celui qui "invente" tout un spectacle pour divertir la compagnie.
Inutile d'insister combien sa maîtrise de l'art militaire et des divertissements
rehausse son éclat et le rapproche des gens de qualité auxquels ces

passetemps étaient réservés! Aucune surprise, donc qu'à la fin ce Belair, "à qui l'on . . . avait expédié des lettres d'une nouvelle noblesse [n'ait] seulement besoin d'un retablissement, et d'une confirmation de l'ancienne" (NC, 344).

L'analyse de ce passage permet de classer et de comprendre le fonctionnement de bien d'autres changements.[22] De nombreuses additions visent à motiver ou à mieux motiver des événements qui pourraient paraître invraisemblables en ajoutant des détails concrets. Par exemple, toujours dans "La Vertu": un long passage pour montrer comment Belair a pu tomber dans le piège tendu par son rival et son Maître, le frère d'Angélique (NC, 238-39); son lieu d'emprisonnement changé pour faciliter sa découverte par Angélique (NC, 56); la conversation entre la suivante et son amant réécrite afin de rendre plus crédible la bonne volonté de ce dernier qui consent à prendre la place de Belair en prison (NC, 288-93). Des changements analogues dans les autres nouvelles: des circonstances qui expliquent mieux comment Edouard (Alério) a pu surprendre la liaison adultère de sa femme et du roi ("Mariages," NC, 730), comment Albert (Clerarque) a pu entretenir sa Maîtresse emprisonnée par un rival ("Amants," NC, 432), etc.

Mais souvent les changements modifient sensiblement les mobiles des personnages et leur évaluation par le narrateur. Le système des noms constitue une première approche évaluative. Sorel se félicitait d'avoir abandonné les noms "à la grecque" conventionnels pour introduire des noms français, et dans certains cas il l'avait réussi dans *Les Nouvelles françoises*. Si les changements qu'il introduit dans le deuxième recueil ne sont pas systématiques, on peut discerner certaines tendances. Dans plusieurs cas, le résultat tend vers l'authenticité: Edouard et Cambrige ("Mariages") sonnent plus anglais que Alerio et Celistée; Albert, Fernand, Enguerrand ("Amants") plus français que Clerarque, Nisarede et Dryante; le sieur de Querasque ("Vertu") plus languedocien peut-être que "le Sieur de Saint-Amour." Cependant d'autres changements sont plus chargés de connotations positives ou négatives. Certaines héroïnes reçoivent des noms qui ressemblent davantage à ceux des jeunes premières dans les comédies de Corneille: Elidore devient Angélique, Orize devient Clymene ("Mariages") et Hermiane, Celinde ("Amants"). L'évaluation est plus marquée lorsque la paysanne Francine reçoit un nom plus élégant, Isabelle ("Jalousie"), et tout à fait évidente dans le cas de ses amants: le sympathique Albert est rebaptisé "Martial," ce qui accentue les qualités qui le distinguent de son rival, Cheron, devenu "Rustan." Des noms allégoriques qui caractérisent et portent un jugement prédominent dans les nouveaux récits: le vieux

Gerileon, le valereux Valeran, l'amoureux Pamphile annoncent déjà des "caractères" de l'époque classique. Tous ces changements ont pour effet de réduire la polyvalence d'un personnage et de le situer plus fermement dans une hiérarchie normative.

Cette tendance s'accompagne d'une autre qui vise à estomper les contrastes extrêmes et à rapprocher du juste milieu les personnages "sympathiques" ou porteurs de valeurs positives. Elle se manifeste par des changements infimes, tels que le remplacement d'une hyperbole par un évaluatif moins emphatique, mais se concentre à des moments critiques. Ce sont les moments où les protagonistes, par leurs paroles ou leur actions, transgressent une norme morale et sociale. Dans ces "lieux névralgiques" les discours sont parfois réécrits de façon à "modaliser" les déclarations péremptoires:[23] lorsque Elidore incite Floran à oser l'aimer, elle lui lance, "En quoi est-ce que nous sommes inégaux? en biens de fortune, n'est-ce pas?" (NF, 20), ce qu'elle exprime avec moins de véhémence dans le deuxième recueil, "Est-ce en biens de fortune?" (NC, 225). De même, l'invective d'Orize contre "le malheureux lien du mariage," un défi à la doctrine de l'église, se mitige par le passage au mode interrogatif:

NF: Malheureux lien qui m'étreint: que celui-là avait peu de raison qui ordonna que tu sois inviolable. Car quelle injustice est-ce de contraindre une personne à demeurer attachée avec une autre qui ne l'affectionne point. (133)
NC: Malheureux lien qui me serre si fort: a-t-on eu raison d'ordonner que tu sois inviolable? N'y a-t-il point quelque injustice . . . point? (690)

Alério, qui en 1623 voulait "causer tant de honte au Roy qu'il se repentit de sa faute" (NF, 165) se contente en 1645 de "montrer au Roy que je ne manquai pas de courage et qu'il ne fallait point qu'il persiste" (NC, 735). Dans de nombreux passages de discours indirect ou de monologue intérieur, la présence médiatrice du narrateur devient plus marquée et multiplie les réserves.

Les passages les plus réécrits se trouvent être les commentaires explicatifs et évaluatifs du narrateur. Si les lamentations d'Elidore/Angélique sur la tombe supposée de son amant ne sont pas modifiées, elles sont suivies d'excuses: "Ainsi l'excès de la passion faisait faire des choses étranges à cette fille, ce que l'on admirera moins quand l'on considèrera que les plus beaux esprits sont souvent capables des plus grandes frénésies"

(NC, 249). Le narrateur remplace un axiologique péjoratif par un mélioratif pour interpréter la réaction de Floran/Belair aux avances de l'héroïne: "La vanité n'eut pas une petite part dans son âme" (NF, 21) devient "La confiance qu'il eut en soi-même le rassura" (NC, 226). Pour prévenir "l'admiration" du lecteur il "motive" une conduite paradoxale: dans *Nouvelles françoises*, Hermiane, qui avait résolu de choisir "le plus aimable," favorise jusqu'au dernier moment ses amants moins méritoires par un sentiment d'incompatibilité avec le héros, dont elle redoute "l'esprit relevé" (NF, 441); la réécriture ajoute six commentaires qui préparent le revirement soudain d'Hermiane/Celinde et introduisent pour expliquer ses "inégalités d'humeur" un mobile plus conforme à ce qu'on pourrait imaginer chez une "fille de Trésorier": elle consent à épouser le financier qu'elle n'aime pas parce qu'elle est touchée "de l'espérance d'avoir beaucoup de biens" (NC, 441). Lorsqu'elle comprendra que l'argent ne fait pas le bonheur, elle récompensera la fidélité du héros. En revanche le narrateur supprime deux longs passages détaillant la passion que le bel inconnu éveille chez Méligène ("Recognoissance", NF, 497-98, 499-500), faisant disparaître ainsi l'avertissement à propos du "plus sale de tous les vices," et fournit une motivation plus honnête: il veut "l'honorer d'une parfaite amitié" (NC, 105) et le poursuit "afin de pouvoir jouir de la conversation d'une personne dont la physionomie lui promettait beaucoup de preuves de vertu" (NC, 107).[24]

Ces exemples de "transmotivation" montrent bien comment les sentiments et comportements que l'on pouvait trouver "extravagants" en 1645 sont réécrits de façon à les rapprocher d'une nouvelle conception de la vraisemblance et des bienséances. En effet, les devisants, qui critiquent Angélique et indirectement Clymene,[25] ne commentent pas la conduite de Celinde et de Meligene. Cet effort est sensible même dans deux longs ajouts qui contribuent, certes, au "naturel," à la "crédibilité" et à la "subtilité psychologique" des nouvelles.[26] Or, il est significatif que les scènes ajoutées se situent au même "lieu névralgique" du texte que le "spectacle militaire" qui rend si séduisant le "fils d'un sergent de village"—à savoir, le moment de l'entrée en scène de l'objet érotique. Dans la réécriture des "Amants" (qui supprime, nous l'avons vu, le discours du narrateur-auteur justifiant Paris comme source d'histoires divertissantes), Albert ne rencontre plus la belle Celinde "sur la porte d'un de ses voisins" mais dans un décor plus actuel et plus spectaculaire. La nouvelle s'ouvre directement sur la description du "cours qui se faisait un soir hors d'une des portes de Paris" et des postures diverses des Dames qui "prennent le frais," démasquées. Tout Paris y est attiré par "la douceur du temps." C'est sur ce fond "naturel" mais combien valorisant, éclipsant tous les "beaux visages" des figurantes, que se présente Celinde aux yeux éblouis du héros qui accompagne "un Seigneur de marque."

> Entre celles qui paraissaient le plus, il y en avait une qui n'était pas dans un char triomphant, que le blason des armes ou les dorures rendent superbes, mais dans un carosse modeste, qui semblait être celui d'une personne de médiocre condition. (NC, 352)

Le carosse "modeste," indice de vraisemblance et anticipation, sert aussi à mettre en relief les "attraits d'une Demoiselle si charmante," qui ne doivent rien aux signes extérieurs, "les armes" et les dorures." En insistant sur cet "objet si agréable," que même le Seigneur regarde avec "tant de satisfaction," la mise-en-scène atténue ainsi le paradoxe de "l'esprit supérieur" qui se dévouera à une fille de condition—et de caractère—médiocre.

Le deuxième passage est encore plus révélateur. Il s'agit du divertissement champêtre long de huit pages qui ouvre maintenant le récit et précède l'épisode de la rencontre des amants paysans. Dans la première version, Albert trouve Francine endormie à l'ombre proche d'une fontaine (NF, 239-42), lieu privé évoquant la pastourelle mais où le "fils d'un Manant" prend la place du chevalier. Au contraire, publique et spectaculaire, la joute aquatique organisée par des "personnes qualifiées" a toute l'allure d'un roman de chevalerie réécrit dans les salons. Elle fait triompher devant Isabelle, placée "avec les plus belles demoiselles," un jeune inconnu

> qui n'avait point la mine d'un paysan, ayant la taille bien faite, et son corps se maniant de bonne grâce, et qui même avait de longs cheveux frisés et une moustache coordonnée de rubans à la mode de la cour. (NC, 519)

Ce Martial, dont le nom bien choisi sera révélé à la fontaine, ne reçoit "une couronne de fleurs et de soie" que pour la mettre sur la tête d'Isabelle sous les regards admiratifs des spectateurs et "même des "Demoiselles de la plus haute condition," dont les "principaux entretiens . . . étaient sur le bonheur de cette villageoise qui avait acquis un serviteur si adroit et qui avait été couronnée en présence d'une si belle compagnie" (NC, 521). Tout y est dans cette présentation éclatante des héros, "foyer normatif" où la description du corps et de l'habit renforce leur supériorité éthique, esthétique, technologique et communicationnelle, et le regard des personnages qualifiés à juger la confirme.[27] Si la scène améliore la structure narrative et la crédibilité, mettant en place les protagonistes et leurs rivaux—Rustan battu par Martial et la sœur jalouse du triomphe d'Isabelle—"un peu comme dans une tragédie classique" (Béchade, 74), elle sert à dévaloriser davantage les actants éloignés des "bonnes grâces" et de "la mode de la cour". En éveillant l'antagonisme des rustauds dès le début, elle rend aussi moins coupables les héros de les avoir trompés par la suite, comportement équivoque atténué par plusieurs ajouts justificatifs du narrateur (NC, 531, 560, 572, 581, 591). S'ils commentent "la cruauté" de la sœur, "la stupidité" du "rustique Rustan" et les "infortunes" des amants, les devisants apprécient surtout la variété et le "mélange agréable" de la nouvelle de "Philandre." L'accent mis sur ses qualités divertissantes est encore plus marqué dans l'ouverture programmatique de son récit et confirme les tendances que nous avons observées dans la réécriture des nouvelles. Ce n'est plus le narrateur-auteur impérieux qui proclame (je souligne):

> *Je veux maintenant pour mon plaisir* tomber d'une extrémité à l'autre (*mes belles Dames*) & vous raconter les passions qui ont possédé les âmes de quelques *gens de basse qualité*, après vous avoir parlé de celles des personnes *des plus relevées*. *Ce sera pour vous faire connaître* que l'Amour n'est pas comme la foudre qui ne se jette que sur les plus hautes tours mais que ressemblant à la mort, il se met aussi bien dans les *pauvres cabanes des paysans*, que dans les *superbes palais des Monarques*. (NF, 236)

L'agréable Philandre des *Nouvelles choisies* fait partie de la compagnie de conteurs et vise avant tout à plaire à son public. Tout en relevant l'intérêt de son sujet, il ménage une transition entre la bassesse et l'élévation.

> *Ceux qui m'ont précédé ont pris plaisir* à raconter des choses arrivées à des personnes, lesquelles, si elles n'étaient toutes d'une fort haute condition, au moins elles étaient d'une médiocre et fort estimée; maintenant, je crois qu'il ne sera point mal à propos de vous entretenir des choses différentes *pour vous plaire davantage* et de tomber d'une extrémité à l'autre, vous racontant les passions . . . relevées. Ce sera . . . Monarques, *ou dans les maisons magnifiques et commodes des Seigneurs et des riches bourgeois*. (NC, 511-12)

Sa nouvelle sert moins à leur apprendre une vérité qu'ils ignorent[28] qu'à leur fournir un passe-temps agréable: "pour vous plaire davantage" précède "pour vous faire connaître."

Entre les paysans et les monarques, pôles établis par la société mais abolis par l'amour, se situent "les Seigneurs et les riches bourgeois," miroirs des devisants et des lecteurs de 1645. La transformation des nouvelles de 1623 rapproche les personnages extrêmes de cette nouvelle société d'honnêtes gens et c'est à ce milieu qu'appartiennent les personnages des deux nouveaux récits. Les interprétations récentes de ces nouvelles encadrantes divergent: l'une relève une thématique commune, des amours malheureux qui semblent montrer que "les grandes passions se modifient avec le temps et qu'il vaut mieux "accepter sans violence des solutions raisonnables," l'autre insiste sur leurs aspects "plaisants," surtout dans "Les Respects nuisibles," où "le conteur se moque complaisamment de lui-même."[29] Ces impressions diverses s'expliquerait, à mon sens, par les procédés de réécriture mis en œuvre par Sorel. Les deux nouvelles semblent reprendre certains schémas des premières mais en les infléchissant: les caractères ne s'opposent plus par des qualités extrêmes et les obstacles s'estompent. Ainsi, dans "Les Amours hors de saison"—reprise des "Trois Amants"—on peut compatir au malheur des deux rivaux, le très jeune Alexis et le vieillard Gerileon, ridicules mais non odieux, tout en célébrant l'union d'Aminte avec l'honnête Valeran que rend possible un événement assez banal, la générosité du vieillard qui sur son lit de mort constitue son neveu Valeran son héritier. Dans "Les Respects nuisibles," la réécriture déconstruit radicalement les éléments qui structurent l'action des autres nouvelles: aucune différence sociale ne sépare le poète Pamphile et la jeune Caliste (tous deux sont des "bergers" aisés de la ville (!) de "Persepolis" (déguisement transparent), les parents sont favorables, le rival, un personnage anodin, n'apparaît que vers la fin. Ce qui est extraordinaire c'est la longueur de la cour qu'il lui fait—cinq ans—au bout de laquelle il n'a pas encore déclaré son amour, étape franchie dès la première séquence par les héros des *Nouvelles françoises*. Lorsque Pamphile s'enhardit, c'est pour arriver à la cérémonie de fiançailles de Caliste et le rival, à laquelle il réagit curieusement, passant soudain "d'une extrême fâcherie à une extrême joie" (NC, 937). L'intrigue est composée d'événements les plus ordinaires— voyages d'affaires, maladies— et de quiproquos dus à la timidité de l'amant et à l'idée fausse qu'il se fait des "respects" et des "services" que le parfait amour exige. Ce qui rend la nouvelle à la fois comique et sentimentale c'est l'habile emploi de la première personne: si Pamphile narrateur "se moque"

de lui-même, il parvient à faire compatir ses auditeurs aux souffrances—
inutiles—du jeune homme qu'il était. Dans sa dernière nouvelle Sorel
propose donc un nouveau genre de fiction, contestataire sur un autre plan,
que ses devisants ne manquent pas d'apprécier:

> chacun avoua que l'on n'en pouvait entendre de plus naïve; qu'ils n'y
> avait pas des aventures étranges comme il en peut arriver à des per-
> sonnes qui courent le pays, ni de grandes intrigues comme à des Cour-
> tisans raffinés, ni des combats & autres entreprises hardies, comme
> celles des hommes âgés et résolus; mais que c'était de vraies affections
> d'un jeune homme qui n'a pas encore appris toute la malice du monde.
> (NC, 938-39)

La nouvelle instance énonciative prévient également le danger de banalité
que comporte la vie de tous les jours. Lorsque la Princesse interroge
Pamphile sur son passé "Persan," il répond malicieusement en soulevant
des doutes sur sa sincérité: "Vous en croirez ce qu'il vous plaira, Madame,
mais si les contes que je vous ai faits ont été ennuyeux . . . ," à quoi la
Princesse, au nom des auditeurs, répond qu'ils souhaiteraient "toujours être
entretenus si agréablement" (NC, 939-40).

Cependant, si la compagnie imaginée par Sorel finit par préférer des
sujets "naïfs" qui s'opposent non seulement à la littérature à la mode mais à
la "naïveté" telle qu'il la concevait vingt ans auparavant, les lecteurs réels,
qui se passionnaient pour les *Ibrahim* et les *Cassandre* et qui tressaient avec
Montausier l'interminable "guirlande de Julie," n'étaient pas prêts à la
suivre. En effet, Sorel avait déjà tenté la nouvelle expérience en 1642 dans
La Maison des jeux, qui représente de manière bien plus développée une
compagnie d'honnêtes gens se divertissant à jouer des jeux de société et à
raconter des histoires de la vie ordinaire.[30] Il la renouvellera avec
Polyandre (1648) dont on connaît l'échec. *La Maison des jeux* sera rééditée
plusieurs fois avec plusieurs "suites" dans les années cinquante, indice
peut-être d'un changement de goût après la Fronde. Mais *Les Nouvelles
choisies*, qui ne proposent que des histoires, n'auront pas cet avenir. Au
moins ce recueil aura-t-il servi à mieux faire comprendre les valeurs éthiques
et esthétiques qui correspondaient à "l'horizon d'attente" en 1645.

NOTES

1 Selon la définition de Jacques Morel, "Il y a réécriture quand une relation peut se discerner entre un texte donné et un ou plusieurs textes antérieurs, celui ou ceux-ci se trouvant, à des niveaux et selon des proportions variables, repris et transformé(s) dans celui-là." Le critique énumère les différentes formes que peuvent prendre la réécriture "de soi" et celle "d'autrui." Celle-là offre des possibilités diverses: "rééditions corrigées, reprises de thèmes obsédants, de figures de scènes, de personnages impliquant le retour, d'une œuvre à l'autre, d'une problématique singulière . . . ; les arguments, les préfaces, dédicaces et avis au lecteur apparaissent souvent comme autant de réécritures;" ("Réécritures," *Cahiers de littérature du XVIIe siècle* 10 [1988], 176-77).

2 *Les Nouvelles françoises* (privilège daté du 27 janvier 1623) sont publiées à Paris chez Pierre Bilaine. Je revoie à la réimpression de Slatkine (Genève, 1972). Le privilège des *Nouvelles choisies*, délivré "à un parent du sieur des Isles," un des pseudonymes de Sorel, est daté du 29 décembre 1641, mais le recueil ne paraît chez Pierre David qu'en 1645 (en deux volumes, pagination continue). Faut-il en conclure que Sorel eut des difficultés à trouver un éditeur? Les références à ces deux recueils, abréviés NF et NC, paraîtront dans le texte. L'orthographe des citations est modernisée.

3 G. Hainsworth, *Les "Novelas exemplares" de Cervantes en France au XVIIe siècle* (Paris: Champion, 1933). Frédéric Deloffre, *La Nouvelle en France à l'âge classique* (Paris: Didier, 1967). René Godenne, *Histoire de la nouvelle française aux XVIIe et XVIIIe siècles* (Genève: Droz, 1970).

4 Judd Hubert, "Les *Nouvelles françaises* de Sorel et de Segrais," in *Cahiers de l'Association Internationale des Etudes Françaises* 18 (mars 1966), 32-40. R. Arbour, "Langage et Société dans les *Nouvelles françoises* de Charles Sorel," *Revue de l'Université d'Ottawa* 41 (avril-juin 1971), 169-91.

5 Pour un bilan récent de la critique, voir Hervé Béchade. "Les *Nouvelles Choisies* de Charles Sorel sont-elles nouvelles?" in *Langue, Littérature du XVIIe et du XVIIIe siècles. Mélanges offerts à Frédéric Deloffre* (Paris: S.E.D.E.S., 1990), 63-77.

6 René Godenne, "Les débuts de la nouvelle narrée à la première personne (1645-1800)," *Romanische Forschungen* (1971), 253-67. Signalons également: l'interprétation autobiographique de Ralph Baldner, "La jeunesse de Charles Sorel," *Dix-septième siècle*, 40 (1958), 273-81; et les remarques de René Démoris, *Le Roman à la première personne* (Paris: Armand Colin, 1975), 32-33.

7 Gabrielle Verdier, "The Art of the Nouvelle in Early Seventeenth-Century France: Charles Sorel." Diss. Yale, 1976.

8 Daniela Dalla Valle, "A propos des *Nouvelles choisies* de Charles Sorel," in *Ouverture et Dialogue. Mélanges offerts à Wolfgang Leiner à l'occasion de son soixantième anniversaire*, ed. Ulrich Déring, et. al. (Tübingen: Gunter Narr, 1988), 83-92. Hervé Béchade effectue ce qu'il appelle des "sondages" (74) pour mesurer les différences tandis que D. Dalla Valle se propose de signaler "quelques aspects" qui lui semblent particulièrement

importants (84). Elle signale en outre une "tesi di laurea" de Roberto Del Prete sur les deux recueils de Sorel.

[9] Gérard Genette, *Palimpsestes. La Littérature au second degré* (Paris: Seuil, 1982) et *Seuils* (Paris: Seuil, 1988). Philippe Hamon, *Texte et idéologie* (Paris: Presses Universitaires de France, 1984).

[10] Sorel commente le genre de la nouvelle dans *La Maison des jeux* (1642), *La Bibliothèque françoise* (1667) et *De la connoissance des bons livres* (1671). A ce sujet, voir les remarques de Godenne (*Histoire*), Verdier et Dalla Valle.

[11] Verdier, 142-46. A l'exception de la deuxième nouvelle, dans laquelle les amants sont nobles, tous les protagonistes de rang social inférieur attirent l'attention par leur esprit, leur culture et leur intelligence. Mes recherches sur les romans sentimentaux antérieurs aux nouvelles de Sorel (Nervèze, Des Escuteaux, Rosset) ont confirmé que leurs protagonistes sont toujours de bonne naissance et qu'il est rarement question de leurs talents intellectuels. L'opposition que Sorel établit entre les "généreux" à l'esprit supérieur et les "brutaux" trahit sans doute une attitude libertine.

[12] Voir les définitions de G. Genette, *Seuils*, 48-85.

[13] Vantardise bien contraire aux habitudes de la plupart des préfaciers, qui s'efforcent de faire valoir l'œuvre pour l'importance ou l'utilité de son sujet, sans paraître valoriser l'auteur. "Talents" et "génie" sont des mots "tabous" (*Seuils*, 184).

[14] Pour un commentaire de l'iconographie planétaire voir Béchade, 75-76, n. 17.

[15] Cependant, je ne puis partager le jugement de H. Béchade: "Le seul intérêt de ces commentaires est, au fond, technique: ils permettent, en nommant une personne de la compagnie qui a participé au débat, de présenter le narrateur suivant" (67).

[16] Cf. la discussion des titres dans l'article de D. Dalla Valle, 84-5.

[17] L'ordre des *Nouvelles choisies* est le suivant (l'ordre et le titre dans le premier recueil sont indiqués entre parenthèses):

I.		"Les Amours hors de Saison"
II.	(5)	"L'Heureuse recognoissance" ("La Recognoissance d'un fils")
III.	(1)	"La Vertu recompensée" ("Le Pauvre généreux")
IV.	(4)	"Les Divers amans" ("Les Trois amants")
V.	(3)	"La Jalousie cruelle" ("La Sœur jalouse")
VI.	(2)	"Les Mal-Mariez" ("Les Mariages mal-assortis")
VII.		"Les Respects nuisibles"

H. Béchade propose une autre interprétation de la nouvelle ordonnance, 71.

[18] La motivation, une des pratiques hypertextuelles analysées par G. Genette, "consiste à introduire un motif là où l'hypotexte n'en comportait, ou au moins n'en indiquait aucun." (*Palimpsestes*, 372). Les variantes de cette pratique, la "démotivation" (élimination de motifs), et la "transmotivation" (substitution de motifs), se rencontrent aussi dans les *Nouvelles choisies*.

[19] "La valorisation d'un personnage consiste à lui attribuer, par voie de transformation pragmatique ou psychologique, un rôle plus important et/ou plus 'sympathique', dans le

système de valeurs de l'hypertexte, que ne lui accordait l'hypotexte." Outre ce terme positif, la transformation axiologique s'analyse en un terme négatif (dévalorisation) et un état complexe (transvalorisation). *Palimpsestes*, 393.

[20] Selon Philippe Hamon, quatre relations principales semblent constituer "les points d'affleurement privilégiés de l'effet idéologie": "celles qui mettent en scène des relations médiatisées entre des sujets et des objets, entre des sujets et des sujets (il y a, répétons-le, valeur là où il y a norme, et il y a norme là où il y a valeur médiatisée entre actants), c'est-à-dire celles qui consistent en manipulations *d'outils* (l'outil est un médiateur entre un sujet individuel et un objet ou matériau utilitaire), en manipulations de *signes* linguistiques (le langage est médiateur entre un sujet individuel et un autre sujet individuel ou pluriel), en manipulations de *lois* (la loi est médiateur entre un sujet individuel et des sujets collectifs), et en manipulations de *canons* esthétiques (la grille esthétique est médiatrice entre un sujet individuel et des collections de sujets ou d'objets non utilitaires)." *Texte et idéologie*, 24.

[21] D'autres changements renforcent cette transvalorisation: "il s'était rendu des plus savants" (NF, 8) est remplacé par "assez savant" (NC, 209); après la phrase, "Cela l'avait convié à rogner la soutane, & à prendre l'épée pour s'en aller à la guerre qui se faisait en Allemagne" (remplacé par "Hollande," plus actuelle), NC ajoute, "Il y fit de si beaux exploits, qu'encore que l'envie s'opposât à sa fortune, elle ne put nuire à sa réputation" (210); et plus loin, ses termes "infiniment courtois" deviennent "fort courtois" (NC, 216).

[22] Je laisse de côté la modernisation de la langue et les variantes surtout stylistiques, fort bien analysées par H. Béchade, 72.

[23] Catherine Kerbrat-Orrecchioni définit ainsi les "modalisateurs": les "procédés signifiants qui signalent *le degré d'adhésion (forte ou mitigée /incertitude/rejet) du sujet d'énonciation aux contenus énoncés.*" *L'Enonciation de la subjectivité dans le langage* (Paris: Armand Colin, 1980), 118. Mes remarques sur les effets des transformations stylistiques s'inspirent de cette étude.

[24] Pour une analyse détaillée de la "psychologie" des personnages et leur transformation dans *Les Nouvelles choisies*, voir ma thèse, 130-64.

[25] Ils se demandent si Clymene quitterait la patrie qu'elle aime pour suivre Edouard en Angleterre et finissent par tomber d'accord sur une maxime qui doit régler la conduite des femmes: "la [sic] vraie amour fait qu'une femme suit librement un mari en tout lieux où il veut aller" (NC, 806).

[26] Ces termes résument pour H. Béchade les fonctions essentielles de ces nouveaux passages, 73-74.

[27] Le corps et l'habit, le regard et le spectacle constituent des "embrayeurs idéologiques" de première importance, ainsi que la parole du personnage et son commentaire évaluatif (Hamon, 36-9, 109-24).

[28] La leçon telle qu'elle est énoncée par le narrateur-auteur en 1623 semble délibérément prendre le contrepied d'un lieu commun qu'on trouve dans une histoire de Rosset: "[Amour], qui tient de la qualité du foudre brise et met en poudre le sommet des superbes

tours, et dédaigne d'exercer sa violence sur un toit de chaume." *Histoires des Amans volages de ce temps* (1617), 315.

[29] La première est de D. Dalla Valle (87), la seconde de H. Béchade (69-71). "Les Respects" surtout a rendu les critiques perplexes: déjà en 1934 G. Hainsworth avait jugé ce récit sentimental "faux" et "manqué" (137) tandis que R. Baldner y trouvera "un Sorel sentimental et idéaliste," un "Sorel romantique" (279-280).

[30] Voir mon "Fiction as Game: Charles Sorel's *La Maison des jeux* and the Dilemma of the Novel in the Seventeenth Century," *French Literature Series* 11 (1984), 11-22.

12

Certaine thématisation de la liberté dans les Fables de La Fontaine

Marcel Gutwirth

LA LIBERTÉ, CE BIEN GRAND MOT, nul doute qu'il ne s'applique de bien des façons à l'art de La Fontaine. A son art de vivre, pour commencer. Son ingénuité légendaire est une façon d'être lui-même sans qu'on y trouve à redire. Bonhomme, que de servitudes lui sont épargnées! celle de briller en société, par exemple, ou de se mettre à dos les confrères (qui le traitent de haut.) On n'attend de lui que des gaffes, et on ne lui connaît presque que des amis. Tous les milieux lui sont ouverts: de ces Messieurs de Port-Royal aux mécréants du Temple, de la fringante duchesse de Bouillon à la peu recommandée Mme Ulrich, de la grande banque protestante (les d'Hervart) à la maîtresse en titre du souverain, Mme de Montespan. S'il se tient à distance respectueuse du maître, il n'en est pas moins personnellement gratifié par son petit-fils, le jeune duc de Bourgogne—et sa liberté ne s'en porte pas plus mal de n'avoir pas à avaler les couleuvres que réserve la vie de cour à un homme de lettres. Quant à ses protecteurs, il se les choisit peu encombrants: Nicolas Fouquet est un parfait homme du monde, Mme de La Sablière une femme de cœur et d'esprit, les d'Hervart sont tout à la dévotion du poète vieillissant. La gloire même, celle qui lui vaut, sur le tard il est vrai, un fauteuil à l'Académie, n'entame guère son indépendance. N'écrit-il pas à son propos, dans une lettre à l'ambassadeur Bonrepaux:

> Quarante beaux esprits certifieront ceci.
> Nous sommes tout autant, qui dormons comme d'autres
> Aux ouvrages d'autrui, quelquefois même aux nôtres. (*OD* 663)

Nous n'avons donc aucun lieu d'être surpris de le retrouver étonnamment libre au sein de son œuvre. Libre de ton, la gaillardise allant jusqu'à l'obscénité des *Contes* s'en porte garante. Quant au choix de ce genre dérivé de Boccace et respirant la joyeuseté gauloise pour s'imposer à un public féru de bienséance, est-ce bien la marque d'un esprit voué au qu'en dira-t-on? S'il paraît hésiter sur le choix du vers libre ou d'une versification délibérément archaïsante mais régulière, il n'en use pas moins à sa guise de la liberté du premier, se réservant d'utiliser le second à chaque fois que le sujet s'y prête. Et s'il soumet ses fables à la censure de l'austère Patru, c'est pour n'en faire qu'à sa tête, quitte à revêtir la nudité antique que ce dernier préconisait de toutes les grâces d'un art qui module du clin d'œil complice à l'apitoiement, de la taquinerie à la véhémence, de la fine plaisanterie au pathétique appuyé. Le choix de la fable, ce genre (dixit Giraudoux) revêche et grognon, ne surprend pas moins que celui du conte chez un poète qui dès l'Avertissement d'*Adonis* annonce son ambition de faire beau et de faire grand:[1] ne témoigne-t-il pas en soi d'une belle indépendance à l'égard de la hiérarchie des genres? N'était-ce pas, d'autre part, se frayer une voie à l'écart qui devait le laisser libre d'adopter tous les tons, de parler de tous sujets, de manier tour à tour le madrigal et l'épigramme, de faire impunément son procès à l'ordre du monde? Et si ce n'est assez de dénoncer la rapacité, la vilénie, la suffisance et l'injustice des grands de la terre, ne se mêlera-t-il pas de dire son fait à la pensée avancée de son temps, de demander des comptes au grand Descartes sur les inepties que l'esprit de système lui a fait proférer sur le compte des animaux?

Enfin ne s'est-il pas donné licence, en dehors de la fable, de chanter tour à tour continence et volupté? les amours de Vénus et la chasteté de Saint Malc? la paillardise de ses Cordeliers, la lubricité de ses nonnains, et la touchante conjugalité de Philémon et Baucis? "Un même encrier, écrit Giraudoux, a tout fourni"[2] et jusqu'à l'audacieuse entreprise de réduire en vers la louange d'un fébrifuge, de composer un poème à la gloire du quinquina. Est-il besoin d'insister? La Fontaine, dans la fable, s'est créé un domaine aux dimensions de l'univers. Tel qu'il est, le poète qui inlassablement chante son humeur inquiète et qui inscrira au fronton de son œuvre: "diversité est ma devise" s'y sentira à l'étroit. De Platon à Epicure, d'Homère à Malherbe, de Rabelais à Baruch son esprit vagabonde, et s'il se donne bien des maîtres (maître Clément, maître François, maître Vincent) il ne se plie à l'autorité de pas un. Bref, ce casanier qui n'aura jamais rien vu au monde de plus distant que Limoges et qui se dit ennemi de l'humeur voyageuse circule on ne saurait plus librement à travers tons, climats, modes, époques et genres, tout au long d'une œuvre qui ne se reconnaît d'entraves que celles que lui dicte le goût le plus délié appuyé sur un sens exquis de la mesure.

Il est donc dans l'ordre que nous tombions, en tête du premier recueil des *Fables choisies mises en vers par M. de La Fontaine*, dès la fable v, *Le Loup et le Chien*, sur l'apologie de la liberté sous sa forme politique la plus fruste. A la fable cinq? Il est à noter que les quatre premières, mettant en jeu l'imprévoyance, la vanité, la sotte démesure, la gloriole punies— cigale, corbeau, grenouille et mulet en faisant les frais respectivement—ne font que taper sur les doigts de nos manquements de moindre envergure. La fable n'entre en matière que précautionneusement: les grands sujets demandent quelques préalables. Et à cinq fables de là veille *Le Loup et l'Agneau* (I, x), où s'énonce la grande loi du monde.

Lupus ad Canem, la fable III, vii de Phèdre, porte un sous-titre qui livre en clair le thème de cette rencontre: *De Arminio et fratre Flavo*. Il s'agirait de la confrontation de ce célèbre Arminius, qui infligea au légat Varus une défaite ignominieuse dans les forêts d'Outre-Rhin ("Varus, répétait Auguste vieillissant, rends-moi mes légions!") et de son frère Flave, qui avait accepté de vivre, pensionné par Rome, dans l'aisance et le déshonneur. Luxe de précision, au vers premier la fable annonce:

> Quam dulcis sit libertas breviter proloquar.

Nous sommes en l'an 16 de notre ère, vraisemblablement.[3] L'Empire en est à son premier demi-siècle et déjà ce sont les Germains qui se voient chargés d'incarner, en prose et en vers, les vertus que les Romains autrefois prê- taient à leur propre République: une âme éprise de liberté dans un corps endurci au manque. Le vieux postulat primitiviste formulé par A. O. Lovejoy et remontant, à tout le moins, à Hérodote est encore pleinement en vigueur: il ne fait pas bon se frotter à ceux qui vivent de peu et n'ont rien à perdre (c'est l'avis que ne prit pas le Lydien Crésus, en déclarant la guerre qu'il perdit contre la Perse rocailleuse de Cyrus et ses hommes revêtant braies de cuir.)[4] Quant à l'amour de la liberté chez ces êtres intraitables la réponse, rapportée par Hérodote, des envoyés de Sparte au satrape qui, se citant en exemple de bons services amplement récompensés, les engageait à rechercher l'amitié de son roi plutôt que de lui résister, dit bien tout ce qu'il faut en dire:

Hydarnès, le conseil que tu nous adresses n'est pas d'un homme qui ait de ceci et de cela une égale connaissance . . . tu sais ce qu'est la sujétion, tu n'as pas encore goûté à la liberté, tu ignores si elle est douce ou non. Si tu y avais goûté, ce n'est pas avec des lances que tu nous conseillerais de combattre pour elle, c'est même avec des haches. (VII, 135)

Du chien au loup il y a en effet cette différence: l'un est la forme aguerrie, mais sauvage, de l'autre. Bien repu, au chaud dans la niche, le chien respire la bonne conscience de qui en s'acquittant de ses devoirs s'emploie à mériter son salaire. Phèdre expédie le contraste en moins de deux vers:

Cani perpasto macie confectus lupus
forte occucurit.

La Fontaine le développe amoureusement:

Un loup n'avait que les os et la peau,
    Tant les chiens faisaient bonne garde.
Ce loup rencontre un dogue aussi puissant que beau,
Gras, poli, qui s'était fourvoyé par mégarde.

Ce loup n'est si efflanqué que parce que ses congénères chiens le tiennent à distance de ce qui lui serait repas. L'état sauvage n'est pas seulement un fait de nature: vivant de rapine l'insoumis est tenu à l'œil par les forces de l'ordre. Tout est donc proie à ses yeux, et ce dogue que le hasard lui envoie rayonne pour cet affamé d'une santé toute comestible.

L'attaquer, le mettre en quartiers,
Sire loup l'eut fait volontiers.

La pensée est rapide comme l'éclair. Peu cartésien, ce loup connaît, tout loup qu'il est, une impulsion *qu'il réprime.*

Mais il fallait livrer bataille;
Et le mâtin était de taille
A se défendre hardiment.
Le loup donc l'aborde humblement,

> Entre en propos, et lui fait compliment
> Sur son embonpoint qu'il admire.

Second thoughts are best! Nous n'en sommes qu'au vers deux chez Phèdre:

> Dein salutati invicem
> ut restiterunt: "unde sic quaeso nites?"

Sans arrière-pensée mauvaise ils s'arrêtent pour échanger le bonjour, et le loup aussitôt interroge: D'où vient que tu brilles ainsi (de santé)? L'égalité règne entre eux, et une certaine bonhomie. Sire loup, lui, se met en frais de compliment, comme pour compenser ce qui s'est passé dans son for intérieur. Il est humble, ce mauvais garçon qui sait comment on parle à Monsieur l'agent. L'autre se rengorge:

> "Il ne tiendra qu'à vous, beau sire,
> D'être aussi gras que moi . . .

Et de lui prodiguer des avis qui sont autant de sentences lancées à la tête de qui n'a pas le bon esprit de faire tout comme lui-même:

> Quittez les bois, vous ferez bien:
> Vos pareils y sont misérables,
> Cancres, hères, et pauvres diables,
> Dont la condition est de mourir de faim.

Voilà le grand mot lâché, avec tout le mépris du tant soit peu nanti pour celui qui vit dans le manque. On en vient à regretter la belle simplicité du chien de Phèdre:

> Canis simpliciter: "Eadem est condicio tibi,
> praestare domino si par officium potes.

Il parle en agence d'emploi, sans poser de grand préalable, sans exhaler d'inutile rancœur.

Incité à la complaisance par la mine respectueuse de son confrère démuni, le chien de La Fontaine, lui, étale sans pudeur la mentalité de son emploi, la mentalité policière. Tout y est: le ton brusque et jovial, l'assurance d'être dans le vrai, la sommation à autrui de changer de vie. Ce chien est bien ce que l'on peut appeler un représentant de l'ordre. Que faire pour être comme lui?

> —Presque rien, dit le chien, donner la chasse aux gens
> Portants bâtons et mendiants;
> Flatter ceux du logis, à son maître complaire.

C'est le programme de la parfaite domesticité, fait à parties égales de rudesse et d'obséquiosité. Houspiller le faible, ramper devant le fort résume en deux points tout l'emploi du bas étage de la société. Promotion certaine pour qui sinon mourrait de faim. Le loup ne sourcille donc aucunement, lui musclé et qui ne sait trop ce que c'est que *flatter*.

A l'énoncé du salaire—os de poulets, os de pigeons: nous sommes loin du *restant des sauces dont personne ne veut plus* que prodigue le chien de Phèdre—sans parler des caresses,

> Le loup déjà se forge une félicité
> Qui le fait pleurer de tendresse.

Ce n'est pas le bien-être seulement que son interlocuteur s'entend à évoquer devant ce meurt-la-faim, c'est le bonheur. Plus éloquent que le satrape Hydarnès, il fait tout ce qu'il faut pour séduire celui qui d'ailleurs ne demande pas mieux que d'échanger sa condition précaire pour un mode de vie plus assuré.

Reste l'écot à payer. La Fontaine encore une fois étire délicieusement la réticence du chien, l'insistance du loup dans l'affaire du collier. Le chien de Phèdre ne se fait prier qu'à une seule reprise:

> "Unde hoc, amice?" "Nihil est." "Dic sodes tamen."
> "Quia videor acer, alligant me interdiu . . ."

et il détourne maladroitement la conversation sur les avantages de sa condition entravée. L'enjeu, chez La Fontaine—chaîne, entrave, collier—ressort d'autant mieux, martelé en trois syllabes, que la gêne du chien, éveillant la suspicion, la met bien en évidence:

> "Qu'est-ce là? lui dit-il. —Rien. —Quoi rien? —Peu de chose.
> —Mais encor? —Le collier dont je suis attaché

De ce que vous voyez est peut-être la cause.
—ATTACHÉ? dit le loup . . .

La syntaxe embarrassée (dont je . . . de ce que . . .), l'inversion, l'adverbe
de mitigation témoignent d'un louable effort de réticence. Rien n'y fait, le
collier absent brille, pris dans les feux d'un participe ignoble. La rançon de
cette idylle domestique c'est le régime de la chaîne, la domestication. Le mot
de liberté n'est jamais prononcé dans la version de La Fontaine. Il aura suffi
de la marque creusée par son contraire pour que cette vérité éclate: être
libre, c'est, pour courir où bon vous semble, renoncer à ce qui pèse et à ce
qui lie. Infiniment allégé, *maître loup s'enfuit, et court encor*.

La liberté du loup est donc une liberté en marge du social et de son
trésor de pacotille—le bonheur des assis. C'est un peu la liberté que Jean-
Jacques fera miroiter aux yeux de son siècle, et c'est même, par une de ces
contradictions dont il avait le secret, ce qu'il trouve à lui reprocher, au livre
II de l'*Emile*:

> Je n'oublierai jamais d'avoir vu beaucoup pleurer une petite fille qu'on
> avait désolée avec cette fable, tout en lui prêchant toujours la docilité.
> On eut peine à savoir la cause de ses pleurs; on la sut enfin. La pauvre
> enfant s'ennuyait d'être à la chaîne, elle se sentait le cou pelé; elle
> pleurait de n'être pas loup.[5]

Etre loup ne se réduit pas tout bonnement à secouer le servage par
un acte de défi interdit à l'enfant bien élevée, mais que chantera la muse
romantique. Le fait d'Arminius nous rappelle qu'il s'agit là d'une image de
la liberté avant tout politique. La condition famélique est celle de qui prise
plus haut son indépendance que la captivité dorée d'une cour.[6] Elle est aussi
le fait de ceux qui n'hésiteront pas au sacrifice de tous leurs biens pour
mettre en échec une grande puissance résolue à les asservir, tels les Hollan-
dais rompant leurs digues lors de l'avance des armées de Louis XIV à
quelques années de là. Si l'image du loup efflanqué colle mal à l'opulente
république batave, souvenons-nous que c'est au bout de près d'un siècle
de combats, au cours d'une guerre d'indépendance menée victorieusement
contre la plus grande puissance de l'Europe, l'Espagne de Philippe II, que
les Provinces Unies ont conquis leur enviable et proberbiale opulence—et
que c'est en *gueux de la mer* qu'ils le firent.

Quant au loup de la fable cinq, qui filait doux devant un dogue, à
cinq fables de là nous le retrouvons confronté à l'agneau, dans son rôle le

plus mémorable. Phèdre avait accordé à cette fable les honneurs de la première place, celle de la fable d'ouverture de son tout premier livre. *La raison du plus fort*, en tête de celle de La Fontaine, tient lieu de morale—morale qui se concilie malaisément avec la course éperdue à la liberté à laquelle aboutissait la rencontre de la fable cinq. Honneur tout d'abord à la *diversité* hautement revendiquée par le poète comme présidant à son inspiration. Le loup qui incarne une des plus chères de nos aspirations se métamorphose en un tournemain, en une figure inoubliable de l'Injustice, la fourbe parlementant avec l'innocence aux abois pour se donner bonne conscience dans le crime. Mais sont-ils si différents l'un de l'autre, ces deux êtres de violence? L'âpre liberté qui ne se plie pas au joug d'une existence réglée, à la renonciation instinctuelle que Freud met au cœur du processus civilisé, ne se porte pas garante d'un comportement respectueux du prochain. Madame Roland a peut-être eu tort de s'étonner que le fanatisme de la liberté engendrât le crime. Parmi les instincts qu'il nous démange de mettre en liberté, l'injustice n'est pas le moindre.

Quoi qu'il en soit, et sans se cacher que la liberté peut être mise à des fins déplorables, convenons que l'art de La Fontaine aura tôt mis en lumière une modalité de la liberté politique, la plus fruste il est vrai, celle qui dit: pour être libre il faut savoir renoncer à l'aisance, rester sur le qui-vive, ne pas se laisser allécher par la pâtée. La liberté de hors-la-loi en un mot, chère au cœur de tout réfractaire à l'ordre établi. Ce n'est pas la seule que les *Fables* nous proposent, nous le verrons par la suite, et c'est vers l'alternative à ce régime de fer instituée par le poète que notre sujet nous conduit.

Une fable se rencontre sur notre chemin qui, de la liberté, nous présente une face tout autre. Il s'agit, au livre VIII, de la fable xvi, *L'Horoscope*. La liberté dont il est traité ici est au premier chef celle qui préoccupe théologiens et philosophes. Elle se dénomme libre arbitre. Ce n'est pas la première fois que La Fontaine s'en prend à ceux qui en font trop bon marché, aux diseurs de bonne aventure, aux tireurs d'horoscopes. Au livre II la fable *treize* met en cause *L'Astrologue qui se laisse tomber dans un puits*. Au livre VII la fable xv, *Les Devineresses*, témoigne de la persistance d'une rancœur, presque d'une hantise. Odette de Mourgues a beau dire,[7] La Fontaine au sein des fables laisse pressentir de loin en loin une prévention, une préférence: il se méfie de la mer et des voyages, l'avarice l'horripile, l'astrologie aussi, et il ne porte dans son cœur ni le maître d'école ni les garnements dont il a la charge.

Y a-t-il lieu de chercher un commun dénominateur à ces trois domaines bénéficiant d'une forme appuyée de la réprobation: la thésaurisation, la mantique, la pédanterie? Je le situerais, quant à moi, dans l'avarice. Le bien, au sens le plus uniment matériel, elle le convertit en un mal, s'en privant, elle-même et les autres. Passion aberrante s'il en fût, elle réussit ce tour de force, de résorber la richesse en manque. La plus corrosive des illusions, elle porte atteinte à l'économie dans son essence même, qui est la circulation des biens. Elle bloque le mouvement, c'est-à-dire la vie—comme le démontre si lumineusement Panurge dans son apologie bien connue de la dette. Or ce blocage de l'*avoir*, le devin et le pédant s'y livrent tour à tour sur le *savoir*, l'un en pré-occupant les esprits d'une connaissance illusoire, l'autre en vidant la science de son suc, ne nous en livrant que l'enveloppe. Détournement de la parole au profit d'un sens ou factice ou parodique, ils s'opposent directement à l'usage que compte en faire la poésie. Le pédant gâte le vrai, le devin impose le faux. Le poète, qui cherche à nous livrer de la vérité une figure, le fabuliste qui la frappe au coin d'une maxime, ne sauraient pactiser avec ces voleurs de langue. Quant aux écoliers soumis à si mauvaise école, quoi d'étonnant s'ils en sortent gâtés?

Pour en revenir à la fable II, xiii, La Fontaine s'amuse à y faire tenir l'apologue entier dans une seule phrase, répartie sur moins de deux vers:

> Un astrologue un jour se laissa choir
> Au fond d'un puits.

Etourderie, inadvertance, *se laissa choir* n'implique pas même l'accident ou l'erreur par la voie active, comme dans *buta* ou *tomba*. La chute est aussi roide que celle d'une pierre, et aussi involontaire. Pur esprit scrutant les hauteurs, il est pur corps soumis aux forces qu'il méconnaît. L'anecdote se conte aux dépens de Thalès, Esope nous en livre une version, mais là c'est du savant distrait—de l'astro*nome*—qu'il s'agit. La morale tient en deux vers elle aussi:

> On lui dit: "Pauvre bête,
> Tandis qu'à peine à tes pieds tu peux voir,
> Penses-tu lire au-dessus de ta tête?"

A cette brièveté qui en remontre à Esope et semble narguer Patru, La Fontaine remédie par un discours en règle, qui en quelque quarante vers réduit à néant les présupposés d'une soi-disant science de la divination. Hasard ou Providence, l'ordre du monde nous échappe: l'un est incalculable, l'autre pour notre bien est soustrait à notre connaissance. Inscrire une prévision assurée des choses à venir dans la configuration des planètes reviendrait à nous ôter nos raisons de vivre: biens rendus insipides, maux connus inévitables. Telle science jurerait avec l'idée même de Providence. La régularité du cours des astres, par ailleurs, est sans commune mesure avec les à-coups, les volte-face, les accidents dont est faite la trame de notre existence. La divination parvient ainsi à être ou impossible ou impensable, et de surplus impraticable . . .

A ce bel ensemble s'ajoute une contrainte: la soumission à la mode. La fable VII, xv, *Les Devineresses*, envisage en effet la question sous l'angle de la sociologie—avant la lettre, s'entend. La foi prêtée à un quelconque déterminisme est à son tour déterminée. L'engouement pour une tireuse de cartes, ne reposant sur rien, se nourrit de sa propre substance, qui est illusion collective, volonté collective d'illusion. Ainsi donc,

> Une femme à Paris faisait la pythonisse.
> On l'allait consulter sur chaque événement:
> Perdait-on un chiffon, avait-on un amant,
> Un mari vivant trop, au gré de son épouse,
> Une mère fâcheuse, une femme jalouse,
>   Chez la devineuse on courait,
> Pour se faire annoncer ce que l'on désirait.

L'ombre de l'Affaire des poisons plane sur cette énumération, mais ce qui surnage, c'est la volonté de s'en faire accroire: toute vogue part de là. Pour aboutir à quoi?

>   Son fait consistait en adresse;
> Quelques termes de l'art, beaucoup de hardiesse,
> Du hasard quelquefois, tout cela concourait:
> Tout cela bien souvent faisait crier au miracle.
> Enfin quoiqu'ignorante à vingt et trois carats,
>   Elle passait pour un oracle.

Miracle rimant à *oracle*, nous y voici. L'anatomie d'une consécration est consommée. Tellement grand est notre besoin de croire à un pouvoir que nous n'avons pas qu'il suffit d'un brin de mise en scène pour nous faire agenouiller. Or mise en scène suppose une scène justement, un lieu consa-cré. De l'oracle au lieu du culte il n'y a qu'un pas; ce pas franchi, l'antre tiendra lieu d'oracle. La mystification désormais fonctionne à vide. En effet,

L'oracle était logé dedans un galetas.
  Là cette femme emplit sa bourse,
  Et sans avoir d'autre ressource,
Gagne de quoi donner un rang à son mari.
Elle achète un office, une maison aussi.
  Voilà le galetas rempli
D'une nouvelle hôtesse, à qui toute la ville,
Femmes, filles, valets, gros messieurs, tout enfin
Allait comme autrefois demander son destin:
Le galetas devint l'antre de la Sibylle.

Physiologie—au sens où l'entendait Honoré de Balzac—d'une ascension sociale, l'*upward mobility* sous le règne du Roi soleil, s'accomplissant par la grâce d'un phénomène d'hallucination collective. Transfert, pourrait-on dire, métonymique du contenu au contenant, de l'oracle à l'antre, faisant tout bonnement litière des ressources d'art et d'industrie qui, la chance aidant, avaient donné quelque justification à la vogue. Plus la chose est illusoire, mieux l'illusion réussit. Il y aurait lieu d'épiloguer—un philosophe du siècle à venir ne s'en fût pas privé—sur les rapports de l'illusionisme et du sacré. La fable se contente de documenter la lubie, de la parer d'un grain de vraisemblance:

  Le meuble, et l'équipage aidaient fort à la chose:
  Quatre sièges boiteux, un manche de balai;
  Tout sentait son sabbat et sa métamorphose.
    Quand cette femme aurait dit vrai
    Dans une chambre tapissée,
  On s'en serait moqué . . .

Allez donc nous parler de *science*, dans ces conditions! Le décor suffit, et l'inextinguible besoin de croire.
    Cela étant dit, on a la surprise de lire au livre VIII la fable xvi intitulée bravement *L'Horoscope*. Cette fable est à vrai dire un conte de fées, du type de *La Belle au bois dormant*, bien qu'elle ait son répondant exact chez Esope. Hérodote déjà relatait, lui le grand maître du folklore de son temps, l'aventure du roi Crésus averti en rêve de la fin prochaine de son fils Atys, et qui s'entremit en vain pour éviter le coup prévu (I, 34-45). C'est le schéma du parricide d'Œdipe, pareillement celui de St. Julien. Bref, la donnée est folklorique, et elle repose sur la véracité inébranlable d'une

prédiction funeste. Le message est livré en clair, et il se révèle incontournable. Dans chaque cas il frappe un père dans ce qu'il a de plus cher, son enfant trop aimé(e). Dans chaque cas l'excès de précaution se retourne contre son auteur, l'enfant meurt, ou tue, ou dort un siècle durant, consacrant l'existence d'une fatalité, le bien-fondé d'un horoscope.

> On rencontre sa destinée
> Souvent par des chemins qu'on prend pour l'éviter.

La morale est tirée d'avance, et elle ne détonne pas au sein de la sagesse fablière. Pour éviter un mal on en tombe dans un pire . . . ou tout simplement on retombe à pic sur celui auquel on se faisait fort d'échapper. Priver son fils d'une occupation qui fait tout le bonheur de son âge et de sa classe, le priver d'aller à la chasse pour empêcher qu'il ne tombe sous la griffe d'un lion, c'est l'inviter à frapper de rage sur un lion en peinture, quitte à se blesser à mort sur un clou que le tableau recouvrait. Là-dessus d'enfiler en guise de confirmation l'anecdote la plus rebattue et la moins sérieusement fiable:

> Même précaution nuisit au poëte Eschyle.
>> Quelque devin le menaça, dit-on,
>> De la chute d'une maison.
>> Aussitôt il quitta la ville,
> Mit son lit en plein champ, loin des toits, sous les cieux.
> Un aigle qui portait en l'air une tortue
> Passa par là, vit l'homme, et sur sa tête nue,
> Qui parut un morceau de rocher à ses yeux,
>> Etant de cheveux dépourvue,
> Laissa tomber sa proie, afin de la casser:
> Le pauvre Eschyle ainsi sut ses jours avancer.

Le malicieux La Fontaine, quant à lui, sut par là sa cause avancer, passant du conte folklrique à la plus cocassement invraisemblable des légendes, dont il aura fait mine d'étoffer sa démonstration. Trois vers débités sur le même ton sentencieux, et il dévoile enfin ses batteries:

> De ces exemples il résulte
> Que cet art, s'il est vrai, fait tomber dans les maux

> Que craint celui qui le consulte.
> Mais je l'en justifie, et maintiens qu'il est faux.

Coup de théâtre, et coup double si l'on ose dire. Le libre arbitre, pour commencer, est remis à l'honneur au détour d'une fable qui feignait d'en prendre le deuil.

> Je ne crois point que la nature
> Se soit lié les mains, et nous les lie encor,
> Jusqu'au point de marquer dans les cieux notre sort.

C'est le temps d'une contre-offensive philosophique, reprenant où la fable de l'astrologue en était restée, alignant les défaillances logiques d'un système ne reposant sur rien. Tout au plus, nous enseigne le galetas de la devineresse, sur l'engouement qui le provoque.

> Il [notre sort] dépend d'une conjoncture
> De lieux, de personnes, de temps,
> Non des conjonctions de tous ces charlatans.
> Ce berger et ce roi sont sous même planète;
> L'un d'eux porte le sceptre et l'autre la houlette:
> Jupiter le voulait ainsi.
> Qu'est-ce que Jupiter? Un corps sans connaissance.
> D'où vient donc que son influence
> Agit différemment sur ces deux hommes-ci?
> Puis comment pénétrer jusques à notre monde?
> Percer Mars, le soleil, et des vides sans fin?
> Un atome la peut détourner en chemin . . .

Les paralogismes, les faux calculs abondent. Celui des déterminations multiples et contradictoires pour commencer; celui aussi des incalculables distances. A même horoscope, sorts tout divers—et comment prêter à l'inanimé volonté, discernement, vue d'ensemble? La liberté humaine est sauve dans ce naufrage d'une doctrine qui ne dogmatise si bien que parce qu'elle invente.

Mais si le libre arbitre en réchappe, s'il lui est donné de faire la nique aux promoteurs de fatalité, que dire de la souveraine liberté du poète s'exerçant ici à l'encontre d'une loi autrement contraignante, celle qui préside à son art? La fable, écrit Théon, est vérité sous figure de mensonge.[8] Il est peu d'exemples aussi flagrants de la liberté que La Fontaine se donne de conduire où il veut l'apologue qu'il remanie que cet abrupt désistement, à même la morale, à l'égard de la trame qu'il a mise sur le métier. Taxée de mensonge sur le plan de la morale que l'on en peut tirer, la fable se retrouve *fable* au sens injurieux qui la convertit en épithète. Elle n'était que prétexte à une morale tout autre, celle du peu de foi à ajouter aux fables qui se donnent pour mathématiquement vraies. A la manière de ces montures dont parle Montaigne au chapitre *Des destries* (I, 48) et que les Romains appelaient DESULTORES, La Fontaine, par une manœuvre qui remplit de point en point le sens de l'adjectif anglais *desultory*, a sauté d'une fable à l'autre.

Or le poète qui, s'érigeant en défenseur du libre arbitre, s'arrange pour témoigner ainsi à l'égard de son art d'une toute souveraine désinvolture, se doit certes de revisiter la liberté politique—liberté par excellence—pour en remettre à jour les données et en parfaire le modèle. La fable du Chien et du Loup avait posé la liberté en partage exclusif de l'*outsider*, relégué par son choix d'une vie nécessiteuse et indifférente au besoin en marge du social et de ses servitudes. Ces dernières sont compensées, plus ou moins généreusement, mais il n'en a cure. *Tout à la pointe de l'épée* est une nécessité dont il fait vertu.

Cela est bel et bien, mais n'en arrive-t-on pas par là à faire son deuil de la liberté dès lors qu'on aura renoncé à la vie des bois, et qu'on aura pris rang dans l'état qui se dit le plus policé de l'Europe, sous le règne du plus glorieux, du plus éclairé des monarques?

A la fable quatorze (justement) du livre VIII, *Les Obsèques de la Lionne*, La Fontaine nous livre, me semble-t-il, la recette d'une liberté compatible avec un régime conférant au chef de l'état un pouvoir absolu de droit divin. Comment mieux représenter ce pouvoir que sous la fauve crinière du lion? Quel milieu en répercute plus puissamment le caractère absolu que celui d'une cour, où s'amplifie le moindre courant émanant de la personne royale? Comment mieux décrire ce que le cérémonial a d'irrésistiblement despotique, pliant tous ces corps à la mimique d'une douleur rien moins que ressentie, sinon par un deuil de cérémonie? C'est dans ce cadre peu prometteur que la fable s'installe.

> La femme du lion mourut:
> Aussitôt chacun accourut
> Pour s'acquitter envers le prince
> De certains compliments de consolation,
> Qui sont surcroît d'affliction.

Les servitudes du pouvoir ne sont pas pour les autres seulement. Qui mieux que Louis XIV éprouva jusqu'à l'heure de sa mort la discipline de fer d'une existence en représentation permanente, dont les peines les plus intimes devaient se jouer en plein théâtre? Ordonner tous les jours dans son moindre détail un cérémonial immuable, statuer sur le tabouret d'une duchesse ou le placement d'un flambeau, telle la partie à ses yeux non la moindre de son devoir de monarque. Ainsi donc,

> Il fit avertir la province
> Que les obsèques se feraient
> Un tel jour, en tel lieu: ses prévôts y seraient
> Pour régler la cérémonie
> Et pour placer la compagnie.
> Jugez si chacun s'y trouva.

Ce que Saint-Simon appelle la mécanique de Versailles est montée, les moindres rouages mis en place, qui n'auraient garde de manquer à l'appel. Ne sont-ils pas, dans la malicieuse définition de la cour qui suit, qualifiés de *simples ressorts*, le fabuliste faisant pièce simultanément à la veulerie courtisane et à l'arrogance cartésienne, qui définit de la sorte à moins juste titre les animaux?

> Le prince aux cris s'abandonna,
> Et tout son antre en résonna.
> Les lions n'ont point d'autre temple.
> On entendit à son exemple
> Rugir en leur patois messieurs les courtisans.

Et ici de placer de la cour une définition célèbre: "peuple caméléon, peuple singe du maître." Modulant de l'antre au temple pour désigner un Louvre, la fable joue supérieurement sur les deux tableaux, rejoignant la férocité de la bête à la hantise solaire, à l'auto-idolâtrie de l'homme Louis. Quant à ses courtisans, "Tristes, gais, prêts à tout, à tout indifférents," nul trait de satire mieux que ce constat de leur parfaite anomie ne saurait nous les immobiliser dans un tableau plus révélateur. Et c'est sur cet arrière-plan de tranche de vie monarchique que se détache l'exemple du Cerf, cet éternel solitaire du monde de la fable. Réfugié dans une étable, à la fable IV, xxi, *L'Œil du maître*, il ne tranche pas plus malencontreusement sur l'aspect de ses hôtes bovins qu'il ne se détache sur ce fond d'obséquiosité courtisanesque, à ne jouer pas le jeu qui s'y impose.

> Pour revenir à notre affaire,
> Le cerf ne pleura point; comment eût-il pu faire?
> Cette mort le vengeait; la reine avait jadis
> Etranglé sa femme et son fils.
> Bref il ne pleura point. Un flatteur l'alla dire,
> Et soutint qu'il l'avait vu rire.

La simple dignité humaine n'est pas de mise dans une cour. Elle porte atteinte à la dignité prétendue qui seule y a place. Elle accuse sans mot dire l'universelle simagrée, ce qui est bien la moins pardonnable des offenses. Ne nous étonnons donc point que le flatteur en rajoute, d'autant que nous sommes en pays de mauvais services à outrance. Et ne suffit-il pas d'un coup de pouce pour faire passer de la simple déréliction au crime pendable? Qui ne flatte point, après tout, met un flatteur à deux doigts du mépris de soi-même.

> "Tel le rugissement du lion, la colère du roi!" (*Prov.* 20:2)

L'Ecriture sainte se met de la partie, amalgamant par avance fauve et souverain sous le signe de la colère, comme pour gloser la scène développée par la fable.

> Mais ce cerf n'avait pas accoutumé de lire.

Autre façon de tourner le dos à la chose, autre marque de sa coupable indifférence. Le style empesé de la sortie du royal félin, tout en inversions solennelles, en antépositions inusitées, en périphrases de commande, n'en paraîtra que plus dérisoire dans son outrance:

> Le monarque lui dit: "Chétif hôte des bois,
> Tu ris, tu ne suis pas ces gémissantes voix.
> Nous n'appliquerons point sur tes membres profanes
> Nos sacrés ongles. . . ."

C'est le prendre de bien haut, mais aussi n'est-il pas lion? Chez tout autre ce discours serait franchement grotesque. On songe à M. de Charlus alléguant ses augustes orteils . . .

Le coupable, sans se démonter, sans non plus rien nier, écarte de sang-froid la menace, renversant la situation par la mémorable invocation d'une leæna ex machina:

> Le cerf reprit alors: "Sire, le temps des pleurs
> Est passé; la douleur est ici superflue."

On ne saurait trop s'émerveiller devant ce ton de calme réprimande. La gueule du fauve, immobilisée en plein rugissement, en a dû se refermer de stupéfaction.

> Votre digne moitié, couchée entre des fleurs,
>   Tout près d'ici m'est apparue,
>   Et je l'ai d'abord reconnue.
> "Ami, m'a-t-elle dit, garde que ce convoi,
> "Quand je vais chez les dieux, ne t'oblige à des larmes.
> "Aux champs Elysiens j'ai goûté mille charmes,
> "Conversant avec ceux qui sont saints comme moi.
> "Laisse agir quelque temps le désespoir du roi.
> "J'y prends plaisir."

Ne voilà-t-il pas un fabulateur de grande volée! Il n'est que de juxtaposer, pour s'en rendre compte, le récit tout nu de cette fabuleuse rencontre chez Abstémius (tel que nous le rappelle en note Régnier):[9]

> Advenienti . . . mihi felix ejus anima ad elysias sedes proficiscens apparuit, dicens ejus discessum non lugendum, quum animam ad amoena vireta fortunatorum nemorum sedesque beatas proficisceretur.

Le cerf de La Fontaine, lui, sait parler à un roi: *couchée entre des fleurs*: à cérémonial, cérémonial et demi. Et pour bien marquer sa place dans l'entourage de celle qu'il est accusé de ne point pleurer, ce *d'abord* à quoi se reconnaît un de ses familiers, ainsi que le confirme l'*Ami* que lui octroie la reine. *Quand je vais chez les dieux* tend au roi le miroir où il est accoutumé de se voir—entre les Olympiens ses pareils. Il ne s'agit pas ici de simple consolation chrétienne (son âme est dans les cieux). La lionne assassine accède aux champs élysiens par grâce d'état, la sainteté lui revient comme autrefois le diadème. A cette mise en scène irrésistible un dernier trait ajoute, comme une suprême impertinence, la permission accordée au roi seul de continuer à la pleurer: coquetterie d'outre-tombe où se devine une imperceptible condescendance—elle est reine, mais elle est femme avant tout.

Irrésistible scénario, disions-nous. Et tous de crier au miracle. D'une part ce cerf, qui sait ce que parler veut dire, ferme très littéralement la bouche (la gueule?) au lion qu'il s'était donné les gants de provoquer, en lui mettant sous les yeux un échantillon de sa propre apothéose (ce qui vaut pour la lionne, à plus forte raison . . .). Il le met hors d'état de le convaincre d'imposture, toute criante qu'elle est, puisqu'elle correspond si exactement à la comédie que se joue un pouvoir qui se veut absolu. Et d'autre part le cerf s'arroge le droit de se moquer de lui bien en face. Rapportons-nous-en à La Rochefoucauld, qui à la maxime 320 fait la pleine lumière: "Louer les princes des vertus qu'ils n'ont pas, c'est leur dire impunément des injures." Mettre un grand carnassier au rang des saints, administrer en face ce pieux mensonge à qui est à même d'en goûter la perfidie sans pouvoir la dénoncer, c'est là se sauver la vie par la plus savoureuse des vengeances. Ce cerf est libre d'une bien rare liberté.

Chanter ainsi la liberté sous les dehors masqués d'une apparente flagornerie, et le faire sans que jamais ce mot subversif soit prononcé, quel plus beau fleuron ajouter à l'art de la fable? Le loup efflanqué de la fable I, v, nous avait fait mesurer ce que la liberté coûte. Il nous en avait représenté une image austère et sauvage, souffreteuse et violente. Belle, malgré tout. Grâce au cerf qui tout de velours vêtu figure pour nous une existence plus large, la liberté s'habille à la mode de Versailles. Elle se fait plus secrète, nécessairement; mais sa victoire n'en est que plus douce. Installer au sein d'une cour le courage de dire la vérité sans, finalement, qu'il en coûte, le courage se doublant de matoiserie, c'est ne devoir qu'à soi une liberté aussi entière au cœur d'un état policé que dans le fond d'un bois. Et le plus beau de cette liberté de l'invention de La Fontaine, c'est qu'elle est fille de cet Imaginaire auquel nous devons et l'art des fables et l'usage infiniment flexible qui en est fait.

NOTES

1 *Œuvres diverses*. Ed. P. Clarac. Bibliothèque de la Pléiade (Paris: Gallimard, 1948). Edition représentée dans le texte par le sigle *OD*. Les fables citées sont prises de même dans l'édition des *Fable, contes et nouvelles*. Eds. R. Groos et J. Schiffrin. Bibliothèque de la Pléiade (Paris: Gallimard, 1954).

2 *Les cinq tentations de La Fontaine* (Paris: Grasset, 1938), 169.

3 Voir l'édition des fables de Phèdre procurée par Alice Brenot (Paris: "Les Belles Lettres," 1969), 39 en note.

4 *A Documentary History of Primitivism and Related Ideas*, eds. A. O. Lovejoy & others (Baltimore: The Johns Hopkins UP, 1935). Voir aussi Hérodote. *Histoires*, ed. & trad. Ph.-E. Legrand, 11 vols. (Paris: "Les Belles Lettres," 1948-61), 2:74.

5 Edition de F. & P. Richard (Paris: Garnier, 1964), 115.

6 Saint-Simon (5: 511) est formel sur les vexations auxquelles sont soumis sur ordre du roi les nobles qui, sous Louis XIV, s'abstiennent de *servir*.

7 Dans un très beau passage que je me fais un plaisir de citer:

> Pas le moindre indice d'une préférence personnelle pour une saison ou pour une fleur, pas un reflet symbolique d'une croyance ou d'une angoisse, le souffle du vent, la fraîcheur de l'ombre, la transparence de l'eau, bref, l'essence même . . . du plein air. *O muse, fuyante proie* . . . (Paris: J. Corti, 1962), 163.

8 Cité par B. E. Perry dans son article "Fable", *Studium Generale* 12 (1959), 17-37.

9 *Œuvres de J. de La Fontaine*. 11 vols. Les Grands Ecrivains de la France (Paris: Hachette, 1882-92), 2:284n.

BIBLIOGRAPHIE

La Bible de Jérusalem. Paris: Editions du Cerf, 1973.

Giraudoux, Jean. *Les cinq tentations de La Fontaine.* Paris: Grasset, 1938.

Hérodote. *Histoires.* Ed. et trad. Ph.-E. Legrand. Vols 1 et 7. Paris: "Les Belles Lettres,"' 1948 et 1951. 11 vols. 1948-61.

La Fontaine, Jean de. *Fables, contes et nouvelles.* Eds. R. Groos et J. Schiffrin. Bibliothèque de la Pléiade. Paris: Gallimard, 1954.

———. *Œuvres de J. de La Fontaine.* Ed. H. Régnier. 11 vols. Les Grands Ecrivains de la France. Paris: 1883-92.

———. *Œuvres diverses.* Ed. P. Clarac. Bibliothèque de la Pléiade. Paris: Gallimard, 1948.

Lovejoy, Arthur O. & others, eds. *A Documentary History of Primitivism and Related Ideas.* Baltimore: The Johns Hopkins UP, 1945.

Montaigne, Michel de. *Essais.* Eds. P. Villey & V.-L. Saulnier. Paris: PUF, 1965.

Mourgues, Odette de. *O muse fuyante proie . . .* Paris: J. Corti, 1962.

Perry, B. E. "Fable," *Studium Generale* 12 (1952): 17-37.

Phèdre. *Fables.* Ed. & trad. A. Brenot. Paris: "Les Belles Lettres," 1969.

Rousseau, Jean-Jacques. *Emile.* Eds. F. & P. Richard. Paris: Garnier, 1964.

Saint-Simon, Louis De Rouvroy, duc de. Vol. 5 des *Mémoires.* Bibliothèque de la Pléiade. Paris: Gallimard, 1985.

13

Madame de Motteville and War

Charles G. S. Williams

Pauline
"Y va-t-il de l'honneur? Y va-t-il de la vie?
Polyeucte
Il y va de bien plus . . ."
(Polyeucte, I, 2, 110-11)

IN AN ANALYSIS OF THE NARRATIVES of a group of seventeenth-century memorialists, which documents a common tendency to exteriorization of experience, Margaret McGowan comments in particular on Mme de Motteville's reactions to "malheur de la guerre." Walking through an improvised shelter for war wounded, at Saint-Denis in 1652, Motteville reflected that among those dying men "quasi tous demandaient à manger avec une avidité non pareille, et pas un ne pensoit à son salut." This amazing indifference, as McGowan characterizes it, is scarcely attenuated by the moralizing commentary following from it. "Ce tableau de la misère humaine," she generalizes, "me fit faire quelques lamentations sur le malheur de la guerre; mais enfin il n'y a rien dans l'univers que le Seigneur n'ait fait; il tire sa gloire de tout."[1] Far from surprising, the Augustinian resonances of this meditation are typical of a disciplined *dévote*. The striking first response may, for us, recall Pascal's stark remark that however fine the comedy may be the last act is bloody. And in line with the proper turn of meditation ("Saint Augustin de même . . .")—seeing each thing by "rapport à la fin pour la montrer toujours"[2]—the writer then fittingly brings her thought to God and his wisdom.

This mature resignation to the spectacle of war was hard won and is not Motteville's only response to it during the years of writing her *Mémoires pour servir à l'histoire d'Anne d'Autriche*. Early on, in 1643, for example, providence may be invoked as explanation for a particular *misère,* in the event actions of the duchesse de Montbazon that ironically favored the consolidation of Mazarin's power at court. But providence does not offer the exasperated young writer full consolation. As with La Fontaine's astronomers, the cause of the war is to be found elsewhere than in the heavens. "Les dames sont d'ordinaire les premières causes des plus grands renversements des Etats; et les guerres qui ruinent les royaumes et les empires, ne procèdent presque jamais que des effets que produisent ou leur beauté ou leur malice" (I, 135).

War came to occupy a larger place in the *Mémoires* than the memorialist had contemplated when she began a diary of the privileged moments with the queen shortly after being recalled to court by her royal protector. That it also occupies a more extensive part of her writing than Motteville wished seems all the more true if the displacement of that "male art" of military description, by a particularizing feminized historical space, is in fact a distinguishing mark of a rescripted history her *Mémoires* shares with those of other women writers of her own time.[3]

I wish to explore, in this essay, the nature and implications of Motteville's changing attitudes toward war over the years 1643-49. During those years, the young widow at first content simply to observe the court, both near the queen and at the distance of a perspective on her place in its grand theatre, is forced to undergo a social and political re-education, whose stakes had not been really calculated in the *imaginaire* of the adolescent who in exile had dreamed of a constant dedication to the queen's service easily transcending all obstacles. War, I wish to show, plays an integral part in that education, visible first in the greater detail and place given to military events in 1645-47, then again in 1649. The changed textualization is, in both instances, linked to a heightened awareness of the horror of war, moments of self-discovery as well as an experience of the wider wilderness of war. At such moments the text of the *Mémoires* displays, with an inward turn, an interference of paradigms or the kind of conflict of "morales" that Paul Bénichou's analyses still powerfully alert readers to discern in post-Fronde writing.[4] Motteville in her search for her own truth remains willingly, even willfully, an "esprit divers," divided by a "Concevez des vœux dignes d'une Romaine," echoing the exhortation of Corneille's noble Roman Julie to the Alban/Roman Sabine and at the same time Julie's reaction to Camille's bellicose joy: "Mais certes, c'en est trop . . ." (*Horace,* I, 1, 24, 127).

In the beginning, Motteville's imagination seems not to have been fired by war itself or by past or currently reported tales of military glory. When the whole of Paris had been aflame with admiration for Condé and his victory at Rocroy, scarcely more than the fact of "a battle" was registered by Motteville (I, 138). After Condé set this "gravestone to Spanish greatness,"[5] however, Motteville's attention is captured by his movements in the field as well as at court. By 1645, she is fully caught up in admiration for him. That spring was animated, she records with a blush of excitement, by the princes' desire "d'aller travailler à la gloire de la France et au bonheur de l'Etat" (I, 232). Glory and happiness for the realm are inextricably linked in and to the war so eagerly desired. Throughout 1647, when Condé is fighting in Spain, and on through his triumph at Lens in August of 1648, Motteville carefully chronicles the dramatic victories and setbacks of the commander who has become for her the exemplar of the noble soldier, embodying the aristocratic ethics of the principles of valor, victory, and vindication (*gloire*).[6]

With Motteville's identification in Condé's life of a superior existence, heroic mode of life, and pure source of morality, there is a fusion of hero and prince of the blood. Political action is consequently an attribute of essence, defined by monarchical ideology. In an allegorization of the court and royal family, which constitutes its nucleus, Condé is bound to the queen and with her to the king's service according to an inalterable logic.[7] The moment of this crystallization may be identified in the *Mémoires* with praise of Corneille, strategically placed after sharing with the queen the pleasures of Corneille's *Polyeucte,* dedicated to Anne in 1643, and *La Mort de Pompée,* dedicated in its turn the following year to Mazarin. "Corneille, cet illustre poëte," Motteville reflected, "avoit enrichi le théâtre de belles pièces dont la morale pouvoit servir de leçon à corriger le dérèglement des passions humaines; et parmi les occupations vaines et dangereuses de la cour, celle-là du moins pouvoit n'être pas des pires" (I, 176). In Motteville's mind and memory, Corneille's theatre of action and high principles, and especially its lessons in history, had special and specific messages for both the queen—who on the one hand was moved naturally to sell her jewels to succor those ravaged by war but on the other "n'aimoit point à lire, et ne savoit guère de choses"[8]—and the devoted *confidente* who became her historian.

At the moment of Motteville's praise of Corneille providentialism is fully evident in the historical world of his theatre.[9] Unlike the "official historians" of her time, who distanced themselves from providence as a master code of historical explanation,[10] Motteville remains faithful to it. But this explanation is not invoked at every turning in a narrative predominantly focused on action in the world and its complex motivation. Corneille's dramatization of heroic testing, of the struggle and victory of *fermeté* of action according to invariable interiorized principles, is what exalts Motteville, on the evidence of the scenarios the memorialist translates into the *Mémoires* both to celebrate Anne and to set reflectively the structure of relations around her that will give proper value to her actions.

A dramatic episode in 1648, one example among many, shows the lasting imprint on Motteville's narrative of Corneille's heroic world (with an echo of *La Mort de Pompée*) and includes a generalized praise of "poets and painters" that draws Motteville's own search after truth closer to that world. Heroic *fermeté* is at the heart of the exemplary scene narrated by Motteville after Anne learns that the Palais-Royal must be evacuated because of its inadequate security against threatening crowds in the streets. Mazarin is cast by Motteville as timorous and disoriented, "si plein d'effroi" that the queen "n'en recevoit nul secours" (II, 176). Anne on the contrary "demeura également constante et ferme, et parut dans ce moment très digne de ses grands aïeux, et parla en petite-fille de Charles Quint." *Fermeté* is there all the more, or indeed essentially, because Anne has put her trust in the Lord. The "belles paroles" Motteville memorializes incarnate the queen's faith and with it the self-abnegating center of her concern—the care of the king that will in Motteville's history harmonize Anne's actions and focus the ultimate meaning of her regency. "Ne craignez point, Dieu n'abandonnera pas l'innocence du Roi; il faut se confier en lui."

Exhibiting the affect in herself of emulation, as she might in response to one of Corneille's "âmes plus pures," for example, a Pauline, Motteville is moved to confess her own error of judgment. Confession to Anne, the really privileged moment repeated ritually in the early years as a consecrating act of friendship, is now internalized.[11] The series of intimate scenes of confession to the queen will continue; so does the moment illustrated here of an inner turn, a modification or adaptation of the *imaginaire* effecting a cathexis of symbolicity. The fullness of this moment includes then also commitment to a certain kind of historical enterprise that is, was, and ever will be the "method" of Motteville's *Mémoires*.

Quand je l'entendis parler ainsi, je fus honteuse, je l'avoue d'avoir cru que sa tranquillité pouvoit être quelquefois causée par l'ignorance du péril. Je l'en avois soupçonnée, parce qu'en effet les rois ne voient jamais leurs maux qu'au travers de mille nuages.[12] La Vérité, que les poëtes et les peintres représentent toute nue, est toujours devant eux habillée de mille façons; et jamais mondaine n'a si souvent changé de mode que celle-là en change quand elle va dans les palais des rois.

En cette occasion, cette grande princesse n'a pu être accusée d'aveuglement. Elle sentit si fortement l'état où elle étoit, qu'elle en fut peu après malade. Mais son âme, plus forte que son corps, la soutint avec tant de fermeté, qu'elle auroit eu honte de montrer ce que la nature n'avoit pu éviter de lui faire souffrir. Et cette honorable fierté fut si grande en elle, qu'elle l'empêcha de donner à ses chagrins d'autres témoins que les horreurs de la nuit. (II, 177)

Motteville will frame the entire year 1649 in Anne's life exactly as she does this episode, with one especially significant exception. Mazarin will not be useless to the queen and is portrayed in a quite different rôle from that assigned to him by the queen's *confidente* during 1645-47. In those years, Georges Dethan has charged,[13] Motteville became so obsessed by the minster-favorite as an obstacle to her just place in faithful service to Anne that she evened the score with a willfully unprincipled and deformed historical account of Mazarin's own service to the queen. To defend the "dame d'honneur" against this charge might seem quixotic and beside the point.[14] War with Mazarin there indeed is, especially before the Fronde. But it is surely fanciful to picture this combat to be driven by a "complexe d'Œnone." The assault led by Motteville in fact initiates a permanent conflict, according to the highest principles, of war waged by a "juste ennemie," as Corneille's Cornélie describes herself in opposition to César (*La Mort de Pompée*, IV, 4, 1386). And it is also, of course, subject to review in the inward turn to a moment of confession that figures penance.[15] To describe Motteville as historian, according to her lights, must include consideration of this privileged particularizing space in which the self-fashioning "dame d'honneur" gave the *Mémoires* their specific shape as history.

Since Motteville was concerned with Anne's tendency to seek *repos,* an ambiguous character trait when its meaning is inactivity or indolence rather than a spiritualizing quietude, she must have welcomed the specific compliments of Corneille's dedicatory celebration with *Polyeucte* of the first glorious year of Anne's regency. The queen's piety is first praised as the sources of the benedictions "sur les premières armes de son roi."[16] But it is Anne's action, following her espousal of "bons conseils," that is finally celebrated as worthy of this reward in the conclusion of the panegyric. Condé is not named there. But it was his military feats, clearly evoked, that were supported, and blessed, and he who was thereby the instrument of Anne's *gloire*. The dedication of *La Mort de Pompée* brought a less welcome association. By a leap of faith Motteville was unable to follow, Corneille casts Mazarin in the place occupied by Condé in the preceding dedication. His virtues are praised as non-Machiavellian; unlike the *mauvais conseillers* who poison Ptolomée in the play to follow, Mazarin's "maximes pour la conduite de cet Etat . . . ne sont fondées sur d'autres principes que ceux de la vertu" (314). Anti-Machiavellian Motteville will always remain and in her own way thus joins an intellectual current of her time.[17] She hastens to assure readers that she has not read Machiavelli in the text, tellingly in 1649 (II, 295); but she has no trouble seeing what passes as its heritage of unprincipled, godless craft in the self-interest identified as the prime mover of the *civitas terena* of the court. And after observation, and reflection, Motteville has little trouble associating Mazarin lastingly with this world.

Motteville's most virulent criticism of Mazarin (and perhaps her most probing), occurring through the years 1644-47, is structured in her thought then by a double play of oppositions. With the clarification of his characteristic tendencies—to conciliation, negotiation that often included covert diplomacy, and skill at the waiting game—Mazarin is cast as the antihero, an antithesis of Condé. Prudence, of a nonheroic sort, may in fact obstruct valor's way; peace at all costs, obscure the glory of France and her commanders. Success at politics, in a second opposition, is as compromising. Scandalized and alarmed as were many of her anti-Machiavellian contemporaries by the claim that the sincere Christian could not succeed in politics,[18] Motteville is unable honestly to counter the argument with the example of a minister she suspects, on the evidence of her observations, of having no firm religious principles. Christian statecraft might be possible for Anne to achieve and is possible for Motteville to conceive; unlike them, Mazarin can do neither.

Early on, with the disgrace of Mlle de Hautefort, Motteville learned "ce que c'est qu'une personne royale quand elle est en colère, et qu'elle peut tout ce qu'elle veut" (I, 146). It is a hard lesson for the young woman who so ardently wished for a perfect friendship between the two women based on full identification in reciprocity. As ambiguities are discovered in

Anne—her indolence and lack of intellectual resources, among others—and
in herself, an adaptation of the early ideal of service and self-fashioning in
its modified terms takes place. The "dame d'honneur," guardian of the
queen's interests and ultimately of her *gloire,* must see through the queen's
eyes and also through her own, combining empathy and detachment. The
final record of the memorialist must all the more maintain this double vision
with which the "pacte biographique" between the two friends was
concluded as founding article for a life whose truth would be historical
rather than solely rhetorical/poetic (1666: IV, 447).

The key to this reconsecrated duty is a constant and difficult vigi-
lance: clear-eyed watchfulness over Anne, a steady gaze of analysis of
Mazarin, and finally a "systematic interior monitoring"[19] of herself. The
risk of this scenario of heroic intentions, Motteville knew, was that of all
too human distortions of vision that would collapse the intention into a pro-
jective delusional scheme.

When the writer and the *Mémoires* enter into History, as in 1647
with the account of Condé's progress toward the long-awaited peace of
1648, or of his movements in Spain in 1645, Motteville does so with a reason of her own. For Anne's benefit, should her *confidente* be called upon
to be a counterbalancing *bon conseiller,* the historian Motteville stockpiles
information for herself that may be a ready arsenal for Anne. She keeps a
wary eye on Mazarin's part in policymaking, especially in 1645 when he
posts Condé to Spain and in so doing might be acting from his well-publi-
cized "inquiétude" over Condé's boldness of command in a manner that
may bury or perhaps disgrace Condé—and with him Anne's and France's
glory. Enthusiasm for Condé and mistrust of Mazarin, Motteville learned
anew, could lead to distorted judgment, notably at the moment of Condé's
victory at Nordlinghen.

With the rumors of the victory of Nordlinghen, Motteville sees in
the queen's eyes "toutes les marques d'une grande joie." "Les victoires
sont les délices des souverains," she generalizes, sharing Anne's joy but at
the same time marking at a distance her own misgivings—for a queen the
joys are the stronger "qu'ils en goûtent les plaisirs sans partager fortement
l'infortune des particuliers." The loyal servant hastens to add that the queen
did not fail to "regretter les personnes de mérite." But when Mazarin appears to confirm the news, and is greeted by the queen's "visage riant et
satisfait," both the queen and her noble *confidente* must and do take to heart
a lesson the minister has to offer them: "Madame, tant de gens sont morts,

qu'il ne faut quasi pas que Votre Majesté se réjouisse de cette victoire"
(I, 234).

It is self-judgment that shapes Motteville's narration of this episode
and gives it the kind of power sought for the moment shaping Anne's heroic
fermeté in 1648. Motteville frames the episode in a manner that will memo-
rialize her own lesson. Before and after Mazarin's account of victory she
confesses that her mind is divided about the cost of war's victory. At the
heart of the episode, with a return to Augustinian generalization there is an
unspoken but understood "je suis honteuse," triggered by the additional information brought by Mazarin that draws Motteville into a new, more direct
experience of war. "Dans cette narration je trouvai que j'avois perdu mes
parens et quelques-uns de mes amis que je regrettai beaucoup," she records.
Restraint here fosters the sense of reading a detail, almost an afterthought,
when in fact it is the experience of being caught out at this moment of dis-
tortion of her own truth—submerged in the queen's as it has been—that articulates the entire narration of the episode in the memorialist's memory and
its recomposition in writing the *Mémoires*. In penance, with her sense of
shame, the narrator is newly ready to admit an error of judgment concerning
Mazarin, to give the minister his due according to her lights. It makes little
difference, she remarks, whether he is playing to the crowd with his edifying words or not, since he is a vehicle of wisdom that is again familiarly
Augustinian: "Un homme qui exerce la vertu, soit que ce soit par sa volonté
plutöt que par son inclination, ne laisse pas d'en être estimable; puisque les
motifs en sont impénétrables, et qu'il appartient seulement à celui qui a
formé le cœur humain de le connaître et le juger" (I, 234).[20]

Again in 1647, while acerbic in judging Mazarin, Motteville pauses
with the same consciousness that heroic demands have blinded her to their
conflictual and obstructing relation with Christian virtues that should always
be clearly before her eyes. "Mais on peut dire le vrai, qu'il a usé de son
pouvoir avec une modération louable; il aimait l'Etat, et servoit le Roi avec
toute la fidélité que méritoit la confiance que la Reine avoit en lui" (I, 273).
During the climactic year 1649, this truth will be expanded to include
Mazarin the "peace maker." That expansion and more constant recourse to
its truth derive from another new and more violent experience of war and its
"malheurs."

Ironically for the sake of her *repos* (II, 287), Motteville does not flee
Paris with the court in January 1649 and remains to be swept up in the full
chaos of civil war. In some of the *Mémoires'* most vivid pages (II, 298-
301) she recounts the depersonalizing horrors of being pursued through the

streets and of finding the doors of absent friends closed to her. Even in the refuge of a church she is threatened by a "fury" who identifies her as a "mazarine." Rescued from this world turned upside down, through the alert actions of the curé of Saint-Roche, Motteville collapses from nervous exhaustion when she gains new refuge with Queen Henrietta Maria in the Louvre. "Je ne suis pas vaillante," the memorialist confesses over these memories and in similar circumstances in 1652: "C'est une terrible aventure pour une femme poltronne" (IV, 19). When she does escape the city, and the disheartening desolation of the countryside on the way to the court at Saint-Germain, she again confesses her weakness to the queen (a confession whose particular significance I shall return to in my conclusion): "J'ai avoué depuis *toutes mes foiblesses* à la Reine: et ma sincérité ne me brouilla pas avec elle, quand après avoir essuyé tant de périls, je lui fis le récit de mes frayeurs et de nos aventures" (II, 306; my emphasis).

Motteville's concern, after this experience likened to martyrdom, is once again for Anne's glory, now felt with new urgency as the hope for a benighted world. She is much relieved when Anne's martial determination to continue civil war is submitted to "doctors" for their judgment. What both women heard from them was essentially a reconfirmation of traditional values, the doctrine of "just war" as derived from Augustine through Aquinas, with a new emphasis on peace that had in the years 1643-49 gladdened the hearts of many war-weary readers of Diego Saavedra's *The Idea of a Christian Prince* (1643; Latin trans. in 1649)—that war was man's worst evil, the exteriorization of his loss of reason's battle with passion (power and wealth in first place), whereas peace is "the sum of the goods God gave to mankind."[21] Anne presented her case as "contrainte à faire la guerre par les cabales du parlement qui le portoient à une désobéissance manifeste, et par la révolte des peuples; et mit pour fondement de sa consultation qu'elle avoit l'intention de faire la paix, aussitôt qu'elle verroit cesser les causes de la guerre." The judgment is that she might continue to wage war, "mais que, pour ne pas confondre l'innocent avec le coupable, elle étoit obligée de rechercher l'accommodement par toutes les voies raisonnables et possibles, et qui manifestement ne lui seroient point désavantageuses" (II, 239). These manifest disadvantages, a price at which no peace may be bought, evidently included indignities suffered by the king (or Anne as regent) or injustices committed by him (or her in his name).

The correctness of views on "just war" eases Motteville's conscience as she hardens that line of interpretation in her retrospective shaping of the history of the Fronde years. But the haunting experience of war continues to play against the steadying recourse to a more rigorous providentialism.[22] At the end of 1648, the historian proleptically prepares readers for the worst of years. Roses yet bloomed among thorns in 1648; only the thorns remain in 1649, she muses, then proclaims the metaphor too weak. War sickness, enveloping in its "souffrance le victorieux et le vaincu" (II, 237), more properly expresses the scandal to the mind experienced in early 1649 and felt to encompass the year: the evils of war, for the victorious, infect an old hero—Condé—and even Anne; and for the vanquished, the king's good city of Paris continues to suffer long after from an "esprit de rébellion" (e.g., II, 425) that makes Motteville queasy throughout the year. The peace of Rueil, the triumph of Mazarin and Anne working in concert, is an uneasy, inconclusive, finally unedifying end to war, as worthy of bitter reflections as the *frondeurs'* spectacle at the battle of Charenton (with a rearguard still hesitant in the Place Royale) is of a mock-heroic sarcasm. Crypto-*frondeuse* Motteville decidedly is not in 1649. But the all-consuming sense of failure catches her up and is internalized to the point that the historian's unquiet mind betrays its disarray. Some curiously discordant appeals to the stars that control men's fate (e.g., II, 420) are uneasily joined with invocations of providence. The constant, daily weight of human suffering, keeping alive Motteville's own experience of it, continues to outweigh any abstract "correctness."

If Mazarin is more kindly—and fairly—treated in 1649, it is as much or more through sympathy for injustices he shares with those experienced by Motteville in civil insurrection as according to the politics and principles of the new power structure that revision is done. That he has proven his fidelity to Anne's service, and shown high courage in doing so, is left in no doubt by Motteville. Deprived of even the common form of men's justice, his property is confiscated and his person put into danger: as "perturbateur de la paix" he is misnamed and misidentified, as Motteville herself had experienced that alienation. Humility, in accepting the noble princes' conditions after the peace of Rueil, is as shockingly rewarded to the historian's mind as she records the *raillerie,* debasement, and prideful acquisitiveness that victimize Mazarin. In the course of watching Condé's *noble fierté* deteriorate, seeing that "il ne voulait pas la paix," and witnessing the transformation of ally of the queen into adversary, Motteville turns around the old antithesis. Mazarin's prudence and valor triumph. Seeking an explanation, Motteville reaches for "women's beauty and malice" in the person of Mme de Longueville. So insistently is this explanation sought and focused (e.g., II, 425), that the historian once more loses both clarity and charity with the queen and through her eyes. Together, at Anne's request, Motteville remains and savors the poetic justice of the spectacle of the sometime conspirator's inarticulate, seemingly guilt-ridden awkwardness when obliged to pay her official call on the queen after Rueil (II, 420-21). Clearly, however, "la joie de la paix fut alors troublée" by internal as well as outer enemies.

If Anne, poetically and truthfully, triumphs over the testing of the civil war at its most rigorous in 1649 as Motteville's framing celebration of her *fermeté* would attest, Motteville also recounts a series of scenes in which the queen is overtaken by the pleasure of revenge, by anger, and by cold scorn, which gives a different lighting to her *noble fierté*.[23] These human failings, whose wretchedness betokens passion's victory over reason, Motteville in part assumes herself without heroic pretense and with the same humility that leads her to provide documents (parlementary papers, peace articles, among others) and more frequently to quote her sources in the history written for 1649.

On her way back to court, charged by Queen Henrietta Maria with a special admonitory political message for the regent, Motteville is especially conscious of a lack in herself, identified in the desolate landscape as her cowardice. When the queen most needed her she had not been there, by her own choice betraying her desire to be the steadfast *bon conseiller*. Beyond all significance attributable to it in a retrospective judgment of the entire civil war, Motteville marks as a black day January 5, 1649, the day of the court's flight from Paris, memorializing it as the date of her abandonment of the queen in her own self-interest. Nor does her half-articulate transmission of the message on the fate of England and its King sound any renewing triumph of heroic service. Perhaps with more than intuition, given the series of scenes of Anne's anger, a sense of her personal failure to stem events (however much a "fantôme du devoir"), and uneasiness before the English lesson ("L'exemple est un miroir trompeur," Corneille's Auguste memorably observed), Motteville knew what a later historian has written about the moment she missed in and for her history. "The flight from Paris did not make civil war inevitable," Lloyd Moote has judged, "the regent's irrational acts during the hours after her arrival at Saint-Germain were therefore especially tragic. In her determination to prevent the pattern of the English civil war from spreading to France, she unwittingly precipitated a civil war which might well have been avoided."[24]

There are more than "some lamentations" on "malheur de la guerre" in 1649 and more than a stylized "tableau de la misère humaine." In the rescripted history composed by Motteville, centered in the space of the friendship of two women and its evolution, both the "malheur"/"souffrance" and the "misère"—eternal human companion of "grandeur" are internalized by the memorialist in that year. Lamentation, sometimes sharp, sometimes muffled and modulated, remains permanently yoked in the textualization of the heroic strivings the two women shared. In peace and at peace in 1661, Motteville declares devotion to be the true glory of "notre sexe" (IV, 259); at war in 1649, she catches herself and allows to stand as admonitory the warring opposite of another devotion, to the queen, to whom—and through whom—at that moment of *misère* she confesses "toutes ses faiblesses" (II, 306).

NOTES

[1] "Découverte de soi ou poursuite de la gloire? le dessein ambigu des mémorialistes." In *Les Valeurs chez les mémorialistes français du XVIIe siècle avant la Fronde* (Paris: Klincksieck, 1979), 215. See F. Riaux, ed., *Mémoires pour servir à l'histoire d'Anne d'Autriche* 4 (Paris: Plon, 1904), 24. Subsequent references to this four-volume edition will be given parenthetically in the text.

[2] Lafuma No. 298; on "comédie," No. 165.

[3] One part of the thesis of Faith E. Beasley, *Revising Memory: Women's Fiction and Memoirs in Seventeenth-Century France* (New Brunswick: Rutgers, 1990). Given the strikingly ambivalent position of Motteville on women, a thorough examination of the *Mémoires* from Beasley's point of view may reveal more a precursor that a companion in the enterprise persuasively presented for Mademoiselle, Villedieu, and especially Lafayette.

[4] *Morales du grand siècle* (Paris: Gallimard, 1949), 102-03 (the "malentendu profond"), 110-11 and passim.

[5] C. V. Wedgwood, *The Thirty Years War* (Garden City, N. Y.: Doubleday Anchor, 1961), 404.

[6] See Paul Bénichou, *Morales*, 19.

[7] This logic is strikingly vectorized for Corneille's *Polyeucte* by Paul Ginestier, "*Polyeucte,* essai de critique esthétique," *Revue d'Esthétique* 13 (1960), 128-39.

[8] I, 177. Through 1647 it becomes clear that one specific application of this general remark is the failure of Anne's pleasure and profit from reading history, which could provide contexts for personal critical judgment of reports. Harlay's dedication of his translation of Tacitus (1644) expresses a similar goal.

9 See Gérard Ferreyrolles, "Augustinisme et conception de l'histoire." *Dix-Septième Siècle* 34 (1982), 228 and n. 67. On "l'augustinien Corneille," see also André Stegmann, *L'Héroïsme cornélien: genèse et signification (Paris: Colin, 1968), 589 and passim.*

10 Cf. G. Ferreyrolles, "Augustinisme et conception de l'histoire," 222.

11 On the ritualization of friendship, see my "Friendship's Duties: Mme de Motteville and the 'femme forte'." *Cahiers du Dix-Septième* 4 (1990), 41-50.

12 Cf. *La Mort de Pompée* (IV, 1, 1094-96).

13 "Madame de Motteville et Mazarin ou le complexe d'Œnone." In *Valeurs chez les moralistes . . . ,*" 103-10; Rpt., without significant change in *Mazarin: un homme de paix à l'âge baroque, 1602-1661* (Paris: Imprimerie nationale, 1981), 300-06.

14 Dethan's psychologizing has been well answered by Ruth Kleinman, who at the same time documents significant historical distortions. See "Mme de Motteville on Mazarin," *Cahiers du Dix-Septième* 3 (1989), 225-42. I have developed here quite differently Kleinman's suggestion (231) that "the picture of Mazarin that she drew owed as much to her notion of politics and good governance as it did to her personal animosity. . . ."

15 My treatment of the dynamism of Pascal's dialectic of "grandeur/misère," proceeding on the side of a consciousness of "misère" toward penance has been drawn from Hugh M. Davidson, "Conflict and Resolution in Pascal's *Pensées,*" *Romanic Review* 49 (1958), 17-21. On the "easing" by the sacrament in the "obstétrique spirituel" of Motteville's time and its relation to self-knowledge, see Jean Delumeau, *L'Aveu et le pardon: les difficultés de la confession, XVIIᵉ-XVIIIᵉ siècles* (Paris: Fayard, 1990), 7-8, 72, and 25-39 passim.

16 Corneille, *Œuvres complètes,* ed. A. Stegmann (Paris: Eds. du Seuil-L'Intégrale, 1963), 290. All references parenthetically in the text are to this edition.

17 See Etienne Thuau, *Raison d'Etat et pensée politique à l'époque de Richelieu* (Paris: Colin, 1966), 54-102 and passim; Michel Prigent, *Le Héros et l'Etat dans la tragédie de Corneille* (Paris: PUF, 1986), 185.

18 Cf. Robert Bireley, *The Counter-Reformation Prince: Anti-Machiavellianism or Catholic Statecraft in Early Modern Europe* (Chapel Hill: The University of North Carolina Press, 1990), 217.

19 According to James R. Farr a "hallmark of the Catholic Reformation's devout self-consciousness." "The Pure and Disciplined Body: Hierarchy, Morality, and Symbolism in France during the Catholic Reformation." *Journal of Interdisciplinary Studies* 21 (1991), 399.

20 On this central topos and its Augustinian resonances, see Jean Lafond, *La Rochefoucauld: augustinisme et littérature* (Paris: Klincksieck, 1977), 26-27.

21 Quoted by Bireley, *The Counter-Reformation Prince,* 207-08. For Augustine, see Henri Paolucci, ed. *The Political Writings of St. Augustine* (Chicago: Regnery, 1965), 162-84.

22 E.g., explicity designating God's punishment, II, 446.

[23] Ruth Kleinman presents a significant number of these scenes from Motteville (and two important ones from Retz and Mademoiselle on anger): *Anne of Austria, Queen of France* (Columbus: The Ohio State University Press, 1985), 205-10.

[24] *The Revolt of the Judges: The Parlement of Paris and the Fronde, 1643-1652* (Princeton: Princeton University Press, 1971), 186.

14

From Hawk to Dove in Seventeenth-Century French Literature

Marlies K. Mueller

As LITERARY SCHOLARS WE ARE INCLINED to forget that early seventeenth-century French civilization was a military civilization and that the culture of the classical age was based on martial habits of thought. In the wake of this century's two catastrophic world wars, the very word 'military' evokes distasteful images of militarism and the cruel excesses of states as 'war machines.' The horror of such memories seems to cause a reluctance on the part of literary critics to address martial issues. Yet in early modern times, war was a co-substantial part of all aspects of existence: professional, aesthetic, and ethical. It was part of the dreams, passions, and hopes of every life.[1] The values of the military order, the "noblesse d'épée," permeated the population as a whole, for the military set the tone for all of society. All eyes were directed toward it. The great thinkers, artists, and literary men and women of this brilliant epoch were products of a culture built on martial values, and the preoccupation with the military ethos was central to the artistic manifestations of French society.[2] A grasp of the contemporary military world view—and its transformation—is hence crucial for our understanding of the culture and literature of the time.

During the first half of the seventeenth century, the most popular texts of the heroic genres[3] portray combat, both private (principally in the form of the duel) and public (civil or international war) as an invigorating, salubrious, in every respect positive undertaking. In theater, poetry, and novel, the ubiquitous duel featured absolute defiance, exhilarating risk, and possibly glorious triumph. War was celebrated for offering drama, camaraderie, and glory, or at least honorable self-sacrifice. It was the great adventure of life.

From the middle of the century onward, however, the concepts of violence and war underwent certain profound changes paralleling other changes in the political, economic, social and military domains. Literary texts featuring combat appear to mirror a growing perplexity over the phenomenon of violence. Increasingly conflictual expressions reveal moral tension, ambivalence, or equivocation about the theory and practice of war. Toward the end of the century, many writers and essayists portrayed war as a tragic exercise filled with futile destruction and vast pain and suffering, no longer justifiable on any grounds.

How did the concept of war change from that of a positive undertaking through a period of ambivalence, to a time when warfare came to be regarded as immoral? In attempting to answer this question, an analysis of cultural changes and changes in the sensibility characteristic of the period[4] may be revealing. Transformations in economic, political, and social conditions and institutions[5] are functionally linked to one another, but they are also linked to a changing system of values. In this paper the primary focus concerns, not the transformation of institutions, but a shift in values—values as they were expressed in the literature of the time. In studying cultural history, one must periodize and categorize, yet boundaries slip and slide, and the resulting characterizations of different mind-sets reflect certain *Idealtypen* in the Weberian sense rather than a rigorous, historically exact, periodization.

The Era of the Hawks

In his poem, *Banquet des Muses,* Jean Auvray (1590?-1622) gives vivid expression to the savage joy with which one went to war:

Nous allons en dansant aux périls de la guerre,
La bruyante trompette au fanfare éclatant,
Le fifre éveille-cœur, le tambour ba-battant,
Le gronder des canons, le cliquetis des armes.
Le hennir des chevaux et le cri des gens d'armes,
Portent à notre oreille un ton plus ravisseur
Que les pleureux accents d'un luth ensorceleur.

Les entrailles des morts nous sont des cassolettes,
La sueur notre bain, le sang nos savonnettes,
Le salpêtre nous est un musc délicieux.

Fiers, fumeux, forts, félons, foudroyants, furieux.
Fendons, fondons, froissons, foudroyons en furie
les scadons plus épais de l'armée ennemie.

Such expressions of active pleasure in warfare were not isolated phenomena. They echoed throughout society, for not even the excesses and cruel-
ties of the Thirty Years' War extinguished the martial ardor and brought
peaceful thoughts to the hearts and minds of men. Embodying the desired
social and emotional model of all strata of society, the aristocracy 'of the
sword' continued to present a powerfully attractive ideal, the alluring image
of the noble warrior. He was master of his fate, vanquished any adversary
(if not physically then morally through stoic acceptance of defeat), gener-
ously offered his life, and achieved immortality through heroism.

This ideal was eloquently accredited by the literature of the times.
During the period of consolidation of monarchical power, increasing
centralization and nascent absolutism, playwrights and novelists responded
to the desire of the ruling elites—the mainly aristocratic public in the entourage of the courts—for confirmation of their political role in the past and
present. This public longed to immerse itself in a self-congratulatory
reliving of their own "heroic past," elegantly clothed in ancient "myth-
history."[6] While celebrating the victories of Caesar, Alexander, and other
superheroes of antiquity through the medium of heroic plays, novels, and
poems, the aristocratic reader and theatergoer perceived a life committed to
military conquest as part of a larger, unfolding drama transcending the
individual. The emulation of the great conquering heroes of the past, which
was the fulfillment of a birthright, the ancestral mission, thus also became
an accession to HISTORY.

Whether set in ancient Rome, Greece, Persia, or fifth-century
Europe, the most popular heroic novels painted a picture of (feudal) military
enterprises, with brushes dipped in the golden colors of a largely imaginary
age of chivalry. At the call to arms, the warriors, magnificently outfitted in
chivalric dress and heraldic armaments, assembled with their retinues. As in
chivalric romances of the medieval and Renaissance tradition, the fighting
force was made up of a collection of aristocratic individuals, and as individuals they fought, often seeking out a personal enemy of equal rank from the

opposite camp. There was no battle order; indeed, there was no army, for after the campaign, everyone galloped back to his castle or went off in search of another hotbed of strife in which to play a decisive role and acquire fame and glory.

Intrinsic to the heroic genre since its Hellenic inception were vivid battle scenes and descriptions of brutal dismemberments. Seventeenth-century authors followed suit, their *tableaux* barely tempered by the dictates of *bienséance*. They delighted in showing men cut in half with a single blow, their arms lopped off or their bodies pierced, and their swords dripping with enemy blood.[7] Such spectacles, involving the great figures of history measuring themselves against one another on the battlefield, were riveting to the contemporary public. A good tragedy or novel of the time offered these obligatory battle scenes as set pieces, which, if executed with panache, greatly contributed to the public success of the work. Theatergoers and readers of novels reveled in depictions of the most savage paroxysms of cruelty and violence; for these served as re-enactments of the birth of the nation in strife and battle.[8] Such fictional high points were read and reread with ardent pleasure and often reverently learned by heart.

In spite of the formulaic plots of chivalric high adventure, heroic texts served a didactic purpose. In accordance with the moralistic aims of seventeenth-century *belles-lettres*, "plaire et instruire," novels, plays, and poems of the elevated genre presented serious models, maxims, counsel for dealing with general affairs of state, as well as examples of conduct in specific conflictual situations within the state and on the international scene.[9]

What are some of the common themes in these novels and plays that reflect the contemporary assumptions about the social and political role of war, the fighting man, and the military enterprise? They were threefold: first, combat played the crucial role of selecting the strongest defenders of the state. In Corneille's *Le Cid,* for instance, Rodrigue emerges as the "fittest" defender of the Spanish throne against the Moorish invaders. Second, war facilitated establishing a "pecking order" within the ranks of the nobility in which dominance and submission depended on relative physical prowess. Again taking *Le Cid* as an example, the old Don Diègue and Chimène's father, Don Gomès, each having had his turn as the foremost warrior of the realm, now must cede to the younger, stronger male, the one destined to be the Cid. Rodrigue's marriage to the most beautiful woman in the kingdom, Chimène, exemplifies what was clearly the third function of war: the selection of the fittest males for purposes of reproduction.

International conflict was portrayed as equally salutary for the kingdom. The literary kings and princes—the Caesars, the Alexanders, the Cyruses—eagerly took up arms to conquer the world, willingly subjecting their countries to war as an acid test for determining where they stood on the ladder of power. War was seen as an occasion to prove and to improve the physical and moral fiber of the realm no less than that of the warriors. Moreover, it offered a welcome opportunity to purge the nation of undesirable elements: the villains, the morally and physically weak, that is, those unfit for the heroic universe.[10] Thus, war was celebrated as a higher form of natural selection. It was the great selector of the fittest, a healthy corrective, an energizing tonic that ensured the continued strength and well-being of the kingdom.

What is the typical biographical sketch of the "fittest," the aristocratic hero? First, his noble heart is seized at an early age by an irrepressible impulse toward all that is martial. He sets off to war when barely more than a child.[11] Second, his early vocation, rewarded by a brilliant victory,[12] transforms him from an ordinary human being into an inviolable hero. Not even a king can henceforth punish the victorious warrior, not even for committing the crime of murder: "De pareils serviteurs sont les forces des rois, / Et de pareils aussi sont au-dessus des lois" (v, 3, 1753-54).[13] Third, his military success turns him into an erotically irresistible male. In fiction, as in the reality of the time, nothing enhanced the erotic appeal of the male more than being covered in blood from head to toe. What later generations would regard as repulsive was then the *nec plus ultra* in sex appeal. Corneille's Cléopâtre, like many of her counterparts in the novels of the time, is erotically aroused by the image of her lover's hand steeped in the blood of his enemies.

> Et de la même main dont il quitte l'épée
> Fumante encore du sang des amis de Pompée,
> Il trace des soupirs, et d'un style plaintif
> Dans son champ de victoire il se dit mon captif.[14]
> (*La Mort de Pompée*, II, 1, 397-400)

In *Horace,* Camille is proud that her fiancé has covered the land with more dead than anyone else: "Autre de plus de morts n'a couvert notre terre" (II, 5, 548). Eriphile in Racine's *Iphigénie* falls in love with the hero when she sees him before her, his arms red with the blood of her people (II, 1, 406, and 475). If the heroine does not find herself in the proximity of the battlefield, narration is enough to stir her erotic impulses. Success in war instantly makes the hero irresistible to women and renders even the middle-aged warrior, otherwise thought too old for romantic love,[15] attractive and exciting. Defeat on the battlefield, on the other hand, immediately extinguishes all sex appeal. The vanquished protagonist shrinks into an erotically uninteresting prospect, (*Mithridate,* III, 5, 1039-40; IV, 4, 1203, 1294) like a Siamese fighting fish that loses its magnificent coloring within seconds of defeat.[16]

What can the exaltation of the hero tell us about the *mentalité* of the seventeenth century? A first hypothesis imposes itself when we compare fictional glorifications and panegyrics written in honor of actual warriors. Whether in ode (Théophile de Viau to Maurice de Nassau, 1619), in *oraison funèbre* (Bossuet's eulogy of le Grand Condé), in tragedy (Corneille, *Le Cid*), or in novel (Mlle de Scudéry, *Artamène ou le grand Cyrus*), the themes, figures of speech, and words used to exalt the fictional hero as the specular image of the real warrior of the time are the same; they refer to the magnetic effect of his presence on the battlefield, which galvanizes his troops and paralyzes the enemy. They refer to his prodigious deeds of valor and noble clemency, which achieve the moral victory of the great general after victory by arms has already been won.[17] The close link between fiction and historiography and the fluid lines of demarcation between the two genres in the early seventeenth-century world view are striking.[18]

A second hypothesis: the more anachronistic the fictional individualistic ideal of feudal warfare became in the early seventeenth century, the closer the nobility attached itself in mentality and often in action to their idealized thirteenth-century forebears (*La Noblesse,* chapter 4). As in the fictional universe, an abundance of rough military men throughout Europe was ready to serve the highest bidder, or in the case of the well-heeled members of the nobility, to fight for honor, glory, and the fun of it.[19] At the news of an outbreak of war between two peoples, the contemporary noble hastens to the site, chooses sides without preconceptions, takes the most dangerous positions, throws himself into the trenches of beleaguered towns, and runs, often unarmed, into enemy fire—without thought of any tactical or strategic advantage (*La Noblesse,* 65). What we would call outrageously foolhardy was praised as courage. The French, nobles and often common soldiers as well, had the reputation of reckless challengers of death. "Ne savez-vous pas," said the Italians, "que les Français vont à la mort comme s'ils devaient ressusciter le lendemain?" (*La Noblesse,* 66). The violent, individualistic ethos of a seemingly uncontrollable aristocracy brought about a high level of violence in European society during the early seventeenth century.[20]

To probe the concepts underlying the warrior ethic of the time, complete with their assumptions, tacit or explicit, it is illuminating to study the socialization process of the young aristocrat.[21] Richelieu, well aware that society transmits its values through education, turned away from the crusty academic learning of the universities (the curricula were still steeped in scholasticism),[22] and fostered military academies where large numbers of young boys from the nobility spent two years of their adolescence. There the knowledge necessary for maintaining the class ethos was transmitted to them. The *summum* of every noble family's dreams was to have their son accepted to be trained in the famous Parisian Academy directed by the renowned Benjamin, who prided himself on providing a thoroughly practical "modern" education. The academy was entrusted with the task of conveying a fixed body of knowledge, the parameters of which varied little during the *Ancien Régime*. The curriculum included instruction in morality, politics, geography, genealogy, heraldry, music, dance, fencing, the elements of fortification, and mathematics (the latter was vital to the design and deployment of siege materiel), in addition to the French language, a modicum of the classics, and a smattering of art and architecture.

Above all, the curriculum of these institutions included, as an essential component of the moral instruction, the sensitization of the child to the twin pillars of the noble ethic: honor and glory. Parents and teachers were concerned that the young nobleman, rather than learning how to "get along" with his peers, to blend in and to conform, learn how to make himself respected, to "stand out." The child was taught to attach high value to the idea of selfhood, to react with immediate outrage to any affront, and to be fiercely competitive.[23] As part of the socialization process, every boy needed to learn the "virtue" of resenting an insult, to weigh the relative gravity of various offenses. The great lesson of sensitization to the system of honor involved the recognition that the seeming trivialities of personal insult or the vainglory of self-aggrandizement were the very essence of public life and the motor of social mobility (*Word of Honor,* 18).

The concept of honor, which has generally been seen by critics and philosophers as ahistorical, static, and unidimensional in its emotive charge, contained within it a historical development, and a tension between passion and reason, impulse and control. During the early century, aristocrats wanted their young to learn but one lesson: the lesson of the passionate ingredient of honor, that is, courage, *la bravoure. Bravoure*, though not

actually "taught," but carefully nurtured through constant practice and
exercise, was perceived as an inborn quality, transmitted through aristocratic bloodlines, and expressed in instinct-based action, not to be acquired
by training the mind and even less by reading school books ("Un prince
dans un livre apprend mal son devoir" *Le Cid,* I, 3, 192). In fact, many
noble families saw book learning as a dangerous pursuit. A young man
could easily become excessively fond of it and acquire too much abstract
knowledge. If he succumbed to this temptation, he ran the risk of ruining
his life, for it was believed that exercising the intellect, "bookishness,"
enfeebled body and will, and was thus detrimental to converting the passion
for honor into action. Honor and *gloire* and the impulse toward them
seemed in the early century pure, self-contained, and self-sufficient, need-
ing no additional help. The use of reason and control appeared inimical to
the exercise of *bravoure.*

Educating the Nobility toward Self-Control

Richelieu, the great promoter of the Academies, while praising the
nobility's courage, chided its impulsive, "sanguine," uncontrolled behavior.
Add calm reflection, patience, and discipline to the "natural" *bravoure* of the
nobility, and France will be the mightiest country in Europe, he predicted.
As minister he strove to do his best to realize these aims, both through administrative measures, such as edicts against the practice of the duel, and
through the pedagogical institutions he founded.[24] Teachers at the aristocratic "pépinières" were eager to carry out the prime-ministerial program.
Knowing well that the concept of honor had since chivalric times contained
a double imperative: that of passion and control, they began to stress the
latter. In transmitting to their pupils the requirements of "honor" as the
quintessential characteristic of the aristocratic soul, they perceived their task
henceforth as twofold: they strove to instill not only the necessity of a passionate self-regard and an unassailable self-esteem, but also a heavy dose of
self-mastery. Self-mastery, self-control, they taught, were essential if one
wanted to attain and retain the inestimable prize of honor. A strong egotistical passion of self-love alone, exploding in impulsive behavior, could easily
lead to disaster and, in an apparent paradox, be fatal to one's honor. Honor,
properly understood, therefore had to be composed of passion and control.
Boys had to be taught that for the love of honor, it was crucial to learn
severity and rigor. The successful graduate was possessed by an ardent

passion—the desire for honor—as well as the power of control over all that would cause a loss of that honor: timidity, fear, cowardice, but also headstrong pride and rash, foolish, reckless action.

The emphasis on self-control was at first a mere appendage to the primary impulse, the "true" essence of honor. It appeared artificially attached. Over time, however, the addition undermined and then supplanted the core concept. At that point, self-control no longer functioned as a contradiction or even as an adjunct value but as an indispensable element in the official formulation of the honor principle. As the century progressed, this element of rational control became a precondition for the existence of honor. Initially, therefore, the concept of reason was an additive suspected of subverting the aristocrat's sense of the natural priority of action. Reason and control gradually gained importance until finally they were the primary condition for achieving honor. Only a life that conquered the self would achieve *gloire* and obtain power over the environment.

Descartes's *cogito ergo sum* was eagerly adopted by the aristocratic schools and given a specifically ethical interpretation. Man had to accept the dominance of resolute will, his actions subject to constant careful scrutiny as to their consequences. The strength of the well-educated aristocrat no longer lay in spontaneity but in the ability to weigh all available factors from within and from without himself, to order them in the proper proportion, to achieve the best adaptation to circumstances. In the religious sphere, this active self-control was the goal of the *exercitia* of St. Ignatius and the basis of rational monastic virtues everywhere.[25] Self-control had become the most important practical ideal of the aristocracy; long before the so-called "rise of the bourgeoisie" with its pride in rational behavior founded on commercial calculation made it the cornerstone of its ethic.[26] Under the aegis of the post-revolutionary, nineteenth-century ethos, rationality was not only appropriated as co-substantial with "the bourgeois," it all but engulfed the very impulse which had given birth to it.

The context in which characters in novels and plays calculate the prospects, costs, and rewards of losing or gaining honor throws a revealing light on the value structures and the entire *Weltanschauung* of the time. What was honorable conduct? Honorable conduct had little to do with acting according to one's conscience. Doing good deeds, such as sparing the life of an enemy or treating a prisoner kindly, were not only acts of altruism imposed by an abstract inner moral imperative, but also the results of having carefully calculated the ways and means of obtaining approval from critical public opinion and recognition of one's superiority over rivals for glory. The monologues of dramatic or novelistic heroes revolve around the question of how a particular action will make them appear in the eyes of the public.[27]

This strong identification of honor with "calcul" supposed that other people were sitting in judgment over every act and required close observation of the signs of peer censure or approval (*Word of Honor,* 100-01). As the nobility increasingly abandoned its independent life in the provinces for the urban constraints in Paris and later for the 'Huis-clos' atmosphere of Versailles, how one appeared to others became of primary importance. Consequently, the emphasis in choosing a course of action fell on external rather than on internal sanctions, and the control of improper behavior relied heavily on the external mechanism of shame rather than on the internal norms of the conscience and the resulting feelings of guilt. In plays and novels, every character was haunted by the fear of ridicule and shame; *la honte* was a feeling of overwhelming intensity from which there could be no escape.[28] Memoirs and letters of the period abound in examples of deaths attributable to shame.[29]

However, seventeenth-century French culture did not rely exclusively on shame to enforce its social norms. Michel Foucault[30] analyzed the effect of the institution of the religious confessional, which since the Middle Ages had played a significant role in guiding European society toward becoming a "guilt culture," that is, to inculcate absolute standards of morality and to rely on members of society developing internal constraints.[31] At the same time that the nobility found itself exposed to an intensified "shame culture," the "guilt culture" received a powerful reinforcement from a movement that was to effect a radical change in attitude toward aggression, violence, and war.

The New Ideal: Restraint and Moderation

The young noblemen, who at the military academies, at court, and in the salons of Paris learned to discipline their thinking, to deduce, calculate, and weigh cause and effect instead of acting on their drives, were ready to embrace a new ideal of manhood proposed by the aristocratic culture of the time. In mid-century, there began to flourish in *le monde* an intellectual and social movement, fostered by the women of the aristocracy and much ridiculed by its opponents, *le mouvement précieux*, which by rationalizing and redefining public tone, good manners, and private morality codified what was thereafter called "l'art de vivre." Decried by their critics as pretentious upper-class prudes, the *précieuses*, led a general educational campaign that was to give society new rules of conduct.

How was it possible that the women of the French *élite*[32] were capable of imposing a new model of the virtuous life upon an entire society? This extraordinary enterprise was successful because *préciosité*, in its mainstream ideology, far from defining itself against the historical movement of the epoch, that is, against absolutist policies (as some twentieth-century critics argue), went hand in hand with social and political objectives emanating directly from the king. By proposing to educate men and women to refine their manners and to subject their impulses to an even greater degree of control, the movement served to reinforce the monarchical policy started under Richelieu, which in its absolutist strivings (especially following the conflicts of the Fronde) likewise attempted to tame the nobility's aggressive drives and to transform the rough, independent, bellicose noblemen, ready to draw the blade at the raising of an eyebrow, into cultivated, civilized, elegant courtiers, more adept at battling with words than with swords.[33] Thus supported by central authority, *préciosité* became a powerful, influential movement that was readily, even eagerly, adopted by all leading groups of society.

The civilizing norms established and enforced by the political centers of the court, the salons, and the academies concerned nothing less than the entire psychic structure of the individual.[34] This new code of behavior covered all aspects of life from table manners to the art of courtship, from the way a handkerchief must be held to the conduct of war. Young and old acquired a code of behavior that prevented them not only from spitting on the table and wiping their mouths and noses on table cloths or hands, but also—and above all—from erupting into violence at every real or imagined slight. Civilized men and women must hencefoth keep their cool in all situations of life: "C'est une dangereuse coustume à prendre, et pour soy, & pour les autres, que de se fâcher aisément."[35] Emotional displays were ridiculed, a show of aggression was censured. Within a generation the internalization of the courtly behavior patterns resulted in the formation of a whole new structure of the ideal personality, that of the *honnête homme*, the honest or honorable man, whose quintessential characteristic was that he was "civilized."

The description and definition of this *honnête homme* was the great preoccupation of all major writers of the time, whether playwrights, moralists, or novelists. Thus moderation and restraint rather than headstrong pride were highlighted by Molière in his *Misanthrope*. Philinte, the sage of the play and model of the "modern" aristocrat, was placed in contrast to the undisciplined, blustering, aggressive Alceste, the outdated, ridiculous protagonist.[36] Applauded by his aristocratic audience of courtiers, princes, and the King, Molière agreed with the "modern" education that sought to enable a man to act calmly upon his constant motives, and saw as the most urgent task the destruction of impulsive action springing from sudden emotion. The aim of the psychological training for *honnêteté* was to give the young nobleman a coherent, stable, unified personality capable of leading an alert, intelligent, examined life.[37]

The elaboration of the new personality traits is evident in the changed structure of the aristocratic novels of the time. The heroic elements dwindled, as the social aspect—the novel as handbook of good manners, refined conversation, and well-bred social interaction—took over the genre. In La Calprenède's *Cléopâtre*,[38] the central plot contains no battle descriptions. Instead, we hear the heroes' *douceur* praised, and court life, where aggression is veiled in politeness, tact, and diplomacy, is foregrounded and analyzed in all its intricacy.[39] The new heroism as defined by the contemporary novel no longer lay in great independent, spontaneous action but in the quality of the motivation and the validity of the reasoning behind well-thought out acts. Such questions as to whether the apparent dissimulation involved in civility was fundamentally dishonest and therefore unheroic, and whether one should be modest about something that is praiseworthy, were the object of intense discussions extending over hundreds of pages. Such issues were of vital interest to the new hero in his endeavor to abandon his aggressive aristocratic individualism and to adapt to the modern, sophisticated social norms of court life.

Aggression, violence, and all activities imbued with their spirit were henceforth condemned.[40] The profound modifications of European sensibility[41] first touch the aristocracy and then filter down to the new class—the bourgeoisie—fascinated by all aspects of the nobility's lifestyle. Writers, essayists, dramatists, economists, moralists, publicists diffuse the new ideas and vie with one another in denouncing war and the profession of the soldier—first *sub rosa*, later on openly—and echo the growing pacifist sentiments circulating throughout the society of the *ancien régime*. Molière's audiences applaud Scapin's denunciation of the "spadassins qui ne font non plus de conscience de tuer un homme que d'avaler un verre de vin." Cyrano de Bergerac satirizes the motives for war in his burlesque *Histoire comique ou Voyage à la lune* (1657). As official court historiographer entrusted with praising the virtues of war during the bitter international conflicts of the waning century, Boileau, even while acclaiming the monarch's victories, injects a subversive note by using the examples of Alexander the Great (*Satire VIII*) and Pyrrhus (*Epître I*) to show that hunger for conquest is madness.[42] From within the military establishment itself, Vauban, the celebrated *Commissaire général des fortifications*, whom Saint-Simon described as "l'homme le plus honnête de son siècle," always readier to expend ammunition than lives, characterizes war as the product of self-interest, ambition, and the blackest of man's passions,[43] and in his *Projet de paix* (*Oisivetés*, I, 50, 508) he salutes an approaching day when war would be no more than a grim memory. La Bruyère, that great demystifyer of the noble ethic, openly blames the ideals of glory and conquest for the poverty of the people (*Du Souverain*, 9). Pierre Bayle accuses "la méchanceté de quelques particuliers et la sottise des peuples" for the outbreak, evils, and miseries of all wars.[44] Even more direct was the moralist Fénelon, who unhesitatingly declares war an unpardonable waste of lives that only serves the King's pride (*Aventures de Télémaque*, Livre X). While the ideas that the Abbé de Saint-Pierre proposes in his *Projet de paix perpétuelle* (1713) go beyond the notions of his age (such as establishing an international organization for the maintenance of perpetual peace, based upon the compulsory membership of all states, and creating a World Court and an international armed force), his aspirations and values were shared to varying degrees by other thinkers of the period.

The entire system of values had been radically changed. Moderation, restraint, defense[45] rather than conquest now were the stated policy aims. When these were not translated into practice, protests against war atrocities arose even from within the offending nation (e.g. many within France objected eloquently to the terrible devastations of the Palatinate). With the opening of the "Quarrel of the Ancients and the Moderns," the opposition to war received a most effective boost from the theory of progress embedded in the dispute. For the "Moderns" the development of commerce and trade was synonymous with civilization and peace; war, on the other hand, characteristic of an earlier, less enlightened stage of human development, must become obsolete.

As we move into the eighteenth century, the voices decrying violence, in whatever form, became at once more powerful and more numerous. Physiocrats proved that war was unproductive, political philosophers that it was a mere instrument of ambition and despotism, moralists that it was barbaric. Wars, it was said and repeated, ruined both victor and vanquished; they were unreasonably expensive; they increased prices and taxes, retarded economic progress, and oppressed the poor. The *philosophes,* Voltaire, Montesquieu, and the *Encyclopédistes* attacked wars' causes and effects.[46] Believers in the power of human reason, they thought of all wars as manifestations of the irrational. Cosmopolitans, as they were, they found resorting to violence against a neighboring country damnable. Nationalism had not yet made its appearance and wars of liberation or annihilation were not considered. All wars were thought of as dynastic wars, that is, disputes between monarchs—disputes that brought untold miseries upon the people.

It is easy to overestimate the importance and influence of these pleas for peace. Military historians Michael Howard, André Corvisier, John Childs, Jeremy Black, and, most recently, John Brewer issue a cautionary word. War remained a normal feature of European life, occupying over half the time between 1659 and 1713. Even in an age when the *galanterie* of Maurice de Saxe characterized the rococo war ("Messieurs, les Anglais tirez les premiers"), warfare for the mass of the soldiers was still a harsh and savage affair. Yet, the conduct of war had altered;[47] it became disciplined, formalized, codified, ritualized, and the civilian population was subjected to less pillage and random violence than before.[48] Violent conflicts were often transferred to sea where they were generally less destructive. Battles, if they were fought at all,[49] became as stylized and limited in their movements as a classical tragedy, and the greatest admiration went to the general who excelled within the narrowest rules.[50] Campaigns, which succeeded *sans coup férir* were esteemed as above any deeds of valor which covered the terrain with corpses.[51]

This happy trend would soon be reversed. Within a few generations, there occurred one of the greatest upheavals in the history of Western civilization, the French Revolution. It marked a complete turnabout in the ethos of war. Soldiers swept through Europe, no longer as the more or less willing instruments in the hands of monarchs, but as militant crusaders of liberation; not just for France but for humanity at large. The new French armies, imbued with revolutionary fervor and fed by universal conscription, ushered in the ideological war and total warfare. Soon Napoleon rushed from victory to victory, as his adversaries persisted in fighting according to the inhibiting rules of the old "limited wars." Embodying the new spirit, he boasted to Metternich: "Un homme comme moi ne regarde pas à la mort d'un million de soldats."[52] The era of restraint and moderation, the era of the doves, seemed to have come to an abrupt end.

NOTES

1 ". . . by the seventeenth century [war] had become almost the livelihood of the masses," states the military historian Michael Roberts, *The Military Revolution* (Belfast: Queen's University of Belfast, 1956), 23.

2 See, for instance, Balzac for a forceful expression of contemporary sentiment: Virtue was synonymous with *gloire* on the battlefield and the thirst for *gloire* was the highest passion. Jean-Louis Guez de Balzac, *Œuvres* (Paris: Louis Billaine, 1665) 2: 158.

3 A division between aristocratic and popular literature, long axiomatic among literary critics, has been shown to be inaccurate. Genres were not sorted by production and consumption into 'high'and 'low' corresponding to social strata. On the contrary, readership and genres were mixed, and disseminated throughout society by such relatively inexpensive circulating libraries as the *Bibliothèque bleue*. See Peter Burke, *Popular Culture in Early Modern Europe* (London and New York: Harper & Row, 1978).

4 See also "Présence de la guerre au XVIIᵉ siècle," *XVIIᵉ Siècle*, 148 (Juillet/Septembre 1985), Société d'Etude du XVIIᵉ siècle avec le concours du C.N.L., du C.N.R.S. et de la ville de Paris.

5 I.e., the sharply increasing money supply and the ensuing inflation which ruined large segments of the nobility between 1500 and 1630; the effects of increasing administrative centralization, which facilitated tax collection and allowed the monarch to hire mercenary armies recruited from the poorer strata of society; the eventual transformation of these troops into a national standing army (commanded by the sovereign's appointees rather than independent nobles); the evolution of military technique and the use of new or improved weapons and the institution of new forms of warfare.

6 See Jean-Marie Apostolidès, *Le Roi-machine* (Paris: Les Editions de Minuit, 1981), 66-92.

7 La Calprenède, *Cassandre* (Paris: A. de Sommaville, 1642-45), 4: 835, 1033-35; 8: 187, 189.

8 See Jean-Marie Apostolidès, *Le Prince Sacrifié* (Paris: Les Editions de Minuit, 1985).

9 For a recent study of the *Ancien Régime* novel as a political genre, see Thomas DiPiero, *Dangerous Truths & Criminal Passions* (Stanford, California: Stanford University Press, 1992), Part One.

10 Moral and physical weakness were equated here, a view still powerfully supported by Montesquieu in the eighteenth century. Jean Bodin underlines this cleansing function of war in the contemporary reality: "Il y a toujours eu, et n'y aura jamais faute de larrons, meurtriers, fait-néants, vagabonds, mutins, voleurs en toute République, qui gastent la simplicité des bons subjects, et n'y a lois, ni magistrats, qui en puissent avoir la raison . . . Il 'y a donc moyen de nettoyer les Républiques de telle ordure, que de les envoyer en guerre, qui est comme une médecine purgative, et fort nécessaire pour chasser les humeurs corrompus du corps universel de la République. Voilà quelques raisons qui peuvent servir pour monstrer que ceux-là s'abusent grandement, qui pensent que le seul but de la guerre

est la paix." Roger Chauviré, *Jean Bodin auteur de la République* (Paris: E. Champion, 1914), 792-93.

11 A disposition for martial tastes from birth is indispensable in establishing heroic quality: Don Rodrigue taunts the count with ". . . aux âmes bien nées / La valeur n'attend point le nombre des années." (Pierre Corneille, *Le Cid,* II, 2, 405-06) and Racine's hero, Bajazet, affected by a typically precocious martial restlessness, refuses to remain in the *molle oisiveté* of the other sultan's children:

> Il vint chercher la guerre au sortir de l'enfance,
>
> . . . .
>
> Emportant après lui tous les cœurs des soldats,
> Et goûter, tout sanglant, le plaisir et la gloire
> Que donne aux jeunes cœurs la première victoire.
> (Jean Racine, *Bajazet,* I, 1, 117, 120-22).

12 All heroes might proclaim with Don Rodrigue: "Mes pareils à deux fois ne se font point connaître, / Et pour leurs coups d'essai veulent des coups de maître" (*Le Cid,* II, 2, 409-10).

13 Pierre Corneille, *Horace* (Paris: Garnier, 1974).

14 Pierre Corneille, *La Mort de Pompée* (Paris: Garnier, 1974).

15 Molière's Arnolphe (*L'Ecole des femmes*) is held up to ridicule for entertaining thoughts of love at his age.

16 The European vogue for high *bravoure* shown in the alarming increase in the practice of dueling, or in foolhardy action on the battlefield, was attributed to the predilection and influence of women. In France especially, where disregard for one's survival and safety was pushed to an extreme, seventeenth-century women, like the fictional heroines, were believed to desire only men who excelled in the martial arts. The more deaths a nobleman had caused, the higher the *gloire* of the lady he wooed. The historian Avenel quotes an Englishman who witnessed in astonishment the progressive rise of a French duellist's erotic stock, as he successively killed seven adversaries: "Les femmes françaises . . . affectionnent par-dessus tout les braves, et pensent qu'elles ne peuvent pas en aimer d'autres sans compromettre leur réputation." Le Vicomte G. d'Avenel, *La Noblesse française sous Richelieu* (Paris: Armand Colin, 1901), 67.

17 See Jacques Morel, "L'Héroïsation des grands chefs de guerre en France au XVIIe siècle," *Revue des Sciences Humaines* (1966), 5-11.

18 For insightful discussions of the relationship between the novel and the early modern vision of historiography, see Marc Fumaroli "Les Mémoires du XVIIe siècle au carrefour des genres en prose" *XVIIe siècle* 94-95 (1971), 7-37; and Faith E. Beasley, *Revising Memory* (New Brunswick and London: Rutgers University Press, 1990), Introduction.

19 There were no standing armies in France at the time. At the beginning of the Thirty Years' War the King had, in addition to a regiment of royal guards he captained himself, only six infantry regiments, a fourth of which could perhaps be assembled at any one time, and five cavalry regiments consisting only of officers. The King hired soldiers

through intermediaries, the captains, or *mestres de camp*, to fight a battle or two, as one might hire plumbers to fix a leak. Such a captain—his regiment bore his name—provided all military structure and commanded the loyalty of those he hired. In 1621 the duke of Montmorency brought together six thousand men for the service of the King. Yet, when shortly after his arrival the duke had the misfortune to fall ill, the troops melted away. Not one was left to the King (see André Corvisier, *La France de Louis XIV* [Paris: CDU et SEDES, 1979], 59-64).

20 See David Kaiser's superb study of early modern warfare, *Politics and War* (Cambridge, Massachusetts: Harvard University Press, 1990), 13-14. For the bellicist nature of early modern society, see also Kristen B. Neuschel, *Word of Honor* (Ithaca and London: Cornell University Press, 1989).

21 For recent studies see W. Frijhoff, D. Julia, *Ecole et société dans la France d'Ancien Régime* (Paris: Armand Colin, 1975); D. Julia, J. Revel, R. Chartier, *Les Universités européennes du XVIᵉ au XVIIIᵉ siècle, vol 1: Histoire sociale des populations étudiantes* (Paris: Ecole des Hautes Etudes en Sciences Sociales, 1986); Roger Chartier, *Cultural History: Between Practices and Representations* (Cambridge, UK: Polity Press in assoc. with Basil Blackwell, 1988) VI; Andy Green, *Education and State Formation: The Rise of the Educational System in England, France and the U.S.* (London: The Macmillan Press Ltd., 1990).

22 See also Emile Durkheim, *L'Evolution pédagogique en France*, vol. 2 (Paris: Librairie Félix Alcan, 1938).

23 See Georges Snyders, *La Pédagogie en France au XVIIᵉ et XVIIIᵉ siècles* (Paris: Presses Universitaires de France, 1965), 51.

24 See R. Gaucheron, éd. *Œuvres du cardinal de Richelieu* (Paris: Plon, 1933), 123-38.

25 This rational self-control was also the underlying principle of Protestantism as analyzed by the genius of Max Weber.

26 See also Jacques Ehrman's analysis of "la comptabilité de l'honneur" in Corneille's *Cinna*: "Les Structures de l'échange dans *Cinna*," *Les Temps modernes* 246 (1966), 929-60.

27 Examples abound. In the first two Acts of Corneille's *Le Cid* alone, from Léonor's "Et que dirait le Roi? que dirait la Castille?" (I, 2, 89) to Rodrigue's "Endurer que l'Espagne impute à ma mémoire / D'avoir mal soutenu l'honneur de ma maison!" (I, 4, 333-344), and Chimène's "Et s'il peut m'obéir, que dira-t-on de lui?" (II, 3, 488).

28 For a discussion of the concepts of "shame culture" versus "guilt culture," see G. Piers and M. B. Singer, *Shame and Guilt* (Springfield, Illinois: Charles C. Thomas, 1953); for the transition from "shame" to "guilt" culture, see Norbert Elias, *Power and Civility* (New York: Pantheon Books, 1982), 292-300. For the use of shame in seventeenth-century pedagogical practices, see Colloque de Marseille, "Le XVIIième siècle et l'Education" in *Supplément au numéro 88 de la revue Marseille* (1er Trimestre 1972), 29-30.

29 See the Cardinal de Retz, *Mémoires* (composed between 1658 and 1662) (Paris: Librairie Gallimard, 1956).
30 Michel Foucault, *La Volonté de savoir* (Paris: Gallimard, 1976).
31 Nevertheless, some of the mechanisms of the use of shame for imposing desirable social behavior have survived to this day. Two conspicuous vestiges of this behavior in continental European culture include the frequent use of shame and ridicule in pedagogy, and the phenomenon of "mauvaise joie", i.e. the censure of ridicule falling on any kind of failure or mishap. Both modes of behavior are practically absent in Anglo-Saxon countries. The English language does not even possess a word to translate the term of "mauvaise joie."
32 Carolyn C. Lougee's valuable research into the social composition of seventeenth-century salons in *Le Paradis des femmes: Women, Salons and Social Stratification in Seventeenth-Century France* (Princeton: Princeton, NJ: Princeton University Press, 1976) shows an upwardly mobile population. I differ with her interpretation in that I see this 'mixed population' as reflecting the processes at work in French society as a whole (see Simon Schama, *Citizens* [New York: Alfred A. Knopf, 1989]), not as defining itself against the rigidly stratified society of the absolutist monarchy, as she suggests.
33 See also Joan B. Landes, *Women and the Public Sphere in the Age of the French Revolution* (Ithaca and London: Cornell University Press, 1988), 22, who writes of the salon as a very impressive social and educational institution "in which women exercised a considerable degree of power—unmatched in subsequent or prior eras." For different readings of *Préciosité* see Joan DeJean, *Tender Geographies* (New York and Oxford: Columbia University Press, 1991); Faith E. Beasley, *Revising Memory;* and Domna C. Stanton, "The Fiction of *Préciosité* and the Fear of Women," *Yale French Studies* 62 (1981), 107-34.
34 See Norbert Elias, *The Court Society* (New York: Pantheon Books, 1983).
35 M. de Scudéry, *Clélie, histoire romaine* (Paris: A. Courbé, 1653-61) 4: 273.
36 Even though the humor of the play for Molière's contemporaries lay in seeing the protagonist, Alceste, behave in the old-fashioned way in his contact with the world, and in matters of friendship and love, Molière's dramatic skill allows each character, however foolish, his or her words of wisdom. Alceste's satire of court life rings true, but ultimately he is ridiculed by Molière for preferring the old straightforward frankness, which was now considered rude, to the new, refined, elegant forms of courtly diplomacy.
37 See Jean-Marie Apostolidès, "L'Ordre identitaire classique" *Ordre et contestation au temps des classiques* I, 73, Biblio 17 (1992), 11-30.
38 Paris: A. Sommaville, 1647-1658.
39 The ideal of *honnêteté* was codified in a great didactic manual of comportment: Castiglione's *Cortegiano* (1528). Though born of the courtly experience in the city states of Renaissance Italy, its translations and imitations, notably N. Faret, *L'Honnête homme ou l'Art de plaire à la Cour* (1630), went through numerous editions in seventeenth-century France, and, together with Gracián's *El Oráculo manual* (1647), became the courtier's

indispensable *vademecum*. The new model of behavior was then diffused throughout Western Europe and beyond by French *Ancien Régime* court culture which under Louis XIV reached paradigmatic stature.

40 This transformation in human sensitivity did not take place without opposition. Conservative voices in the realm bitterly decried what they perceived as the emasculating education at court, in the salons, and at the academies: "Pour qu'un jeune homme soit aimable il faut qu'il soit . . . une jeune fille." (quoted by Georges Vigarello, *Le Corps redressé* (Paris: J. P. Delarge, 1978), 92. Many an aristocrat harbored deeply ambivalent feelings. He inclined to resist compulsion and discipline; he was nostalgic for the free knightly rivalry of the past, with its unrestrained violence, where the right of the stronger, not the ruse of the negotiator, prevailed. On the other hand, he took pride in the new self-control and delight in the more refined sophisticated pleasures.

41 See also Michel Foucault *Discipline and Punish: The Birth of the Prison* (New York: Pantheon Books, 1978) where he analyzes the social disciplining process in early modern Europe.

42 For the change in the interpretation of the figure of Alexander the Great from the ideal of the conquering hero at the beginning of the century to cruel despot in the heroic novel of the mid-century, see Marlies K. Mueller, *Les Idées politiques dans le roman héroïque de 1630 à 1670* (Harvard Studies in Romance Languages, 40, French Forum: 1984), 119.

43 See *Vauban: Sa famille et ses écrits, les Oisivetés et sa Correspondance* ed. A. de Rochas d'Aiglun (Paris: Berger-Leurault, 1910), 1: 267.

44 *Dictionnaire historique et critique* (Amsterdam: P. Brunel, 1730), vol 6, *Erasme*.

45 See L. Bély, J. Bérenger, A. Corvisier, *Guerre et Paix dans l'Europe du XVIIe siècle* (Paris: SEDES, 1991), Chapter VIII (Louis XIV et la stratégie défensive) for a reevaluation of Louis XIV's warfare.

46 The juxtaposition of two descriptions of armies facing each other before a battle is revealing. The first is from the best seller *Le Grand Cyrus:* "Jamais on n'a rien veu de si magnifique, que l'estoit cette grande Armée: car non seulement Cyrus, le Roy d'Assirie, Mazare, & tous les autres Princes estoient superbement armez; mais encore tous les Capitaines; & il n'y avoit pas mesme un simple Soldat, qui du moins n'eust rendu ses armes claires & luisantes, s'il ne les avoit pû avoir belles & riches: de sorte que le Soleil estant ce jour là sans aucun nuage, fit voir en la marche de cette Armée, le plus bel objet qui soit jamais tombé sous les yeux . . ." Madeleine de Scudéry, *Artamène, ou Le Grand Cyrus* (Paris: A. Courbé, 1649-53), V, 636. The second is Voltaire's famous sarcastic tableau in Candide: "Rien n'était si beau, si leste, si brillant, si bien ordonné que les deux armées. . . ." Voltaire, *Candide* (Paris: Bordas, 1977) III, 48.

47 For the perspective of military historians on the difference between the two halves of the century in the conduct of warfare, see Jeremy Black, *A Military Revolution? Military Change and European Society, 1550-1800* (Atlantic Highlands, NJ: Humanities Press International, Inc., 1991); and L. Bély, J. Bérenger, A. Corvisier, *Guerre et Paix.*

48 See John Brewer, *The Sinews of Power* (Cambridge, MA: Harvard University Press, 1990), 47.

49 See Jean-Marie Apostolidès,"L'Année 1674," *Actes de Baton Rouge. Papers on French Seventeenth Century Literature,* ed. Selma A. Zebouni (Paris, Seattle, Tübingen: Biblio 17, 1986), where he analyzes the passage from battles to the new rationalized, calculable, and restrained siege warfare.

50 While Turenne, the greatest French general of the second half of the century, did not shirk battles, he was a master of the art of manoeuver, for the manner of conducting wars at the time was so much imbued with the idea of restraining one's forces, conserving one's energy, and the belief in the superiority of maneuver, that—as in a game of chess—one considered the adversary beaten if he was outflanked. At his death in 1678, contemporaries could think of no higher praise than to laud him as a general whose defensive skills had saved the kingdom from invasion and the miseries of war. See Jean Bérenger, *Turenne* (Paris: Fayard, 1987), 417. Clausewitz, analyzing the eighteenth-century limited warfare from a post-Napoleonic perspective, lamented that during the period of the "Kabinetskriege," the warrior element slowly devoured itself.

51 A worsening financial situation may offer a partial explanation for the increasing moderation in warfare, but it was hardly the decisive factor. Recent studies (see Paul Kennedy, *The Rise and Fall of the Great Powers* [New York: Vintage Books, 1989], 121) have shown that France's financial situation, did not improve until *after* 1815, i.e. *after* the great Napoleonic victories and defeats, after the wars in which—in spite of France's near catastrophic economic conditions—all restraints, all limitations on human brutality, had been swept away by revolutionary fervor.

52 Quoted by Gaston Bouthoul, *Sauver la guerre* (Paris: Grasset, 1961), 108.

15

From Folklore to Hyperbole in the French Fairy Tale

Judd D. Hubert

MANY SCHOLARS HAVE POINTED OUT that the vast majority of French fairy tale writers at the end of the seventeenth-century belonged to the nobility and, more often than not, had frequented at one time or another Louis XIV's ostentatious court. Charles Perrault, who started the vogue, had played, at the very least since the1662 "Courses de Têtes et de Bagues," a prominent part in official cultural and artistic productions. As Jacques Barchilon succintly states, "le merveilleux des contes était souvent une évocation de la vie au château de Versailles."[1] Although six of Perrault's ten tales deal with royal personages, only two, "Sleeping Beauty" and "Cinderella," portray courtly behavior. Actually, his contemporaries will go much further in involving royalty in their tales and also in their predilection for superlatives: not only do they frequent the highest circles and dwell as a matter of course on the adventures of kings, queens, princes, and princesses, but they rarely fail to regale their readers with hyperbolic descriptions of magnificent palaces, sumptuous costumes, lavish festivities, and priceless jewelry. One of these storytellers, Préchac, goes so far as to recount in *Sans Parangon ou la reine des fées* the life of the incomparable Sun King in terms of fairy literature, thus making explicit a connection taken for granted in many a contemporary tale intent on depicting its triumphant prince as though only Louis le Grand could have served as model for his peerless behavior.[2] Madame d'Auneil in *La Tyrannie des fées détruite* relies on the dedicatee of her work, "la duchesse de Bourgogne," designated in her story as "une grande princesse," to subdue the evil fairies, whose punishment will consist in assuring through perpetual but invisible hard labor that the gardens of Versailles will receive each day an abundant supply of water.[3] By scrupulously conforming to courtly manners, the fairies in most of these tales provide more often than not an aristocracy hierarchically superior to, and far more powerful than, human monarchies. It goes almost without saying that Fairyland festivities easily surpass those provided by the kings and queens of the real world. Instead of giving all the details, the omniscient narrator of *Cornichon et Toupette* lets her readers imagine the rejoicings taking place at the fairy court: ". . . on est seulement averti de donner à chacune de ces choses le degré de perfection qui manque chez nous, & qu'on se doute bien qui ne manquoit pas chez les fées."[4] And in asserting the hierarchical superiority of fairies, no one could go further than Madame de Villeneuve. In "La Belle et la bête," it turns out that the heroine, the daughter of a king and a fairy and not, as everyone had thought, of mere merchants, paradoxically outranks the metamorphosed prince whose life and kingdom she has saved.[5]

Barchilon has commented on the preciosity of seventeenth and of several eighteenth-century tales as well as on their continued adherence to the stylistic and amorous values of French classical drama.[6] All these trends reach a contrived climax in an anonymous story entitled "Le Mariage du prince Diamant et de la princesse Perle" published in 1707 together with four other tales, two of which would warrant inclusion in *Le Cabinet des fées:* " Le Singe favori," located in tropical Abyssinia, and "Le Merle blanc," which takes place in frigid Lapland.[7] Neither Barchilon nor Robert have admitted these three stories in their corpus, perhaps because of the book's extreme rarity. Indeed, major libraries, including the Bibliothèque Nationale, do not list it. The narrative frame in which "Le Mariage" appears provides interestingly enough a severe critique of fairy literature. Cléante, a member of an aristocratic company having nothing better to do than discuss current literary fashions and invent stories, reads a tale he has deliberately composed for the occasion as proof that any literary wit acquainted with the formula can write in a matter of hours a *conte de fées* capable of pleasing the most discriminating audience. Hence, the chief interest of "Le Mariage" may lie, if we can believe Cléante, in its strict adherence to the conventions or, more precisely, the clichés of the genre. We constantly move from one *locus amœnus* and from one architectural marvel to the next. All the while, the narrator leads us through throngs of the most beautiful maidens and the most handsome knights ever assembled, each one attired in finery the cost of which would beggar the wealthiest courtier in Europe. As we might expect, the author through his systematic abuse of hyperbole, triggered even before the narrative can begin by the names of his two protagonists, Perle and Diamant, meticulously conforms to the accepted standards of the genre. The title indeed provides a *mise en abyme* for the entire narrative. The hero and the heroine, born exactly at the same moment and both absolutely beyond compare even in Fairyland, belong to neighboring but steadfastly friendly kingdoms that metaphorically complement one another, for l'Empire d'Orient derives its identity from the rising and l'Empire d'Occident from the setting sun. Moreover, the former bases its wealth on an unlimited supply of gold and precious stones, the latter on a boundless quantity of silver and pearls. And while one nation displays an eight-foot-high altar sculpted from a single diamond, the other flaunts an equally large statue carved out of a single pearl, extracted no doubt from an oyster big enough to feed the entire population during the nuptial festivities. We might even describe l'Empire d'Orient as solar and male, l'Empire d'Occident as female and lunar. Obviously, the two nations can hardly avoid relating to one another by a *mariage de raison* this time made in heaven, since it by no means excludes love. As always in tales of the marvelous, an obstacle comes between the prince and the princess as well as between the two kingdoms. A powerful, evil, but stunningly beautiful fairy, intertextually descended from two of the most redoubtable sorceresses in literature, Medea and Armida, wants Diamant for herself, while her handsome brother has amorous designs on Perle. Regrettably, the author refrains from introducing captivating monsters or even those immeasurably old, grossly repulsive, and superlatively ugly fairies bound to make a brave prince's adventures not only perilous but intolerable. Cléante, with little thought of parody, insists on keeping everything and everybody beautiful, even the dark and precipitous stretches of landscape that the protagonists have to cross. But this tale, which appropriately begins and ends with a ceremony, lacks the grotesque and carnivalesque elements capable of enhancing its obvious festive qualities. Both the prince and the princess easily resist the illusory attractions proposed by the sorceress and her brother simply because they have chosen once and for all to remain faithful to one another. Married but unconsummated love thus triumphs over temptation and overcomes formidable obstacles. Obviously, Cléante has not forgotten that in order to conform to the more edifying examples of the genre, his concocted fairy tale should provide a moral lesson. Interestingly enough, it also offers its readers a political and anti-colonialist lesson, for Cléante broadly hints that he has situated the two friendly nations, whose true location the defeated sorceress has revealed to enterprising Europeans, in pre-Columbian America: "Enfin l'avarice inspira à des hommes avides de tenter tous les périls pour découvrir ces heureux climats, où ils porterent ensuite une guerre aussi injuste que cruelle" (63).

Raymonde Robert rightly sees in seventeenth- and eighteenth-century fairy literature an idealized, and one might even say perfected, self-image of the aristocrats who had composed and made them fashionable.[8] Although Robert may not have considered this possibility, idealization in the vast majority of tales coincides with an inordinate use of hyperbole. In this respect if no other, the *conte de fées* has much in common with an earlier and far more intellectual aristocratic parlor game, that of *maximes,* played with such consummate skill by La Rochefoucauld that it soon transcended its playful origins to become part of the literary canon. But whereas fairy tales purport more often than not to maintain heroic values, maxims as a rule tend to undermine them.[9] In classifying both *maximes* and fairy tales as parlor games, as *jeux,* I have chosen to follow the example of Charles Sorel, who indeed reserves for fictional narrative the most important place in *La Maison des jeux* and subsequent game collections.[10] It so happens that several authors and compilers of these tales of the marvelous have set their stories within a narrative frame quite similar to that of Sorel: a select society of guests who idle away pleasant spring, summer, or fall days in their host's country estate, described as a *locus amœnus* beyond compare, both from a natural and an architectural point of view. The various narrators in *La Maison des jeux* specialize in love stories concerning people belonging to the same class as themselves and, not infrequently, personal acquaintances. Early in the eighteenth century, Robert Challe in *Les Illustres françoises* will go far beyond such conventional settings by plunging both the narrator and his audience into highly charged and sometimes scandalous adventures of direct concern to each one of them.[11]

Fairy tales both in their frame—when they happen to have one—and in content move of course in the opposite direction from that of *Les Illustres françoises,* for they tend to avoid connections with ordinary human experience even when they make a show of psychological verisimilitude in matters of love. They lend themselves to gamesmanship far more readily than do Sorel's romances, for they adhere even more rigidly to generic conventions. As a matter of fact, they favor formal considerations to such an extent that we might compare them to sonnets or, better still, to *bouts rimés,* a purely playful enterprise practiced in aristocratic circles in the 1660s, somewhat to the detriment of lyrical poetry. Not surprisingly, several narrators and collectors of fairy tales disparagingly refer to their stories as *bagatelles,* a term equally suited to *bouts rimés.*

* * *

Superlatives, a feature of seventeenth- rather than eighteenth-century literature, continue to abound in fairy tales if nowhere else long after the reign of the Sun King and of Sans Parangon, his fictional derivative. Who during the eighteenth century but a writer of fairy tales would dream of beginning a novel: "La magnificence et la galanterie n'ont jamais paru en France avec tant d'éclat que dans les dernières années du règne de Henri second." But in Madame de La Fayette's generous dissemination of superlatives throughout *La Princesse de Clèves,* the reader can usually discern an ironic twist in keeping with La Rochefoucauld's deconstructive practice in his *Maximes.* Authors of fairy tales, whether in the seventeenth or the eighteenth century, do not use hyperbole in quite so corrosive and unmasking a manner, perhaps because the genre they have chosen to prac- tice happens to require this stylistic convention. Nevertheless, the presence of hyperbole in some of the erotic fairy literature composed during the Age of Enlightenment produces by displacement or misplacement a sense of incongruity rarely found in earlier tales. *Gaudriole,* one of the most gro- tesquely erotic of these stories, begins in the usual manner with exaggerated praise of the king, belatedly blessed with a daughter: "Elpenor Roi de Thessalie sans contredit le meilleur Prince de son temps. . . ."[12] The author uses the same sort of superlative when he first mentions the island where most of the action will take place: "De toutes les Isles qu'on trouve sur les vieilles cartes qui nous restent encore de l'ancien et vaste Empire des Fées, il n'en est pas sans contredit de plus fameuse, que l'*Isle Grise* (31). The author wittily takes advantage of the fact that his (or perhaps her) readers can have no previous knowledge of so celebrated a place or of the maps that would allow them to locate or even visit it. And he can hardly avoid hyperbole in characterizing the relationship between the hideous fairy and her husband, an equally repulsive genie: "C'étoit bien le couple le mieux assorti qu'il y eut alors, qu'il y ait eu depuis & qu'il y aura peut-être jamais" (34). In this particular instance, the superlative functions, by means of a play on words, as a radical understatement, for Gaudriole and Moragrandy, who show little affection for one another, pursue in utter contempt for their spouses monstrous love affairs. Many *contes de fées* feature a frightfully ugly, mean, and repulsive old crone who has erotic designs on a prince charming inevitably endowed with every human perfection. It would seem that fairy literature thrives on antithetical exaggerations, frequently brought about by confrontations between a superlatively attractive and virtuous heroic couple and incredibly repugnant aggressors completely lacking in redeeming features either physical or moral. In short, stories such as *Gaudriole* often succeed in pushing hyperbole to extreme limits with the help of antithesis. This juxtaposition of antithetical superlatives in beauty and hideousness enhances through the introduction of carnivalesque episodes the festive qualities characteristic of the genre. Indeed, many a fairy tale readily lends itself to the Bakhtinian analysis of carnival because of the paradoxical combination of grotesque realism with escapist preciosity.[13] Indeed, fairies turn the rational world upside down in manners reminiscent of *la fête des fous* but without really challenging hierarchical order. Although Bakhtine shows little concern for fairy literature, he nevertheless singles out Diderot's *Les Bijoux indiscrets* as Rabelaisian.[14]

In keeping with its decrepit but immortal king and queen, l'Isle Grise serves as a retirement community for doddering senior citizens from all over the world. As young people may not gain admittance, the heroine with the aid of a supportive fairy metamorphoses herself into an eighty-year-old woman and soon becomes Gaudriole's favorite lady in waiting. She has gone to the island in order to retrieve her beloved prince, a difficult assignment since Moragrandy out of jealousy has severed his body into three unequal parts, metamorphosing each one into a plant. He has transformed a crucial but habitually hidden fragment of the prince's anatomy into a curiously shaped flower named *l'onyny*. While mutilation of one sort or another occurs in many a fairy tale, the anonymous author of *Gaudriole* seems to have pushed segmentation a step further than his rivals. He has indeed hyperbolized mutilation in the same way he has exaggerated erotic repulsiveness in his nymphomaniacal fairy and dirty old genie. But hyperbole may not fully account for the cruel quartering of the prince, since the discussion of androgynous love in *The Symposium* seems to have provided a sardonic intertext for the heroic couple's misadventures. Even though the impotent Moragrandy has in desperation borrowed *l'onyny* to have his way with the princess, true love can come into being only when the prince has become whole again. Love as opposed to sex depends, so to speak, on the reunification of the heroic couple. And we can safely claim not only that the result must exceed the sum of its parts but that multiplicity and division inevitably lead to failure. Thus even a ribald fairy tale manages, however ironically, to provide a moral lesson.

* * *

Parody with or without eroticism, as both Barchilon and Robert have shown, plays a major role in fairy tales, notably in those of the eighteenth-century.[15] Although Anthony Hamilton no doubt initiated the systematic, as opposed to the occasional, use of satire in four fairy tales written early in the century but published only in 1730, some ten years after his death, we owe the first methodical parody of the genre to appear in print to an obscure writer, the Marquis de Culant, author of a folkloric fairy tale written, like Perrault's *Peau d'âne,* in *vers libres: Les Trois chiens* (1722).[16] The publisher, or perhaps the author, can hardly have spared expenses, for this elegant octavo volume boasts of a frontispice and three other full-page engravings. It has nonetheless escaped the attention not only of the editor of *Le Cabinet des fées* but of Barchilon and Robert, who lists (25) very few fairy tales published between the turn of the century, when the vogue began, and the 1730s, when the marvelous returned to favor. She goes so far as to describe the period 1715-30 as "la plage du silence" (311). Although Culant may lack La Fontaine's or Perrault's talents as poet and storyteller, his *Trois chiens* shows at the very least considerable originality in making satirical use of elements borrowed from folklore or, more exactly, from seventeenth-century fairy tales. His hero, a superlatively handsome but, unlike the usual run of prince charmings, hopelessly stupid young man, has received as his part of the king's inheritance an enormous flock of sheep but with no pastures where they might graze and no money to buy land:

> Jamais ne mourut si bon Pere,
> Des Fils voici le caractere;
> L'aîné sçavant dans l'art de régir un Etat,
> Avoit sans être scelerat
> La conscience large & mince,
> Et son frere l'homme à l'argent
> A peine eût servi d'Intendant
> Dans la plus chétive Province,
> Et le troisiéme étoit bon Prince;
> C'est-à-dire que ce Cadet,
> Auroit dans le siecle où nous sommes
> Passé pour l'homme le mieux fait,
> Mais pour le plus sot de tous les hommes (2-3).

Forced by his siblings to seek greener pastures in foreign lands, he soon witnesses, but without undue regret, the complete depletion of his timorous flock which, in spite of all his martial encouragements, fails to rise to the occasion and defend itself against packs of wolves. Deep down, he sides with the beasts of prey, as should any brave prince who has had pastoral obligations foisted upon him. He gleefully replaces his lost sheep with three hounds, each one certain of winning top prize in a dog show, and in obedience trials. Descended from one of Diana's divine hounds who broke all the rules by consorting with a mortal bitch, the three dogs not only enjoy, like Puss in Boots, magic powers, but invariably show far more intelligence than their master whom they repeatedly save from the catastrophic end he has richly earned by his blunders. They climax their fidelity and devotion by securing for their master the Philosopher's Stone, which accomplishes a far more difficult task than the transformation of lead into gold, for it bestows enough intelligence and wit upon the hero to make him acceptable to the utterly beautiful but sophisticated princess he has saved from a monster and duly married. In the course of parodying "Peau d'âne," "Le Chat botté," "Le Voyage des trois fils du roi de Sérendip" and other tales, the author has made clever intertextual use of myths, involving not only Diana the huntress, but Perseus and Andromeda together with the amorous transgressions of the Immortals. Thanks to his hounds, the hero hardly requires the Gorgone's head or even a magic sword. Not only does Culant poke fun at Greek mythology, but he frequently lampoons contemporary customs and especially the timeless incompetence of government. Throughout his complex parody, he deliberately multiplies superlatives and makes inordinate use of exaggeration, particularly in narrating the miraculous exploits of the three dedicated dogs.

* * *

Without unduly relying on superlatives at least in the grammatical sense of the term, Mademoiselle de Lubert pushes the use of hyperbole to the limit. Whereas most other authors reward the prince and the princess with long, happy, and fruitful lives if only to make up for the impossible ordeals they have inflicted upon them, she goes several steps further in *La Princesse Lionnette et le Prince Coquerico:* "Ils vécurent des millions d'années, & le roi & la reine donnèrent au monde des fées et des génies bienfaisans, qui sont actuellement occupés à faire le bonheur de l'humanité."[17] Previously, a stroke of the good fairy's wand had rejuvenated

Lionette's pitifully decrepit foster parents henceforth entitled to remain as long as they wish of the same age as Lionette and Coquerico. Nonetheless, the princess's royal father, previously metamorphosed into a lion, fails to regain his youth in reassuming after so many years his human shape. No doubt de Lubert realized the social necessity, even in Fairyland, of maintaining a proper generation gap between parents and their offspring.

In de Lubert's highly imaginative and extravagant tales, hyperbole usually coincides with humor and on several occasions with parody.[18] The heroine of *La Princesse Camion* must undergo three quite different metamorphoses at the hands of a remarkably imaginative evil fairy metonymically named Marmotte. Camion, whose name refers, because of her diminutive size at birth, to a collar pin, appears antithetically to prince Zirphile as Baleine, a mermaid weighed down with a huge cetacean tail but graced with an irresistibly beautiful face. When he next sees her, but without fully recognizing her, she has become a tiny enameled live doll enclosed at night for the sake of her own protection in a toothpick case. During her third metamorphosis the prince fails to locate her among some fifteen thousand garrulous crayfish all of whom he has received orders to grind in a mortar during the weeks to come for the codfish king's—"le Roi des Merlans"— evening chowder. He thus finds himself for the second time in a situation that hyperbolically combines paradox with antithesis, for when he had first encountered and immediately fallen in love with the radiantly beautiful Baleine in her underground retreat he had to choose between immediately marrying her or skinning her alive. Although the mermaid would have much preferred the latter treatment, for it would have freed her forever from Marmotte's clutches and restored her normal identity, the kindly prince in spite of her urging stubbornly insists on matrimony. De Lubert, perhaps for the sake of parody, has gone even further, from the standpoint of cruelty as well as complexity, than Madame d'Aulnoy in "La Chatte blanche," where the prince must merely lop off his beloved feline's head and tail.[19] And when Zirphile carries off a dozen crayfish destined for the codfish king's soup of the evening, they invariably laugh joyfully all the way to the mortar. It would appear at first that de Lubert has established an antithetical relationship between their horrendous situation and their playful behavior in keeping with the paradoxes that predominate throughout the story. Actually they laugh so happily because they know that their only means of escape and rehabilitation must pass through the mortar. We might even construe their journey from slavery and suffering to bliss less as a parody than as an unconscious echo of Christian beliefs concerning salvation. After all, the reliance on ordeals, so characteristic of fairy literature, derives in part from romances of chivalry, in which we can often discern the laicization of a Christian view of the world.

Forgoing a lengthy introduction in the manner of Madame de Villeneuve in "La Belle et la bête," de Lubert usually starts out with a challenging event, only slightly more concocted than those found in the general run of contemporary fairy tales. Far from using this initial event merely as a means of thematically structuring and coordinating the story, de Lubert invariably gives free play to her imagination so that her tale becomes a perpetual crescendo of surprising adventures, each one more astonishing than the previous. The mermaid basking in an oversize basin leads up to the transformation of an entire population into the variegated denizens of a vast aquarium functioning in every respect as a court. Although de Lubert's pike- and shark-headed attendants have much in common with Lewis Carroll's frog footmen, they function thematically as part of the seafairing confusion that predominates throughout the story, a confusion antithetically contrived by the mountaineering Marmotte, duty bound to help her fish-headed nephew win the hand of the reluctant Camion.

A carnival atmosphere prevails in *Cornichon et Toupette*.[20] The narrative exploits, though in the most decorous manner possible, a grotesque theme emphasized by Bakhtine, that of libidinousness in old age, where death and pregnancy conjoin. A hopelessly stupid fairy, appropriately named Dindonnette, in her attempt to insure the happiness of the islanders assigned to her care, not only gives the waters of their only available fountain the power to rejuvenate the old at full speed but to make the young sink swiftly into senescence. As a result of her blunder, the entire population perishes. Cornichon and Toupette, happily betrothed and protected by an aeronautically minded fairy, land on the desert island and drink from the magic fountain. Selnozoura, the good fairy, although unable to undo the evil wrought by Dindonnette, makes unsuccessful attempts, with the consent of her stupid colleague, to mitigate the catastrophe by various compromises. Fortunately, both Cornichon and Toupette happen to have supernatural forebears who save them in extremis from the horrible fate that had destroyed an entire people (446-47). But before this discovery, the heroic couple had lived through a series of grotesque and humiliating misadventures similar to those experienced by the islanders. In depicting their tribulations, the author actually hyperbolizes old age. She follows, but with far greater decorum, the lead of the satirical poets of the preceding century, notably Régnier and Sigogne, who had emphasized, in conjunction with eroticism, its most repulsive aspects. According to de Lubert, old age must inevitably coincide with second childhood. The senile Cornichon has no awareness whatsoever of his role as bridegroom and of his surroundings when they marry him in front of the entire court to his rejuvenated and disdainful bride. Likewise, the total ignorance and feebleness accompanying both extreme age and early childhood account for the death of all the islanders: "l'imbécillité étoit l'apanage des deux extrêmes" (388). Moreover, "Celui qui tomboit dans l'enfance au sortir de la vieillesse, n'emportoit aucun souvenir de ses connoissances passées" (389). It would appear that de Lubert, in keeping with most of her contemporaries, has found her own peculiar method for rejecting the past, but in this instance with unfortunate consequences rather than the exhiliration that may derive from the elimination of original sin.

Her originality appears even more clearly in the various ways senescence throughout the tale combines or clashes with youth, for she excels in the confrontation of extremes. Dindonnette reaches even greater absurdity than when she had poisoned the island fountain by proposing to the heroic couple: ". . . la moitié de votre corps va reprendre la vigueur & les grâces de la jeunesse, tandis que l'autre moitié éprouvera la décadence à laquelle le tout étoit destiné. C'est à vous de choisir quelle partie de vous-même vous est la plus chère, & doit subir cette heureuse métamorphose" (454). In spite of the uproarious laughter of the entire court, the fairy indicates to her astonished victims an additional geometrical option in their pending *métamorphose*. They alone must decide "Si elle s'opérera par une ligne perpendiculaire, qui séparant le corps dans toute sa longueur, lui fera réunir deux profils opposés; ou si une ligne horizontale tracée en ceinture sera le terme de ces deux états, & à laquelle enfin de ces deux moitiés ainsi distinguées en supérieures et en inférieures, sera attachée la jeunesse" (434-35). We may even consider the fairy's strange proposal a parody of science fiction, already a fashionable genre at that time. The fact that Dindonnette makes known her impossible plan in the midst of court festivities adds considerably to the carnivalesque atmosphere of the event.

The wise Selnozoura falls back on a plan hardly more satisfactory than that of her colleague but far less ridiculous: either Cornichon or Toupette will become youthful once again while the other will continue to lapse into senescence. When the devoted Cornichon consents to sacrifice himself for his beloved, "Toupette, comme un serpent qui se dépouille de sa vieille peau, se vit dépouillée de ses rides, & fit voir à leur place les traits d'une beauté parfaite, & la taille d'une nymphe" (436). Instead of receiving a fitting reward for his generosity, the hero loses the last shreds of his dignity: "La surprise de Cornichon, quoique préparé à cet événement, fut si grande, qu'il tomba à la renverse, criant de toute sa force, à moi, chère Toupette" (437-38). Before Toupette's rejuvenation, Cornichon had reiterated many of the clichés of idealized and disinterested courtly love so prevalent in the literature of the previous century. He had promised Toupette that if the fairies should choose to restore them, he would offer his youthful graces as

> un hommage éclatant aux rides & aux infirmités de votre vieillesse. Quelle joie pure ne devrez-vous pas éprouver vous-même de reconnoître alors que l'illusion de la beauté n'entrera pour rien dans l'hommage que je vous rendrai; il ne pourra se rapporter qu'à vos vertus, qu'à la plus belle âme du monde (426-27).

Because of his advanced years and Toupette's coquettish vanity, such sentiments strike the reader as doubly displaced, and for this reason even his heroic self-sacrifice will produce no more than a pathetically comic effect. In his old age, Cornichon stubbornly displays an attitude toward love deemed hopelessly out of date and therefore ridiculous during the reign of Louis le Bien Aimé. And his praise of the virtuous but wrinkled Toupette as blessed with "la plus belle âme du monde" makes his use of a superlative particularly ironic. Toupette angrily rejects Cornichon's Platonic homage to her beautiful soul encased in a decaying body, as well she should, for in spite of its reliance on an idealistic conception of love, such respect clearly betrays its male chauvinist origins and thus provides a most unusual example of unconscious hypocrisy or bad faith. To nobody's surprise, she considers herself no less worthy than her lover of regaining her lost youth and making a mark in the world. Unlike de Lubert and her contemporary, Madame de Villeneuve, Crébillon, fils, in his long fairy novel, *L'Ecumoire, ou Tanzaï et Néadarné, Histoire japonoise,* indulges on the contrary in blatant male chauvinism.[21] He disparages the fairies seen primarily as women: "Leur sexe, les intérets qui l'animent, peu importans quelquefois, mais toujours vifs; la jalousie du commandement, celle de la beauté, l'envie de faire parler d'elles, la fantaisie qui, pour des Déités femelles, est un mobile considérable, faisoient naître entre ces Puissances les guerres les plus sanglantes" (13). Their status as fairies allows the witty Crébillon to hyperbolize faults traditionally ascribed to women. And hyperbole plays an important part throughout the tale, for, unlike Diderot in *Les Bijoux indiscrets,* he rarely departs from the conventions of the genre. Indeed, one can hardly imagine a more accomplished prince than Tanzaï.

Although the fairy tale as a genre originates in folklore, nonetheless many of the tales owe their existence to the authors' peculiar imagination together with borrowings from other storytellers rather than to popular literature. But it would appear that the overdetermination of superlatives and other forms of hyperbole has little or nothing to do with folklore. Perrault, who systematically derives most of his stories from folklore and attempts, but not without irony, to preserve their popular flavor, makes only moderate use of hyperbole even in tales dealing with royalty.[22] Madame d'Aulnoy's "L'Ile de la Félicité," the earliest in date of seventeenth-century fairy tales, already makes far greater use of hyperbole than does Perrault. Although folkloric in origin, it relies on classical mythology and shows a strong aristocratic bias: for instance, the hero overcomes his fear upon entering an inauspicious cavern simply because ". . . les ames des Princes ont quelque chose de plus noble & de plus fier que celles des autres hommes.."[23] The aristocratic and mythological twist of d'Aulnoy's narrative should hardly surprise us, for the inserted tale purports to entertain a select gathering of adults rather than the urchins sitting at the feet of "Ma Mère l'Oye" in the frontispice of seventeenth-century editions of Perrault's tales. Authors of fairy literature tend of course to embroider and expand folkloric tales to suit themselves and perhaps even their readers, as Mlle l'Héritier readily admitted in a remark concerning "L'Adroite princesse" and addressed to Madame la comtesse de Murat: "Je vous avoue que je l'ai brodée, & que je vous l'ai contée un peu au long."[24]

In one of d'Aulnoy's most famous stories, "La Chatte blanche," hyperbole runs rampant, not, as in Lubert's tales, to heighten an already unbridled imagination, but to enhance the esthetic or decorative aspects of her narrative. In a recent article, Michèle L. Farrell has persuasively analyzed this fairy tale as an expression of feminine—and aristocratic—desire. Indeed, the heroine plays so active a part that all by herself she contrives and imposes a happy ending in accordance with her fondest wishes.[24] Farrell has revealed the sociological and psychological basis of "La Chatte blanche" without any need to delve into its rhetorical ramifications. She has thus shown far greater interest in the author's motives than in her literary talent. Nothing, however, would prevent feminine desire from transforming itself into ornate exaggeration.

The esthetic overdetermination of hyperbole appears most clearly in the second ordeal the king imposes on his three sons in order to avoid choosing a successor. They have to bring back within a year a cloth fine enough to pass through "le trou d'une aiguille à faire du point de Venise" (471). In short, each prince must accomplish a humanly impossible task. Fortunately, the feline heroine immediately supplies the prince with a piece of cloth manufactured by expert cat paws and lodged in a walnut. When the prince breaks the shell in the presence of the entire court, he finds only a cherry stone. He nevertheless continues his deconstructive operations through several phases until he pulls from a millet seed

> une pièce de toile de quatre cens aunes, si merveilleuse, que tous les oiseaux, tous les animaux & les poissons y étoient peints avec les arbres, les fruits & les plantes de la terre, les rochers, les raretés & les coquillages de la mer, le soleil, la lune, les étoiles, les astres & les planètes des cieux: il y avoit encore le portrait des rois et des autres souverains qui régnoient pour lors dans le monde; celui de leurs femmes, de leurs maîtresses, de leurs enfans & de tous leurs sujets, sans que le plus petit polisson y fût oublié. (479)

The author has playfully combined a concretized offshoot of Pascal's "deux infinis" with the explosive display of a jack-in-the-box. Instead of a small piece of plain cloth, Chatte Blanche has provided the prince with a painting representing the entire universe! Works of art, each one more beautiful than the next, play an important part in the narrative together with intertextual allusions to other fairy tales and to La Fontaine's fables. The author goes so far as to adapt a scene from *L'Ecole des femmes,* for the heroine confined by decrepit fairies to a tower makes the same naïve gestures as Agnès when she beholds a handsome young man for the first time in her life.

In spite of some unimportant inconsistencies in the narrative, "Chatte Blanche" displays a metaphorical coherence absent from the vast majority of fairy tales including those of de Lubert, which so skillfully combine a wide variety of incredible adventures. The idea of breaking out of an enclosure appears in a number of events. In the first quest, consisting of bringing to the king the most ingratiating "petit chien" imaginable, Chatte Blanche gives the hero a dog so small that he carries it back to his father in an acorn from which it suddenly sallies forth to perform a dance. In the third ordeal, consisting of returning to court with the most beautiful princess, Chatte Blanche comes into the presence of the king enclosed in a cristal rock from which she bursts forth in such dazzling splendor that she easily surpasses her two rivals. Since in all three of the quests, containment leads to an explosive display, it would seem that Chatte Blanche, who has engineered each one of these scenarios, tends to repeat the story of her own existence characterized essentially by constraint while compensating for her mother's pathetic visit to the fairies' forbidden orchards and her first husband's illicit penetration into her tower. Rash entrances as well as explosive exits possess strong erotic connotations.

By taking into account the interests, prejudices, and cultural background of their readers, writers of fairy tale, whether of the seventeenth or the eighteenth century, find ways and means to manipulate and please their audience. Hyperbole provides them with a particularly effective rhetorical tool, for not only does it help create a make-believe universe recognizable as a vastly improved version of the world in which their readers would desire to live, but it lends itself to innumerable elaborations, nuances, and ironic twists, particularly in the licentious and parodic tales of the Age of Enlightenment. In spite of their deviant content, the latter continue to adhere to conventions established in the previous century, though not quite in the same way that Voltaire's dramas follow the rules of classical tragedy. Indeed, authors of fairy tales do not have to take formal considerations as seriously as dramatists even when they scrupulously observe and even flaunt generic conventions. Unlike dramatists duty bound to observe convention, authors of fairy tales stick to the rules because they happen to provide the best means to lift their readers into a purely fabricated universe having very little in common with their own. Conventions, including systematic indulgence in hyperbole, pave the way not so much toward suspension of disbelief but in the direction of marvelling unbelief.

NOTES

[1] Barchilon, Jacques, *Le Conte merveilleux français de 1690 à 1790* (Paris: Honoré Champion, 1975), 45.

[2] Préchac, *Contes moins contes que les autres* (Paris: Barbin, 1698). For a commentary on this tale, see Robert, Raymonde, *Le Conte de fées littéraire en France de la fin du XVIIe à la fin du XVIIIe siècle* (Nancy: Presses Universitaires, 1981).

[3] D'Auneuil, Louise de Bossigny, *La Tyrannie des fées détruite* (Paris: Chevillon, 1702). See Robert, 228.

[4] [De Lubert?], *Cornichon et Toupette*, histoire fée, in *Le Cabinet des fées* (Amsterdam et se trouve à Paris, Rue et Hotel Serpente, 1785), 34, 432. First edition: La Haye: P. de Hondt, 1752.

[5] Villeneuve, Gabrielle-Suzanne Barbot de Gaalon de, *La Jeune Amériquaine et les contes marins* 5 vols. (La Haye: Aux dépens de la Compagnie, 1740-41). Reprint of *La Belle et la bête* in *Le Cabinet des fées*, 36, 29-214. For Villeneuve's feminism, see Judd D. Hubert, "A Reactionary Woman Novelist: Gabrielle de Villeneuve," in *Women, Gender, Genre*, in *L'Esprit Créateur*, 29 (1989), 65-75.

[6] Barchilon, 63-76.

[7] *Contes et nouvelles* (Rotterdam: Reiner Leers, 1707).

[8] Robert, notably 327-81.

[9] Bénichou, Paul, *Morales du grand siècle* (Paris: NRF, 1948), 97-111.

[10] Sorel, Charles, *La Maison des jeux* (Paris: Sercy, 1642), 2 vol.

[11] Challe, Robert, *Les Illustres françoises*, ed. Frédéric Deloffre, 2 vols. (Paris: Les Belles Lettres, 1959). First published at the end of the Sun King's reign in 1713.

[12] *Gaudriole, conte* (La Haye: Isaac Beauregard, 1746).

[13] Bakhtin, Mikhail, *Rabelais and his World* (Bloomington: Indiana University Press, 1984).

[14] Bakhtin, 118.

[15] Barchilon, notably in connection with Anthony Hamilton, p. 81. Robert, 222-23 and 233-85.

[16] [Culant, Marquis de], *Les Trois chiens, conte en vers distribué en trois chants* (Paris: Jean Pépingué, 1722).

[17] *Cabinet des fées*, 33, 104. First published at La Haye in 1743.

[18] In "Le Prince glacé et la princesse étincelante," her strange imagination provides a sort of anticipation of Condillac's famous statue. Prince Adonis, metamorphosed into a statue, tells Etincelante: "Malgré ma transformation, il me restoit l'usage des yeux & du sentiment" (33, 131). Seeing the princess induces in him a feeling of love much in the same manner that the sense of smell, the only sense granted him, induces in Condillac's statue the thought: "Je suis odeur de rose" when presented with that flower. Presumably the philosopher's imaginary work of art had previously undergone the same sort of metamorphosis as the fairy prince.

[19] *Le Cabinet de fées*, 3, 484.

[20] Attributed to de Lubert because it displays the same exuberant imagination and humor so characteristic of her tales.

[21] Crébillon, Claude-Prosper Jolyot de, *L'Ecumoire, ou Tanzaï et Néadarné, histoire japonoise*, in *Collection complette des œuvres* (Londres: 1772). First published in 1734.

[22] Robert, 436-37.

[23] *Histoire d'Hypolite, comte de Duglas* (Paris: J. B. Lamesle. 1726), vol. 2, 102.

[24] *Le Cabinet des fées*, 1, 115.

[25] "Celebration and Repression of Feminine Desire in Mme d'Aulnoy's Fairy Tale: 'La Chatte blanche,' " *L'Esprit Créateur*, 29 (1989), 52-64.

16

Tartuffe, Dufresny et Dancourt

Gérard Gouvernet

*T*ARTUFFE EST SANS CONTESTE l'une des pièces de Molière les
plus audacieuses et les plus controversées, en même temps qu'une de ses
plus grandes réussites. Il n'est donc nullement surprenant que cette comédie ait inspiré nombre d'auteurs, comme l'a constaté notamment W. D.
Howarth dans son étude sur le thème de *Tartuffe* au dix-huitième siècle.[1]
Se basant sur les travaux d'Henri C. Lancaster,[2] il signale brièvement que,
dès la fin du dix-septième siècle, le sujet en avait déjà été repris, en particulier par Dufresny dans *La Malade sans maladie* (1699) et *Le Faux Honnête
Homme* (1703), ainsi que par Dancourt dans *Madame Artus* (1708).[3]
Comme ces deux auteurs n'ont jamais caché leur admiration pour Molière,
Dufresny, non sans un agacement certain, Dancourt, avec l'intention avouée
d'être reconnu comme son successeur,[4] il semble intéressant de considérer
comment ces deux auteurs ont traité le sujet de *Tartuffe,* en partant d'un
point de vue général avant d'en aborder l'aspect religieux.

Dufresny et Dancourt ont suivi Molière, chacun à sa manière. C'est
ainsi qu'au dix-neuvième siècle, Victor Fournel a pu noter que la pièce de
Dancourt rappelait *Tartuffe*.[5] A l'opposé, Dufresny s'est inspiré de Molière
d'une manière beaucoup plus détournée. En fait, c'est par l'intrigue, même
si Dufresny la complique davantage, que ses deux comédies se rapprochent
de *Madame Artus* et de *Tartuffe.* Et l'intrigue de ces quatre pièces peut se
présenter comme une variante des scénarios traditionnels des comédies de
l'époque. Le schéma de la plupart des comédies du dix-septième siècle est
le suivant: les amours de deux jeunes gens sont contrariées pour des raisons diverses par leurs parents; un valet astucieux ou une servante dévouée
se charge généralement de supprimer les obstacles qui empêchent le mariage. Sans vouloir, bien entendu, réduire *Tartuffe* à ce genre de comédie, il

est quand même possible de faire entrer la pièce de Molière dans ce moule. L'aveuglement d'Orgon et les menées de Tartuffe, qui menacent aussi toute la famille, font obstacle au bonheur de Valère et Mariane qui ne pourront réaliser leurs projets matrimoniaux que lorsque l'imposteur aura été finalement confondu. Il en va de même dans les trois pièces de Dufresny et Dancourt qui, cependant, restent plus que Molière dans les limites du comique; ils n'ont en effet retenu ni le rebondissement de la fin de l'acte IV ni l'acte V de *Tartuffe,* à l'exception du consentement d'Orgon au mariage des jeunes gens. Le problème qui se pose dans leurs pièces est résumé ainsi dans *Le Faux Honnête Homme* de Dufresny où la servante Frosine déclare à la jeune Angélique: "Votre tante est entichée d'Ariste . . . ; il faut la désentêter de cet homme-là, c'est le nœud de l'affaire" (II, 1). Commentant *Tartuffe,* Jacques Guicharnaud apporte un jugement légèrement plus nuancé: "Orgon désabusé! voici un des grands événements de la pièce."[6] Dans l'ensemble, il suffit donc que le chef de famille ait en main les preuves de la perfidie du fourbe pour que, sortant de son aveuglement, il le chasse et cesse de s'opposer à l'union des jeunes amoureux. Néanmoins, comme dans *Tartuffe,* l'intrigant (ou l'intrigante) n'échoue que lorsqu'il (ou elle) se croit sur le point de triompher.

L'établissement d'un parallèle entre *Tartuffe* et *La Malade sans maladie* semble, a priori, délicat à effectuer. Pour pouvoir épouser Valère, la jeune Angélique espère être dotée par sa tante, La Malade, ou hériter d'un vieux cousin. Mais, d'une part, La Malade hésite entre céder son bien à l'insidieuse Lucinde, sa prétendue amie, ou épouser . . . Valère. Convaincue par un faux médecin que le mariage lui serait fatal, elle décide alors d'unir Lucinde à Valère et de lui léguer toute sa fortune. D'autre part, certes le vieux cousin meurt, mais en laissant tout son bien à La Malade. Il remet son testament à son ami Faussinville. Celui-ci prévoit, soit de montrer le testament si La Malade consent à le prendre pour époux, soit de le détruire si Angélique, devenant ainsi héritière, l'accepte pour mari. Apprenant le projet de donation au bénéfice de Lucinde, dont il connaît certaines malversations, il la force à lui signer une promesse de mariage dans laquelle le bien de La Malade constitue la dot de l'intrigante. Lorsque Lucinde accepte d'épouser Valère, Faussinville intervient et montre la promesse à La Malade qui chasse Lucinde et consent à l'union de Valère et Angélique.

Certes, Dufresny brouille les cartes en introduisant le Normand Faussinville, marquis plaideur et épouseur universel, et un problème de testament. En plus, ne serait-ce que par le titre, sa pièce évoque inéluctablement *Le Malade imaginaire.* D'ailleurs, comme le signale François

Moureau,[7] après Lancaster,[8] si l'on en croit Dangeau, la pièce aurait été jouée une fois sous le titre: *La Malade imaginaire.* Mais n'existe-t-il pas quelques similitudes entre les deux pièces de Molière? Béline rappelle Tartuffe. C'est une hypocrite qui vise la fortune d'Argan dont elle veut faire enfermer les deux filles au couvent; elle est finalement démasquée et Argan accepte qu'Angélique épouse Cléante.

On ne saurait donc s'étonner que Dufresny ait puisé tour à tour dans les deux comédies de Molière. Certains sentiments que manifestent ses personnages ou certaines situations dans lesquelles ils sont placés, ont leur source dans *Le Malade Imaginaire.* Béline et Lucinde ont plusieurs points en commun: toutes deux veulent s'enrichir aux dépens de leur dupe et en lésant l'héritière légitime; toutes deux aussi placent mal leur confiance: Béline se confie à Toinette qui s'est juré de la prendre à son propre jeu (I, 8), cependant que Lucinde a choisi pour confidente Lisette qui cherche à protéger la jeune Angélique (I, 1). La scène dans laquelle cette dernière échange des mots assez vifs avec Lucinde (I, 2) rappelle la scène de piques entre Béline et sa belle-fille (II, 6). La Malade et Argan font preuve du même égoïsme forcené. Ainsi que l'affirme François Moureau: "Comme Argan, La Malade est un monomane" (*Dufresny,* 318). Argan, lorsqu'il décrète qu'il veut un médecin pour gendre, ne songe qu'à sa santé; La Malade, après avoir déclaré en toute simplicité à Lucinde: "Quand je serai morte, nous n'aurons plus besoin de rien" (IV, 5), décide d'unir par un mariage d'intérêt les deux personnes qu'elle juge les plus aptes à s'occuper de sa petite personne (V, 7). Les deux pièces offrent un dénouement analogue. Les deux "Malades" reconnaissent enfin qui les aime et qui les hait. Argan, en feignant d'être mort, découvre la perfidie de Béline ainsi que l'affection sincère que lui voue Angélique (III, 12, 13 et 14). Quant à La Malade, c'est à une double intervention de Faussinville, qui joue ici le rôle de détonateur, qu'elle doit d'être éclaircie; d'une part, lorsqu'il lui montre la promesse de mariage, elle se rend compte de la duplicité de Lucinde; d'autre part, lorsqu'il propose à Angélique de plaider contre sa tante, le refus indigné qu'elle lui oppose, amène La Malade à reconnaître l'attachement fidèle que lui porte la jeune fille (V, 9). Ce même Faussinville, lorsqu'il se présente à La Malade, a le tort de commencer par la complimenter sur son "coloris" et son "embonpoint" (II, 5). Cléante avait commis la même erreur envers Argan (II, 2). Enfin, la satire des médecins, qui est exprimée dans *Le Malade imaginaire* par Béralde et Toinette (III, 3 et 10), est reprise, dans la pièce de Dufresny, par le serviteur La Valée qui, comme Toinette, revêt temporairement l'habit médical (V, 4).

De *Tartuffe,* Dufresny a retenu certains détails plus ou moins significatifs. Comme Dorine (I, 4), Lisette se plaint d'avoir dû veiller toute la nuit (I, 2). Le train de vie que promet La Valée à Angélique si elle accepte d'épouser son maître Faussinville (II, 8), apparaît aussi ridiculement ennuyeux que celui que, selon Dorine, mènerait Mariane, si elle acceptait de se laisser tartuffier (II, 3). L'éloquence que déploie Valère pour persuader Faussinville que son attitude est indigne d'un honnête homme, connaît le même échec que celle de Cléante, lorsqu'il reprochait à Tartuffe son manque de probité: Tartuffe éludait et se retranchait derrière ses obligations religieuses (IV, 1); lorsque Valère hausse le ton et parle duel, Faussinville, tout marquis qu'il est, répond procès (III, 1). Mais surtout, Tartuffe et Lucinde se trouvent placés dans une situation assez semblable. Tartuffe, choyé et dorloté par Orgon qui lui promet la main de sa fille (II, 1) et lui offre tous ses biens (III, 7), se retourne contre son bienfaiteur. Lucinde, qui règne en maîtresse dans la maison de La Malade qui est sur le point de lui léguer sa fortune (III, 3) et envisage de la marier (V, 7), ne songe qu'à payer d'ingratitude sa protectrice. Les qualificatifs qu'emploient à leur égard les personnages qui ne sont pas dupes de leur malhonnêteté, sont aussi voisins que peu flatteurs. Les raisons de leur échec sont toutefois différentes. Dans ce domaine, Dufresny s'éloigne de Molière. Tartuffe, trahi par sa concupiscence, est amené à baisser le masque. La position de Lucinde, qui semblait assurée au début de la pièce, se dégrade très vite, sans qu'elle en soit directement responsable. D'une part, si aucun désir charnel ne l'agite, il n'en va pas de même pour La Malade qui, loin d'être insensible au charme du jeune Valère, envisage de l'épouser. D'autre part, elle doit faire face à un autre adversaire, Faussinville, qui, à même de la faire chanter, l'obligera à se compromettre avec lui et causera sa disgrâce finale.

Certes, Dufresny n'a pas su, comme l'a finement remarqué François Moureau, maintenir le ton de la comédie de caractère et a vite transformé sa pièce en "une comédie d'intrigue financière" (*Dufresny,* 318). Cependant, sa comédie et *Tartuffe* présentent plusieurs thèmes communs: dissimulation, hypocrisie, fausse amitié, ingratitude. Et il est curieux de constater que Lancaster et Moureau sont à nouveau d'accord pour rattacher *La Malade sans maladie* à *Tartuffe* par l'intermédiaire du *Faux Honnête Homme.* Selon François Moureau, Lucinde et Faussinville annoncent les "faux honnêtes hommes" (*Dufresny,* 318). Lancaster, lui, s'était appuyé sur les frères Parfaict qui pensaient qu'Ariste rappelait fortement Lucinde et que les deux pièces de Dufresny descendaient de *Tartuffe* (*Sunset,* 203).

Dans *Le Faux Honnête Homme,* l'amour d'Angélique et Valère semble sans espoir. En effet, La Marquise, mère du jeune homme, veut que son fils épouse un riche parti, sous peine d'être déshérité. Elle accepterait Angélique pour bru, si celle-ci entrait en possession de la fortune de sa tante, La Veuve, dont le défunt mari a écrit deux testaments; dans le premier, il lègue ses biens à son nouvel ami, Ariste; dans le second, qui annule le premier, c'est son vieil ami Le Capitaine, qui devient son légataire. Informé de l'existence du deuxième testament, l'intrigant Ariste change son plan initial, qui était d'épouser La Veuve, ce qui réduisait Angélique au couvent. Il décide de se rabattre sur la riche Marquise, qui a un faible pour lui, et pousse Valère à la désobéissance en lui conseillant d'épouser secrètement Angélique. Le Capitaine, lui, n'entend rendre son bien à La Veuve qu'après l'avoir désabusée d'Ariste, à qui il propose un feint accommodement: si ce dernier l'aide à épouser La Veuve, il ne l'empêchera pas de convoler avec La Marquise, et ils se partageront la fortune du défunt. Ariste tombe dans le panneau et se trahit devant La Veuve qui, déjà ébranlée par l'éclaircissement que la servante Frosine lui avait procuré avec La Marquise et Valère, renonce au mariage et chasse Ariste. Angélique et Valère pourront se marier.

De prime abord, *Le Faux Honnête Homme* semble donc fort différent de *Tartuffe.* En fait, par certains aspects, cette pièce peut se situer à mi-chemin entre *Tartuffe* et *La Mère coupable* de Beaumarchais. Surtout si l'on considère le personnage d'Ariste. Comme Bégearss et avant lui, il a l'oreille de presque tous les autres personnages tout en étant desservi par la maladresse de son valet. Et lui aussi, pour reprendre l'expression de Beaumarchais, apparaît comme un "Tartuffe de la probité." Il vante lui-même ses vertus (II, 2), et La Veuve "aime sa sincérité, son désintéressement, sa probité" (I, 1). Il n'est pas sans rappeler Tartuffe. Le portrait physique qu'en trace Frosine: "Sa probité a le teint vermeil, les yeux vifs" (I, 1) fait écho à celui de Tartuffe par Dorine: "Gros et gras, le teint frais et la bouche vermeille" (I, 4, 234). Si Tartuffe a attiré l'attention d'Orgon par d'ostentatoires actes de dévotion (I, 5), la première rencontre entre Ariste et le défunt mari de La Veuve n'a pas été fortuite: elle a été longuement préparée par le fourbe qui, après avoir pris des renseignements sur sa future dupe qui "était si bonhomme, si bon, si bon, qu'il n'avait point d'esprit du tout," l'a alors subjuguée en faisant preuve d'une feinte générosité (I, 11). Lorsque les deux hypocrites entrent en scène au milieu de la pièce, le spectateur sait à quoi s'en tenir sur leur compte. Tous deux se justifient avec aisance des premières accusations qui sont portées contre eux, Tartuffe de celles de

Damis (III, 6), Ariste de la teneur d'une lettre compromettante que Frosine avait remise à La Veuve (II, 11). On fait aussi allusion à leur passé, brièvement chez Molière (V, 7), avec beaucoup plus de détails chez Dufresny (I, 11 et II, 6). Enfin, de même qu'Orgon, pour reconnaître la vilenie de Tartuffe, a besoin de le prendre, pour ainsi dire, sur le fait (IV, 5 et 6), de même, La Veuve, bien qu'informée par Valère et La Marquise de la fausseté d'Ariste, doit l'entendre se rétracter devant elle, pour y croire (III, 12).

Dans cette comédie, ". . . l'amour est constamment bafoué et la cupidité élevée à la hauteur d'une passion universelle," constate mélancoliquement François Moureau, avant de regretter que Dufresny soit encore une fois passé à côté ". . . de ce qui aurait pu être une grande pièce à la manière de *Tartuffe*" (*Dufresny*, 323-24). C'est surtout le personnage d'Ariste, sorte de chevalier d'industrie sur le retour et qui entend faire une fin, qui permet d'effectuer un rapprochement significatif entre les deux pièces.

A son tour, Dancourt va, dans *Madame Artus*, tenter de camper un Tartuffe en jupons. Jules Lemaitre a abruptement résumé la pièce en ces termes: "Le sujet rappelle *Tartuffe*. Mme Argante, une bourgeoise avare et dure (cf. Orgon), est dominée par Mme Artus, une intrigante hypocrite (cf. Tartuffe) . . . Mme Artus, qui a jeté son dévolu sur le fils de la maison, est mystifiée et démasquée par un notaire trop malin."[9] De fait, les manigances de l'intrigante éponyme viennent traverser les amours de Célide et Dorante, les deux enfants de sa bienfaitrice. Alors que la jeune fille a donné sa foi à Eraste, l'ami de son frère, et que ce dernier est follement épris d'une jeune fermière, Rosette, au point de lui avoir signé une promesse de mariage, ils se voient informés que Mme Argante a l'intention d'épouser Eraste, tandis que Mme Artus deviendra sa bru et héritière en se mariant avec Dorante.[10] Obligée toutefois de composer avec Eraste qui est au courant de certaines de ses escroqueries antérieures, Mme Artus lui promet que, sur le contrat de mariage, le nom de Célide remplacera celui de Mme Argante. Le notaire qui dresse les contrats n'étant autre, ce que Mme Artus ignore, que l'oncle de Rosette, va donc tromper la trompeuse en procédant à une double substitution de nom sur les contrats. Les jeunes amoureux se trouveront mariés par ses soins, cependant que Mme Artus sera déconfite et chassée.

L'imitation de Dancourt ne semble pas tellement servile. On pourrait même considérer que sa pièce traite de la mésaventure ou du désabusement d'un personnage qui apparaît avec une certaine fréquence dans d'autres de ses comédies ou dans certaines de Regnard, la vieille amoureuse, la dame d'un certain âge, tourmentée par le démon de midi. Ceci est vrai aussi, dans

La Malade sans maladie, pour la maîtresse de maison qui s'éprend d'un jeune homme et devient la rivale de sa nièce. En ce qui concerne l'intrigante, que ce soit Lucinde ou Mme Artus, elle est menée plus par l'intérêt que par la concupiscence, même si la déclaration de Mme Artus à Dorante (IV, 7) laisse quelque place à l'équivoque.

En outre, Dancourt semble s'être souvenu de *L'Avare.* La rivalité amoureuse entre la mère et la fille semble être une transposition de celle qui existait entre Harpagon et Cléante. Le valet Merlin présente Mme Argante comme une vieille ladre qui refuse de céder à son fils, pourtant majeur, la part d'héritage qui lui revient (I, 1). Ce dernier, comme Cléante, est endetté et sur le point de se mésallier.

Le personnage même de Mme Artus diffère, dans une certaine mesure, de celui de Tartuffe. Plus froide et calculatrice comme Lucinde, elle monnaie ses services (IV, 3) et n'hésite pas à baisser le masque successivement devant Eraste (IV, 3), Dorante (IV, 7) et le notaire Mr. Ludet (V, 11), avant de révéler finalement sa fausseté devant Mme Argante. Dancourt lui a prêté une vocation de marieuse: si on l'écoutait, tous les personnages se retrouveraient mariés, bon gré mal gré, à la fin de la pièce. Enfin, Dancourt s'est écarté de Molière en introduisant le personnage du notaire. L'action de ce dernier, en tant que *deus ex machina,* n'est pas sans rappeler, mais dans une faible mesure, l'intervention de l'exempt du dénouement de *Tartuffe,* intervention qui constitue un véritable coup de théâtre, alors que, dans *Madame Artus,* dès le troisième acte (III, 13), le spectateur est informé que Mr Ludet est en train de duper Mme Artus. Ce faisant, Dancourt a, dans une grande mesure, déplacé le centre de l'intérêt dramatique. Dans sa pièce, il ne s'agit plus de se demander si le personnage inquiétant connaîtra l'échec ou le succès, mais comment il sera battu à son propre jeu par le notaire. Dancourt maintient néanmoins une certaine incertitude en faisant exprimer à Célide des doutes sur la réussite du plan de Mr Ludet (V, 9). Dans ce contexte, le ton et l'ambiance sont différents: alors que les membres de la famille d'Orgon redoutent, à juste titre, Tartuffe, ceux de la famille de Mme Argante se permettent de railler ouvertement Mme Artus, dès qu'ils apprennent ses projets matrimoniaux (V, 10).

Il n'en reste pas moins qu'en dépit de ces divergences, Dancourt s'est largement inspiré de *Tartuffe.* Ne serait-ce déjà que par le titre. Selon Lancaster, le nom de l'héroïne éponyme dérive de Tartuffe, cependant que Mme Argante sonne comme Orgon (*Sunset,* 154-55). Pour André Blanc, Mme Artus est "un amalgame entre AR(sinoé) et (Tar)TUFFE."[11] De par leur attitude, certains personnages ressemblent à ceux de Molière. Ainsi,

Merlin et Finette donnent-ils des avis semblables à ceux qu'émettait Dorine. Comme elle (II, 4), ils conseillaient à leurs maîtres d'essayer de gagner du temps (II, 2). Et, si la servante de Molière avait dû abréger la réconciliation de Mariane et Valère (II, 4), la soubrette de Dancourt se verra obligée d'écourter les protestations amoureuses de Dorante et Rosette (V, 4). Quant à Damis, le frère de Mme Argante, il vient, au début de la pièce, réprimander ses neveux, mais il faut bien reconnaître qu'il est loin de posséder la pétulance de l'irascible Mme Pernelle; par la suite, son rôle se rapproche de celui de Cléante dans *Tartuffe;* ce dernier reprochait au faux dévot son attitude après la querelle entre Orgon et son fils (IV, 1): Damis, lui, soupçonne bien vite Mme Artus d'entretenir volontairement la mésentente entre son neveu et sa sœur (I, 5). Celle-ci est aussi aveugle qu'Orgon. Il avait choisi Tartuffe pour gendre, elle offre la main de son fils à Mme Artus.[12]

Mais c'est surtout avec le personnage de Mme Artus que l'imitation de Dancourt devient flagrante. Comme Tartuffe, Mme Artus n'apparaît qu'au troisième acte. Molière évoque à deux reprises le passé de Tartuffe, la première par l'intermédiaire d'Orgon (I, 5), la seconde par celui de l'exempt (V, 7). Dancourt ne manque pas de faire tracer par Eraste un portrait fort édifiant de Mme Artus (II, 3). Comme Laurent, le valet de Tartuffe, Ursule, la domestique de Mme Artus, demeure invisible. Si l'on en croit Dorine (I, 4) et Finette (II, 2), les deux parasites partagent le même amour du confort et de la bonne chère. Les expressions injurieuses qu'emploient les autres personnages pour les désigner sont peut-être plus nombreuses et variées dans *Madame Artus*. Le jugement méprisant que porte Mme Artus sur Damis: "C'est un assez sot homme, espèce d'imbécile, / Encore plus que sa sœur à gouverner facile" (V, 11), n'est qu'un souvenir de la piètre opinion que Tartuffe avait d'Orgon: "C'est un homme, entre nous, à mener par le nez" (IV, 5, 1524). Tartuffe affirmait à Elmire: "Je vous réponds de tout et prends le mal sur moi" (IV, 5, 1496). Mme Artus lui fait écho: "Mettez le tout sur moi," précise-t-elle au notaire (V, 11). Enfin, certains vers de Molière se retrouvent, à peine transformés, sous la plume de Dancourt. Lorsque les deux hypocrites sont démasqués, ils se voient sommés de quitter la place en des termes fort semblables. Orgon menaçait ainsi Tartuffe: "Allons, point de bruit, je vous prie / Dénichons de céans et sans cérémonie," avant d'ajouter: "Il faut, tout sur-le-champ, sortir de la maison" (IV, 7, 1553-54, 1556). Chez Dancourt, Dorante déclare sèchement: "Allons, Madame Artus, décampez de céans" (V, 14), avant que sa mère n'intervienne à son tour: "Et sortez de chez moi sans éclat et sans bruit" (V, 15).

La dette de Dancourt envers Molière est donc bien plus lourde que celle de Dufresny et il y a, entre *Tartuffe* et *Madame Artus* plus que la certaine ressemblance mentionnée par Victor Fournel.

En définitive, en dehors de ces imitations ou similitudes, les principaux éléments qui permettent d'effectuer un rapprochement entre ces différentes pièces, se trouvent rassemblés dans le personnage central et la situation dans laquelle il se trouve. Chaque fois, il s'agit d'un aventurier, homme ou femme, dénué de scrupules, d'un intrigant au passé douteux, d'un parasite insidieux qui s'incruste dans une maison aisée, et qui, après avoir capté, en affichant hypocritement des dehors respectables et vertueux, la confiance aveugle du trop crédule chef de famille, vise à s'établir bourgeoisement grâce à un mariage avantageux qui entraînerait la ruine totale de la famille qui l'a accueilli. Heureusement, il échoue. Toutefois, cet échec n'est pas dû aux mêmes raisons dans *Tartuffe* et dans les autres pièces. Dans ces dernières, le fourbe est démasqué ou dupé par une tierce personne, Lucinde par Faussinville, Ariste par Le Capitaine, Mme Artus par le notaire. Sans vouloir minimiser le rôle d'Elmire, on peut affirmer que Tartuffe, lui, en fait, se trahit lui-même. Sa concupiscence l'emporte et il se découvre. Ce conflit que se livrent en lui la froide raison, l'intérêt, l'ambition et les exigences des sens est une des raisons qui rendent son personnage infiniment plus vivant et intéressant que celui des autres imposteurs. C'est ce que Jacques Guicharnaud appelle "la dualité fondamentale" de Tartuffe, à savoir: "sa tendance consommatrice et sa volonté de paraître ce qu'il n'est pas" (*Molière,* 102). L'art de Molière a consisté à peindre un homme qui se voit obligé de professer une rigueur ascétique, alors qu'il est naturellement doté d'une sensualité exigeante, à tel point que Harold C. Knutson n'hésitera pas à affirmer: "Pleasure for him is but the violent coupling of animals."[13] La nature l'emporte et il succombe. En comparaison, ses successeurs, uniquement calculateurs et menés par le désir de s'enrichir à tout prix, paraissent bien fades. Même Mme Artus, si elle est vraiment sincère, lorsqu'elle résume ainsi leurs aspirations: "Un rang, un nom, du bien, voilà ce que je veux" (IV, 7). C'est pourquoi, dépourvus de la richesse psychologique de Tartuffe, à la fois paradoxale, contradictoire et donc plus réelle, plus humaine, ils n'en apparaissent que comme de pâles répliques.

Il reste maintenant à aborder l'autre problème posé par *Tartuffe,* le moins négligeable d'ailleurs, celui qui a longuement retardé la parution de la pièce et a fait couler le plus d'encre, à savoir le problème religieux. Dans ce domaine, le grand reproche qui a été adressé à Molière concerne l'équivoque qui a plané sur ses réelles intentions, en dépit de ses protestations. Même s'il ne voulait que dénoncer l'hypocrisie des faux dévots, il a porté atteinte à la vraie religion. Paul Bénichou l'a bien vu, qui déclare: "les porte-parole les plus divers du christianisme au dix-septième siècle, quel que fût leur caractère ou celui de leur secte, ont jugé *Le Tartuffe* dangereux," avant de s'expliquer sur l'ambiguïté de la position adoptée par Molière: "Or, on ne peut nier que ce soit une forme de pensée bien peu édifiante que de charger de tous les vices quiconque fait profession de censurer le vice."[14] A côté du faux dévot, Molière a introduit deux personnages sincères qui représentent deux pôles opposés de la religion: Orgon et Cléante. Le premier, qui essaie, avec sa mère, de mettre en pratique les préceptes prônés par Tartuffe, symbolise une forme de religion austère, rigide, bornée, envahissante et qui tend au fanatisme; avec Cléante, la religion reste sincère et authentique, mais prend la forme d'un humanisme chrétien plus souriant. Il sert de contre-poids à Tartuffe auquel il est le seul à pouvoir asséner des arguments imparables dans le domaine religieux.

Chez Dufresny et Dancourt, les personnages qui s'opposent à l'imposteur et le démasquent ou le dupent, ne se posent aucun problème religieux. Faussinville ne songe qu'à plaider, Mr Ludet n'a en tête que le mariage de sa nièce; quant au Capitaine du *Faux Honnête Homme,* c'est un personnage haut en couleur et pittoresque, qui va battre Ariste à son propre jeu en lui laissant croire qu'il est aussi fripon que lui. Tous trois se soucient peu de la morale chrétienne et se montrent dénués de scrupules; pour eux, la fin justifie les moyens.

Cléante n'a donc pas d'équivalent dans ces comédies de Dufresny et Dancourt. En est-il de même pour le personnage central dans le domaine religieux? Il est hors de doute que Molière a peint dans Tartuffe le prototype de l'hypocrite en matière de religion. Selon Gérard Ferreyrolles, "Il existe sans doute un bon usage de l'hypocrisie—c'est "l'abêtissement" pascalien avec son eau bénite et ses génuflexions—mais nulle métamorphose de Tartuffe ne vient témoigner que l'hypocrite se serait laissé prendre à son propre jeu . . . ."[15] Loin de là! En fait, le personnage de Tartuffe apparaît comme une parodie et une réfutation de l'hypocrisie pascalienne. A la fin de l'argument du Pari, Pascal, on s'en souvient, conseillait au libertin qui n'avait pas la foi, d'en adopter les signes extérieurs pour s'y habituer, de faire semblant de croire pour la gagner. Plus Tartuffe affecte des dehors dévots, moins il se montre chrétien et fait peser sur Orgon et sa famille, comme l'a noté Jacques Scherer, des périls croissants d'ordre sentimental d'abord, financier ensuite et enfin politique.[16]

Dans *La Malade sans maladie,* la flatteuse Lucinde affiche quelques qualités très chrétiennes: "Ce n'est point vertu chez moi d'aimer ceux qui me haïssent . . . " déclare-t-elle à Angélique, qui voit clair dans son jeu (I, 2). Et, plus tard, elle avance: "Je ne vois jamais que l'utilité d'autrui" (II, 6). Tartuffe, lui aussi, avait pardonné "l'offense" de Damis et n'avait soi-disant en vue que l'intérêt public en acceptant la fortune d'Orgon (IV, 1).

Dufresny, on l'a vu plus haut, se retranche derrière le mot de probité dans *Le Faux Honnête Homme.* Ariste prétend et passe pour être la probité faite homme. Il est toutefois un incident trivial qui rappelle la casuistique de Tartuffe, quand il avance qu'une bonne intention peut excuser une mauvaise action. Lorsque le dévot voulait séduire Elmire, il s'efforçait de la persuader que

> Selon divers besoins, il est une science
> D'étendre les liens de notre conscience,
> Et de rectifier le mal de l'action
> Avec la pureté de notre intention
>   (IV, 5, 1489-92)

avant d'ajouter: "Et ce n'est pas pécher que pécher en silence" (1506). Chez Dufresny, Ariste justifie, par un raisonnement semblable que rapporte son valet, l'indélicatesse qui consiste à ouvrir le courrier d'autrui. Elle est, selon lui, légitime, si l'on a en vue les intérêts du destinataire et si le procédé demeure indécelable. La suivante Frosine s'empressera donc de lire une lettre qui était destinée à l'intrigant en s'écriant: "Dès qu'il n'y paraît pas, cela est permis" (II, 6).

De tous ces hypocrites, Mme Artus demeure le personnage qui se rapproche le plus de Tartuffe sur ce point aussi. Pourtant, André Blanc pense qu'elle n'est "nullement dévote, ou à peine et si discrètement! . . . Seules, ses "vertus" et son feint détachement du monde rappellent la piété chrétienne" (*Dancourt,* 112). Il précisera plus loin: " Enfin, *Madame Artus* s'en prend moins à la dévotion officielle qu'à une certaine forme de direction laïque, en rapport avec une déviation de la mentalité janséniste" (*Dancourt,* 181). Mme Artus présente néanmoins beaucoup de caractéristiques d'une fausse dévote. Bien qu'ayant été mariée et ayant pratiqué la coquetterie et même la galanterie, elle prône, tout comme Tartuffe chez Orgon, une morale austère et se mêle de régenter la conduite des enfants de

Mme Argante. Elle condamne ainsi notamment les écarts de jeunesse de Dorante et déplore que Célide ne soit nullement attirée par les choses spirituelles et n'aime guère passer ses journées à filer et faire des nœuds (II, 4). Comme, à l'instar de Tartuffe, elle "n'a point d'autre objet / Que le bien du public dans tout ce qu'elle fait" (II, 4), elle pratique aussi la charité, en même temps que l'usure d'ailleurs. Elle prête de l'argent (qu'elle a soutiré à Mme Argante bien entendu) à seize pour cent, en conserve cinq pour cent et fait distribuer le reste aux pauvres (IV, 5). Elle se montre donc plus rouée que Tartuffe et soigne ainsi à la fois sa bourse et sa réputation. Et si Elmire peut dire à Tartuffe: "C'est que vous n'aimez rien des choses de la terre" (III, 3, 929), Madame Artus affirme à Dorante: "Et de ce monde-là je voudrais m'arracher" (IV, 7). Mme Argante en était persuadée: "Au monde son dessein était de renoncer", avait-elle expliqué à Finette (II, 4). Mais, tout comme Tartuffe, Mme Artus se heurte à un dilemme. Il reconnaissait devant Elmire que l'abstinence lui pesait: "L'amour qui nous attache aux beautés éternelles / N'étouffe pas en nous l'amour des temporelles" (III, 3, 933-34). Mme Artus, pour être dévote, n'en est pas moins femme. Chez elle, la vanité et le désir de paraître sont en conflit avec ses intentions religieuses:

> Telle de notre sexe est l'erreur sans seconde
> Qu'il n'offre guère au Ciel que le rebut du monde;
> Ce n'est qu'à soixante ans que l'on songe à quitter
> Ce monde où jusque-là on se plaît de rester.

Mais, à la différence de Tartuffe, elle a trouvé une solution morale et avantageuse: la retraite à deux dans le mariage,

> On peut, du vrai bonheur se faisant une étude,
> Jouir du monde ensemble, et de la solitude,
> Et s'unir à quelqu'un, qui légitimement
> Fasse tous nos plaisirs, tous nos attachements. (IV, 7)

Enfin, Mme Pernelle était convaincue, à propos de Tartuffe: "Que le Ciel, au besoin, l'a céans envoyé" (I, 1, 147), Finette, la soubrette, lorsqu'elle parle de Mme Artus, n'hésite pas à évoquer Dieu ou . . . le démon. Devant Mme Argante, elle affirme ironiquement: "Le Ciel exprès pour vous a fait Madame Artus" (II, 4). Mais, seule avec Merlin, elle espère la voir chassée de la place et souhaite que "Le diable qui l'y mit, quelque jour ne l'en chasse" (I, 2).

En dépit de ces quelques audaces, Dancourt se garde bien de faire tenir à Mme Artus le langage des dévots. Il reste bien loin du ton qu'emploie Molière pour dénoncer la pudibonderie et l'hypocrisie religieuses et pour mettre en cause la cagoterie du parti dévot et la casuistique jésuite, tout en s'amusant à affubler son personnage central d'au moins six des sept péchés capitaux.[17]

On peut s'étonner devant la timidité ou la pusillanimité que manifestent Dufresny et Dancourt. Pourtant, dans d'autres pièces, Dancourt a porté à la scène des abbés galants et pomponnés, mais les petits-collets restent dans la tradition gauloise et farcesque du moine paillard et demeurent amusants, alors que Tartuffe est inquiétant. Et il était certainement moins dangereux pour le pouvoir et la société de voir le public rire des abbés mondains que de laisser ridiculiser et attaquer la foi et les croyants, même si telle n'était pas l'intention de Molière. De plus, les circonstances avaient changé. Le jeune Louis XIV protégeait Molière et ne voyait pas d'un mauvais œil diminuer l'importance du parti dévot. Au moment où Dancourt et Dufresny écrivent, Louis XIV a vieilli et, sous l'influence de Madame de Maintenon, est apparemment devenu profondément croyant. Il cesse de protéger les comédiens. En 1697, la troupe des Comédiens Italiens est bannie de Paris, très certainement pour avoir représenté une pièce de Lenoble intitulée *La Fausse Prude,* que Madame de Maintenon avait jugée scandaleuse et sacrilège et dans laquelle elle s'était sentie visée. Ceci explique peut-être pourquoi Dufresny et Dancourt, lorsqu'ils ont repris le sujet de Tartuffe, en ont, sans doute volontairement, négligé l'aspect religieux ou, plus exactement, qui pouvait paraître anti-religieux, et pourquoi Dancourt a résisté à la tentation de peindre Madame Artus sous les traits d'une fausse dévote.

En définitive, le jugement que W. D. Howarth porte sur les imitations de *Tartuffe* par les dramaturges du dix-huitième siècle: "Needless to say, the similarity of these plays to Moliere's is limited to a resemblance of theme: they do not reproduce the character of Tartuffe as a 'faux dévot,' but as a rogue of some other sort" (*The Theme of Tartuffe,* 114), peut très bien s'adapter aux trois comédies de Dufresny et Dancourt. Avec ces deux auteurs, on assiste à une laïcisation prudente du sujet principal de *Tartuffe,* plus flagrante chez Dufresny; la fausse probité et le faux dévouement remplacent la fausse dévotion.

NOTES

[1] W. D. Howarth, "The Theme of *Tartuffe* in Eighteenth-Century Comedy," *French Studies* 4 (1950), 113-14.

[2] Henri C. Lancaster, *Sunset, A History of Parisian Drama in the Last Years of Louis XIV, 1701-1715* (Baltimore: The John Hopkins Press, 1945), 154 et 203.

[3] Je considère que le dix-septième siècle ne finit qu'à la mort de Louis XIV.

[4] Dufresny, dans le Prologue du *Négligent* en 1692; Dancourt à deux reprises: dans le Prologue de *Céphale et Procris* (1711) et dans l'Epitre à Monseigneur le duc de Mortemart qui prélude à *Sancho Pança, gouverneur* (1712).

[5] Victor Fournel, *Le Théâtre au dix-septième siècle, La Comédie* (Paris: Lecène, Oudin et Cie, 1892), 392.

[6] Jacques Guicharnaud, *Molière, une aventure théâtrale* (Paris: Gallimard, 1963), 127.

[7] François Moureau, *Dufresny, auteur dramatique (1657-1724)* (Paris: Klincksieck, 1979), 71-72.

[8] Henri C. Lancaster, *A History of French Dramatic Literature in the Seventeenth Century* 1940 (New York: Gordian Press, 1966), IV, II, 761.

[9] Jules Lemaître, *La Comédie après Molière et le théâtre de Dancourt* (Paris: Hachette, 1882), 206-07.

[10] Ces dames trichent sur leur âge: Mme Artus prétend avoir 35 ans (IV, 7); Mme Argante n'en avance que 30 (III, 9). Pourtant, son fils Dorante a bel et bien 25 ans (I, 1).

[11] André Blanc, *F. C. Dancourt (1661-1725), La Comédie française à l'heure du soleil couchant* (Tübingen: Gunter Narr, 1984), 112.

[12] Toutefois, leurs raisons sont différentes. Orgon veut prouver son attachement à Tartuffe en lui donnant sa fille. Mme Argante pense seulement à essayer de justifier devant l'opinion publique son propre mariage avec Eraste. Comme le dit Mme Artus, "Chacune a sa faiblesse; elle veut que la mienne / Autorise, ou du moins fasse excuser la sienne" (IV, 7).

[13] Harold C. Knutson, *Molière, An Archetypal Approach* (Toronto and Buffalo: University of Toronto Press, 1976), 82.

[14] Paul Bénichou, *Morales du Grand Siècle* 1948 (Paris: Gallimard, 1988), 275 et 280.

[15] Gérard Ferreyrolles, *Molière. Tartuffe* (Paris: Presses Universitaires de France, 1987), 89.

[16] Jacques Scherer, *Structures de Tartuffe* (Paris: SEDES, 1974), 185.

[17] A savoir l'orgueil (I, 5 et II, 12), la luxure (III, 3 et IV, 5), la gourmandise (I, 2 et 5), la colère (I, 5). De plus Tartuffe est paresseux et certainement envieux. En revanche, il ne semble pas être avare.

BIBLIOGRAPHIE

Bénichou, Paul. *Morales du Grand Siècle*. 1948. Paris: Gallimard, 1988.

Blanc, André. *F. C. Dancourt (1661-1725)*. *La Comédie française à l'heure du soleil couchant*. Tübingen: Gunter Narr, 1984.

Dancourt, Florent Carton. *Madame Artus,* in *Œuvres de théâtre*. Tome 10. Paris: Aux dépens des Libraires associés, 1760.

Dufresny, Charles Rivière. *La Malade sans maladie* et *Le Faux Honnête Homme*, in *Œuvres*. Vol. 2. Paris: Briasson, 1731.

Ferreyrolles, Gérard. *Molière, Tartuffe*. Paris: Presses Universitaires de France, 1987.

Fournel, Victor. *Le Théâtre au dix-septième siècle. La Comédie*. Paris: Lecène, Oudin et Cie, 1892.

Guicharnaud, Jacques. *Molière, une aventure théâtrale*. Paris: Gallimard, 1963.

Howarth, D.C. "The Theme of *Tartuffe* in Eighteenth-Century Comedy," *French Studies* 4 (1950), 113-27.

Knutson, Harold, C. *Molière, An Archetypal Approach*. Toronto and Buffalo: University of Toronto Press, 1976.

Lancaster, Henri, C. *A History of French Dramatic Literature in the Seventeenth Century*. 1940. New York: Gordian Press, 1966.

———. *Sunset, A History of Parisian Drama in the last years of Louis XIV, 1701-1715*. Baltimore: The John Hopkins Press, 1945.

Lemaître, Jules. *La Comédie après Molière et le théâtre de Dancourt*. Paris: Hachette, 1882.

Molière. *Tartuffe* in *Œuvres complètes*. Ed. Robert Jouanny. Vol. 1. Paris: Garnier frères, 1962.

———. *Le Malade imaginaire* in *Œuvres complètes*. Vol. 2.

Moureau, François. *Dufresny, auteur dramatique (1657-1724)*. Paris: Klincksieck, 1979.

Scherer, Jacques. *Structures de Tartuffe*. Paris: SEDES, 1987.

17

Molière républicain: La Réception critique et scolaire de son œuvre au dix-neuvième siècle

Ralph Albanese, Jr.

SAISIR LA TRANSFORMATION DE MOLIÈRE en objet de lecture au dix-neuvième siècle, c'est-à-dire, sa constitution définitive en classique scolaire, c'est tenir compte, au préalable, de l'histoire de l'enseignement littéraire à cette époque. Ces deux pratiques institutionnelles sont à tel point enchevêtrées qu'elles en viennent à représenter une forme suprême d'acculturation visant, à partir des années 1870, à "républicaniser" les esprits. On ne s'étonne guère que l'idéologie de la Troisième République se soit appuyée sur la notion de survie nationale afin de programmer les valeurs de certitude, de cohésion et de permanence en véritables fondements de l'identité culturelle de la France. Dans la mesure où cette idéologie s'inspirait d'une foi laïque, elle attachait une importance primordiale à l'Ecole au sein d'une société se voulant "moderne": il s'agissait avant tout d'enraciner la République par le biais de l'instruction publique, de scolariser en quelque sorte des valeurs et des modes de comportement. Garante la plus sûre de l'unité et de la reconstruction nationales, l'éducation se donnait pour tâche alors de surpasser l'ancien système de privilèges. Si nous envisageons l'enseignement secondaire de cette époque comme un processus de socialisation, c'est qu'il faisait preuve d'une dimension anthropologique et même ethnologique en ce sens que la mise en place des programmes littéraires témoignait de cette problématique fondamentale de toute culture moderne, c'est-à-dire, la transmission du savoir.

Dans cette perspective, l'Ecole républicaine constitue un appareil heuristique de premier ordre nous permettant de comprendre l'évolution culturelle de la France de la fin du dix-neuvième siècle, évolution marquée par un ensemble de bouleversements idéologiques et socio-culturels:

1) *L'éveil du nationalisme*—l'exaltation du patriotisme, valeur suprême dépassant les antagonismes politiques entre la Droite et la Gauche, d'où l'idéalisation du passé national, la genèse concomitante du concept d' "ethnie." Ainsi s'explique la volonté d'instaurer une défense et illustration de la culture classique, liée à une valorisation du "génie" national: la langue et la littérature françaises incarnent le mieux cet idéal.

2) *L'essor de la bourgeoisie*—l'avènement définitif de cette classe coïncide avec le règne de Louis-Philippe (1830-1848). Se définissant comme les héritiers légitimes de la culture, les bourgeois de cette époque sont animés d'un désir profond de distinction. Ils fondent leur identité sociale sur leur prise en charge, dès 1808, de l'enseignement secondaire et supérieur, ce qui leur permet de constituer une nouvelle élite. Dès lors, le lycée devient l'institution qui légitime la sélection sociale, permettant ainsi la formation de futurs notables: le baccalauréat représente une véritable barrière socio-culturelle. Attachée à la préservation des valeurs traditionnelles, cette classe adopte la morale du juste milieu, fondée sur les vertus de probité, de travail et d'épargne. A l'élitisme social s'ajoute du reste un élitisme moral, une justification sereine de son propre enrichissement.[1]

3) *La politique de laïcité*—cette politique cristallise la dimension idéologique de la querelle scolaire lors de la fondation de l'Ecole républicaine. La laïcisation de l'Etat suppose la création d'une nouvelle société, libérée à jamais du pouvoir d'un cléricalisme toujours redoutable; l'unité spirituelle et morale des Français doit s'accomplir, selon Jules Ferry, en dehors de toute référence au christianisme.[2] On assiste alors à l'émergence d'une "sacralité" d'ordre laïc, les vérités religieuses cédant la place à une nouvelle sacralisation, celle de la culture nationale. La mise en place d'un canon artistique et littéraire entraîne la transformation du musée et de l'école en "espaces sacrés." Désireuse de faire l'éloge du "grand homme" de la nation, la culture académique privilégie les textes du programme chargés d'illustrer le culte des lettres et fonde en même temps l'éducation morale des Français.

4) *L'avènement d'une "démocratie" républicaine*—la Troisième République exalte l'idéal de l'unité des classes par l'intermédiaire d'une démocratisation à la fois sociale et pédagogique. Telle que la préconise Lanson, l'histoire littéraire vise à mettre en valeur un patrimoine culturel de moins en moins connu vers la fin du siècle. L'égalitarisme se heurte toutefois à l'élitisme d'un public scolaire détenteur de privilèges sociaux.

5) *L'enseignement du français*—il s'agit d'institutionnaliser un "français national" à la portée de tous les citoyens de la République. Bien national et culturel par excellence, le français assure de la sorte l'unité linguistique du pays. De plus, la grammaire scolaire s'insère dans un enseignement littéraire normatif: on aspire à la perfection linguistique, s'apppuyant en l'occurrence sur des modèles prescriptifs afin de discipliner, voire de moraliser les élèves. Grâce aux réformes scolaires des années 1880, le français est élevé au statut d'une discipline autonome au point de devenir le "centre de gravité" du système d'enseignement secondaire. Langue littéraire, le français contribue de façon décisive à la formation d'un classicisme scolaire, et les lettrés seront de plus en plus détenteurs d'un savoir canonique.

Fondé sur la rhétorique, l'enseignement traditionnel prône une lecture de textes fort dirigée—la récitation des "morceaux d'éloquence"—supposant ainsi une expérience essentiellement mimétique où la mémoire joue un rôle essentiel. L'avènement de la notion d'histoire littéraire en 1840 coïncide avec l'émergence d'un "discours français," où l'on puise de manière systématique des sujets de composition dans l'œuvre des auteurs du patrimoine. Les pratiques scolaires se ramènent, en gros, à la narration (la rédaction moderne), à la maxime à développer, au lieu commun de morale et de critique et, dans les années 1880, à l'explication de texte. Permettant la vérification des significations admises, ce dernier exercice met en jeu une démarche inductive propre à la méthode expérimentale; il développe l'esprit critique de l'élève et assure en même temps une compréhension satisfaisante d'un français classique de moins en moins intelligible, autant dire, de plus en plus académique. . . . Alors que l'histoire littéraire constitue un appareil conceptuel s'adressant à l'enseignement supérieur, l'explication de textes représente, elle, une expérience pratique destinée aux élèves du secondaire. Grâce à l'apport fondamental de Lanson, l'enseignement littéraire, fondé sur la promotion d'une certaine idée de la littérature nationale, acquiert droit de cité au sein de l'Ecole républicaine. Tous les "grands écrivains" personnifient, à des degrés divers, les traits de l'identité nationale: le "bon" La Fontaine, le "glorieux" Corneille, le "tendre" Racine et l' "aimable" Molière symbolisent autant d'icônes culturelles du panthéon scolaire français. Etant donné la valeur esthétique et éthique incontestable que l'on attache à la littérature classique, le dix-septième siècle finit par devenir la source primordiale d'un enseignement littéraire désireux de formuler un classicisme scolaire. Signalons, toutefois, que Lanson n'a pas manqué de souligner la difficulté de réconcilier une littérature inspirée d'un siècle monarchique et catholique avec les principes de la laïcité républicaine.[3]

Ce qui caractérise peut-être le mieux la nouvelle orientation de l'éducation libérale en France au dix-neuvième siècle, c'est le triomphe des humanités "modernes" (le français) sur les humanités classiques (le latin). L'humanisme littéraire traditionnel s'avère particulièrement apte à former les citoyens, que l'on considère la Monarchie constitutionnelle, le Second Empire ou bien la Troisième République. Férue de l'idéal d'une "culture générale" qu'il s'agit de dispenser, cette idéologie académique affiche un mépris profond pour l'enseignement technique ou spécialisé. Le vrai, le beau et le bien, voilà les valeurs suprêmes de cet idéalisme—Nisard exalte à ce sujet les "vérités durables"[4]—qui crée en fin de compte une barrière culturelle empêchant toute incursion du réel, toute référence aux courants politiques et philosophiques du dix-neuvième siècle, tels l'utilitarisme, la démocratie, le matérialisme, etc. On ne saurait trop insister, dans cette perspective, sur le sens d'une mission à la fois professionnelle et civique propre aux "hussards noirs de la République," ainsi qu'aux professeurs de l'enseignement secondaire: ils s'érigent en défenseurs ardents de la culture classique, en serviteurs de la mission civilisatrice de la France.[5] La littérature se transforme, chez eux, en un vaste programme de moralisation, et le professeur de lettres sert, plus précisément, de médiateur privilégié des chefs-d'œuvre du patrimoine; les "écrivains de génie," eux, servent à diriger la conscience nationale. On assiste, en somme, à un souci d'évangéliser une culture perçue sous forme d'une nouvelle religion laïque.

Ce qui légitime le choix de Molière dans cette enquête, c'est le fait qu'il apparaît, de manière encore plus nette que d'autres classiques scolaires, tels La Fontaine, Corneille ou Racine, comme le génie universel dont l'œuvre prend une large signification symbolique au sein de la culture française. En fait, il semble incarner le mieux les traits caractéristiques de l'identité nationale; Sainte-Beuve et Nisard l'érigent en dramaturge français par excellence, voire en symbole officiel de tout le théâtre.[6] Si l'on s'interroge sur la "rentabilité" de Molière en tant qu'objet de consommation culturelle, on s'aperçoit que son œuvre illustre le bon sens et la modération, valeurs centrales d'un classicisme scolaire en voie de codification au dix-neuvième siècle. Représentant attitré de l'ethnie française, cet auteur essentiellement gaulois fait l'objet d'une adulation qui atteint des proportions mythiques vers la fin du siècle. De toute évidence, le culte académique de Molière fait partie intégrante de la stratégie commémorative entreprise par la Troisième République.

Afin de saisir ce culte particulier dans toute son ampleur, il importe de faire ressortir la relation organique entre la critique littéraire et les pratiques scolaires ou, plus précisément, les médiations par lesquelles le discours critique s'est transformé en discours scolaire. Grâce à la dialctique entre la production du savoir et sa diffusion subséquente par l'intermediaire des manuels scolaires, on décèle mieux le point d'articulation entre l'enseignement supérieur et l'enseignement secondaire. La critique et la pédagogie constituent, en fait, des pratiques institutionnelles partageant un corps de références et de valeurs communes qui seules permettent l'acquisition de la compétence littéraire au dix-neuvième siècle. Il convient de signaler, dans cet ordre d'idées, l'émergence du statut professionnel de la critique en France vers 1850: on assiste, depuis La Harpe, à la publication de nombreux cours de littérature, c'est-à-dire, à la mise en place d'une critique professorale soucieuse de s'adresser à un public scolaire de plus en plus large. Un recensement des manuels démontre à l'évidence l'influence réelle des jugements de Nisard et de Sainte-Beuve non seulement sur le choix des sujets de composition française, mais aussi sur l'organisation et l'évolution des programmes littéraires; du reste, les professeurs formés à l'Ecole normale supérieure ont dû inculquer à leurs élèves les techniques nécessaires à l'art d'un "savoir-lire."

Il n'est pas question, dans les limites de cet article, d'évoquer la totalité des jugements critiques sur Molière au dix-neuvième siècle. Nous nous proposons plutôt d'opérer une sélection de quelques-unes des lectures les plus représentatives de cette époque, ceci afin de montrer à quel point le discours scolaire prend à son compte ces diverses lectures en vue des finalités de l'Ecole républicaine.

Dans ses *Cours de littérature dramatique,* publiés en 1819, Geoffroy fait un diagnostic de la société française sous l'Empire en fonction des valeurs sociales et morales du dix-septième siècle.[7] Le critique dramatique se livre en fait à une réflexion sur la "modernité," à laquelle il impute la dissolution générale des mœurs depuis la Révolution. Alors qu'il loue la sagesse paternelle de Chrysale dans *Les Femmes Savantes,* il insiste sur les conséquences néfastes de l'avarice d'Harpagon, vice qui préfigure le matérialisme croissant de son époque. "Poète philosophe," Molière apparaît ici comme le chantre d'une conception plus libérale de l'honnêteté; mais sa raillerie gauloise à l'égard de l'institution conjugale dans *l'Ecole des Femmes* et dans *George Dandin* nuit, toutefois, à l'autorité traditionnelle du mari.

Jouissant d'une place privilégiée dans l'histoire de la critique littéraire au dix-neuvième siècle, Nisard a exercé, grâce à son rôle de directeur de l'Ecole normale supérieure à partir de 1857, une influence capitale sur la formation des professeurs sous le Second Empire. La vision du classicisme qui se dégage de son *Histoire de la littérature française* est si étroite que, selon lui, seuls les grands écrivains du dix-septième siècle ont bénéficié de l'époque de "maturité" historique pendant laquelle ils ont vécu. La valorisation nisardienne de l'idéal classique s'accompagne d'une condamnation systématique de l'individualisme romantique, qui a abouti, à ses yeux, à la décadence de la culture contemporaine. D'où l'efficacité des valeurs du classicisme—discipline, sens de la contrainte, bon goût—voilà l'unique remède pour un pays en voie de dissolution. Au surplus, Nisard fonde son histoire littéraire sur sa classification des grands écrivains, ceux-ci étant définis en fonction de sa notion figée d'"esprit français." Quant à l'œuvre moliéresque, le critique s'attache notamment à l'analyse des comédies de caractère, et il dégage une forme de correction morale qui opère dans chaque pièce, une sorte de justice distributive susceptible d'évaluer le caractère des grands personnages de Molière: une théorie du châtiment s'esquisse ici, et le sort d'un Tartuffe ou d'un Alceste trouve sa justification suprême dans les rires du parterre. Dans cette perspective, si le plaisir théâtral que l'on tire des comédies moliéresques est d'ordre éthique, ceci tient aux rapports d'affectivité liant le dramaturge à son public. Ce dernier adopte spontanément l'amour du bien et du vrai, embrasse l'idéal du naturel et de la bienveillance qui se manifestent dans le théâtre de Molière: homme de génie, celui-ci excelle à communiquer un ensemble de vérités communément admises. Nisard souligne enfin les liens de parenté entre la bourgeoisie du dix-neuvième siècle et celle du siècle de Louis XIV.

Fondateur de la critique professionnelle au siècle dernier, Sainte-Beuve recourt d'abord à une méthode subjectiviste visant à déchiffrer l'œuvre moliéresque à la lumière des traits de biographie, d'où la mise en valeur de l'image romantique du dramaturge en proie à des déboires conjugaux et à une mélancolie profonde. Mais l'exégèse beuvienne vaut avant tout par sa formulation d'un classicisme moderne,[8] symbolique des auteurs du Grand Siècle en tant que modèles exemplaires, signes de ralliement pour des lettrés contemporains. Grâce à l'impulsion donnée par Sainte-Beuve à la notion d'"ethnie" littéraire—on sait l'importance chez lui des termes tels que "famille d'esprits," "caractère national," "génie" et "race"—les grands écrivains s'inscrivent dans une culture littéraire française qui marquera l'organisation des programmes de l'Ecole républicaine.

Grand génie dramatique intemporel, Molière prend une place exceptionnelle dans le panthéon littéraire de Sainte-Beuve. Tout en gardant des liens avec les auteurs du seizième siècle et, en particulier, Rabelais, le dramaturge apparaît comme un précurseur de la Révolution, car il esquisse les conséquences néfastes d'un ordre social fondé sur des préjugés de caste. Sainte-Beuve signale, d'autre part, la fantaisie irrépressible du rire moliéresque et il finit par dégager de ce théâtre une "poésie du comique." Son éloge célèbre du poète comique témoigne d'une véritable moliérophilie: pour des raisons à la fois dramaturgiques, morales, politiques et humanitaires, le "premier farceur de la France" mérite pleinement l'adoration commune que l'on éprouve à son égard.[9]

L. Veuillot est peut-être le meilleur représentant du courant religieux de la critique moliéresque au dix-neuvième siècle.[10] Prenant la relève de Bossuet, dont la position orthodoxe considérait la comédie comme une école de perdition, Veuillot s'en prend à l'immoralité foncière du *Misanthrope* et à la diffamation de la charité chrétienne dans *Tartuffe*. Cette pièce-ci sert en fait la politique anticléricale et aboutit à une perversion de la "vraie morale." Le polémiste tourne en ridicule la réputation de sainteté laïque qui s'est créée autour de Molière, soulignant en l'occurrence les multiples bassesses de la vie personnelle du dramaturge, poussé, selon lui, par un véritable machiavélisme. D'autres commentateurs catholiques, tels E. Doumergue, A. Charaux et Camille de la Croix, dénoncent "l'âme pécheresse" de Molière, qui l'amène tantôt à se faire le chantre cynique de l'adultère dans *Amphitryon,* tantôt à pervertir les relations familiales dans *L'Avare* et dans *Les Femmes Savantes*.[11]

La lecture polémique de Camille de la Croix, frère franciscain, s'inscrit en faux contre l'idée du naturalisme moliéresque chère à Brunetière. Représentant de la tradition universitaire des années 1880, ce dernier estime que l'œuvre de Molière est à la fois nationale et bourgeoise, réaliste et naturaliste; de plus, chaque comédie réussit à démontrer une thèse.[12] Le critique signale aussi la primauté dans ce théâtre de la comédie de caractère. Chose plus importante, peut-être, Brunetière dégage les lignes de force d'une "philosophie" moliéresque: celle-ci se ramène aux platitudes d'une morale excessivement médiocre. Il déplore l'insuffisance de la peinture de types féminins chez Molière, et le dramaturge est jugé en l'occurrence antiféministe. L'auteur des *Epoques du théâtre français* érige en système le naturalisme de ce dernier, hérité de Rabelais et de Montaigne. Tous ceux qui refusent de se conformer aux exigences de la nature—Philaminte, M. Jourdain, M. Diafoirius et M. Purgon—sont voués au ridicule: ces personnages grotesques et odieux se détournent volontairement du chemin de la "bonne nature." Le libertinage intellectuel du poète comique le pousse à s'attaquer, dans *Tartuffe,* aux vrais dévots, et il finit par mettre en question le principe même de la contrainte sous-jacente à toute religion établie. Ainsi, "l'école de Molière" célèbre le triomphe des instincts, le respect total des lois de la nature. *Le Malade imaginaire* représente en fait "une apologie de la nature." La philosophie de Molière suit, en fin de compte, une évolution continue, malgré le caractère problématique de sa production théâtrale entre 1664 et 1669, aboutissant à un pessimisme de sa vision de la nature humaine vers la fin de sa carrière.

Quant à E. Faguet, il réduit l'ensemble des comédies à une série de thèses, de préceptes de vie qui devraient constituer des points de repère pour tout bourgeois soucieux de mener une existence honnête.[13] Mais l'observation de la vie de tous les jours se révèle souvent décourageante, d'où le besoin de remédier à une morale moliéresque jugée défectueuse. Faguet incarne peut-être le mieux l'universitaire moraliste de la fin du siècle dernier en ce sens qu'il projette une image volontairement bourgeoise du dramaturge, au point de le désigner comme "le Sancho Panza de la France."[14] Ce qui contribue en particulier à la codification d'un discours scolaire avide de leçons exemplaires, c'est l'utilisation que fait ce critique des "raisonneurs" de Molière transformés en modèles normatifs, excellant à véhiculer des vérités prudhommesques, bref, des poncifs traditionnels de la classe moyenne. On a affaire ici au triomphe d'une vision éminemment pragmatique, qui rejette le principe de vertu héroïque, dans la mesure où il constitue une violation de l'idéal de *mediocritas.* Cette morale se ramène pour l'essentiel à une attitude bornée à l'égard des autres, à un profond repliement sur soi qui s'accompagne d'une volonté d'éviter à tout prix le ridicule. Ce que Faguet transmet, en dernière analyse, au corps enseignant de la génération précédant la première guerre mondiale, c'est une gestion systématique des risques dans l'expérience quotidienne de la vie, c'est-à-dire, le goût d'un conformisme social de la part de ceux qui se laissent diriger par un souci excessif du "qu'en dira-t-on, " goût lié à une peur congénitale du ridicule. Faguet exalte au surplus la supériorité des "comédies-écoles" (c'est-à-dire, les comédies de caractère) par rapport aux divertissements de cour. Cette perception communément admise de la bassesse de la farce dans la hiérarchie des genres rend compte de l'absence relative de la dimension carnavalesque du théâtre de Molière—scatologie, jeux de scène gratuits, dénouements fantaisistes, etc.—dans les éditions scolaires de cette époque.[15]

Le cas de Faguet est particulièrement révélateur car il illustre, à l'instar de maints autres critiques du dix-neuvième siècle, le recrutement systématique des professeurs distingués, en vue de la production massive des manuels et des anthologies scolaires. Cette double fonction met en évidence la distribution de la culture littéraire du haut en bas, c'est-à-dire, de l'enseignement supérieur à l'enseignement secondaire. Dans la mesure où ils vulgarisent les données fondamentales de l'histoire littéraire, les manuels visent à la codification, plutôt qu'à la création, d'un savoir donné. Ils font preuve d'une dimension pratique grâce aux exercices permettant à l'élève de perfectionner ses compétences littéraires et en même temps de développer son jugement, son goût et sa morale; c'est précisément de cette manière que l'élève devient littéralement bien "élevé." D'autre part, si Nisard, Sainte-Beuve, Brunetière et Faguet valorisent, à des degrés divers, les classiques scolaires du dix-septième siècle, les érigeant en quelque sorte en maîtres à penser, c'est que ces derniers servent de base à l'acquisition d'une compétence à la fois linguistique et littéraire. De l'exégèse nisardienne au discours scolaire de J. Demogeot, par exemple, il n'y qu'un pas: dans son *Histoire de la littérature française,* celui-ci projette, lui aussi, une vision idéalisée du Grand Siècle, perçu comme la période de maturité française, marqué par une incontestable prépondérance culturelle.[16] Nous essaierons maintenant d'analyser les permutations de l'œuvre de Molière en fonction du discours scolaire du dix-neuvième siècle; il s'agit, en gros, de l'assimilation des principaux arguments de la critique exégétique aboutissant à une sorte de réécriture programmée par l'Ecole républicaine.

L'exploitation de l'œuvre moliéresque dans les manuels met en lumière, d'abord, la primauté du problème de la laïcité, qui a donné lieu à une polémique politique et culturelle permanente pour les Français du dix-neuvième siècle. Qu'il s'agisse des manuels destinés à l'enseignement confessionnel ou bien de ceux qui s'adressent à l'enseignement laïc, on assiste à une volonté profonde d'édifier la jeunesse, c'est-à-dire, de s'assurer d'une clientèle essentiellement bourgeoise en vue des impératifs de l'Eglise ou de l'Etat. Dans l'ensemble, les auteurs des livres scolaires se réclament de l'autorité des critiques afin de justifier leur choix de morceaux cités ou bien afin de renforcer leur argumentation. Il en est ainsi des *Etudes littéraires sur les auteurs français* du Père Fernossole, et du manuel du Père M., qui s'inspirent du catholicisme doctrinaire de L. Veuillot pour mettre en doute la valeur morale et philosophique du théâtre de Molière.[17] Le Père Fernossole s'en remet à l'autorité religieuse suprême, à savoir, le Christ—qu'il qualifie de "Divin Pédagogue"—afin de fonder son manuel sur la "formation des âmes."[18] Malgré l'absence de religion chez Molière, on peut néanmoins dégager une morale qui légitime les droits de la raison, et le critique s'appuie ici sur la notion de "justice distributive" chère à Nisard: la peinture comique d'Harpagon, de M. Jourdain et de Tartuffe s'explique par des défauts précis de caractère (avarice, vanité, hypocrisie.)

Quant au Père M., il évoque l'autorité de Bossuet pour mieux faire ressortir la licence effrénée de ce théâtre. Se réclamant des analyses de L. Veuillot, il met en lumière l'invraisemblance de ces portraits-charge que sont Tartuffe et Orgon, ainsi que le comportement peu reluisant des autres membres de la famille. Loin d'être un maître à penser pour la jeunesse, Molière apparaît, à ses yeux, comme un maître d'inconscience morale: *Tartuffe* sert mieux que tout autre document la cause anticléricale. Le Père M. déplore, en plus, l'absence de conversion, c'est-à-dire, de correction morale, dans la comédie moliéresque, tout aussi bien que l'inefficacité des "leçons" suggérées par le dénouement. Il signale que le conseil de modération prôné par Philinte est inspiré d'une maxime de Saint-Paul, qui souligne la nécessité de prendre son mal en patience. Enfin, ce professeur de rhétorique engage l'élève à mettre en question l'intention sacrilège du dramaturge, à l'accuser carrément de trahison. La faute de ce dernier serait, dans cette perspective, à la fois esthétique: "vous avez agi en *maladroit*," et éthique: "vous avez agi en *traître*" (c'est nous qui soulignons).[19]

Les commentateurs catholiques insistent, en particulier, sur les faiblesses de la morale chez Molière, illustrées tantôt par le portrait invraisemblable des jeunes filles, tantôt par les conséquences néfastes de l'avarice au sein de la famille, ou par la représentation faussée de la dévotion dans *Tartuffe*.[20] Ces déficiences sont si flagrantes que le Père Caruel en arrive à taxer le dramaturge d'anti-patriotisme; il dégage des écrits de Saint-Marc Girardin une notion de critique-sermon qui érige le critique en moraliste exemplaire. Il en est ainsi du *Tableau d'histoire littéraire* des Pères Sévère-Jacques Bizeul et P. Boulay, qui présente une structure fort didactique. La dialectique question-réponse, supposant une série de jugements catégoriques et orthodoxes, fait penser irrésistiblement à un catéchisme scolaire.[21]

Parmi les manuels d'inspiration laïque, on peut citer *Les Lettres françaises depuis leurs origines* de M. Gellion-Danglar.[22] Celui-ci offre l'image d'un Molière doué d'une conscience politique et, plus précisément, d'une "verve révolutionnaire"; la tirade de Dom Juan sur l'hypocrisie lui permet de prendre à partie, de manière oblique, une société corrompue privilégiant une caste nobiliaire dépravée; de même, la morgue des Sotenville les amène à humilier publiquement George Dandin, représentant du peuple. Dans un manuel maintes fois réédité au dix-neuvième siècle, E. Géruzez loue la morale de Molière, qui constitue à ses yeux un enseignement humaniste fondé sur l'alliance entre le vrai, le beau et le bien.[23] Au demeurant, par la place qu'elle accorde à la notion du juste milieu, la dramaturgie moliéresque se révèle essentiellement thérapeutique. Ainsi, Cléante incarne une sagesse modérée, l'idéal de la charité chrétienne s'opposant à la démesure que représente l'hypocrisie de Tartuffe. Le poète comique exerce une fonction pédagogique en ce sens qu'il fournit des "cours de morale dramatique" à l'adresse des gens du monde, une sorte d'apprentissage supérieur dans l'expérience quotidienne.[24]

Dans ce même courant d'idées républicaines, J. Demogeot considère Molière comme partisan de l'idéal humanitaire justifiant l'avènement d'une France laïque. Plus précisément, il l'appelle "poète national," qui prend pour cible particulière l'hypocrisie religieuse et va jusqu'à situer la crainte du ridicule au centre de l'expérience collective des Français.[25] On s'explique ainsi la place exceptionnelle dont jouit Molière dans la mémoire culturelle de la France. Si le lecteur/spectateur s'identifie de manière immédiate avec ses personnages, c'est qu'il partage avec eux un vécu commun. Dans l'anthologie de C. Berville, destinée à dispenser des leçons pratiques, Molière est présenté comme un "grand moraliste" qui soutient l'idéal humaniste traditionnel.[26] Le dramaturge s'attaque de front à l'ensemble des vices, et C. Berville met en valeur l'influence dégradante de l'avarice d'Harpagon lors de la scène du vol (IV, 7). MM. Tarsot et Charlot reconnaissent, eux aussi, que l'auteur du *Misanthrope* enseigne la vertu en dramatisant les conséquences fâcheuses des divers vices.[27] Ils s'occupent de fixer les traits de caractère d'une personnalité particulière en fonction de leur valeur morale: les personnages ont-ils droit à l'admiration de l'élève ou bien méritent-ils la réprobation de ce dernier? Ainsi, l'élève est engagé à porter un jugement sur les démarches peu scrupuleuses de Valère et de Cléante, "vulgaire libertin" dans *L'Avare*. Alors qu'Elise est proposée en modèle, le comportement de Marianne ne laisse pas d'être immoral.

Quoique les manuels confessionnnels et laïcs partagent le souci profond de filtrer les valeurs idéologiques et morales à travers la comédie moliéresque, l'idéal d'un enseignement secondaire essentiellement humaniste consiste à promouvoir la mise en place d'un Molière universel, maître à penser de la jeunesse française. On a affaire, en fait, à un discours scolaire qui transmet des valeurs de référence culturelle. Le sujet de composition suivant, par exemple, situe Molière—auteur gaulois par excellence—dans un contexte ethnologique:

> Rabelais et Régnier lui ont fourni des caractères; Larivey, Boisrobert,
> Rotrou et Cyrano de Bergerac, des scènes. Mais surtout on peut dire
> qu'il s'est nourri de la substance et de la sève de nos vieux auteurs; par
> le caractère de sa raillerie et par sa manière d'envisager la vie humaine,
> il doit passer à bon droit pour un continuateur de l'esprit gaulois.[28]

Représentant exemplaire de la race française, le poète comique assure de la
sorte la continuité culturelle de la nation, et sa survie même en tant qu'entité
ethnique. Génie dramatique incomparable, il jouit d'une excellente
"rentabilité" dans le marché des biens culturels dans la mesure où il
s'exporte à merveille:

> Il n'est peut-être pas de génie qui fasse plus d'honneur à notre pays.
> Partout Molière est connu, joué et étudié. Les étrangers nous l'envient
> et ils ont raison: 'Molière est tellement grand,' disait Goethe, 'qu'on est
> toujours frappé d'étonnement lorsqu'on le relit. C'est un homme
> complet. Ses pièces touchent au tragique: elle vous captivent, et
> personne n'a le courage de marcher sur ses traces. . . .'[29]

Afin d'arracher l'œuvre moliéresque aux interprétations étroitement sec-
taires, l'enseignement humaniste a célébré la convergence de discours sur
cette œuvre, au point d'en dégager une lecture œcuménique embrassant à la
fois les partisans de la Gauche républicaine, épris de modernisme et de
laïcité, et les défenseurs de la Droite, qui exaltent, dans ce théâtre, les
valeurs traditionnelles de la France: ordre, mesure, sagesse. Grâce à
l'exemple de Molière, on comprend à quel point l'Ecole républicaine
s'appuie sur des modèles culturels afin de s'acquitter d'une fonction ethnologique, et la pertinence des analyses de P. Bourdieu et de J-C. Passeron—
notamment en ce qui concerne la "reproduction culturelle"—se manifeste ici
avec vigueur.[30] Leçons de tolérance et de civilité, éléments d'une morale
familiale fondée sur le bon sens, voilà quelques principes-clefs de la sagesse
moliéresque. Il en est de même de l'image fictive d'une harmonie de classes
créée par ce théâtre, image qui s'intègre dans une vision idéalisée de la
modernité républicaine; l'idéal de reconstruction nationale a pour objet la
formation des citoyens par le biais d'une volonté de consensus. De sur-
croît, la transformation d'un Molière monarchique en un Molière républicain
suppose la mise en évidence d'une nouvelle cohérence imaginaire au dix-
neuvième siècle: la notion de modernité se fonde, on l'a vu, sur une reconstruction idéologique des valeurs du Grand Siècle.

Molière à l'Ecole républicaine souligne l'insertion institutionnelle de l'œuvre du dramaturge dans une culture française post-révolutionnaire; le circuit d'intelligibilité se situe au carrefour de la critique exégétique et des manuels scolaires.[31] Plus précisément, nous envisageons la relation texte-commentaire dans une perspective d'intertextualité, sous forme de réseaux de transmission et de redistribution d'un savoir codé. Dans la mesure où tout écrit scolaire est nécessairement lié à une pluralité d'autres textes, où il renvoie à l'existence d'un pré-texte, la critique se définit comme une "relecture incessante" des textes. La mise en place d'un classicisme scolaire suppose la constitution d'un programme d'œuvres canoniques destinées à transformer les écrivains en de saints patrons de la culture littéraire de la France, bref, à en faire des directeurs de la conscience nationale. Mis au premier rang par l'histoire littéraire, ces textes fondateurs s'insèrent, de toute évidence, dans l'imaginaire culturel français. On s'explique ainsi que l'enseignement littéraire ait joué un rôle tout aussi formateur que l'enseignement historique ou scientifique au dix-neuvième siècle: l'identité de l'élève est intimement liée à la notion de mémoire culturelle. Entreprise de vulgarisation républicaine, la promotion scolaire de Molière fait donc partie intégrante d'un classicisme visant avant tout à acculturer l'élève, à le former selon une stratégie pédagogique normative; le poids de l'expérience scolaire finit par marquer les structures cognitives et affectives de ce dernier.

L'avènement au pouvoir de la bourgeoisie entraîne le triomphe d'une idéologie spirituelle laïque qui situe la littérature dans une zone de justification scolaire, d'où les mécanismes de consécration des "grands écrivains" du patrimoine.[32] La mission éducatrice des élites bourgeoises relève, à n'en point douter, de la sacralisation de la culture entreprise par ces élites. Dès lors, nous pouvons nous interroger sur les médiations sous-jacentes à la création d'un savoir légitime, en l'occurrence les appareils de production et de consommation de ce savoir. Les œuvres jugées "canoniques," c'est-à-dire, dignes d'être transmises au sein de l'institution scolaire, mettent en évidence une dimension sociale et idéologique particulière. Saisir les significations codées de ces œuvres qui sont constamment lues et relues, citées et (re)citées par le professeur et ses élèves, c'est en même temps faire ressurgir l'archéologie du savoir en France au dix-neuvième siècle. Purger la critique de cet amas d'interprétations figées, transformer l'icône littéraire en texte pur, susceptible du jeu libre de signifiants, voilà le propre d'une pédagogie déconstructionniste. De tels propos nous amènent à envisager, à l'instar de Foucault, la discipline scolaire comme l'expression privilégiée d'une évidente volonté de pouvoir. Dans la mesure où l'enseignement littéraire fonctionne à la manière d'une entreprise correctionnelle, les pratiques discursives ressortissant des manuels contribuent évidemment bien à la formation du sujet/élève. Dans cette perspective, les professeurs se donnent pour tâche la production systématique de la notion de vérité, qu'ils transmettent à leurs élèves sous forme d'objet de consommation. Les exercices scolaires soutiennent, de la sorte, une pédagogie corrective du français aboutissant, en somme, à la normalisation linguistique et morale de l'élève. C'est ainsi que l'Ecole républicaine a tâché, en dernière analyse, de régulariser les conduites marginales, voire anomiques des élèves français du siècle passé.[33]

NOTES

[1] Le tableau de M. Bertin par Ingres constitue la meilleure représentation iconographique de cette bourgeoisie conquérante.

[2] Voir à ce sujet P. Robiquet, *Discours et opinions de Jules Ferry* (Paris: Colin, 1893-98).

[3] Voir Antoine Compagnon, *La Troisième République des lettres* (Paris: Seuil, 1983).

[4] C'est en ces termes que H. Bourgoin définit la doctrine nisardienne, *L'Enseignement du français* (Paris: F. Alcan, 1911), 4-5.

[5] Charles Péguy évoque à ce sujet le "vieux civisme classique et français" qui anime le corps enseignant à cette époque (cité par J. Bessière dans *L'Ecole* [Paris: Larousse, 1978], 106).

[6] Charles-Augustin Sainte-Beuve, *Portraits littéraires*, 2 (Paris: Didier, 1852); *Œuvres complètes de Molière*, 5 (Paris: Calmann-Lévy, 1884); D. Nisard, *Histoire de la littérature française* (Paris: Firmin-Didot, 1849).

[7] *Cours de littérature dramatique*, 1 (Paris: Blanchard, 1819).

[8] R. Molho évoque à juste titre le "mythe critique du XVIIème siècle" qui a été élaboré par l'auteur des *Causeries du Lundi* (*L'Ordre et les ténèbres ou la naissance d'un mythe chez Sainte-Beuve* [Paris: Colin, 1972]).

[9] "Aimer Molière, c'est être guéri à jamais, je ne parle pas de la basse et infâme hypocrisie, mais du fanatisme, de l'intolérance et de la dureté en ce genre, de ce qui fait anathématiser et maudire. . . . Aimer Molière, c'est être également à l'abri . . . de cet autre fanatisme politique, froid, sec et cruel, qui ne rit pas, qui sent son sectaire, qui . . . trouve moyen de pétrir et de combiner tous les fiels et d'unir dans une doctrine amère les haines, les rancunes et les jacobinismes de tous les temps. . . . Aimer et chérir Molière, c'est être antipathique à toute *manière* dans le langage et dans l'expression; c'est ne pas s'amuser et s'attarder aux grâces mignardes, aux finesses cherchées, au marivaudage en aucun genre, au style miroitant et artificiel. Aimer Molière, c'est n'être disposé à aimer ni le faux bel

esprit ni la science pédante; c'est aimer la santé et le droit sens de l'esprit chez les
autres comme pour soi" (*Œuvres complètes*, 5, 277-78).

10 *Molière et Bourdaloue* (Paris: Palmé, 1877).

11 E. Doumergue, "La Religion dans le théâtre de Molière," *Revue chrétienne*, 16 (1869),
725-44; "La Philosophie dans le théâtre de Molière," *Revue chrétienne*, 17 (1870), 326-
47; A. Charaux, *Molière: la critique idéale et catholique* (Lille: Lefort, 1882); le Frère
Camille de la Croix, "La Morale de Molière," *Etudes franciscaines*, 2 (1899), 69-86, 298-
309, 624-32.

12 *Histoire de la littérature française classique* (Paris: Delagrave, 1912); *Les Epoques du
théâtre français* (Paris: Hachette, 1906).

13 *Dix-septième siècle* (Paris: Boivin, s.d.); *En lisant Molière* (Paris: Hachette, 1914).

14 *Œuvres complètes de Molière*, 1 (Paris: Lutetia, 1919), 12.

15 Dans ses *Œuvres complètes de Molière*, Faguet montre une nette préférence pour les
comédies sérieuses, au détriment des divertissements de cour et des farces. Grâce à leur
évidente valeur éthique, les œuvres canoniques telles *L'Avare* et *Les Femmes Savantes*
(classes de seconde), *Le Misanthrope* et *Tartuffe* (classes de rhétorique), servent mieux les
finalités de l'Ecole républicaine.

16 *Histoire de la littérature française* (Paris: Hachette, 1852).

17 Le Père Fernossole, *Etudes littéraires sur les auteurs français*, 1 (Paris: Beauchesne,
1914); le Père M., *Etudes littéraires sur les auteurs français* (Paris: Delhomme et Briguet,
1886).

18 *Etudes littéraires*, I.

19 *Etudes littéraires*, 206.

20 R. Canat, *La Littérature française par les textes* (Paris: Delaplane, 1906); G. Long-
haye, *Histoire de la littérature française*, 2 (Paris: Retaux, 1895); le Père Caruel, *Etudes
sur les auteurs français* (Tours: Cattier, 1901).

21 *Tableau d'histoire littéraire* (Paris: Poussielgue, 1885).

22 *Les Lettres françaises depuis leurs origines* (Paris: Degorce-Cadot, 1882).

23 *Histoire de la littérature française* (Paris: Didier, 1861) I.

24 E. Géruzez, *Histoire*, 164.

25 E. Géruzez, *Histoire*, 412.

26 *Belles pages littéraires et morales à l'école* (Paris: Larousse, 1912), 287.

27 *Etudes biographiques et critiques* (Paris: Delalain, 1900)

28 Charles Urbain et Charles Jamey, *Etudes historiques et critiques sur les classiques
français du baccalauréat*, 2 (Lyon: Vitte et Perneuil, 1884), 608.

29 A. Mouchard et C. Blanchet, *Les Auteurs français du baccalauréat* (Paris: Poussielgue,
1894), 230.

30 *La Reproduction: éléments pour une théorie du système d'enseignement* (Paris:
Minuit, 1964).

31 Les données principales de cet article se réfèrent directement à *Molière à l'Ecole républicaine: De la critique universitaire aux manuels scolaires (1870-1914)* (Saratoga, Ca.:

Anma Libri [Stanford French and Italian Studies], 1992). Nous voudrions signaler que le présent article a été soumis bien avant la publication du livre.

[32] Voir à ce propos Paul Bénichou, *Le Sacre de l'écrivain, 1750-1830. Essai sur l'avènement d'un pouvoir spirituel laïc dans la France moderne* (Paris: Corti, 1973).

[33] Nous tenons à remercier Michel Gueldry d'avoir bien voulu nous faire bénéficier de ses excellents commentaires d'ordre stylistique.

18

Tropes of Stage Writing: Aspects of Roger Planchon's Classical Stagings

Laurence Romero

Délirant ou réfléchi, le théâtre
concentre, l'architecture extériorise.
—*Michel Parent*

DURING AT LEAST THE PAST TWENTY YEARS, theatre practice has spun out in various directions. The thrust toward performance is marked by the liberation of once unified staging components, allowing discrete nontextual elements (decor, light, sound) to develop their own metadiscourses within the director's global project of stage writing (écriture scénique), the conceptual framework of *mise en scène*. The evolution toward what Bernard Dort called "la représentation émancipée" had been anticipated in part by the semioticians of the Prague School. For the concerns of this essay, J. Honzel reminded us as early as 1940 that, "One should recognize the invalidity of the notion of the 'relative nonparticipation of the scenic image' . . . [and] that sound can be a stage . . . and scenery can be a text."[1] The growing appreciation of the intricate network of theatrical signification operating through strategies of theatricality (nontextual codes and signs) goes implicitly against the Wagnerian concept of *Gesamtkunstwerk:* a grand illusionistic fusion around the text (or music in opera) of all artistic components of the production functioning toward preconceived closure. The more liberated performances and stage productions conceive of production as process, accentuating the specificity of certain codes in the production which operate sometime with, sometime against the text for the desired effect on stage and in reception (within the audience). While Roger Planchon's stage work is not at the extreme limits of recent postmodern innovations in *mise en scène,* he has employed certain strategies of theatricality—his own tropes of *mise en scène*—which have enlivened his stagings of the classics and made them clearer and closer to us. In all his directorial work, Planchon has been attentive both to past staging traditions and to academic criticism, especially in his productions of *Tartuffe.* While he seems not to have mentioned directly P. Bénichou's seminal *Morales du grand siècle,* a close collaborator did while indicating parallels between the essay's implied leftist critique of the *ancien régime* and Planchon's determination in his *Tartuffe* "de rendre compte le plus clairement possible du contexte social et historique."[2] After a few contextual opening remarks, this essay will propose a brief presentation of Planchon's dialectical concept for his staging of Molière's *Tartuffe,* along with aspects of "architecture parlante" (signifying architecture or decor) and the innovative "espace sonore" in his production of Racine's *Bérénice.*

Born in 1931, Roger Planchon began his career in Lyon, first at the Théâtre de la Comédie in 1953 before being called in 1957 to direct the Théâtre de la Cité in nearby Villeurbanne. For fifteen years he staged classics and moderns and began playwriting and producing his own scripts. In 1972 Planchon was named director of the French national theatre, the TNP. Since then he has continued producing and writing, has toured extensively and forged his own idea—after Jean Vilar—of "théâtre populaire."

Even in the past two decades during which Planchon has done his major work, theatre practice and criticism have changed, in part because of several well-known phenomena: the waning of the historical avant-garde, the encrochment of postmodernism (performance, dance, opera) and its attraction to practitioners like Chéreau, Mnouchkine, Lavaudant, and the late Antoine Vitez, as well as the rise of unconventional playwrights like Cormann, Deutsch, Koltès, and Wenzel. But other factors have impinged more directly on Planchon's stage work and our appreciation of it: the diminished authority of Brecht in contemporary French theatre praxis, and the retreat of Brechtian "théâtre populaire" and Planchon's direct association with it. "Théâtre populaire" was a powerful idea—and ideal—of what theatre could and should be beginning with the "Front populaire" of the mid-1930s and with renewed impetus after 1950 under Jean Vilar. Polemics aside, there is general agreement that, due in large part to Vilar, Planchon and others involved in the cultural decentralization, many new theatres and audiences were created, along with an artistic engagement in history, politics, and social issues; that alone realized the main agenda of "théâtre populaire." While popular theatre practice continues today by those committed to it, the critical discourse on the concept and its role has run its course. This has effectively left production criticism free to examine the process and functioning of Planchon's stage writing strategies without the obligation to read them into "théâtre populaire" esthetics or justify them within French cultural politics.

Along with new perspectives from performance and postmodernism, semiotic research has provided a detailed inventory of the constituent components of *mise en scène* and a critical descriptive vocabulary. The concept of theatricality (*théâtralité*) has also enhanced our appreciation of the specificity of the theatrical in stage production. Here is Barthes's well-known definition: "C'est le théâtre sans le texte, une épaisseur de signes et de sensations qui s'édifie sur la scène à partir de l'argument écrit [et] qui submerge le texte sous la plénitude de son langage extérieur."[3] This exterior language operates in a kind of sub-staging, a "mise en espace" to accompany the "mise en parole" (Pavis). Traditional theatre practice took the "langage extérieur" for granted, assuming it to be but an accessory to the major component, the script. In his essay, *La Représentation émancipée*,[4] Bernard Dort argues that in recent practice, the univocal discourse of the script opens onto a complexity of voices, usually compatible and similarly directed but not necessarily and not always. In the most ambitious productions, these new discourses maintain a creative tension with the text which can interact very effectively with their differences in a kind of metaplay, a playing within the play, that challenges the script in its literality and its authority as unique source of signification. These are some of the considerations informing our investigation of certain strategies and techniques of Roger Planchon's stage writing for his productions of *Tartuffe* in 1973 (there was an earlier one in 1962), and *Bérénice* in 1970 (earlier ones in 1966 and 1969).[5]

Implied in Planchon's *mise en scène* for *Tartuffe* are two dialectical concepts: one a metaphor for the fable, the other a superstructure of place. In the first, the director has Molière's story unfold within the binary possession/dispossession, in both a sexual and material sense. In the second, beyond the private realm of Orgon's home where the anecdote of his family plays out, Planchon reinforces the presence of the public sphere which Molière indicates specifically only in the dénouement when the State intervenes. In this locus as we shall see, History will transgress the anecdote and inscribe itself. Here are a few aspects of Planchon's stage writing, examples of the Barthian "épaisseur de signes et de sensations."

Instances of possession/dispossession are numerous in this staging, either *in virtu* or realized. Orgon lusts after—a will to possess—Tartuffe;

twice Tartuffe attempts to possess Elmire (III, 3 and IV, 5); there is the father's dispossession of his son (the disinheritance in III, 6), and the near
possession of the family fortune by Tartuffe (IV,7 and dénouement). The
playful lovers' quarrel (II,4), a subtle game of lust and coyness (forms of
possession/dispossession) between Mariane and Valère, is orchestrated by
Dorine who, moments earlier, had intervened in the potentially more serious
attempted dispossession of Mariane by her father, to be possessed by
Tartuffe (II, 1,2). As indexical functions on a micro level, Planchon has
members of Orgon's family change clothes often, mostly from formal to in-
formal attire, to emphasize the routine small rituals of a rich and privileged
bourgeois family. This transfer of clothing also implies a momentary material dispossession/possession. These actual or virtual exchanges operate
within the intimacy of the family home, within the anecdote of Orgon's
story. During this unfolding Planchon has strewn the stage with signs of a
larger world outside, creating through a "théâtre sans texte" the context of
Molière's script, a superstructure of another place. Orgon's house is filled
with large reproductions of tableaux from the period, many of swooning
saints, ambiguously suggesting the thin line between religious agony and
sensual ecstasy, an ambiguity not only rampant in the primary script but
also in religious texts and iconography of the French seventeenth century.
(The paintings were also a brilliant reminder of the baroque fascination with
replication and proliferation.) In the midst of major renovations within
Orgon's house, there are two statues: one evidently being discarded of a
dejected, anguished Christ ("un Christ-aux-outrages"—Planchon), and another larger one not yet fully uncovered of a triumphant king mounted on a
powerful rearing steed, clearly waiting to find its central place in the reno-
vated bourgeois mansion. In Planchon's *mise en scène,* these contextual
signs make the intervention of the State at the dénouement much less the
arbitrary *deus-ex-machina* it is often thought to be. At the end of the play
Tartuffe is dispossessed of his liberty, an act that closes the anecdote. But,
that Orgon is then allowed to repossess his family fortune transgresses an
anecdote in which nothing has happened to predict or justify the outcome.
That final exchange is made possible only by the intervention of the State
and accomplished by the brutal Royal Secret Police in the person of
L'Exempt and his *Gardes* but masterminded by an omniscient, all-powerful
Monarch. Since there are serious political implications in Orgon's past ties
to his friend, the *frondeur* Argas, the former's repossession of the family
fortune is assured only by grace of the King. Through the example of
Orgon, an entire class is delegitimized politically, largely through the

machinations of a vast network of absolute, clandestine power. At the end of Planchon's staging, the bourgeoisie is dispossessed by the *ancien régime,* an act which is no longer an anecdote but a moment in French history. The play's last long rejoinder is a grand discourse on absolute royal power, but the final irony comes from Molière: his script ends on two adjectives, "généreux et sincère."

Another stage writing strategy in *Tartuffe* is Planchon's implicit "architecture parlante" or signifying architecture, which develops its own intertextual discourse with Molière's script, creating a rich oscillation between mimesis and diagesis, show and tell. As an autotextual form, "architecture parlante" develops its own signifying practice which transforms set design into something more than a mere aesthetic frame supporting an assumed preexisting textual meaning, as suggested earlier. In Planchon's *mise en scène,* the against-the-grain tensions between stage architecture and script are not so much a *mise en question* of Molière's text, but of the accumulated conventions of staging and critical exegesis of *Tartuffe,* the most popular play in the classical repertory. Traditionally, Orgon is played as a rich bourgeois, as fixed in his mentality as his social class is established in its smug, secure upper-mobility. Conventional stagings replicated these affectations by scenic designs that emphasized solidity and security to the point of boredom. Planchon and his set designer Hubert Monloup conceived of their scenic architecture as a reflection of the realities of the 1660s when Molière produced his three versions of *Tartuffe.* And in fact that period was anything but a time of lethargy in French society: Louis XIV was fast organizing and coalescing power, construction on Versailles was begun, the Royal Police was put in place. Louis's ascension to full power was abetted by the successive departures of several sometime antagonists: Foucquet is arrested in 1661; the President of the Parliament of Paris, Lamoignon, bans *Tartuffe* in 1664 but by 1668 fades from the scene; Mazarin dies in 1661 and the austere Queen Mother in early 1666. The bourgeoisie, prominent under Mazarin and Colbert, draws in somewhat but retains its substantial wealth. All of this to recall that the time of *Tartuffe* was a period of considerable movement and change. Thus the scenic architecture for Planchon's staging imagines Orgon's house in a state of transition. From what appears to have been a comfortable late Renaissance home, extensive renovations are transforming it into a magnificent modern residence. The set depicts a vast interior construction site: scaffolding, ropes, pulleys, carpenter and mason tools lie around, and dustcovers shield large pieces of furniture. Here is Planchon's explanation of his intent: "Le monde est donné en transformation, le passé est détruit, une époque s'installe. Ce qui est mis en avant: une instabilité qui, nous l'espérons, dit quelque chose de profond sur le déséquilibre des forces, des comportements, des valeurs en présence dans l'œuvre."[6] Earlier we alluded to the iconography of illusive, transitory forms: the figures of the dejected, discarded Christ and the emerging triumphant Monarch, complemented by numerous paintings of religious figures in ambiguous, fluxuating states of agony/ecstacy. Not only are these micro-elements of Planchon's stage architecture in implicit constant motion, even the macrostructure moves, literally. As the fable progresses, entire sections of richly polished wood, the panelled walls and partitions of Orgon's house, fly up into the vaulted stage-house, creating a striking visual mimesis of the incremental exposing of Orgon's true self and a stripping of his paternal and political legitimacy. By the time of the dramatic dénouement, the trappings of Orgon's power and prestige have disappeared with the partitions. What remains are the rough exterior brick walls of the theatre, Orgon's ground zero; in real time, they are also a reminder of the anti-illusionist aesthetic of post-war stage praxis. But with the crashing intervention of the Super Cops (*Exempt et gardes*), heretofore unseen doors and trapdoors open violently as the police raiders manhandle not only Tartuffe and string up his manservant Laurent (a mute presence during the second half of the play), they also confine Orgon and family to dungeon-like slits in the floor. This raid targets not only Tartuffe, but Orgon as well—to intimidate him—and it is conducted by a State with ultimate power, commanding even unknown features of Orgon's own house; the new *régime* fashions it own architecture. Here the final grand exchange takes place with Tartuffe's dispossession and Orgon's repossession of his "new" house by personal gesture of the King. Of course what is solved by this dramatic police action is only Tartuffe's criminality which was just exposed and was never a problematic of the play. What is, Tartuffe's immorality, his hypocrisy, lubricity, and boorishness, these are problems that no work of literature would ever resolve, as Molière well knew. So the real *coup de théâtre* at the end of *Tartuffe* is the subtle slippage from the protagonist's indomitable immorality to his more banal criminality, a slight of hand that allowed the dramatist to bring his show to a conventionally comic end. In this production, Planchon's effective stage writing makes the *dénouement* more convincing and satisfying.

Another aspect of "architecture parlante" here transforms mute characters into elements of scenic architecture, from *dramatis personae* to *adramatis personae,* each one emitting, silently, its own signification.

Tartuffe's manservant Laurent appears in the flesh, albeit mute, enriching the Brechtian fundamental *gestus* of both Tartuffe and *Tartuffe*. Bare-chested, sweaty, smirking ominously, he prowls in the margins of the set as he had lurked in the interstices of Molière's text. Planchon makes him an indexical signifier—like any piece of decor—of Tartuffe's moral and physical, sexual presence. Laurent is not so much the protagonist's *Doppelgänger* as he is the receptacle and reflector of his master's *caractère,* a typical theatrical redundancy. Molière had already provided a model for this in Mme Pernelle's domestic, Flipote. Listed as one of the *dramatis personae,* she is in fact an *adramatis persona:* mute, passive, redundant. Her unique function is to receive Mme Pernelle's arbitrary and gratuitous violent slap at the end of the play's opening scene. Also an index for Mme Pernelle, Flipote's brilliant redundancy allows her mistress to reveal a violent, unpredictable nature, which prepares the spectator for Orgon's comportment while also hinting at Damis's impetuosity; psychological coherence over three generations. Flipote also allows Molière an act of violence not normally tolerated under the requirements of *bienséances.* But seventeenth-century audiences and we accept the violence to Flipote because of her anonymity, her empty presence, just as we laugh unashamedly at the violent mishaps of the Keystone Cops, those animated puppets of whom we have only distant visual knowledge. In similar fashion, Planchon incarnates Laurent—in disincarnate form—on whom he wreaks considerable havoc through the harsh *Exempt* and his *Gardes*. While Tartuffe is bound and gagged, Laurent is more roughly trussed and hanged (in effigy of his master), lexically a clear suggestion of what the future might hold for the *faux dévot*. The director's highly effective use of theatricality enlightened the script and disengaged his *mise en scène* from the heavily encrusted conformity of *Tartuffe* staging tradition.

Planchon's stage writing for Racine's *Bérénice* also moves his *mise en scène* out of the conventional interpretation of the play as a majestic, lyrical tragedy of love foiled by duty, "malgré lui, malgré elle." For a change, the director invites us to take Titus not for what he says—that he loves Bérénice eternally—but for what he does—banishes her abruptly and unceremoniously at the very moment he would be free to marry her as he had promised. Why? As Planchon tells it, because Titus is tired of Bérénice and being young, immature, deeply narcissistic and ambitious, he wants to rule Rome and the world without problems from a Roman senate wary of foreign princesses. (The players in this production appear in fine Louis XIII costumes: Titus is evolving toward a model of the Sun King but is not quite there yet.) As we listen to an egotistical and ambitious Titus, we must be distrustful of his discourse. Planchon's stage architecture, designed by René Allio who had also done the sets for the first *Tartuffe* in 1962, established and exploited a strong reciprocal relationship between environment and comportment, between Rome and Titus's will to rule. One of the major components of the set was a long hall of mirrors—recalling Versailles—in the main playing space, the area between the emperor's chambers and Bérénice's apartments. These large reflecting surfaces, "une énorme baignoire narcissiste"[7] (the bath, where the body is narcissistically stroked and preened), reflected incessantly the characters' gestures: those of Titus especially were exposed as being highly stylized, self-conscious, studied, almost mechanical. Here the pitiless discourse of stage architecture contests systematically Titus's own discourse and gesturality, endlessly reflecting and refracting (deconstructing) them, revealing them as false and the ambitious young emperor as paranoid, deceptive, and self-deluding, trapped between altruistic intentions and overpowering selfishness. Moreover, the natural symmetry of the neoclassical *palais à volonté* was proliferated such as to produce a shimmering oblique typography calculated to project a sense of imbalance and instability in the anti-hero and his world.

Another Planchon strategy in renewing Racine for contemporary audiences concerned the conventionalized delivery of the Racinian alexandrine, the "dire Racine" habit (Barthes), especially in the tradition of the Comédie Française. This practice establishes an intonation pattern that puts in relief certain privileged lines of the text that collectively build toward a preordained effect. These lines are the ones committed to memory by *lycée* students in France, retained for life, and refreshed with every visit to the Comédie Française. To break this pattern, Planchon devised another kind of delivery mode which he referred to as *la principale:* principal verses considered key to his *écriture scénique* were to be clearly declaimed, while lesser lines were spoken in neurotic rapid-fire, especially in the case of Titus. In the protagonist's famous three lines beginning with "Ah, lâche! fais l'amour, et renonce à l'empire" (IV, 4), that line, with emphasis on *lâche,* is *la principale* and would be stressed.[8] Here is Jean Jourdheuil's apt characterization of this technique: "Dans un jeu décousu, où le texte est morcelé, l'acteur accentue tel mot, glisse sur un autre, rétablit son équilibre sur un troisième, les assortissant d'effets propres à signifier l'état intérieur du personnage à l'instant qu'il les profère."[9] In the process of re-presenting Titus and his entourage of hedonistic wastrels, Planchon's stage writing indicts an entire class, the aristocracy of the *ancien régime,* toying indolently with even their language, swooning in their self-reflected immeasure and ostentation: "oisives gens abusifs." The aristocratic courtisans are displayed here in a manner that disenchants their aura, demythologizes their presence and standing, delegitimizes their command of our respect; it is of course primarily Titus who is diminished in his substance and credibility. Rome is but a pretext for his lack of courage to tell Bérénice the truth, just as his allusions to honor and duty are but hypocritical affectations.

In Titus's palace, not only are forms and figures replicated but sound too, in Planchon's "espace sonore." At five moments in the action, a taped track extended sounds beyond the gestures that occasioned them. At the end of his searching monologue in act IV, Titus decides to go to Bérénice and announce their imminent marriage. He starts walking toward her apartment where she waits anxiously. Close to her door, he stops and goes no further, having clearly changed his mind. At this point we hear a recording replicating his footsteps as they resound in the palace, ironically suggesting what Titus should but will not do. Abruptly the taped march stops because it cannot do Titus's duty, to go to the end of the truth. The faithful princess will be dismissed, "malgré elle mais non pas malgré lui."[10] Just as the mirrors deflected and deconstructed the characters to reveal their inner motives, here too the replicated sound of Titus's footsteps unmasks and impugns his pretended noble intentions and reinforces the spectator's view of his diminished stature. Once again imaginative stage writing brought disparate elements of text and subtexts into a clear unity of vision.

Planchon's original, provocative stagings create not only a "bold redefinition of the play's visual field" (Bradby, 1984), but generate a rich cultural discourse between the classics and us, past significance and present meaning. Planchon's stage writing has been controversial because his *mises en scène* are not simply unimaginative, overly deferential records of the original script, but sometimes a bold reconstellation of its parts. Although his work as playwright has been mostly a "succès d'estime," Planchon's real contribution to contemporary French theatre has been his "écriture scénique," a process he characterized as "cette espèce d'hésitation entre le sens et la sensibilité."[11]

NOTES

[1] J. Honzel, "Dynamics of the Sign in Theater," in L. Matejka and I. Titunik, eds. *Semiotics of Art* (Cambridge: MIT Press, 1984), 76 and 91.

[2] Emile Copfermann, *Théâtres de Roger Planchon* (Paris: Union générale d'éditions, 1977), 225-26; see also "Propos de Roger Planchon sur sa mise en scène de *Tartuffe*," in Molière, *Tartuffe* (Paris: Classiques Hachette, 1967), 198 sq. See also Bénichou's reflections on his *Morales* . . . and other works in "Conversation with Paul Bénichou," in T. Todorov, *Literature and its Theorists,* tr. Catherine Porter (Ithaca: Cornell University Press, 1987), 122-54; the volume appeared originally as *Critique de la critique* (Paris: Le Seuil, 1984).

[3] Roland Barthes, *Essais critiques* (Paris: Le Seuil, 1964), 41-44; also quoted in P. Pavis, *Dictionnaire du théâtre* (Paris: Editions sociales, 1980), 409-10. The basic work on semiotic typology is still T. Kowzan, *Littérature et spectacle* (The Hague: Mouton, 1975). See also Keir Elam, *The Semiotics of Theatre and Drama* (London: Methuen, 1980), and J. Féral, et. al. eds., *Théâtralité, écriture et mise en scène* (Lasalle, Québec: Editions Hurtubise, 1985); the English version had appeared in *Modern Drama,* 5 (1982).

[4] Bernard Dort, "La Représentation émancipée," in *La Représentation émancipée* (Avignon: Actes Sud, 1988), 171-84. The essay had appeared in slightly different form in *Théâtralité, écriture, et mise en scène* and *Modern Drama,* noted above.

[5] For descriptions of Planchon's major stagings, see Yvette Daoust, *Roger Planchon: Director and Playwright* (Cambridge: Cambridge University Press, 1981), especially 88-97 and 104-09. For one detailed exegesis, see Alfred Simon, ed., *Tartuffe. Dans la mise en scène de Roger Planchon* (Paris: L'Avant-Scène, 1972).

[6] Roger Planchon, "Correspondance avec une spectatrice," *La Nouvelle critique* (85), 31; see also in the same number, the "Dossier Planchon," 21-29. David Bradby cites the letter in his *The Theatre of Roger Planchon* (Cambridge: Chadwyck-Healy, 1984), 52; see also Bradby's *Modern French Drama 1940-1990* (Cambridge: Cambridge University Press, 1991), and Bradby and D. Williams, *Directors' Theatre* (New York: St. Martin's Press, 1988), especially 51-83. Also useful are Emile Copfermann's *Planchon* (Lausanne: La Cité, 1969), David Whitton, *Stage Directors in Modern France* (Manchester: Manchester University Press, 1987), and Michel Corvin's semiotic study emphasizing theatrical redundancy: *Molière et ses metteurs en scène d'aujourd'hui* (Lyon: Presses Universitaires de Lyon, 1985), especially chapter 6.

[7] Roger Planchon, "Une Lettre à Richard Demarcy," *Travail théâtral* (January-March 1971), 161. On architecture and theatre, see André Villers, ed. *Architecture et dramaturgie* (Paris: Flammarion, 1950), and Michel Parent, *Création théâtrale et création architecturale* (London: Athlone Press, 1971).

[8] Jean-Pierre Léonardini, "La Cage à miroirs," in *Travail théâtral* (December 1970), 85; see also E. Copfermann, *Théâtres. . . ,* 229.

9 Jean Jourdheuil, "Que faire des classiques?" in *Travail théâtral* (December 1970), 88; See also Alain Girault, "Pourquoi monter un classique?" in *La Nouvelle critique* (December 1973), 78-80.
10 Raymonde Temkine, "Racine et Shakespeare . . . ," in *La Pensée* (153), 132.
11 J. Mambrino, "Entretien avec Roger Planchon," in *Etudes,* 347 (August-September 1977), 223.

Notes on Contributors

RALPH ALBANESE, JR., is Professor of French and Chairman of the Department of Foreign Languages and Literatures at Memphis State University. He is the author of *Le Dynamisme de la peur chez Molière: Une Analyse socio-culturelle de "Dom Juan," "Tartuffe," et "L'École des Femmes"* (1976), *Initiation aux problèmes socio-culturels de la France au XVIIème siècle* (1977), and assorted articles on seventeenth-century French literature. His *Molière à l'Ecole républicaine: De la critique universitaire aux manuels scolaires (1870-1914)* has recently been published by Stanford French and Italian Studies.

HARRIET RAY ALLENTUCH, Professor of French at the State University of New York at Stony Brook and Coordinator of the French Program, is the author of *Madame de Sévigné: A Portrait in Letters* and numerous articles on seventeenth-century French literature, particularly on Madame de Lafayette, Corneille and Madame de Sévigné.

SUSAN READ BAKER is Professor of French at the University of Florida. Her books include *Collaboration et originalité chez La Rouchefoucauld* and *Dissonant Harmonies: Drama and Ideology in Five Neglected Plays of Pierre Corneille*. She is the author of articles on Racine, Marivaux, Cyrano de Bergerac, and Saint-Evremond. Her current research concerns Montaigne's relationship to seventeenth-century French moralists.

RICHARD E. GOODKIN, Professor of French at the University of Wisconsin-Madison, is the author of *The Symbolist Home and the Tragic Home: Mallarmé and Oedipus* (John Benjamins, 1984); *The Tragic Middle: Racine, Aristotle, Euripides* (Wisconsin, 1991); and *Around Proust* (Princeton, 1991). He is also the editor of a volume devoted to Racine entitled *Autour de Racine: Studies in Intertextuality* (Yale French Studies 76, 1989). He is currently working on a book-length study entitled *Generations of French Classicism 1635-1671*.

GERARD GOUVERNET is an Associate Professor and Chair of the Foreign Language Department at SUNY Geneseo. His dissertation, entitled *Le Type du valet chez Molière et ses successeurs: Regnard, Dufresny, Dancourt et Lesage, Caractères et évolution,* written under the direction of Paul Bénichou, has been published by Peter Lang. He also has contributed the analysis of seventeen plays by Hauteroche, Molière, Regnard and Scarron to the *Dictionnaire analytique des œuvres théâtrales* to be published by José Feijoo. He is currently preparing an annotated edition of the works of Madame de Saliès, a French seventeenth-century feminist.

MARCEL GUTWIRTH, John Whitehead Professor Emeritus at Haverford College (1948-87) is now Distinguished Professor of French at the Graduate School and University Center of the University of the City of New York (CUNY). He is the author, *i.a.,* of *Un merveilleux sans éclat: La Fontaine ou la Poésie exilée* (Droz, 1987).

JUDD D. HUBERT is Professor Emeritus at the University of California, Irvine. Among his works are *L'Esthétique des Fleurs du mal: Essai sur l'ambiguïté poétique* (Cailler, 1953); *Essai d'exégèse racinienne* (Nizet, 1956); *Molière and the Comedy of Intellect* (U. of California Press, 1962); *Metatheater: The Example of Shakespeare* (U. of Nebraska Press, 1991).

MICHAEL S. KOPPISCH is Professor of French and Chair of the Department of Romance and Classical Languages at Michigan State University. The author of *The Dissolution of Character: Changing Perspectives in La Bruyère's 'Caractères',* and essays on seventeenth-century French literature, he is currently writing a book on Molière.

JOHN D. LYONS is Commonwealth Professor of French at the University of Virginia. His books include *Exemplum: The Rhetoric of Example in Early Modern France and Italy* (1989) and *The Tragedy of Origins: Tragedy and History in the Work of Pierre Corneille* (in press). He is currently preparing a book on dramatic theory in seventeenth-century France.

MILORAD MARGITIC is Professor of French at Wake Forest University. Among his publications are an *Essai sur la mythologie du "Cid"* (1976), and critical editions of Corneille's *La Suivante* (1978), *La Galerie du Palais* (1981), and *Le Cid* (1989); he has also edited a collection of essays on *Corneille comique* (1982). French seventeenth-century drama continues to be his principal research interest and he is currently working on a study of power in Corneille's theater.

MARLIES K. MUELLER is Senior Preceptor in Romance Languages and Literatures at Harvard University since 1978. She is the author of *Les Idées politiques dans le roman héroïque de 1630 à 1670,* (Harvard Studies in Romance Languages, 1984); *Ethics Then and Now,* a series of videotapes focusing on the interplay between changing cultural institutions and values from the seventeenth to the twentieth century, published by the Kennedy School of Government, Program on Ethics, Harvard University, 1992. An article entitled "The Taming of the Amazon: The Changing Image of the Woman Warrior in *ancien régime* fiction," is forthcoming in vol. 42 of *Papers on French Seventeenth-Century Literature* (Jan. 1995). She is currently finishing a book on the influence of neo-stoic teachings on *ancien régime* culture.

TIMOTHY J. REISS is Professor and Chair of Comparative Literature at New York University, author of *Toward Dramatic Illusion, Tragedy and Truth, The Discourse of Modernism,* his most recent books are *The Uncertainty of Analysis* (Cornell, 1988) and *The Meaning of Literature* (Cornell, 1992), which has just won the 1992 Forkosch prize for intellectual history. He is working on a sequel to this last, as well as on several other volumes: one on sixteenth-century debates about language, meaning, and method, another on Racine and political thought, and a third on the place of Descartes's work in the political and social controversies of the time.

SYLVIE ROMANOWSKI is Associate Professor at Northwestern University and specializes in French literature of the seventeenth, eighteenth, and twentieth centuries. She has published a book, *L'Illusion chez Descartes: la structure du discours cartésien* (Klincksieck, 1974) and articles on Molière, Racine, *préciosité,* Montesquieu, Colette, and Malraux. She is now writing a book on Montesquieu's *Lettres persanes.*

LAURENCE ROMERO is Professor of French at Villanova University. His research interests are neo-classical French theatre, modern stagings of the classics, European dramaturgy, decentralization and post-war French theatre, and performance. He is the author of a book, *Molière: Traditions in Criticism,* and essays on Molière, Racine, La Bruyère, Roger Planchon, Robert Wilson, Claus Peymann, among others.

GABRIELLE VERDIER is Associate Professor of French at the University of Wisconsin-Milwaukee. She is the author of *Charles Sorel* (G. K. Hall, 1984) and numerous articles on seventeenth-century prose fiction, women novelists, memorialists and letter-writers, the literary fairy tale, and eighteenth-century women dramatists.

CHARLES G. S. WILLIAMS is Professor of French and Chair of the Department of French and Italian at the Ohio State University. He is the author *Madame de Sévigné* (1981) and *Valincour: The Limits of honnêteté* (1991). He is a past president of the North American Society for the Study of Seventeenth-Century French Literature and a member of the *French XVII* bibliography group.

BARBARA R. WOSHINSKY is Professor of French at the University of Miami. She is the author of *La Princesse de Clèves: The Tension of Elegance* and *The Linguistic Imperative in French Classical Literature,* as well as numerous articles on seventeenth-century literature and thought. Her current work involves the use of allegorical figures in the classical period.

ELÉONORE M. ZIMMERMANN is Professor of French and Comparative Literature at SUNY Stony Brook. She is author of *La Liberté et le destin dans le théâtre de Jean Racine* (Anma Libri, 1982) and *Magies de Verlaine* (Corti, 1967), and numerous articles on seventeenth-century drama, nineteenth-century poetry, romanticism, and Proust. She is currently writing a book on *Les Fleurs du mal.*

Publications by Paul Bénichou

Books

Morales du grand siècle. Paris: Gallimard, Collection "Bibliothèque des Idées," 1948. Reprint. "Idées," 1967. Reprint. "Folio," 1988. *Man and Ethics: Studies in French Classicism.* Trans. Elizabeth Hughes. Garden City, New York: Anchor Books, 1971.

L'Ecrivain et ses travaux. Paris: Corti, 1967.

Romancero judeo-español de Marruecos. Madrid: Editorial Castalia, 1968.

Creación poética en el romancero tradicional. Madrid: Editorial Gredos, 1968.

Nerval et la chanson folklorique. Paris: Corti, 1970.

Le Sacre de l'écrivain: Essai sur l'avènement d'un pouvoir spirituel laïque dans la France moderne. Paris: Corti, 1973.

Le Temps des prophètes: doctrines de l'âge romantique. Paris: Gallimard, "Bibliothèque des Idées," 1977.

Les Mages romantiques. Paris: Gallimard, 1988.

L'Ecole du désenchantement: Sainte-Beuve, Nodier, Musset, Nerval, Gautier. Paris: Gallimard, 1992.

Articles

"Le Monde de J. L. Borges." *Critique* (1952).

"Le Monde et l'esprit chez J. L. Borges." *Les Lettres nouvelles* (1954).

"Corneille," "La Rochefoucauld," "Racine." *Encyclopaedia Universalis,* 1968.

"Jeune-France et Bousingots: essai de mise au point." *Revue d'histoire littéraire de la France* (1971).

"A propos du 'Guignon', note sur le travail poétique chez Baudelaire." *Hommage à W. T. Bandy. Etudes baudelairiennes,* 3 (1973).

"Le grand œuvre de Ballanche: chronologie et inachèvement." *Revue d'histoire littéraire de la France* (1975).

"El romance de la muerte del Príncipe de Portugal." *Homage to Raimundo Lida. Nueva Revista de Filología Hispánica,* 24 (1976).

"Réflexions sur l'idée de nature chez J.-J. Rousseau." *Annales de la Société Jean-Jacques Rousseau* 39 (1972-1977).

"Sur quelques sources françaises de l'antisémitisme moderne." *Commentaire,* 1 (1978).

"Sur la *Pandora* de Nerval." *Revue d'histoire littéraire de la France* (1978).

"Sur Mallarmé." *Le Surnaturalisme français, actes du colloque organisé à l'Université Vanderbilt* (1978). Neuchâtel: La Baconnière, 1979.

"Mallarmé y Vasco de Gama," with Sylvia Roubaud. *Homenaje a Raimundo Lida. Nueva Revista de Filología Hispánica,* 29 (1980).

"Vigny et l'architecture des *Destinées.*" *Revue d'histoire littéraire de la France* (1980).

"Réflexions sur la critique littéraire." *Le Statut de la littérature: Mélanges offerts à Paul Bénichou.* Ed. Marc Fumaroli. Genève: Droz, 1982.

"A propos d'ordinateurs." *Commentaire* 19 (1982).

"Sobre una colección de romances de Tánger." *Hispanic Review* 51 (1983).

"Poétique et métaphysique dans trois sonnets de Mallarmé." *La Passion de la raison: Hommage à Ferdinand Alquié.* Ed. Jean-Luc Marion. Paris: Presses Universitaires de France, 1983.

"Formes et significations dans la *Rodogune* de Corneille." *Le Débat* (septembre 1984).

"Littérature et critique. Entretien avec Tzvetan Todorov." *Le Débat* (septembre 1984)

"Victor Hugo et le Dieu caché." *Hugo le Fabuleux,* Colloque de Cerisy. Paris, 1985.

"Sur un sonnet de Mallarmé, 'Petit air II.' " *Du romantisme au surnaturalisme: Hommage à Claude Pichois.* Ed. James S. Patty. Neuchâtel: La Baconnière, 1985.

"Romancero español y romanticismo francés." *Hispanic Studies in Honor of Joseph H. Silverman.* Ed. Joseph V. Ricapito. Louisiana State University Press, 1988.

"La Prose pour des Esseintes." *Saggi e ricerche di letteratura francese* 27 (1988).

"Le Parcours de l'écrivain." *Le Débat* (mars-avril 1989).

"Sur deux sonnets de Mallarmé ('Petit air I' et 'Petit air guerrier')." *L'Esprit et la lettre: Mélanges offerts à Jules Brody.* Ed. Louis Van Delft. Tübingen: Gunter Narr, 1991.